The Traveller in the Evening

The Traveller in the Evening

THE LAST WORKS OF WILLIAM BLAKE

MORTON D. PALEY

OXFORD

UNIVERSITY PRESS

OXFORD
UNIVERSITY PRESS

Great Clarendon Street, Oxford OX2 6DP

Oxford University Press is a department of the University of Oxford.
It furthers the University's objective of excellence in research, scholarship,
and education by publishing worldwide in

Oxford New York

Auckland Bangkok Buenos Aires Cape Town Chennai
Dar es Salaam Delhi Hong Kong Istanbul Karachi Kolkata
Kuala Lumpur Madrid Melbourne Mexico City Mumbai Nairobi
São Paulo Shanghai Taipei Tokyo Toronto

Oxford is a registered trade mark of Oxford University Press
in the UK and in certain other countries

Published in the United States
by Oxford University Press Inc. New York

© Morton D. Paley 2003

British Library Cataloguing in Publication Data

Data available

Library of Congress Cataloging in Publication Data

Data available

ISBN 0-19-925562-8

1 3 5 7 9 10 8 6 4 2

Typeset by SNP Best-set Typesetter Ltd., Hong Kong
Printed in Great Britain
on acid-free paper by
Biddles Ltd.
Guildford and King's Lynn

For MARTIN *and* FRANCES BUTLIN

Acknowledgements

I CAN HARDLY imagine having written this book without the generous aid of three friends and fellow scholars: Martin Butlin, Detlef W. Dörrbecker, and Robert N. Essick. For their generous advice and criticism I am deeply grateful.

For additional help and suggestions I am indebted to G. E. Bentley, Jr., David Bindman, Pamela Clemit, Morris Eaves, Tim Fulford, Alexander Gourlay, Nelson Hilton, Tim Hoyer, Grevel Lindop, Rosamund A. C. Paice, Sheila Spector, Joseph Viscomi, David Wagenknecht, David Worrall, and Alex Zwerdling.

I have also greatly benefited from the advice and encouragement of Sophie Goldsworthy at Oxford University Press, from the expert assistance of Frances Whistler, from the skilful editing of Mary Worthington, and from the expert proofreading of George Tulloch.

My thanks to the institutions at which I did my research: the libraries of the University of California at Berkeley, the Bancroft Library, the British Library, the Department of Prints and Drawings of the British Museum, the New York Public Library and its Print Room, the Watson Library of the Metropolitan Museum of Art, the Butler Library of Columbia University, the Henry E. Huntington Library and Art Gallery, the Zentralbibliothek of Zürich, the English Seminar Library of the University of Zürich, the National Art-Collections Library of the Victoria and Albert Museum, and Tate Britain. I am grateful to staffs of these libraries and museums, and especially to Frances Carey, Marianne Kaempf, Anthony Bliss, Peter Hanff, and Michaelyn Burnette.

I appreciate the opportunity to give some parts of this book in an earlier form as papers at the Tate Gallery Blake Conference, the Blake Society (London), the North American Society for the Study of Romanticism Conference (Seattle 2001), and the Arts Club of Berkeley. I also wish to acknowledge the kindness of the editors and publishers of *Studies in Romanticism* and of *Prophetic Character: Essays on William Blake in Honor of John E. Grant*, in which parts of chapters first appeared.

I wish to express appreciation for the assistance I received in support of travel and other research expenses from the Committee on Research and the Chancellor's Office of the University of California at Berkeley. At the Berkeley English Department I received invaluable help from Beverley Scherf and Mary Melinn, both of whom it is a pleasure to thank.

My single greatest debt is, as always, to my wife, Gunnel Tottie.

Morton D. Paley

Berkeley, California
17 March 2003

Table of Contents

List of Illustrations

Abbreviations

Blake	*Blake: An Illustrated Quarterly* [previously *Blake Newsletter*]
BR	G. E. Bentley, Jr., *Blake Records* (Oxford: Clarendon Press, 1969)
Butlin [+ no.]	Martin Butlin, *The Paintings and Drawings of William Blake* (2 vols., New Haven and London: Yale University Press, 1981). Butlin numbers are given for Blake's paintings and drawings
Concordance	David V. Erdman, ed., *A Concordance to the Writings of William Blake* (2 vols., Ithaca, NY: Cornell University Press, 1967)
DNB	*Dictionary of National Biography*, ed. Sir Leslie Stephen and Sir Sidney Lee (26 vols., London: Oxford University Press, 1959–60)
E	*The Complete Poetry and Prose of William Blake*, ed. David V. Erdman (Berkeley and Los Angeles: University of California Press, rev. edn., 1982); cited with page numbers following; where necessary plate and line references precede the page number
Essick and Viscomi	Blake, *Milton a Poem* and the Final Illuminated Works: *The Ghost of Abel, On Homer's Poetry* [and] *On Virgil, Laocoön*, ed. with Introductions and Notes by Robert N. Essick and Joseph Viscomi (London: William Blake Trust/Tate Gallery, 1993)
Gilchrist, *Life*	Alexander Gilchrist, *Life of William Blake*, ed. Ruthven Todd (rev. edn., London: J. M. Dent & Sons, New York: E. P. Dutton, 1945). References to the first (1863) and second (1880) editions of this work are indicated by those dates.

Introduction

I

IN 1820 WILLIAM BLAKE completed the printing of the first complete copy of *Jerusalem*, his greatest illuminated work. Its creation had been an enormous labour, and one that had interlocked with two other ambitious projects: *The Four Zoas* and *Milton*. Blake gave up work on *The Four Zoas* manuscript around 1807.[1] *Milton* was issued *c.*1810, and Blake probably worked on *Jerusalem* all through those years and afterwards. In 1807 Blake's friend George Cumberland noted that 'Blake has engd. 60 plates of a new Prophecy!'[2] and the remaining forty plates were written and designed in the years following. Two more monochrome copies were printed in 1820, and by the time of Blake's death in 1827 there was a total of four monochrome copies, one complete coloured copy, and one coloured copy comprising the twenty-five plates of chapter 1. Printing the plates and colouring copies B and E was artistically demanding work, but it was work of a different kind than the writing of poetry, the execution of designs, and the elaboration of a mythological and symbolic framework that supported both. In the new poetry and art that Blake produced during his remarkably productive remaining years, he might sometimes employ terms and images derived from preceding works, but he would not continue, in the words of his poet-prophet Los, to 'Create a System' (*Jerusalem* 10: 20, E 153).

Los's famous words are usually taken as a statement on Blake's part, and so they are if we rightly understand what 'a System' in this context means. Blake had been in the process of creating a System ever since the mid-1790s. Two of the great pioneer works of Blake criticism—S. Foster Damon's *William Blake: His Philosophy and Symbols*[3] and Northrop Frye's *Fearful Symmetry*[4]—are largely

---

[1] See E 817.
[2] See G. E. Bentley, Jr., *Blake Records* (Oxford: Clarendon Press, 1969), p. 187. This work will be cited as *BR*.
[3] Boston: Houghton Mifflin, 1924; repr. Gloucester, Mass.: Peter Lang, 1958.
[4] Princeton: Princeton University Press, 1947.

devoted to exploring its meaning and structure—an enterprise particularly necessary because many once believed it had none. However, for some readers the demonstration that Blake's mythology had a coherent meaning implied that Blake had created a fixed, sustained framework of symbolism all the parts of which were interrelated, and which was not subject to change. Nothing could be further from the truth. Blake's System was never stable or, as he might have said, 'petrified'. It was continually in progress, evolving, changing. It included at one time or another, among other entities and places, the four Zoas and their Spectres and Emanations, Albion the Eternal Man, Albion's twelve sons and twelve daughters, Vala, the twenty-four Friends (cathedral cities) of Albion, four levels of reality, Satan, Milton and his emanation Ololon, the Council of God, Rintrah and Palambron, Jerusalem (a City yet a Woman), and the Mundane Shell. Symbols such as these were to play a much reduced role in the new works that Blake produced during the last years of his life.

It would be convenient if periods in the lives of poets and artists always followed strict lines of demarcation. In that case, Blake's last works would begin after the printing of copy A of *Jerusalem* in 1820. However, Blake was seldom engaged in only one project, and as he neared the realization of his great task, he was probably engaged in other, less ambitious works. For more than one reason it would be more accurate to regard 1818 as the year in which a new epoch of Blake's life began. First and most important, it was in June of that year that he met John Linnell.[5] Blake was 60 years old and in poor health. He had no source of steady patronage, and he supported himself and his wife as a professional engraver. For the years 1814 through to 1817 his total known earnings were £242. 18*s.*, of which £207. 18*s.* was for engraving the plates of John Flaxman's *Hesiod*.[6] The Blakes lived in decent poverty in a small apartment in Fountain Court, off the Strand. According to W. M. Rossetti, had

[5] See G. E. Bentley, Jr., *The Stranger from Paradise: A Biography of William Blake* (New Haven and London: Yale University Press, 2001), pp. 366–7. On the Blake–Linnell relationship, see Geoffrey Keynes, 'The Blake–Linnell Documents' and 'William Blake and John Linnell', in *Blake Studies* (rev. edn., Oxford: Clarendon Press, 1971), pp. 205–20; Robert N. Essick, 'John Linnell, William Blake, and the Printmaker's Craft', in *Essays on the Blake Followers*, ed. G. E. Bentley, Jr. (San Marino, Calif.: Huntington Library, 1983), pp. 18–32; and *BR*, *passim*.

[6] See *BR*, pp. 607 and 618.

Blake not met Linnell, 'Blake's last years would have been employed [in] making a set of Morland's pig and ploughboy subjects'.[7] Linnell would not make Blake rich, nor would he make him famous during his lifetime. What he would do was to provide Blake with a steady income for drawing and engraving subjects in the worth of which he wholeheartedly believed, help him enrich his style of engraving, introduce him to other prospective employers, take him out into the world of art exhibitions and gatherings (such as those at the home of Charles and Elizabeth Aders, where Blake probably met Coleridge), and even take him to the theatre. Linnell was connected in one way or another with every major work that Blake produced from 1818 on. Furthermore, with the security of weekly payments from Linnell, Blake was able to embark on some less ambitious projects that were entirely his own. These last productions, as we might well expect, display, in addition to much that is familiar in Blake's thought, some new interests or a new emphasis on old ones.

2

After his first meeeting with Blake, at a dinner given by Elizabeth and Charles Aders, Henry Crabb Robinson wrote in his Diary for 17 December 1825:

We spoke of the Devil And I observed that when a child I thought the Manichaean doctrine or that of two principles a rational one. He assented to this—and in confirmation asserted that he did not believe in the *omnipotence* of God.—The language of the Bible on that subject is only poetical or allegorical[.] Yet soon after he denied that the natural world is any thing. It is all nothing and satan's is the empire of nothing[.][8]

Much later, Robinson recalled in his 'Reminiscences' Blake's comments on Wordsworthian Nature on 24 December 1825:

---

[7] See *BR*, p. 274 n. According to Rossetti, this information was given by the sculptor Alexander Munro, 'who told me this Nov./1863 as if he knew it from some authentic source'. The expression 'pig and ploughboy' pictures is unnecessarily disparaging to Morland, who was a painter of very great ability and interest; but Blake was by artistic temperament and belief no more suited to engrave after him than he would have been to execute *English Landscape Scenery* after Constable.

[8] See *BR*, p. 316.

The eloquent descriptions of Nature in Wordsworth's poems were conclusive proof of Atheism, for whoever believes in Nature said B: disbelieves in God—for Nature is the work of the Devil[.] On my obtaining from him the declaration that the Bible was the work of God, I referred to the commencemt of Genesis—In the beginning God created the Heaven & the Earth[.]—But I gained nothing by this for I was triumphantly told that this God was not Jehovah but the Elohim, and the doctrine of the Gnostics repeated with sufficient consistency to silence one so unlearned as myself[.][9]

In later years Blake's one-time disciple Samuel Palmer wrote that he considered Blake a 'great man' but found it necessary to add 'disavowing, however, all adherence to some of the doctrines put forth in the poems, which seem to me to savour of Manicheism'.[10] Some modern scholars have also suggested that Blake was influenced by Manichaeanism or the doctrine from which it derived, Gnosticism.[11] If Blake wanted to learn about the Manichaeans, he could have found information in the widely available *General Dictionary* of Pierre Bayle.[12] There he would have read that the Manichaeans were 'an infamous sect of Heretics founded by one MANES, sprung up in the third century', that they believed there were two principles of good and evil that had fought together, 'and in the conflict there was a mixture made of good and evil, since that time the good principle has been endeavouring to recover what formerly belonged to him: he infused his powers through the elements in order to select the good from the evil in them'. According to Bayle, the doctrine was 'much older than Manes', having been 'introduced into Christianity by the Gnostics', who were not themselves its inventors. Bayle regards Manichaeanism as being extremely widespread, including Zoroastrianism with its opposition of light and darkness, and the

---

[9] *BR*, p. 545.

[10] From a letter to L. R. Valpy dated June 1864, from A. H. Palmer, *The Life and Letters of Samuel Palmer* (London: Seeley & Co., 1892), p. 244.

[11] See, among others, Stuart Curran, 'Blake's Gnostic Hyle: A Double Negative', *Blake Studies*, 4 (1972): 117–34; Stuart Crehan, *Blake in Context* (Dublin: Gill and Macmillan, 1984), pp. 204, 285; Pierre Boutang, *William Blake manichéen et visionnaire* (Paris: La Différence, 1990); François Piquet, *Blake et le sacré*, Études Anglaises, 98 (Paris: Didier, 1996), pp. 161–216; Stuart Peterfreund, *William Blake in a Newtonian World* (Norman, Okla.: University of Oklahoma Press, 1998), pp. 95–104.

[12] See Bayle, *A General Dictionary, Historical and Critical,* ed. and trans. John Peter Bernard, Rev. Thomas Birch, John Lockman, et al. (rev. edn., 10 vols., London, 1734–41), viii (1735): 396–402.

Kabbala, which he does not name but ascribes to 'rabbins' who 'say that God unites himself with pure intelligences called Sefirà, and that he operates with them in such a manner, that all the variations and imperfections of effects must be ascribed to them'. He finds examples of it in Heraclitus, Plutarch, and Euripedes, and concludes that 'the ancient heresy of two principles prevails at this day in some of the eastern countries, and some are of the opinion that it was very common among the ancient barbarous inhabitants of Europe'. Blake may not have consistently believed the doctrine of the two principles, but his statements to Robinson and such writings as 'The Everlasting Gospel' (see Chapter 4) make it easy to see why someone could infer that he was a Manichaean.

As for Gnosticism itself, once more if Blake had wished to read about the subject, the materials were ready to hand. He need have gone no further than J. L. Mosheim's *Ecclesiastical History*, first published in English in 1794, or to Joseph Priestley's *Disquisitions Relating to Matter and Spirit*, brought out by Joseph Johnson in 1777, as I have pointed out elsewhere,[13] or to Mosheim's *Commentaries*. According to Mosheim:

By none of its adversaries or corrupters was Christianity, from almost its first rise, more seriously injured; by none was the church more grievously lacerated, and rendered less attractive to the people, than by those who were for making the religion of Christ accommodate itself to the principles of the oriental philosophy respecting the Deity, the origin of the world, the nature of matter, and the human soul. We allude to those who, from their pretending that they were able to communicate to mankind, at present held in bondage by the Architect of the World, a correct knowledge (γνῶσις) of the true and ever-loving God, were commonly styled Gnostics.[14]

Mosheim summarized the tenets of Gnosticism as follows:

that the Deity had nothing at all to do with matter, the nature and qualities of which they considered to be malignant and poisonous—that the body was held in subjection by a being entirely distinct from him to whom the dominion over the rational soul belonged—that the world and all terrestrial

---

[13] See *Energy and the Imagination: A Study of the Development of Blake's Thought* (Oxford: Clarendon Press, 1970), pp. 66–7.

[14] John Laurence Mosheim, *Commentaries on the Affairs of the Christians Before the Time of Constantine the Great*, trans. Robert Studley Vidal (2 vols., London, 1813), i. 299–305.

bodies were not the work of the Supreme Being, the author of all good, but were formed out of matter by a nature either evil in its origin, or that had fallen into a state of depravity—and, lastly, that the knowledge of the true Deity had become extinct, and that the whole race of mankind, instead of worshipping the Father of Light and Life, and source of every thing good, universally paid their homage to the Founder and Prince of this nether world, or to his substitutes and agents.[15]

Some, though not all, of these beliefs are entirely compatible with Blake's late views as expressed in such works as *The Everlasting Gospel*, the aphorisms engraved on his separate plate depicting the *Laocoön* group, and the inscriptions on some of the Dante designs. Especially interesting to Blake would have been Mosheim's statements that the Gnostics 'persisted in maintaining that the creator of this world was a being of a nature vastly inferior to the supreme deity, the Father of our Lord, and that the law of Moses was not dictated by the Almighty, but by this same inferior being, by whom also the bodies of men were formed'; and that 'Strange, however, as it may appear . . . it is most certain that some of this sect conceived themselves to be warranted by these self-same principles in plunging, with the most barefaced effrontery, into every species of libidinousness and excess'.[16]

Blake could never have accepted the Gnostic and Manichaean doctrines in full because they denied that Christ really became a man, suffered, died, and was resurrected. This was, indeed, what made Gnosticism fail in its competition with Christianity.[17] However, it is doubtful that Blake ever accepted any of his intellectual sources in full: his way was to absorb elements of them into his own 'System'. Nor would he have been troubled by apparent contradictions between Gnosticism and antinomianism, even though according to the latter God is to be found within man. He could declare on the same plate that 'The outward ceremony is Antichrist', that 'Adam is only the Natural Man & not the Soul or Imagination', and that 'the Eternal Body of Man is The IMAGINATION'[18] (E 273), bringing together Gnostic, Pauline, and antinomian beliefs.

---

[15] Mosheim, *Commentaries*, i. 309–10.
[16] Ibid., i. 313, 315.
[17] See Elaine Pagels, *The Gnostic Gospels* (New York: Random House, Vintage Books, 1981).
[18] See Chapter 2, יהוה *& his two Sons Satan & Adam*.

It should also be emphasized that Blake need not have been especially influenced by any one of the heresies of which he had, or could have had, knowledge. The reader who searches for specific sources in this regard will find himself in the position of the novice Adso in Umberto Eco's novel *The Name of the Rose*, who, after hearing disquisitions on the various millenarian sects of his time, tells his master William: 'I can no longer distinguish the accidental differences among Waldensians, Catharists, the poor of Lyons, the Umiliati, the beghards, Joachimites, Patarines, Apostles, Poor Lombards, Arnoldists, Williamites, Followers of the Free Spirit, and Luciferines.'[19] What is important is that Blake had a temperamental affinity for Gnosticism, and that this tendency increased in his very late works. Along with this came some other characteristics, including a sharply polarized view of women, an equivocal and sometimes self-contradictory attitude toward human sexuality, a dismissal of all institutions, the complete identification of true religion with Art, a vehement rejection of money and the idea of commerce, opposed tendencies to divide and to reconcile God the Father and God the Son, and a withdrawal from the political realm.[20] It is true that none of these beliefs or combinations of seemingly opposed beliefs was entirely new to Blake. They are all present somewhere or other in *Jerusalem*, but they take on a different aspect when they are no longer part of an overall symbolic structure that ends with the recuperation of all fallen forms. Each of Blake's last works creates its own context, its own frame of reference, and they sometimes are inconsistent with one another and even within themselves. This does not, of course, invalidate them as imaginative creations. Much of the best art and writing of Blake's last years shows the truth of Yeats's statement: 'We make out of the quarrel with others, rhetoric, but of the quarrel with ourselves, poetry'.[21]

[19] Umberto Eco, *The Name of the Rose*, trans. William Weaver (New York: Harcourt Brace, 1983), p. 197.

[20] It is true that at heart Blake still considered himself a practitioner of 'Republican Art', and stated that 'since the French Revolution Englishmen are all Intermeasurable One by Another . . .' (Letter to George Cumberland, 12 April 1827, E 783). However, one need only compare the political content of his works during the early years of the French Revolution with that during the years of the Blanketeers, Peterloo, and the struggle for Reform to recognize the striking difference.

[21] William Butler Yeats, 'Per Amica Silentia Lunae', in *Mythologies* (New York: Macmillan, 1959), p. 331.

3

One of the works that Blake began about this time[22] was *For the Sexes: The Gates of Paradise*, which serves as a good point of entry to Blake's late productions, taking as it does a much earlier work as its starting point: the emblem book *For Children: The Gates of Paradise*, dated on its title page 1793. *For Children* comprises seventeen small engravings,[23] each with its own title. Using this as a base, Blake turned it into an entirely new work. He also reworked the original engravings, creating stronger contrasts of light and darkness.[24] He made a new title page with ten lines of verse and a design, added a fifty-line poem entitled 'The Keys of the Gates', and concluded with an eight-line epilogue addressed 'To the Accuser who is the God of This World'. He also added to the captions of some of the engravings. Although to some extent the new material may grow out of and amplify meanings implicit in *For Children*, it is remarkable for introducing themes, concepts, and terminology uncharacteristic of the Blake of 1793. Probably begun when Blake was close to completing work on copy A of *Jerusalem*, it serves as a good introduction to the creations of Blake's last decade.

The frontispiece displays a caterpillar on a dark oak leaf, and a pupa with a child's head on a leaf below. *For Children* had as text only 'What is Man!' but *For the Sexes* adds the couplet:

> The Sun's light when he unfolds it
> Depends of the Organ that beholds it

The original caption makes it possible for the reader/viewer to see the image in two possible ways: humanity is both a 'devouring appetite' (*Jerusalem* 54: 24, E 204) and a (metaphorically) winged being in an early stage of its development. The new couplet underlines this by bringing in a belief Blake held all his life. Reality is shaped by the

---

[22] See G. E. Bentley, Jr., *Blake Books* (Oxford: Clarendon Press, 1977), pp. 194–5. The earliest watermark (three leaves in copy B) is 1818. Bentley suggests that 'The dates of 1825 and 1826 in all but the first watermarked copy suggest that it was not until several years after 1818 that he was sufficiently satisfied with the work to pull prints'. The William Blake Archive dates the copies A and B *c.*1820.—The William Blake Archive, ed. Morris Eaves, Robert N. Essick, and Joseph Viscomi, 2 January 2003, www.blakearchive.org.

[23] For the measurements of each plate, see Bentley, *Blake Books*, p. 67.

[24] On Blake's 'burnishing, darkening, and outlining' of the plates, see Robert N. Essick, *William Blake, Printmaker* (Princeton: Princeton University Press, 1980), pp. 186–8.

perceiver—the sun can be 'a round Disk of fire somewhat like a Guinea' or 'an Innumerable company of the Heavenly host crying Holy Holy Holy is the Lord God Almighty'.[25] Then, in 'The Keys of the Gates', Blake introduces an entirely different aspect of the caterpillar image:

> The Catterpiller on the Leaf
> Reminds thee of thy Mothers Grief

This couplet, which virtually repeats one in *Auguries of Innocence*,[26] brings in the pain both of birth and of separation, in line with the generally pessimistic colouring of *For the Sexes*.

Where the title page of *For Children* showed a single flying figure inviting the reader to enter the book, *For the Sexes* has two flying in opposite directions, three small flying forms rising below each, and a pair of angels hovering on either side of the rising sun's disc as he unfolds his light.[27] This invites us to expect a hopeful beginning, and indeed the first two lines accord with this:

> Mutual Forgiveness of each Vice
> Such are the Gates of Paradise

'Mutual Forgiveness' is a conjoining peculiar to the later Blake, to be found elsewhere only in *Jerusalem* (five times) and once in *The Everlasting Gospel*, which was begun at about the same time as *For the Sexes*. It is opposed to the Law mistakenly written by Jehovah:

> Against the Accusers chief desire
> Who walkd among the Stones of Fire
> Jehovahs Finger Wrote the Law

Copies A and B originally read 'Fingers',[28] but the image of one finger of God writing, as again in *The Everlasting Gospel* ([f]: 23, E 521), is the more striking. The Accuser is of course Blake's Satan, associated with the figure of the Covering Cherub that Blake had derived from Ezekiel's 'Thou art the anointed cherub that covereth;

---

[25] *A Vision of the Last Judgment*, E 565–6.

[26]
> The Catterpiller on the Leaf
> Repeats to thee thy Mothers grief
> (E 491, lines 37–8)

[27] For a high-quality facsimile reproduction, see *William Blake: The Gates of Paradise*, ed. Geoffrey Keynes (3 vols., London: Trianon Press for the William Blake Trust, 1968). David Erdman, *The Illuminated Blake* (Garden City, NY: Anchor Books, 1974), pp. 268–73, conveniently reproduces both sets.

[28] For all textual variants, see E 813.

and I have set thee so: thou wast upon the holy mountain of God; thou hast walked up and down in the midst of the stones of fire' (28: 14). The dead letter of the Law only serves the Accuser by creating laws to be broken, and Blake's Jehovah immediately repents what he has done:

> Then Wept! then rose in Zeal & Awe
> And the Dead Corpse from Sinais heat
> Buried beneath his Mercy Seat

The Mercy Seat was placed above the Ark of the Tabernacle (see Exod. 25: 21), with a cherub of gold on either side of it, 'And the cherubims spread out their wings on high, and covered with their wings over the mercy seat' (Exod. 37: 9). For Blake this is a highly equivocal image, one that can in some contexts be positive but in others, as here, constitutes a manifestation of the Covering Cherub, Satan. Jehovah's attempt to bury the corpse in the desert—copies A and B have the weaker 'And in the midst of Sinais heat'—fails, for it has been reified as an object of worship independent of his will:

> O Christians Christians! tell me Why
> You rear it on your Altars high

This idea of a Jehovah who makes mistakes and is powerless to prevent their taking effect is typical of the very late Blake, although, as we shall see, only one of several conceptions. The ending of the prologue with what is in effect a cry of despair, shows how far *For the Sexes* is from *For Children*.

The verses in 'The Keys of the Gates' are cued to the emblems that follow the prologue. The first of these shows a woman in a flowing dress plucking a human-headed mandrake from the ground, while she holds others in a fold in her garment. The caption in both versions is: 'I found him beneath a Tree', but this is amplified in 'The Keys'. The woman is the Eve to Blake's Adam, created in a parody of Gen. 2: 21–2:

> 1 My Eternal Man set in Repose
> The Female from his darkness rose
> And She found me beneath a Tree
> A Mandrake & in her Veil hid me

Blake also refers to the mandrake in *Jerusalem* 93: 8: 'As Reuben found Mandrakes in the field & gave them to his mother', alluding to the story in Gen. 30: 14–16:

And Reuben went in the days of wheat harvest, and found mandrakes in the field, and brought them unto his mother Leah. Then Rachel said to Leah, Give me, I pray thee, of thy son's mandrakes.
And she said unto her, Is it a small matter that thou hast taken my husband? and wouldest thou take away my son's mandrakes also? And Rachel said, Therefore he shall lie with thee to night for thy son's mandrakes.
And Jacob came out of the field in the evening, and Leah went out to meet him, and said, Thou must come in unto me; for surely I have hired thee with my son's mandrakes. And he lay with her that night.

The sexual and fertilizing power of the mandrake is evident here, as Blake clearly recognized.[29] The birth of the speaker as a human vegetable is in *For the Sexes* the beginning of a cycle of the life of man.

The next four plates are devoted to the traditional four elements, represented by four naked male figures; in *For Children* they bore simply the names of each: 'Water', 'Earth', 'Air', and 'Fire'. In reworking these plates, Blake also added to their titles. Plate 2, showing a man sitting in the rain beside a withered tree and vainly trying to calm the rising waters below him with a palms-down gesture, now bears the caption 'Thou waterest him with Tears'. Plate 3, 'Earth' in *For Children*, shows a powerfully built naked man exerting himself against enclosing rocks, and to the caption is added 'He struggles into life'. (Very similar is the male seen from behind at the top of plate 10 of *The [First] Book of Urizen*, first published in 1794.) Next, the figure hunched on a cloud in the night sky, with his hands meeting over his forehead in a gesture of puzzlement, previously was labelled simply 'Air', but *For the Sexes* adds: 'On Cloudy Doubts & Reasoning Cares'. And 'Fire', showing a Satanic figure brandishing sword and spear among flames, now bears the additional text: 'That end in endless Strife'. In *For the Sexes,* scales, not present in *For Children*, cover his belly and crotch, and even some of the flames appear to be scaly. The four additions to the captions, as John Beer points out,[30] form a quatrain:

> Thou waterest him with Tears
> He struggles into life
> On Cloudy Doubts & Reasoning Cares
> That end in endless Strife.

[29] See Damon, *William Blake: His Philosophy and Symbols*, p. 84; and Frye, *Fearful Symmetry*, p. 369.
[30] See John Beer, *Blake's Humanism* (Manchester: Manchester University Press, 1968), p. 233.

The corresponding lines of 'The Keys', 9–12, amplify the futility of the speaker's passing through the four elements.

> 2 Doubt Self Jealous Watry folly
> 3 Struggling thro Earths Melancholy
> 4 Naked in Air in Shame & Fear
> 5 Blind in Fire with shield & spear

Interestingly, in *The [First] Book of Urizen*, Urizen embarks on the same quest:

> 5 First I fought with the fire; consum'd
> Inwards, into a deep world within:
> A void immense, wild dark & deep,
> Where nothing was: Natures wide womb
>
> And self balanc'd stretch'd o'er the void
> I alone, even I! the winds merciless
> Bound; but condensing, in torrents
> They fall & fall; strong I repell'd
> The vast waves, & arose on the waters
> A wide world of solid obstruction
>
> (4: 14–23, E 72)

Although the order—fire, earth, air, and water—differs, the process is in both cases a fruitless passage through the four elements.

The speaker and the Woman have become parts of the same composite being, 'a dark Hermaphrodite' subject to 'Doubt' resulting from 'Two Hornd Reasoning Cloven Fiction' (ll. 13–15); and her Veil freezes, becoming the 'Mundane Shell' (19). These conceptions are of course absent from *For Children* but are familiar to us through Blake's later works. They all involve the idea of doubleness. The hermaphrodite is a being in a state of unresolved contradictions.[31] Reason is associated by Blake with Satan's horns and cloven hoof because of its tendency to divide everything into binary, either/or categories. The Mundane Shell, formed from the Veil of Vala in *Jerusalem* 59: 2–3 (E 208), encloses the egg-shaped material world, as we know from the full page-diagram of *Milton* 32. In the sixth emblem, captioned in both sets 'At length for hatching ripe he bursts the shell', it appears as if the speaker, shown as a winged putto emerging from the broken egg, is about to emerge from the material

---

[31] See S. Foster Damon, *A Blake Dictionary: The Ideas and Symbols of William Blake* (Hanover, NH: University Press of New England, rev. edn., 1988), p. 181.

world. This is a positively charged image that Blake had used before: *Night Thoughts* illustration 13 shows a butterfly-winged putto emerging from a crack in a huge shell, and 16 depicts a naked female floating upward from a broken shell, illustrating Young's 'Embryos we must be, till we burst the shell, | Yon ambient azure shell, and spring to life'.[32] The caption for emblem 6, however, comes from an entirely different source—Dryden, as Blake indicates in his Notebook drawing, specifically *Palamon and Arcite*, Dryden's version of *The Knight's Tale*. John Beer[33] has convincingly argued the relevance of the passage in which it appears, outlining Boethius's philosophy of Necessity according to which Man is viewed as part of what Blake would call the 'Vegetable World'. Indeed, the passage linked to emblem 6 in 'The Keys' gives only minimal grounds for optimism:

> 6 I rent the Veil where the Dead dwell
> When weary Man enters his Cave
> He meets his Saviour in the Grave
> Some find a Female Garment there
> And some a Male, woven with care
> Lest the Sexual Garments sweet
> Should grow a devouring Winding sheet

The speaker enters a place where human identities are, through divine mercy, clothed in garments of flesh that will act as a buffer between them and the elemental forces of the world. The danger, according to this poem's pessimistic view of material existence, is that the wearers will consider their true identities to be these gendered garments, a point to which the poet will return in the Epilogue.

In emblem 7 the speaker, now a thoughtless smiling boy, has killed a tiny female with his hat, as another flies upward to try to escape the same fate. Blake must have seen children commit such cruelties, and he twice described similar situations in verse. In the Notebook poem 'The Fairy', the fairy is 'in my hat caught' (E 475), and in two copies of *Europe*, the poem is narrated by a fairy after the poet 'caught him in my hat as boys knock down a butterfly' (E 60). In these instances the entrapped victims survive, but emblem 7 is more in the spirit of the words of Shakespeare's blind Gloucester: 'As flies to wanton

---

[32] See Damon, *William Blake: His Philosophy and Symbols*, p. 85 n. 8.
[33] See Beer, *Blake's Humanism*, pp. 238–41.

boys, are we to th' Gods; | They kill us for their sport'.[34] The caption
in *For Children* was simply 'Alas!' but in *For the Sexes* Blake worked
it into: 'What are these? Alas! The Female Martyr | Is She also
the Divine Image[?]' Presumably the answer is affirmative, and
the martyred female counterbalances the Vala-figure of emblem 1.
The wanton boy has grown into a lithe, parricidal adolescent in
emblem 8, and is about to throw his spear at a long-bearded man
slumped on a massive throne, too tired or too despondent to defend
himself with the sword gripped in his right hand. 'My Son! my Son!'
reads the caption, which in 'The Keys' is expanded into:

> 8   In Vain-glory hatcht & nurst
>   By double Spectres Self Accurst
>   My Son! my Son! thou treatest me
>   But as I have instructed thee

After this act of Oedipal aggression, the subject will assume the
patriarchal role in emblem 11. But first he will try to climb a ladder
to the moon in emblem 9,[35] labelled 'I want! I want!', and then
drown 'In Times Ocean' in emblem 10.

> 10 In Times Ocean falling drownd
>   In Aged Ignorance profound
>
> 11 Holy & cold I clipd the Wings
>   Of all Sublunary Things

The speaker, now a bespectacled Urizen figure, wields a pair of shears
to clip the right wing of a naked cupid headed toward the rising sun.
This scene is related to the neo-classical visual theme of the selling of
cupids, as rendered by artists such as Joseph-Marie Vien and Henry
Fuseli, in which the vendor holds the captive cupid by the wings.[36]
Like the male protagonist of 'The Mental Traveller', Blake's speaker

---

[34] *King Lear*, ed. Kenneth Muir (Cambridge, Mass.: Harvard University Press,
1959), IV. i. 36–7 (p. 149).

[35] David V. Erdman convincingly suggests a source for Blake's image in James
Gillray's print *The Slough of Despond: Vide the Patriot's Progress*, dated 2 January
1793. See Erdman, *Blake: Prophet Against Empire* (Princeton: Princeton University
Press, 1977), pp. 202–4.

[36] See Kazuya Okada, 'Orc Under a Veil Revealed', *Blake*, 34 (2000): 41–2. For a
discussion of this visual topos see Robert Rosenblum, *Transformations in Late
Eighteenth Century Art* (Princeton: Princeton University Press, 1967), pp. 3–9 and
plates 1–5.

has gone through a cycle from infancy to age. A long-held view of Blake's is expressed in the caption added to the original 'Aged Ignorance' of emblem 11: 'Perceptive Organs closed their Objects close'. The old man's eyes are shut behind his spectacles and he therefore cannot see the glorious sunrise. He wants to reduce the winged boy to his own earthbound state.

The speaker's tyrannic nature is further emphasized in emblem 12, which pictures without naming them (as does plate 16 of *The Marriage of Heaven and Hell*) Dante's Count Ugolino and his two sons and two grandsons,[37] starving to death in prison. Massive blocks of stone, not in *For Children*, compose the walls. 'Does thy God O Priest take such vengeance as this?' asks the caption, alluding to Archbishop Ruggieri, who put them there, and whose identity the speaker now assumes:

> 12 And in depths of my Dungeons
> Closed the Father & the Sons

This was neither the first nor the last time Blake would take up Ugolino's story, as we will see in discussing his Dante illustrations (Chapter 3). Here the scene marks the speaker's lowest point of degradation, for in emblem 13 a conversion takes place. A mother with three children, one nearly adult, cluster at the head of a deathbed, looking at the Spiritual Body of a white-bearded old man who rises from the feet of the corpse and points upward. Keynes notes that this plate in *For the Sexes* 'appears to have been completely re-engraved'.[38] The rising figure has been given a luminous halo and the background considerably darkened, creating a much more dramatic effect. This design resembles in content (though not in compositional structure) Blake's illustration for Blair's *Grave*, *The Death of the Good Old Man*.[39] Below his Notebook sketch, Blake had written 'What we hope we see' (N61), but in both versions of *The Gates* he substituted the more powerful 'Fear & Hope are—Vision'. This example of dying into spiritual life transforms the speaker, as the cause-and-effect narrative of 'The Keys' indicates:

---

[37] Although often referred to as Ugolino's 'sons', and apparently regarded as such in *Marriage* 16, they belong to two different generations. Erdman, *The Illuminated Blake*, p. 274, regards the smaller pair as girls, which I think doubtful.

[38] Introductory volume for *The Gates of Paradise*, p. 4.

[39] See Robert Blair, *The Grave* (London, 1808), facing p. 30.

FIG. 1. William Blake, 'The Traveller hasteth in the Evening',
For the Sexes: The Gates of Paradise, 14. Engraving, second
state, *c*.1818.

13 But when once I did descry
     The Immortal Man that cannot Die

14 Thro evening shades I haste away
     To close the Labours of my Day

In emblem 14 (Fig. 1), captioned 'The Traveller hasteth in the
Evening', he is a pilgrim-like walker wearing a broad-brimmed hat
and tailed coat, striding purposefully forward with the aid of a stick as
the shadows lengthen. (Blake would execute for Thornton's *Virgil* (see
Chapter 1) a very similar wood engraving in which the traveller bears
unmistakable reference to himself.) Next, the now-aged Traveller,
aided by a crutch, reaches his goal. In emblem 15 we see
an image Blake also used in *America* 14 and in his great white-line
etching *Deaths Door*.[40] Surprisingly, considering the conversionary

---

[40] Blake's design, intended for *Blair's Grave*, was in the event engraved by Louis
Schiavonetti; for reproductions see Robert N. Essick and Morton D. Paley, *Robert
Blair's* The Grave *Illustrated by William Blake* (London: Scolar Press, 1982), supple-
mentary illustration 13 and illustration facing p. 32 of the text of the poem. The
America plate is reproduced in William Blake, *The Continental Prophecies*, ed. D. W.
Dörrbecker (London: William Blake Trust/Tate Gallery, 1995), p. 106.

experience of 13, 'The Keys' points us toward not spiritual regenera-
tion but corporeal death: '15 The Door of Death I open found |
And the Worm Weaving in the Ground'. Both the emblem series and
'The Keys' then end with the reintroduction of the Female of emblem
1 in the form of a cowled figure who is partly human and partly a huge,
reticulated worm presiding over dead bodies whose faces are
glimpsed barely above the earth.[41] 'I have said to the Worm: thou art
my mother & my sister', reads the caption, a condensation of Job 17:
14: 'I have said to corruption, Thou art my father: to the worm, Thou
art my mother, and my sister'. Significantly, Blake omits the masculine
allusion, though when he first sketched the image he wrote out the en-
tire line below it.[42] 'The Keys' amplifies this gendering of death:

> 16 Thou'rt my Mother from the Womb
> Wife, Sister, Daughter to the Tomb
> Weaving to Dreams the Sexual strife
> And weeping over the Web of Life

This conclusion expresses a deep fear of the female principle, one
that in *Jerusalem* was balanced by its positive aspect as embodied in
Jerusalem herself, but which finds no such contrary here.

For the Sexes concludes with an additional page bearing an eight-
line epilogue with accompanying images. Between the title and the
text of the poem stretches a coiling serpent (ten of its coils numbered
so as to remind us of the Decalogue) that suggests Satan's identity as
the Tempter in the Garden. At the bottom a larger design depicts a
sleeping, naked traveller (as indicated by his walking stick, so dis-
used that a spider has woven its web at the top of it), oblivious to the
dawn behind him. From his body there emerges a dark figure very
like the Spectre of Los as pictured in *Jerusalem* 44 [30], with bat
wings containing the sun, moon, and stars. As Nelson Hilton
remarks, 'The starry spectre's foot is drawn so as to suggest the
Traveller's snaky penis rising in his sleep. . . . We see a spectrogram
of the fallen Los ready to copulate ("sleep") with his own nocturnal
emission, the dream of the starry universe of generation.'[43] At the

---

[41] A related drawing, though lacking the worm, is *A Crouching Woman* (Butlin
133, Pierpont Morgan Library), dated by Butlin *c*.1780–1785; see *William Blake: The
Gates of Paradise*, ed. Keynes, i. 19–20, 39.

[42] See *The Notebook of William Blake*, ed. David V. Erdman with the assistance of
Donald K. Moore (Oxford: Clarendon Press, 1973), N45.

[43] Nelson Hilton, *Literal Imagination: Blake's Vision of Words* (Berkeley and Los
Angeles: University of California Press, 1983), p. 166.

same time there is something almost comic about this Spectre, especially in the way his hands protrude from his wings. Satan is, after all, 'but a Dunce', the poem tells us. His foolishness consists in not recognizing what Blake elsewhere calls Individuals and States, between the Sexual Garments found in the Grave and the human identities who (temporarily) wear them.

> Distinguish therefore States from Individuals in those States.
> States Change: but Individual Identities never change nor cease:[44]

Despite his power on Earth, the realm of this 'Son of Morn'—Lucifer, the morning star—is declared illusory, like the dream world of a sleeper in a ballad.

> . . . thou art still
> The Son of Morn in weary Nights decline
> The lost Travellers Dream under the Hill[45]

The beauty of this concluding lyric cannot, however, disguise the radical bifurcation of human experience that both it and *For the Sexes* as a whole express. Blake's title, 'To the Accuser Who is | The God of This World' (E 269), recalls the Satanic accuser of the prologue, and at the same time alludes to 2 Cor. 4: 3–4:

> But if our gospel be hid, it is hid to them that are lost:
>   In whom the god of this world hath blinded the minds of them which believe not, lest the light of the glorious gospel of Christ, who is the image of God, should shine unto them.

As we can see, the 'God of This World' need not be a 'Manichaean' concept—here Paul contrasts such a God to the Gospel of Christ. However, in Blake's poem it is the God of this World who is 'Worshipd by the Names Divine | Of Jesus & Jehovah', just as in the prologue the law is reared on Christian altars. Whether or not Blake derived this conception from the Gnostics, it is entirely congruent with their beliefs.

   The original *Gates of Paradise*, comprising only the emblems with their captions, was a rather sombre book to address to children—

---

[44] *Milton* 32: 22–3; E 132.
[45] Nelson Hilton suggests another dimension of meaning for 'under the hill' in Exod. 24: 4 'And Moses wrote all the words of the Lord, and rose up early in the morning, and builded an altar under the hill . . .'. See Hilton, ' "Under the Hill" ', *Blake*, 22 (1988): 16.

more in the spirit of the Brothers Grimm than of Mary Woll-
stonecraft's *Original Stories from Real Life*. Some of the meanings
to which Blake gave voice in *For the Sexes* may have been in his
mind from the start, while others were undoubtedly an expression of
his later thought. Images and phrases such as the 'Eternal Man',
'Serpent Reasonings', 'Cloven Fiction', 'Hermaphrodite', 'Sexual
Garments', and Individuals and States are familiar to us largely
through Blake's later writings. It is not surprising that we should
encounter them in a work he recast in 1818 or later; what is perhaps
surprising is the relative scantness of positive views of life in the
realm of what Blake called Generation. In *Jerusalem* Blake could
write 'O holy Generation! [Image] of regeneration!'[46] and the fron-
tispiece to *The Gates* might be read that way, since the pupa will
develop into a butterfly—but if so the fate of the flying babes in
emblem 7 is not reassuring, and neither is the clipping of the cupid's
wings in emblem 11. Though the luminous example of 'The
Immortal Man that cannot Die' causes the Traveller to haste in the
evening, weary Man meets his Saviour only in the Grave; there is no
active participation of Jesus in this world, either through the Sacrifice
of Self or through the human Imagination. This does not, of course,
indicate a complete change of world-view on Blake's part around
1818. We could also find many instances to the contrary among the
works of his last decade. Rather, it shows that at this point Blake did
not think it nesessary to make a small volume such as *For the Sexes* a
microcosm of his beliefs. He could develop the work in its own
terms, and in those terms the world is sharply polarized, both liter-
ally and metaphorically, between light and darkness, with the latter
often preponderating. Such dramatic oscillations are characteristic
of Blake's late works, as we will see in discussing the first series of
new engravings that Blake produced after his epochal meeting with
John Linnell, even though this was a commission on a pastoral sub-
ject and therefore limited in the scope of its subject matter.

---

[46] 7: 65, E 150. 'Image' was deleted but then restored in two copies (E 809), which
may indicate some ambivalence toward the idea on Blake's part.

1 Dark Pastoral: Illustrations to Thornton's *Virgil*

IN 1821 THERE APPEARED the third edition of Dr Robert John Thornton's *The Pastorals of Virgil, with a Course of English Reading, Adapted for Schools*.[1] The first edition of this work, unillustrated, had been published in 1812.[2] Eighty-one pages of illustrations for it, from one to five on a page, were published separately in 1814,[3] and a second edition with these included appeared in 1819.[4] The 1821 *Pastorals* had a greatly increased number of illustrations—117 pages of small woodcuts, 230 engravings in all, executed by 'the most eminent engravers on wood', to use Thornton's own words.[5] Most of these could be characterized in the words the *DNB* uses of those published previously—'worthless little woodcuts'.[6] It is fair to say that Thornton's *Pastorals of Virgil* is known today for one reason alone: the seventeen wood engravings by William Blake that appear in it.

Though Robert John Thornton was a medical doctor by profession, his true passion was for botany, more specifically for publishing elegantly illustrated botanical books such as *The Temple of Flora*

[1] Published by a conger including F. C. & J. Rivingtons [*sic*] and Longman & Co. 'Copies may be had of Mr. Harrison, 13, Little Tower Street, Agent for Dr. Thornton'. The book was entered at Stationers' Hall on 12 February 1821 as the 'Property of Wm Harrison'.

[2] *School Virgil whereby Boys Will Acquire Ideas As Well as Words etc.* (London, 1812). 'Published at the Linnaean Gallery, Hinde-street, Manchester-square; F. C. and J. Rivingtons, Joseph Johnson', etc.

[3] *Illustrations of the School-Virgil in Copper-Plates, and Wood-Cuts . . .* (London: F. C. and J. Rivington, Joseph Johnson, etc., 1814).

[4] See Geoffrey Keynes, Introduction to *The Illustrations of William Blake for Thornton's Virgil* (London: Nonesuch Press, 1937), pp. 7–20. This essay is reprinted in Keynes's *Blake Studies: Essays on His Life and Work* (2nd edn., Oxford: Clarendon Press, 1971), pp. 136–42.

[5] 'Address to School-Masters & Parents', p. vi. Blake does not appear among the eleven engravers named, but Blake was a newcomer to wood engraving; his name, along with those of Thurston, Craig, Cruickshanks [*sic*], and Varley, is among those mentioned by Thornton among the artists who made the designs.

[6] *DNB*, s.v. 'Thornton, Robert John'.

(1799) and *New Illustrations of the the Sexual System of Linnaeus* (1799–1807).[7] Blake had no role in these elaborate projects, although his beautiful renditions of flowers in such works as the design for 'Infant Joy' of *Innocence* and the full-page picture in *The Song of Los* (plate 5[8]) of a tiny king and queen in the blossoms of lilies might have recommended him, had Thornton seen them. Blake must have come by the *Virgil* commission through John Linnell, whose family doctor Thornton was. Blake, Thornton, and Linnell are recorded as being together on 19 September 1818.[9] This was before the publication of the second edition. It has been suggested that Blake may have begun his illustrations to the *Pastorals* in 1820.[10] In any event, Blake produced for the third edition twenty-seven drawings and twenty-six engravings of various kinds. These were meant by Thornton, as was the mass of other illustrative material—the subtitle of his book is 'in which all the Proper Facilities Are Given, Enabling Youtm [*sic*] to Acquire the Latin Language, in the Shortest Period of Time'. The engravings were but one of these 'Facilities'. Each Eclogue is presented with an introduction by Thornton, illustrations interspersed with the text, the Latin interspersed with English paraphrases by Thornton, a Moral by Thornton, and a modern English imitation with its own introduction and illustrations. There are also other literary texts in English scattered throughout. The whole is designed to engage the student, to make him see each Eclogue as a poem to be enjoyed.

However laudable these aims—so at variance with the mere rote memorization often associated with classical education in the early nineteenth century—may appear to many of us, it is unlikely that Blake would have admired them. First of all, Blake was opposed to formal education, early and late. In 'The School Boy', first published in *Songs of Innocence*, the speaker laments:

> But to go to school in a summer morn,
> O! It drives all joy away;
> Under a cruel eye outworn,

---

[7] According to the *DNB*, Thornton 'ruined himself' by the expensive projects and died leaving his family 'very poor'.

[8] Unless otherwise indicated plate references follow the numbering of G. E. Bentley, Jr., *Blake Books* (Oxford: Clarendon Press, 1977).

[9] See *BR*, p. 258.

[10] See Keynes, Introduction to *The Illustrations of William Blake for Thornton's Virgil*, p. 7.

The little ones spend the day
In sighing and dismay.

Ah! then at times I drooping sit,
And spend many an anxious hour.
Nor in my book can I take delight,
Nor sit in learnings bower
Worn thro' with the dreary shower.[11]

Such remained Blake's view late in life. In contrast to Dr Thornton, who asked his reader to contemplate 'the *advantages of Education* in its fullest point of view', Blake told Henry Crabb Robinson in 1825 that 'There is no real use in education', and continued: 'I hold it wrong—It is the great Sin . . . the eating of the tree of the knowledge of good & evil.'[12] For Blake, classical education must have held an especially low place, for after his conversionary experiences at Felpham Blake rejected the classics entirely, and he associated the study of the classics with the cult of the nation-state and its wars. This view became if anything more vehement in his last works. 'The Classics, it is the Classics! & not Goths nor Monks, that Desolate Europe with Wars', he wrote in the broadsheet *On Homers Poetry | On Virgil*, produced a year or so after Thornton's third edition was published.[13] At the time that he agreed to illustrate part of Thornton's book, Blake can hardly have had sympathy with its aims.

There are two mistaken ways of looking at Blake's attitude toward participating in such a project. One would be to think that he somehow became reconciled to the basic idea, despite his antipathy to the classics in general and to Virgil in particular, the other to imagine that the experience was a continued ordeal for him. Neither of these views would be true to the life of a man who had to make his living as an engraver, supplementing it by the sale of his drawings and illuminated books. We know very little about Blake's income during the years immediately preceding Linnell's paying him regular advances for the *Job* engravings, but the little we do know tells us something about Blake's situation. In 1818 Blake received from Linnell 15

---

[11] E 31.   [12] Preface to *Pastorals*, p. v; *BR*, p. 311.
[13] It is unlikely to have been produced earlier than 1821, as copy C (untraced) was recorded by Keynes as having an 1821 watermark (see Bentley, *Blake Books*, p. 335); and the copies of it owned by Blake's friends Thomas Butts and Frederick Tatham were paired with *The Ghost of Abel*, which bears the date 1822. See Essick and Viscomi, p. 240.

guineas for Blake's part of the work in engraving a portrait of James Upton, while in 1819 Linnell paid Blake £2. 13s. 6d. for a copy of *Songs of Innocence* and an uncoloured copy of *Jerusalem*.[14] The differences between what Blake could earn from commercial engraving and what he could realistically expect to earn by selling his own works is remarkable. He simply could not afford the luxury of turning down whatever Thornton paid him (the amount is unknown). There are, moreover, two different aspects to the commission. One comprises the workaday heads of classical figures, the other the illustrations to Ambrose Philips's 'Second Pastoral'; and these two groups need to be discussed separately.

As a working engraver, Blake had frequently had the experience of executing commissions toward which he felt indifference or antipathy. Take, as one of many examples, the head of David Hartley that Blake engraved as the frontispiece for a new edition of David Hartley's *Observations on Man*, published in 1791.[15] We know what Blake thought of Hartley: in 1798, Blake seized upon a mention of Hartley among 'men of judgment' in Bishop Watson's *Apology for the Bible* to note 'Hartley a Man of Judgment then Judgment was a Fool what Nonsense' (E 619). Examples could be multiplied, but the main point is clear: Blake had to accept or reject commissions on practical grounds. He also had to develop a strategy for coping with the feelings generated by spending his time and labour on such subjects. Blake's engraving classical heads is virtually an allegory of one aspect of the relationship of Los and his Spectre: the imaginative man ruling the workaday self within him. Such control had, as Blake himself intuited, a terrible price, as expressed in the Spectre's outbreaks of rebellion, 'Watching his time with glowing eyes to leap upon his prey'.[16] Nevertheless, this myth must have given Blake a sense of being in control of his internal world when by necessity he undertook subjects he disliked or even despised.

The copperplate portraits that Blake executed for Thornton's *Virgil* are certainly a case in point, beginning with the second (the first, *Theocritus*, would not have been problematic), *Publius*

[14] Information from *BR*, p. 607. These are the sole financial records extant for those two years.

[15] London, Joseph Johnson, 1791 (after John Shackelton). See Robert N. Essick, *William Blake's Commercial Book Illustrations* (Oxford: Clarendon Press, 1991), no. XXII and pl. 75.

[16] *Jerusalem* 8: 22, E 151.

Virgilius Maro, facing page 4 of volume I.[17] Blake's view of what
Virgil represented is expressed in *On Homers Poetry | On Virgil*,
where Blake expresses his conviction that the classical tradition is a
conduit for the exaltation of war and commerce. He also vehemently
identifies the latter with the art market of his own day:

> Rome & Greece swept Art into their maw and destroyd it a Warlike State
> never can produce Art. It will Rob & Plunder & accumulate into one place,
> & Translate & Copy & Buy & Sell & Criticise, but not Make. (E 270)

Greece and Rome as well as Babylon and Egypt 'were destroyers of
all Art', and 'Homer Virgil & Ovid confirm this opinion . . .'. 'Virgil
in the Eneid Book VI. line 848', Blake acidly remarks, 'says Let
others study Art: Rome has somewhat better to do, namely War
& Dominion' (E 270). Although it is the *Aeneid* that is cited here, we
must not think the *Eclogues* were exempted. When Blake later
came to annotate Dr Thornton's new translation of the Lord's
Prayer, he wrote 'Caesar Virgils Only God See Eclogue I' (E 670).
'Eclogue I' is of course the one that Philips loosely imitated in
his 'Second Pastoral', which Blake illustrated for Thornton. The
lines Blake has in mind are (like most of Virgil's original) not in the
Philips text, but they are in the original Latin, as Blake evidently
knew. The passage is usually taken to allude to Octavian, the
Augustus Caesar to be:

> O Meliboee, deus nobis haec otia fecit:
> namque, erit ille mihi semper deus . . .

---

[17] These engravings are described and reproduced by Essick in *William Blake's
Commercial Book Illustrations*, pp. 112–14. The head of Virgil evidently caused a
temporary reappraisal of the project on Thornton's part. In a letter to Linnell dated
15 September 1820 and enclosing a proof of the plate, Thornton wrote 'I long to see
your Virgil transferred upon the Stone' (*BR*, pp. 266–7). Bentley takes this to
mean that Thornton was dissatisfied with Blake's wood engravings and wanted them
redone as lithographs. Although the work enclosed by Thornton is a proof taken from
Blake's copperplate engraving, he does seem to advocate a change of medium to
lithography for the whole project. Bentley observes that on 2 October 1820 Linnell
went with Thornton to the Lithography Press at Dartmouth Street, Westminster 'to
prove a head of Virgil' (*BR*, p. 267), and he elsewhere suggests 'that Linnell had made
the reduced drawing for the "head of Virgil" which Blake engraved and that Thornton
wished Linnell to draw them [*sic*] directly on the lithographic stone' (*Blake Books*,
p. 259). This is a reasonable supposition—that 'your Virgil' applies to the head, not
to the illustrations for the Philips poem. In the end, of course, none of these were
published as lithographs, though there are two lithographically printed maps in
volume I.

O Meliboeus, it is a god who wrought for us this peace—for a god he shall ever be to me . . .[18]

In addition, Thornton's paraphrase of lines 37–40 of Eclogue I begins: 'He [Tityrus] calls Augustus "a God . . .".'[19]

Augustus himself is the subject of Blake's third plate, *Octavius Augustus Caesar,* bound immediately after the second. 'If Caesar is Right Christ is Wrong', Blake wrote in his annotations to the *Essays of Sir Francis Bacon,* 'both in Politics & Religion since they will divide them in Two' (E 620). This is actually a more uncompromising view than that ascribed to Jesus in the discussion of Caesar's coin in the Synoptic Gospels. Blake would go even further when he later attacked Dr Thornton's *The Lord's Prayer, Newly Translated,* beginning his merciless parody of Thornton's translation 'Our Father Augustus Caesar who art in these thy ⟨Substantial Astronomical Telescopic⟩ Heavens Holiness to thy Name' (E 669). Aware of Thornton's note saying that Tityrus calls Augustus a god, in the paraphrase Blake transfers such a view to Thornton himself. In response to Thornton's characterization of God as *'uncontrolably powerful',* Blake writes, in words that might be taken as a retroactive condemnation of the entire *Virgil* project: 'So you See That God is just such a Tyrant as Augustus Caesar & is not this Good Learned & Wise & Classical' (E 669).

The ancient coins engraved by Blake in his fourth plate include heads of Agrippa, 'a famous General to Augustus', and of Gallus, *'who slew himself having ruled Tyranically'.* As for Julius Caesar, the subject of plate 5,[20] he was one of the alien invaders of Britain in Blake's early series of watercolours of the History of England: 'The Landing of Julius Caesar', preceding 'Boadicea inspiring the Britons

[18] *Virgil,* trans. H. Rushton Fairclough (rev. edn., 2 vols., Cambridge, Mass.: Harvard University Press; London: William Heinemann, 1960), i. 2–3, ll. 6–7. See Andrew Wilton, *The Wood Engravings of William Blake for Thornton's Virgil* (London: British Museum, 1977), p. 21 n.

[19] Far from being uncritical of Augustus, and Blake's later marginalia notwithstanding, Thornton was, as Annabel Patterson observes, highly critical of him and, by analogy, of some of the policies of the Castlereagh administration. See Patterson, *Pastoral and Ideology* (Berkeley and Los Angeles: University of California Press, 1987), pp. 258–9. Thornton's actual view is that calling Augustus 'a God' was 'flattery of a degrading nature, but suited to the times' (p. 6).

[20] This illustrates 'the Fifth Pastoral, Named Julius Caesar', ii. 215–356, and a quotation about Caesar from Lucan's *Pharsalia,* ii. 228–9. See Essick, *William Blake's Commercial Book Illustrations,* p. 114.

against the Romans' and 'Alfred in the countryman's house' (E 672).
Julius, a man of war by profession, is no doubt to be included
in Blake's allusion in *Jerusalem* 52, where Blake accuses 'the
Alexanders & Caesars, the Lewis's & Fredericks' of being alone
the causes of war 'and its actors' (E 201). And whether the
verses in *Auguries of Innocence*—'The Strongest Poison ever
known | Came from Caesars Laurel Crown' (E 492)—refer to Julius
or to his nephew, they express Blake's attitude toward Caesarism.
(Thornton's own view was not very different: 'Julius Caesar, indeed,
properly fell, having violated his country's liberties'.)[21]
    The sixth and last of the copperplate engravings (facing ii. 360)
depicts Epicurus, whose philosophy is the subject of the 'Sixth
Pastoral, the Epicurean Philosophy' (ii. 357–452) and of a quotation
from Lucretius (ii. 360–2) praising Epicurus. Thornton considered
Epicurus 'the greatest philosopher of the age', and beneath Blake's
portrait are eight lines of engraved script, concluding 'He placed the
summum bonum on Tranquility of Mind, arising from Virtue, and
the Contemplation of Nature'.[22] Considering that Blake believed
that 'Moral Virtues do not Exist' and that Nature was a 'Delusive
Goddess',[23] this would hardly have counted in Epicurus' favour for
him. Blake detested the Epicurean philosophy because of its view of
life as a fortuitous concourse of atoms, and he links Epicurus with
more than one of his own *bêtes noires*. In annotating Reynolds's
Discourses, Blake says 'he Thinks Imagination not to be above
the Mortal & Perishing Nature. Such is the End of Epicurean or
Newtonian Philosophy it is Atheism' (E 660). Elsewhere in the
Reynolds marginalia, Blake remarks 'Bacons Philosophy has Ruind
England ⟨Bacon is only Epicurus over again⟩' (E 645). In *Jerusalem*
67 the Daughters of Albion engage in a ritual of human sacrifice,
'Calling the Rocks Atomic Origins of Existence; denying Eternity |
By the Atheistical Epicurean Philosophy of Albions Tree' (12–13; E
220). This portrait, as well as the preceding five engravings, must
have been mere hackwork for Blake.
    In contrast, in illustrating Philips's poem Blake had the opportu-

---

[21] ii. 228. The passage on Caesar from Lucan that Thornton chose to include,
declares: 'But 'twas a valor restless, unconfin'd, | which no success could sate, nor
limits bind' (ii. 228).
[22] Facing ii. 360.
[23] [*A Vision of the Last Judgment*], E 563; Letter to George Cumberland, 12 April
1827, E 784.

nity to exercise his creative imagination. Two specific aspects of the commission are likely to have appealed to him: the challenge of working on an almost gem-like scale, and the pastoral content of the poem he was to illustrate. Blake had worked on a very small scale before: the plate size of the first illuminated books averages 5.4 × 4 cm,[24] while the *Virgil* wood engravings' average size (excepting the frontispiece) is 3.5 × 7.5 cm.[25] Engraving on such small woodblocks is likely to have reminded Blake of the art of gem engraving, the techniques of which he well understood, as we see in part of a plate entitled *GEM Engraving*, which he executed for Rees's *Cyclopaedia*, picturing three views of the cutting of an image of the bust of Jupiter Serapis.[26] Blake had great respect for this art: 'The Greek Gems are in the Same Style as the Greek Statues', Blake wrote in his Annotations to Reynolds (E 651). The content of Philips's *Pastorals* would also have appealed to Blake, whose attraction to the pastoral mode is demonstrated by *The Book of Thel* and by the long pastoral section of Night the Ninth of *The Four Zoas* (126–32, E 395–400). As these works show, Blake had a fine intuitive understanding of the complexities of pastoral, something that affects the world of his *Virgil* illustrations.

Blake may have begun by making a relief etching comprising illustrations 2–5 on a single plate. As Robert N. Essick points out, a comparison of these with the corresponding drawings and the published prints suggest that the drawings were done later in preparation for the wood engravings.[27] There are two main differences between the images in the relief etching and their counterparts in the wood engravings. One is that instead of a supposed shepherd's gown, Colinet (the unhappy shepherd) wears a leotard of the sort familiar to us from many other Blake designs, closely revealing his muscles and the outlines of his body. (In the drawings, he wears a

[24] See Blake, *The Early Illuminated Books*, ed. Morris Eaves, Robert N. Essick, and Joseph Viscomi (London: Tate Gallery for the William Blake Trust, 1993), p. 21.

[25] Martin Butlin, *William Blake* (London: Tate Gallery, 1978), p. 138.

[26] Abraham Rees, *The Cyclopaedia; or, Universal Dictionary of Arts, Sciences, and Literature* (39 text volumes and 6 plates volumes, London: Longman, Hurst, Rees, Orme, & Brown), vol. iv of the plates, Plate XVIII, published 1819. See Essick, *William Blake's Commercial Book Illustrations*, LII, 3a and 3b, p. 110 and fig. 274.

[27] Essick, 'A Relief Etching of Blake's Virgil Illustrations', *Blake*, 25 (Winter 1991/2): 117–26. The relief-etched sheet, in the collection of Professor Essick, is reproduced on p. 117.

gown.) The other is that these four images are much brighter than their wood-engraved counterparts, a point to which we must return later.

In preparation for his engravings on wood, Blake produced at least twenty drawings in pencil, pen, and sepia wash.[28] One of them, showing Thenot and Colinet together, was never engraved, and three were engraved by another hand. The reason for the first omission may have been merely the formatting of the pages of illustrations, but the second involved a threat to Blake's entire participation in the project. According to Alexander Gilchrist, Dr Thornton was almost persuaded to abandon Blake's wood engravings:

> The publishers, unused to so daring a style, were taken aback, and declared 'This man must do no more'; nay, were for having all he *had* done recut by one of their regular hands. The very engravers received them with derision, crying out in the words of the critic: 'This will never do'.

Blake's wood engravings were saved, says Gilchrist, by the intervention of some of Blake's fellow artists at one of the dinners held by the art collectors Charles and Eliza Aders:

> It fortunately happened that meeting one day several artists at Mrs. Charles Aders's table—Lawrence, James Ward, Linnell, and others—conversation fell on Virgil. All expressed warm admiration of Blake's art, and of those designs and woodcuts in particular. By such competent authority reassured, if also puzzled, the good doctor began to think there must be more in them than he and his publishers could discern.[29]

The first part of Gilchrist's story derives from a 'very intelligent article', now known to have been written by Henry Cole, in *The Athenaeum* for 21 January 1843.[30] As the reliability of the Cole and Gilchrist anecdotes has been challenged, something further should be said about them, especially as regards Gilchrist's credibility in this

---

[28] Butlin 1–20. The drawing for the frontispiece is not known to exist. Butlin places the unengraved drawing after Blake's fourth wood engraving.

[29] Gilchrist, *Life*, p. 245. 'This will never do' is of course the first sentence of Francis Jeffrey's famous review of Wordsworth's *Excursion*.

[30] Gilchrist, *Life*, p. 280. [Henry Cole], '*The Vicar of Wakefield*. With thirty-two Illustrations. By W. Mulready, R.A. Van Voorst', *The Athenaeum* (1843), pp. 65–8. Cole is identified as the author of this review by Bentley, *BR*, p. 267 n. 2.

matter.[31] It is true that we do not know the source of Cole's story, published sixteen years after Blake's death. However, even if we for some reason wish to dismiss Cole's account, it is important to note that Gilchrist's depends only partly upon it. The second part, concerning Linnell and three other named artists at the Aderses' dinner, does not appear in Cole. The likelihood is that Gilchrist got this information, as he did much else about Blake's later years, from Linnell himself.[32] Ward and Lawrence would have been likely to have joined Linnell in defending Blake, as these two artists were among the Royal Academicians who later joined in praising Blake's *Job* engravings, and Lawrence later acquired two of Blake's watercolours at 15 guineas each.[33] Furthermore, the second part of the story develops from the authenticity of the first. There would have been no need for the artists to persuade Thornton to publish Blake's wood engravings had the three substitutions not been intended as the prelude to more, and indeed one additional substitute was cut but not used. The indubitable existence of the three 'comparison' wood engravings by another hand means that the scholar who doubts that Thornton intended to replace Blake in the project must conclude that their presence 'remains a mystery'.[34]

The episode of the three 'comparison' illustrations brings the subject of the Thornton–Blake relationship to the fore. In the 1821 volume, the following statement appears under Blake's frontispiece: 'The Illustrations of this English Pastoral are by the famous BLAKE, the illustrator of *Young's* Night Thoughts, and *Blair's* Grave; who designed and engraved them himself. This is mentioned, as they

---

[31] The accounts are dismissed as 'hearsay evidence' by Michael J. Tolley, and Ted Gott states that 'There is . . . not a single piece of evidence to indicate Thornton's reaction to Blake's wood engravings'. See Tolley, 'Thornton's Blake Edition', *University of Adelaide Library News*, 10 (1988): 7; and Gott, 'Thornton's *Virgil*', in Martin Butlin and Ted Gott, *William Blake in the Collection of the National Gallery of Victoria* (Melbourne: National Gallery of Victoria, 1989), pp. 135–6.

[32] Here we may distinguish between the degree of confidence we can have in Gilchrist's unattributed accounts of Blake in the 1790s and those of Blake in the last years of his life. Gilchrist no doubt accumulated his material conscientiously, but in the mid-19th c. very few people were alive who could have known Blake sixty years before, while for information about Blake's late years Gilchrist was able to interview a number of Blake's younger contemporaries.

[33] See *BR*, p. 460 (the source is John Thomas Smith's reliable early life of Blake); Gilchrist, *Life*, p. 349; and Butlin 481 and 559.

[34] Gott, 'Thornton's *Virgil*', p. 138.

display less of art than genius, and are much admired by some eminent painters'. Having decided not to scrap the remaining seventeen illustrations after all, Thornton wants to reassure the reader (and perhaps himself) that although Blake's work may appear strange, he was after all the illustrator of two editions of famous eighteenth-century poets.[35] It is a version of the view that Blake had fought against all his working life: that he was capable of invention but not of execution. Thornton may have wanted to benefit Blake by giving him the commission in the first place, and it has been asserted that the Blake wood engravings are 'grouped together at the front of the first volume'[36] in recognition of the importance of Blake's work. However, the reader who opens the book for the first time does not find Blake's engravings at the very beginning. The first picture is a frontispiece of Virgil, engraved by Hughes after Canova. Then, facing page [v], come two anonymous woodcuts on one page (illustrating 'Fables in Dilworth's Spelling-Book'). Blake's engravings of Virgil, Augustus, and heads from antiquity come after page 4, followed by a map of ancient Italy. Then the illustrations to Virgil's First Eclogue begin with a full-page design engraved by Lee, facing page 5, and continue with thirty-three wood engravings on eleven pages, plus a two-page map of the ancient world, before we encounter Blake's frontispiece to Philips's poem. As the 1814 *Illustrations* contains twelve illustrations on seven pages before that frontispiece, we can see that, far from placing Blake's wood engravings as much to the fore as possible, Thornton added a considerable number of prints by other hands preceding the point where Blake's 'Thenot and Colinet' would appear, followed by his other original designs. Blake appears in the book as one among many illustrators, and he must have felt keenly the indignity of having almost been dropped from the project altogether, of having three of his wood engravings replaced by those of an anonymous hack, and of having his work accompanied by an apologia when it was published. Furthermore, his original wood-blocks had been cut down to fit the page size of Thornton's edition,

[35] On this subject see Geoffrey Keynes, *A Bibliography of William Blake* (New York: Grolier Club, 1921), p. 214; David Bindman, *Blake as an Artist* (Oxford: Phaidon, 1977), pp. 204–5; Butlin, *William Blake*, p. 139; Robert N. Essick, *A Troubled Paradise: William Blake's Virgil Wood Engravings* (San Francisco: John Windle, 1999), p. 10. For a different view, see Tolley, who interprets Thornton's statement as meaning 'not that Blake's work lacks art but that it shows more genius (even) than it shows art' ('Thornton's Blake Edition', p. 5).
[36] Gott, 'Thornton's *Virgil*', p. 134.

with consequent loss of detail and imbalancing of composition. A few words should be said about the effect of this on the published designs.

The extent of what was lost can be appreciated by comparing the woodblocks with the proofs that were taken before the blocks were cut down.[37] The difference is not a matter of size alone, although the reduction in size is one indicator. The sizes of the eight wood engravings in proof compared with those of the woodblocks[38] are as follows, in cm:

2 Proof 3.9 × 8.8; block 3.9 × 7.4.
3 Proof 3.4 × 8.5; block 3.3 × 7.4.
4 Proof 4.5 × 8.6; block 3.2 × 7.3.
5 Proof 4 × 8.7; block 3.7 × 7.4.
6 Proof 4 × 8.4; Thornton edn. 3.4 × 7.3.
7 Proof 3.6 × 8.6; block 3.6 × 7.4.
8 Proof 3.3 × 8.7; block 3.3 × 7.3.
9 Proof 3.9 × 8.7; block 3.4 × 7.3.

As we can see, some of the differences are considerable. For example, number 6, the most famous of the *Virgil* designs, originally measured 33.6 square cm but was reduced to 24.82 square cm for publication. What is eliminated is the extension of the landscape to the viewer's right and the upper part of the blasted tree's middle branch, but in addition to the loss of details, the overall effect of the composition is altered. In the proof of number 3 we can see the fruit on the left side of the left-hand tree as well as on the right side, and the whole trunk of the tree at the right is visible. The proof shows that there were originally two trees at the right in 7, of which only one remained after the block was cut down. Other examples will be mentioned in the course of discussing the individual designs, but what is generally clear is that

---

[37] The blocks were acquired by John Linnell in 1825, and Linnell also owned at least two proof sheets made before the blocks were cut down. These blocks and proofs are now in the Department of Prints and Drawings of the British Museum. The two BM proof sheets (nos. 2–5 and 6–9) are reproduced by Keynes in *The Illustrations of William Blake for Thornton's Virgil*. After Linnell acquired the blocks, he and his friends took a number of prints from them, and these must of course be distinguished from the original proof sheets. At least one group of seven wood engravings was coloured, though not in a manner characteristic of Blake, by the Linnell circle (see G. Ingli James, 'Blake's Woodcuts Illuminated', *Apollo*, 94 (1974): 194–5).

[38] The measurements of the woodblocks rather than those of the published designs are given because it is more feasible to obtain precise measurements from the blocks than from the pages of a book. In the case of no. 6 the block was not available because on loan, and there the dimensions of the wood engraving as published are given.

the blocks were cut down in the workshop with little regard for the consequences for Blake's designs. This must have been yet another blow to Blake's pride in his work. It is very likely that the vehemence of Blake's acidulous comments on Dr Thornton's 'Tory Translation' (E 669) of the Lord's Prayer in 1827 owes something to this and his other experiences in the course of working on Thornton's project, especially when those marginalia end, as we have seen, with a reference to Virgil's First Eclogue.

In a surprisingly short time, these small wood engravings became some of Blake's most celebrated works. Samuel Palmer's characterization set the tone for discussion of them in the nineteenth century:

> I sat down with Mr. Blake's Thornton's *Virgil* woodcuts before me, thinking to give to their merits my feeble testimony. I happened first to think of their sentiment. They are visions of little dells, and nooks, and corners of Paradise; models of the exquisitest pitch of intense poetry. I thought of their light and shade, and looking upon them I found no word to describe it. Intense depth, solemnity, and vivid brilliancy only coldly and partially describe them. There is in all such a mystic and dreamy glimmer as penetrates and kindles the inmost soul, and gives complete and unreserved delight, unlike the gaudy daylight of this world. They are like all that wonderful artist's works the drawing aside of the fleshly curtain, and the glimpse which all the most holy, studious saints and sages have enjoyed, of that rest which remaineth to the people of God.[39]

Such an idealized view was typical of Blake's nineteenth-century admirers, but some time later critics began to recognize the disturbing elements in these wood engravings.[40] Some of this is of course due to Philips's poem, which Blake followed closely for the most part, but accentuating the dark side of his subject, both metaphorically and literally. To convey his vision Blake used a combination of white and black line technique, emphasizing the contrast of light and darkness. He described the white line aspect of his method in two undated memoranda in his Notebook (E 694):

---

[39] Quoted from a sketchbook of 1825 by A. H. Palmer, *The Life and Letters of Samuel Palmer* (London: Seeley & Co., 1892), pp. 15–16.

[40] For example, Jean H. Hagstrum, after quoting Palmer's words, declares that these wood engravings are 'not . . . merely picturesque . . . but powerful moral emblems in which the blasted wheat, the agitated shepherds, the dead trunk, the darkened moon are signs of a fallen world'. See *William Blake: Poet and Painter* (Chicago: University of Chicago Press, 1964), pp. 52–3.

MEMORANDUM

To Woodcut on Pewter. lay a ground on the Plate & smoke it as for Etching, then trace your outline⟨s⟩ [& *draw them in with a needle*]. and beginning with the spots of light on each object with an oval pointed needle scrape off the ground. [& *instead of etching the shadowy strokes*] as a direction for your graver then proceed to graving with the ground on the plate being as careful as possible not to hurt the ground because it being black will shew perfectly what is wanted [*towards*]

MEMORANDUM

To Woodcut on Copper Lay a ground as for Etching. trace &ᶜ. & instead of Etching the blacks Etch the whites & bite it in

As Laurence Binyon described Blake's procedure in an essay first published in 1917, 'Instead of conceiving the design in black on a white ground, he took the black ground which would result from taking an impression from the unengraved block and using that as the foundation of his design, worked, like a mezzotint, from black to white'.[41] The effect was accentuated by Blake's flick work—'seemingly careless flicks', as Essick puts it, '—actually placed with great skill—to capture the play of light and shadow'.[42] The dramatic impression of light emanating from darkness, which Blake had created in his previous works in white line, was now achieved on wood. The overwhelming effect of the series is of darkness. Only one of Blake's wood engravings is predominantly bright, six are night scenes while six take place at sunrise or sunset, and even in full day the blacks are pervasive. It is instructive to compare Blake's engraving 3 with the 'amendment' that Thornton at one time intended to replace it with, printed by Henry Cole as an illustration of his argument that 'amid all drawbacks there exists a power in the work of a man of genius, which no one but himself can utter fully'.[43] The 'amendment' is clearer and cleaner than Blake's, and much less dark; Thenot's posture is different—he leans forward and extends his right

---

[41] Binyon, 'The Engravings of William Blake and Edward Calvert', *Print Collector's Quarterly*, 7 (1917): 305–32; repr. in Robert N. Essick, ed., *The Visionary Hand* (Los Angeles: Hennessey & Ingals, 1973), p. 61.

[42] See Essick, *William Blake, Printmaker* (Princeton: Princeton University Press, 1980), p. 227. Essick's entire chapter on the *Virgil* series, pp. 224–33, is of great importance.

[43] [Henry Cole], '*The Vicar of Wakefield*', pp. 65–8.

FIG. 2. William Blake, Illustrations to Thornton's *Virgil*,
frontispiece to Eclogue I: 'Thenot and Colinet'. Wood
engraving, *c*.1820.

arm bent at the elbow, perhaps indicating the bright, radiant
sun. The three anonymous 'comparison engravings' are also much
less dark than all but one of Blake's, though in this case we unfortu-
nately do not have Blake's as comparisons. The prevailing darkness
in Blake's series is of course very deliberate. Its thematic power
will become more evident as we discuss the individual wood
engravings.

Blake's first three illustrations show the pastoral world in three dif-
ferent phases of the rising sun. In the frontispiece (Fig. 2) the sun is
seen just rising above hills in the background, where a shepherd's
cottage is visible. 'Lonesome' and 'in woful plight', Colinet leans
against a tree in a pathos-formula of melancholy, his left hand to his
head (rather than 'with folded arms' as in Philips's text[44]), and his
shepherd's pipe and syrinx hang unused on the tree trunk, like the
unused musical instruments in *Job* engraving 1. (Both cottage and
tree will become important motifs in this series.) Thenot, the older
shepherd, makes an admonitory gesture with his left palm down and
right palm extended toward the viewer, as a visual equivalent of

---

[44] Quotations from Philips's 'The Second Pastoral' are from Thornton's edition
(i. 13–17) because, although this text is corrupt in at least one passage (see below), it
is the one Blake illustrated. For a modern edition, the reader may consult *The Poems
of Ambrose Philips*, ed. M. G. Segar (Oxford: Blackwell, 1937).

Philips's 'Why in this mournful manner art thou found, | unthankful lad, when all things smile around?' Both wear gowns (Colinet's tighter-fitting and a bit shorter) of the kind worn by shepherds only in the land of pastoral. Sheep graze between them, with a ram in the centre staring out at us. This visual equivalent of the verbal dialogue continues as the sun continues to rise in 2 (Fig. 3*a*), which begins the first full sheet of four wood engravings. Colinet, still beneath the tree, floridly gestures with his right arm to express his feeling: 'Waking, at midnight, I my woes renew, | my tears oft mingling with the falling dew'. Thenot responds with outspread arms in a palms-out gesture usually asssociated in Blake's imagery with the generous giving of self, as in *Albion rose* and *Jerusalem* 76. In what can only be called a picturesque detail, a shepherd dog sniffs Thenot's left foot. Although singing birds—'lark and linnet', both active at dawn—are contrasted to the 'mournful' shepherd in Philips's poem, Blake has not attempted to render them, perhaps because of the inherent difficulty of representing songbirds in a very small engraving in which full-length human figures must appear. With the sun fully risen over the hills in 3 (Fig. 3*b*), the two sit under trees on either side of the image, the sheep again between them, and the cottage again in the background. Thenot, arms raised oratorically, discourses on age and youth. A branch of the tree to his side bends over him in illustration of Philips's trope:

> Yet though with years my body downward tend,
> as trees beneath their fruit in autumn bend,
> spite of my snowy head and icy veins,
> my mind a cheerful temper still retains.

Significantly, no fruit appears on the tree under which Colinet slumps dejected. In 4 (Fig. 3*c*) it is full day, and the sheep have changed positions—two appear to be baaing at Colinet while others appear in a row in the background, legs bent identically like an ovine corps de ballet. Thenot extends his right arm palm up, indicating the arrival of a youth who appears running down a hill, much like the messenger in the background of *Job* engraving 4, with a leaping dog following him. This is 'Lightfoot', who will tend Thenot's sheep so that the older shepherd may have leisure to hear about Colinet's 'inward ailment'. In the last wood engraving on this page, 5 (Fig. 3*d*), Colinet, almost a mirror image of himself as shown in 2, gestures with both hands, the right one extended towards the sky (and almost cut off by

FIG. 3*a*. 'Colinet'

FIG. 3*b*. 'Thenot'

FIG. 3*c*. 'Colinet and Thenot'

FIG. 3*d*. 'Colinet'

FIG. 3*a, b, c, d*. William Blake, Illustrations to Thornton's
Virgil. Wood engravings, *c*.1820.

the trimming of the woodblock), the left one holding his staff, as he expresses his unhappiness.

> Where to begin I know not, where to end.—
> Does there one smiling hour my youth attend?—
> Though few my days, as well my follies show,
> yet are those days all clouded o'er with wo:
> no happy gleam of sunshine doth appear,
> my low'ring sky, and wint'ry months, to chear.—

Thenot reacts with a palms-down gesture expressing surprise and horror (cf. the woman looking down at the dead baby in the 'Holy Thursday' of *Experience*). The tree at our right, which up to now has displayed a leafy bough, is now leafless as if in sympathy with Colinet's lament, and a cleft has appeared in it, anticipating Philips's lines a little further on. The sheep have again changed position and are now feeding, tended by a dog, between Colinet and the tree. These four images and the frontispiece are like the panels of a comic strip—the reader can easily fill in what happens between the pictures, and while they illustrate a text, one could easily reconstruct the basic situations without any words at all.

The first five wood engravings give an overall impression of darkness unlike anything to be found among the works of the other engravers in these two volumes. Even though in the course of 1–5 the sun's disc rises over the hills into the morning sky, the hills, most of the ground, the cottage, and the trees are predominantly black with flecks of white. This effect is carried much further in 6 (Fig. 4*a*), opening the second page of four illustrations with what has become one of Blake's most famous images. The tree to the viewer's left is even more 'naked' than the one to our right in the previous design. Its form suggests a human being in torment. As the fruitful tree in 3 mirrored Thenot's state, this 'Ill-fated tree' mirrors Colinet's, a parallel central to Philips's text:

> My piteous plight in yonder naked tree,
> which bears the thunder-scar too plain I see:
> quite destitute it stands of shelter kind,
> the mark of storms, and sport of every wind:
> the riven trunk feels not the approach of spring;
> nor birds among the leafless branches sing:
> no more, beneath thy shade, shall shepherds throng
> with jocund tale, or pipe, or pleasing song.—

FIG. 4a. 'Thenot'

FIG. 4b. 'Thenot'

FIG. 4c. 'Colinet'

FIG. 4d. 'Colinet'

FIG. 4a, b, c, d. William Blake, Illustrations to Thornton's
Virgil. Wood engravings, c.1820.

> Ill-fated tree! and more ill-fated I!
> from thee, from me, alike the shepherds fly.—

Further details of Blake's design are provided in Thenot's reply:

> Sure thou in hapless hour of time wast born,
> when blighting mildews spoil the rising corn,
> or blasting winds o'er-blossom'd hedge-rows pass,
> to kill the promis'd fruits, and scorch the grass;
> or when the moon, by wizard charm'd, foreshows,
> blood-stain'd in foul eclipse, impending woes.—
> Untimely born, ill-luck betides thee still.—

Closely following Philips, Blake shows the moon in eclipse, making the night even darker; and as in *America* 9 the wheat has been beaten down by winds, and slant rain falls.[45] This design may also be compared with plate 12 of *Europe*, in which two beautiful trumpeters personify, in the words of a contemporary annotator who may have been George Cumberland, 'Mildews blighting ears of Corn'.[46] Beneath the beauty of these designs lies a ravaged world symbolized by the spoiling of the harvest. Another night scene of destruction follows. Thenot seems at this point to have become as melancholy as Colinet:

COLINET.

And can there, THENOT, be a greater ill?—

THENOT.

> Nor fox, nor wolf, nor rot among our sheep;
> from these good shepherd's care his flock may keep
> against ill-luck, alas! all forecast fails;
> nor toil by day, nor watch by night, avails.—

In 7 (Fig. 4*b*) all three disasters appear to be happening at once. The animal at our left has a Reynard-like face and is presumably the fox, while the one bearing away a sheep despite the shepherd's gesticulation must be the wolf. At the shepherd's feet, outside the sheepfold, lies a sheep presumably dead or dying of rot.

At this point in Philips's poem Colinet begins the recital of his own personal story (as distinguished from the shepherd's lot in general),

---

[45] As noted by Tolley, 'Thornton's Blake Edition', p. 15.
[46] See Bentley, *Blake Books*, pp. 158–9.

which will become one with which Blake closely identifies. Illustration 8 (Fig. 4*c*), however, is a landscape. It shows, indeed, that a successful landscape engraving is possible even on such a small scale. In the centre, flowing into the foreground, meanders a river, emanating from what may be a lake before a hill at the rear, and reflecting almost supernally the light of an unseen moon. Sheep safely graze to our left, one suckling a lamb; and there is a tree on either side, the one on the right sheltering a cottage like the one seen earlier but nearer at hand. (Before the block was cut down, the foliage of the tree extended considerably further to our right, giving the cottage an even more protected feeling.) The rural cottage here is, as in some of Coleridge's poems of the 1790s, potentially a millennial world in miniature,[47] one which Colinet laments that he has abandoned:

> Unhappy hour! when fresh in youthful bud,
> I left, Sabrina fair, thy silv'ry flood.—
> Ah, silly I! more silly than my sheep,
> which on thy flow'ry banks I wont to keep.—
> Sweet are thy banks: oh, when shall I once more,
> with ravish'd eyes review thine amell'd shore?—
> When, in the crystal of thy waters, scan
> each feature faded, and my colour wan?—
> When shall I see my hut, the small abode
> myself did raise and cover o'er with sod?—
> Small though it be, a mean and humble cell,
> yet is there room for peace and me to dwell.—

'Sabrina fair', a deliberate echo by Philips of Milton's *Comus*, alludes to the River Severn, which flows through Philips's native Shropshire. However, Blake may here be remembering the three years that he himself spent in the English countryside, in Sussex at the very beginning of the century, and it may be that echoes of his failed attempt to live under the patronage of William Hayley begin at this point. Robert Essick sees a parallel here between Colinet's 'hut' and Blake's cottage at Felpham,[48] and this and other comparisons to Blake's

---

[47] See my *Apocalypse and Millennium in English Romantic Poetry* (Oxford: Clarendon Press, 1999), pp. 83, 85, 116, 120–1, 123–4.

[48] 'Like Colinet's house, Blake's had a thatched roof, second-story windows well within the pitch of the roof at the end, and a wood fence with diagonal members'.— Essick, *William Blake, Printmaker*, p. 231. The idea that Blake's recollection of the Felpham period figures importantly in these illustrations begins, as Essick mentions,

Felpham experience work well if we bear in mind that what is involved is not a systematic, one-on-one analogy. How complex the allusions can be may be seen in the next picture. Illustration 9 (Fig. 4*d*) takes place at the last moment of sunset—there is a sliver of setting sun behind the hills, and its light strikes and illuminates a church steeple in the background. The traveller, who has just passed a wayside cross (a relic of medieval England), is a cryptic self-portrait of Blake himself, wearing the kind of hat that Blake wore at this time of his life, '*rather* broad brimmed but not quakerish',[49] to use Samuel Palmer's words, and that he is shown wearing in Linnell's late portrait sketch (Fitzwilliam Museum). (Interestingly, in Blake's preparatory drawing the figure wears no hat, and there is no church spire.[50]) This design echoes in reverse 'The Traveller hasteth in the Evening' from *The Gates of Paradise*. In that engraving the Traveller wears a similar hat but has a walking stick rather than staff in his right hand, and he seems to be striding forward with alacrity in contrast to the more measured step of the shepherd figure. In the wood engraving a personal reference is introduced by the milestone (which looks very like a gravestone) that the shepherd is passing. It is inscribed 'LXII | miles | London', and as Blake was 62 at the time of the Thornton commission, we may interpret the figure as Blake himself. Blake may well have been thinking of the verses he had inscribed for the Traveller in *For the Sexes*: 'Thro evening shades I haste away | To close the Labours of my Day' (43–4, E 269). A possible additional meaning may lie in the fact that the distance from Felpham to London is about 62 miles, which leads to the suggestion that the traveller may be walking that route. The spire could then be that of Chichester Cathedral, which Blake had pictured in the closing vignette for Hayley's Preface to the 1802 *Ballads*.[51] Of course the mile marker would then be facing the wrong way as the traveller

with Laurence Binyon in his Introduction to *Little Engravings Classical & Contemporary Number II. William Blake, Being All His Woodcuts* (London: Sign of the Unicorn, 1902). It has been endorsed by, among others: David Wagenknecht, *Blake's Night: William Blake and the Idea of Pastoral* (Cambridge, Mass.: Belknap Press, 1973), p. 8; Tolley, 'Thornton's Blake Edition'; Patterson, *Pastoral and Ideology*, pp. 253–9; and Gott, 'Thornton's *Virgil*'.

[49] See Gilchrist, *Life*, p. 283.

[50] He may be carrying the hat in his right hand, unless the object there is a scrip.

[51] See Essick, *William Blake, Printmaker*, p. 232; and Leopold Damrosch, *Symbol and Truth in Blake's Myth* (Princeton: Princeton University Press, 1980), pp. 229–30 n.

passes it, but that may be a mere visual convenience. (If Blake were thinking of Felpham as a deviation from his true path, the Traveller would be walking away from it.) Here Colinet's course is not quite the same as Blake's.

THENOT.

And what enticement charm'd thee far away
from thy lov'd home, and led thy heart astray?—

COLINET.

A fond desire strange lands and swains to know.—
Ah me! that ever I should covet woe.—[52]
With wand'ring feet unblest, and fond of fame,
I sought I know not what besides a name.—

Before going to Felpham, Blake had lived all his life in London, so returning there could hardly correspond to Colinet's 'fond desire strange lands and swains to know'. However, we may recognize in this and some other *Virgil* designs elements of Blake's 'three years slumber on the banks of the Ocean'[53] rather than a sustained parallel narrative. What is undoubtable here is that Blake now thought of himself as the Traveller in the Evening passing the milestone of his sixty-second year.

The third set of four wood engravings begins with one of Blake's less successful *Virgil* designs, illustrating Thenot's words:

Or, sooth to say, didst thou not hither rome
in search of gains more plenty than at home?
A rolling stone is ever, bare of moss;
and, to their cost, green years old proverbs cross.—

Thornton may possibly have directed the artist to illustrate the metaphor, as he almost certainly did with respect to the three 'Comparison' designs to come. The illustrations were after all meant to stimulate students, although literalizing a sententious trope as Blake does in 10 (Fig. 5a) may not have been the best way to accomplish this. Blake makes the 'rolling stone' a roller pulled by a young man, bent almost double with exertion, over the drive of a stately

---

[52] Perhaps to protect the innocent student reader, these lines have been altered from: 'A lewd desire strange lands, and swains, to know: | Ah God! that ever I should covet woe'.

[53] *Jerusalem* 3, E 145.

FIG. 5*a*. 'Thenot'

FIG. 5*b*. 'Colinet'

FIG. 5*c*. 'Colinet'

FIG. 5*d*. 'Thenot'

FIG. 5*a*, *b*, *c*, *d*. William Blake, Illustrations to Thornton's
Virgil. Wood engravings, *c*.1820.

mansion. Unlike the shepherds, he wears tights, and the image breaks the line of visual narrative that has succeeded so well thus far and that is immediately resumed afterwards. In the very dark night scene of 11 (Fig. 5*b*) we see Colinet lamenting his situation on the banks of the Cam:

COLINET.

> Small need there was, in random search of gain,
> to drive my pining flock athwart the plain
> to distant Cam.—Fine gain at length, I trow,
> to hoard up to myself such deal of wo!—
> My sheep quite spent through travel and ill fare,
> and like their keeper ragged grown and bare,
> the damp cold green sward for my nightly bed,
> and some slaunt willow's trunk to rest my head.—

Blake represents all these details. Colinet lies against a tree, his sheep visible along the river bank. The effect of the moonlight reflected from the water is wonderful. On the other side, in the background, the waning moon bathes in light the spires of a Gothic building which, it has been suggested, is King's College Chapel.[54] The obvious reference here is to Philips, who was a Fellow of St John's College, Cambridge. However, as Blake well knew, Dr Thornton had been a student at King's College, Cambridge, before he went to Guy's Hospital—the title page of the *Virgil* identifies Thornton as 'Member of the University of Cambridge'—and Blake may be implying that Thornton's studies were as fruitless as Colinet's. In 12 (Fig. 5*c*), however, we are back to Colinet-Philips-Blake, as shepherd and poet.

COLINET.

> Untoward lads, the wanton imps of spite
> make mock of all the ditties I endite.—
> In vain, O COLINET thy pipe, so shrill,
> charms every vale, and gladdens every hill:
> in vain thou seek'st the coverings of the grove,
> in the cool shade to sing the pains of love:
> sing what thou wilt, ill-nature will prevail;

---

[54] Andrew Wilton remarks: 'Colinet rests by "distant Cam" and the Gothic pinnacles of King's College Chapel glitter under the moon in a scene of dim chiaroscuro that recalls Elsheimer's nocturnal landscapes'.—*The Wood Engravings of William Blake for Thornton's Virgil*, p. 27.

This theme is entirely absent from Virgil's First Eclogue and was introduced by Philips. As Philips wrote his pastorals very early in his career, prior to Pope's, and could not have known that Pope would savage his work, 'the wanton imps of spite' may have been fellow Cambridge undergraduates, or perhaps this part of Colinet's lament is purely conventional. Blake, however, had certainly encountered derision of his poetry and could identify with Colinet, who stands helplessly between two trees with his pipe in his left hand while two youths gesture mockingly at him. (Only a cottage in the background reminds us that tranquillity may be found somewhere.) When Blake's *Poetical Sketches* were printed in 1783, they were preceded by an anonymous deprecatory 'Advertisement' stating that the poems 'were the productions of untutored youth' and that 'he has been deprived of the leisure requisite to such a revisal of these sheets, as might have rendered them less unfit to meet the public eye'.[55] In 1803, when Blake showed William Hayley part of *Vala*, which Blake considered 'the Grandest Poem that This World Contains', Hayley 'lookd with sufficient contempt to enhance my opinion of it';[56] and when he let Robert Southey see part of *Jerusalem*, Southey considered it 'a perfectly mad poem'.[57] After he rented his cottage at Felpham, Blake declared 'I can be Poet Painter & Musician as the Inspiration comes',[58] but by the time he executed the *Virgil* designs there is little to indicate that he was thought of as a poet even by his friends, and he must have feared that like Colinet's his music might be stilled.

A sudden change of tone marks the last image of this page, no. 13 (Fig. 5*d*). The world has become very bright for the moment. We are witnessing an outdoor musical event at which three women in revealing dresses, one holding a tambourine over her head, dance gracefully (cf. the dancing women in the top part of Blake's full-page

---

[55] E 846. It should not be thought that the *Poetical Sketches* were ancient history to Blake: he continued to give away copies late in life and possessed some at the time of his death.

[56] Letter to Thomas Butts, 6 July 1803, E 730.

[57] As reported by Henry Crabb Robinson, *BR*, p. 229. Of course Southey may not have used these words to Blake himself, but, considering Southey's characteristic bluntness in such matters, he is likely to have given Blake some inkling of his judgement.

[58] Letter to George Cumberland, 1 September 1800. See Robert N. Essick and Morton D. Paley, ' "Dear Generous Cumberland": A Newly Discovered Letter and Poem by William Blake', *Blake*, 32 (1998): 4–13.

Milton 15 design). The music is produced by a seated, well-dressed couple, he playing a violin, she a lyre. A girl and a small boy look on, but the main audience is imagined to be viewing the performance from our own perspective. In the background is what may be the other façade of the Palladian mansion pictured in 10. We may assume that the seated man is Menalcas, praised by both shepherds:

COLINET.

> But yet, though poor and artless be my vein,
> MENALCAS seems to like my simple strain:
> and, while that he delighteth in my song,
> which to the good MENALCAS doth belong,
> nor night nor day shall my rude music cease;
> I ask no more, so I MENALCAS please.

THENOT.

> MENALCAS, lord of these fair fertile plains,
> preserves the sheep, and o'er the shepherds reigns:
> for him our yearly wakes and feasts we hold,
> and choose the fairest firstlings from the fold;
> he, good to all who good deserves, shall give
> thy flock to feed, and thee at ease to live,
> shall curb the malice of unbridled tongues,
> and bounteously reward thy rural songs.—

Menalcas in the original Eclogue is thought to be Octavian, who restored to Virgil an estate that had been taken away from him; in the Philips version, he stands for Joseph Addison, who praised Philips's *Pastorals* and served as his literary defender. If we wish to pursue an autobiographical element here, who would have been Blake's Menalcas? It is unlikely that after his experiences at Felpham Blake could have regarded Hayley in such a way. However, there is another Sussex candidate. According to Gilchrist, 'Hayley, desiring the artist's worldly advancement, introduced him to many of the neighbouring gentry; among them, Lord Egremont of Petworth'.[59] The Earl of Egremont's benefactions to the poor were almost legendary: according to the *DNB*, he disbursed £20,000 a year for charity over a period of sixty years, and he gave annual fêtes for the poor on an extraordinary scale—Charles Greville, who attended one of them,

---

[59] *Life*, p. 139.

said there were six thousand people present, 'and declared it to be the gayest and most beautiful spectacle he had ever seen. . . . Not the least impressive part of the entertainment was the keen pleasure shown by the host himself . . .'.[60] Blake executed a *Vision of the Last Judgment* (Butlin 642) for the Countess of Egremont in 1808, and she was also the owner of his *Satan Calling Up His Legions* (Butlin 662). The Earl appears to have thought of himself as at least Blake's potential Menalcas, for he visited Mrs Blake some time after her husband's death 'and, recalling Blake's Felpham days, said regretfully, "Why did he leave me?" '[61] Blake may well have intended 13 as a graceful compliment to the Egremonts, in which case the mansion in the background could be the late seventeenth-century great house at Petworth, which, like the house in Blake's design, has three storeys, and one façade of which had a pediment until 1814.[62]

After the temporary uplift of 13 come the three unfortunate 'Comparison' pictures (Figs. 6a, 6b, and 6c), engraved by an unknown hand. These follow, though not in every detail, the corresponding drawings by Blake, but it is difficult to imagine Blake as having chosen such unpromising passages for illustration:

COLINET.

> First then shall lightsome birds forget to fly,
> the briny ocean turn to pastures dry,
> and every rapid river cease to flow,
> ere I unmindful of MENALCAS grow.

Perhaps Dr Thornton set these *adynata*[63] as examples to be illustrated. Only two other designs in the series have no human figures in them—6 and 8—but, although both of those are memorable, the tasks of showing birds not flying, the ocean drying up, and rivers not

---

[60] *DNB*, s.v. [61] Gilchrist, *Life*, p. 356.

[62] The pediment appears clearly in Samuel Hieronymus Grim's watercolour *West and South Fronts of Petworth House* (1780), and although there is no portico, the section of the house below the pediment is thrust out; these details can be seen, although less distinctly, in J. M. W. Turner's *Dewy Morning* (1810). See Martin Butlin, Mollie Luther, and Ian Warrell, *Turner at Petworth* (London: Tate Gallery, 1989), figs. 106 (p. 110) and 35 (p. 43). The house extends much farther on either side than it does in Blake's picture, but closing off the entire background would not have been to Blake's purpose artistically.

[63] Paul Alpers points out that this is 'the rhetorical term for such a catalogue of impossibilities'. See Alpers, *The Singer of the Eclogues* (Berkeley and Los Angeles: University of California Press, 1979), p. 70. Although this is a point of contact between Philips's poem and Virgil's, the images are different in each.

(a)

(b)

(c)

FIG. 6a, b, c. Anonymous wood engraver, Illustrations to
Thornton's *Virgil*. Wood engravings, c.1820. (a) 'First
Comparison'; (b) 'Second Comparison'; (c) 'Third
Comparison'.

flowing was beyond even Blake. He did not attempt this in his drawings (Butlin 769.14, 15, 16) but rather showed the state of things before each event occurred (see reproductions in Butlin ii, figs. 1009–11). Nevertheless, the subjects did not lend themselves to representation on such a small scale, much as we wish we had Blake's own renditions.

In the fourth sheet of Blake's own wood engravings, which brings the series to its conclusion, the designs fall into two pairs. No. 14 (Fig. 7*a*) is a sunset scene with the land darkening as the last remnant of the solar disc slips behind the hills. In contrast to 7 the sheep are safe in their fold, a few laggards entering under Thenot's protecting right arm, with a cottage in the midground behind the sheepfold. Flourishing his shepherd's crook in his other hand, the older shepherd leans toward the younger invitingly.

THENOT.

This night thy care with me forget, and fold
thy flock with mine, to ward th' injurious cold.—

Colinet makes a gesture of acceptance with his right hand, palm out; and in 15 (Fig. 7*b*) we find him enjoying Thenot's hospitality:

New milk, and clouted cream, mild cheese and curd,
with some remaining fruit of last year's hoard,
shall be our ev'ning fare; and, for the night,
sweet herbs and moss, which gentle sleep invite:[64]

We see into Thenot's hut from outside, the 'fourth wall' being removed, following a convention widely used in thirteenth- and fourteenth-century painting. (Blake had done this earlier in the first illustration of Milton's Nativity Ode, where the front of the stable is cut away—especially striking in the Whitworth Art Gallery version.[65]) It is night, and outside we see the stars and a sliver of a waxing moon, while within the two shepherds sit at supper near a glowing hearth. What is depicted is an image of protection and containment, yet it is at the same time constricting—Colinet even has to tilt his head slightly to accommodate to the slanting roof above him. This perhaps reminds us that Colinet is protected from cold and care

---

[64] A passage, for once, close to some lines in Virgil's Eclogue: see *Virgil*, trans. Fairclough, p. 9, ll. 80–3.
[65] Executed 1809. Butlin 538.1 (reproduced pl. 660).

FIG. 7a. 'Thenot'. 'To illustrate lines 1, 2'

FIG. 7b. 'Lines 3, 4, 5, 6'

FIG. 7c. 'Lines 7, 8, 9'

FIG. 7d. 'Line 10'

FIG. 7a, b, c, d. William Blake, Illustrations to Thornton's
Virgil. Wood engravings, c.1820.

for one night only, and that the vicissitudes of the shepherd's life await him the next day.

The last two designs shift back in time to sunset, illustrating Philips's:

> and now behold the sun's departing ray,
> o'er yonder hill, the sign of ebbing day:
> with songs the jovial hinds return from plow;
> and unyok'd heifers, loitering homeward, low.

In **16** (Fig. 7*c*) as the sun sets behind the dark hills, a boy removes the yoke from two 'heifers', though as represented by Blake they appear to be oxen. All cast long shadows, a wonderful touch. Before the animals walk two men wearing hats and carrying musical instruments—the one at the left a pipe, the one at the right a syrinx— Colinet's musical instruments are back in use, though not by him. In the left foreground is the plough that the heifers or oxen were pulling when yoked. In **17** (Fig. 7*d*) a boy younger than his predecessor, wearing a hat and carrying a crook, looks back at the animal immediately behind him, which appears to be lowing while its companion flicks its tail. The disc of the sun has moved to our right and sunk even lower.

Scenes like those on this last page of wood engravings are, as is generally recognized, in some ways reminiscent of the level of existence Blake calls Beulah:

> There is a place where Contrarieties are equally True
> This place is called Beulah, It is a pleasant lovely Shadow
> Where no dispute can come. Because of those who Sleep.[66]

Beulah is typically associated with human love, the moon, the starry night, and flowers. It is one aspect of the pastoral. But it is 'a mild & pleasant rest'[67] from the labours of Eternity, a rest that cannot be prolonged for ever without terrible results (as shown by the examples of Har and Heva in *Tiriel*, who in old age still devote themselves to childish pursuits). As we have seen, the content of Blake's *Virgil* includes deprivation, destruction, and the rejection of the poet—all subjects that can be accommodated by the pastoral mode but that can find no place in that 'pleasant lovely Shadow'. The last images in the series again remind us of the limitations of Beulah. In *Songs of*

---

[66] *Milton* 30: 1–3, E 129.   [67] *The Four Zoas*, Night I, 5: 29, E 303.

Experience Blake had presented the chimney sweep as an indictment of his entire society. The boy of 17 seems a terribly frail figure in contrast to the two draft animals he leads, suggesting that Blake's awareness of the injustice of child labour did not stop at the edge of the countryside. The yoke that is held aloft by a slightly older boy close to the centre of 16 may take on an additional meaning in this context, and the agricultural labourers who walk home in the lengthening shadows will, we know, have to rise at dawn to resume their work. These magnificent last scenes, rendered in a deliberately archaic or 'primitive' manner, provide in their ambiguity a fitting end to Blake's dark pastoral.

In engraving his designs for Thornton's *Virgil*, Blake fulfilled his commission in an unusually imaginative way, but was not free to go beyond his subject matter, except by implication. Another major work of his last years also had its origin as one of a group of book illustrations, but in this instance Blake was stimulated to make further use of the subject in a work uniquely his own, one of which he is said to have declared 'You will find my creed there'.[68] For a full discussion of this subject, we must go back to its origin.

[68] See Bentley, *The Stranger from Paradise*, p. 498. Bentley quotes from the journal of John Clark Strange, who owned some Blake pictures and knew Samuel Palmer, to whom, according to Strange's journal, Blake made the statement.

2 יהּ & his two Sons Satan & Adam

I

SOME TIME IN 1815 an obscure artist and engraver came to the
Royal Academy's antique school for the purpose of drawing from a
cast of the *Laocoön* group (Fig. 8), in preparation for an engraving
he had been commissioned to make. Henry Fuseli, Professor of
Painting and Keeper, recognized an old friend. 'Why! Mr Blake,' he
said, 'you a student! You ought to teach us!' Alexander Gilchrist,
who had this anecdote from Blake's much younger friend Frederick
Tatham, continues: 'Blake took his place with the students, and
exulted over his work . . . like a young disciple; meeting his old
friend Fuseli's congratulations and kind remarks with cheerful, sim-
ple joy.'[1] However cheerful William Blake may really have been in
doing this commercial job, he produced at least two drawings of the
Laocoön, and then an engraving that was, with three others by
Blake, published illustrating John Flaxman's article on sculpture in
Abraham Rees's *The Cyclopaedia; or, Universal Dictionary of Arts,
Sciences, and Literature.*[2] The drawing that has survived (Fig. 9)[3]
corrects the position of the right arm of the younger son, bending it
back over the figure's head in a manner similar to that of the second
restoration that would be completed in 1960, and the stomach mus-
cles of the father are more contracted than in the Royal Academy cast

[1] Gilchrist, *Life*, p. 261.
[2] Abraham Rees, *The Cyclopaedia; or, Universal Dictionary of Arts, Sciences, and
Literature* (39 text volumes and 6 plates volumes, London: Longman, Hurst, Rees,
Orme, & Brown) was first published in fascicles from 1802 to 1820. Blake engraved
at least seven plates for this work. The one depicting the *Laocoön* and two other stat-
ues, dated 1 October 1815, appears as plate 3 for 'Sculpture' in the fourth plate vol-
ume. The article, attributed to John Flaxman, John Bacon, and Prince Hoare, appears
in text volume xxxii. See Robert N. Essick, *William Blake's Commercial Book
Illustrations* (Oxford: Clarendon Press, 1991), pp. 109–12.
[3] Butlin 679. Another, larger drawing (Butlin 680), once the property of Mrs Blake,
was exhibited in 1876 but has been untraced since 1885.

FIG. 8. Cast of the *Laocoön*.

FIG. 9. William Blake, copy of the *Laocoön* for Rees's
Cyclopaedia. Pencil, 1815.

that Blake copied (or in the original it was taken from).[4] The stippled line engraving that Blake produced for *The Cyclopaedia* (Fig. 10) was first published in 1816. Doing this work evidently put him in mind of the *Laocoön* as a possible subject for one or more of his own creations.

One of these was a large pen, pencil, and watercolour drawing (Fig. 11) that Martin Butlin has dated as being 'stylistically close to the Dante illustrations of 1824–7'.[5] The bearded central figure is fully clothed, unlike the one in the *Laocoön* sculpture, although his garment is, as so often in Blake, diaphanous, revealing the body beneath. Again unlike the sculpture, his mouth is opened in a cry. His two sons, more lightly sketched, are on either side of him, almost of the same height as each other. His left foot, emerging from his gown, has been outlined and the toes delineated in pen and ink. Perhaps not all bearded patriarchs in Blake's works are to be identified with Urizen, but the anguished expression and the prominent left foot of this figure (compare Urizen's left foot in the frontispiece to *Europe*) make such an identification likely here, as Keynes suggests.[6] The fact that the serpents tower over the figures and that the central figure is crying out, suggests that the subject is Virgil's description of the scene in the second book of *The Aeneid*. In Dryden's translation, this reads in part:

> We fled amaz'd; their destin'd Way they take,
> And to *Laocoon* and his children make:
> And first around the tender Boys they wind,
> Then with sharpen'd Fangs their Limbs and Bodies grind.
> The wretched Father, running to their Aid
> With pious Haste, but vain, they next invade:
> Twice round his waste their winding Volumes rowl'd,
> And twice about his gasping Throat they fold.
> The Priest thus doubly choak'd, their crests divide,
> And towring o're his Head, in Triumph ride.
> With both his Hands he labours at the Knots;
> His Holy Fillets the blue Venom blots:
> His roaring fills the flittering Air around.
> Thus, when an Oxe receives a glancing Wound,

[4] See Sir Geoffrey Keynes, ed., *William Blake's Laocoön: A Last Testament: With Related Works: On Homers' Poetry and On Virgil, The Ghost of Abel* (London: The Trianon Press for the William Blake Trust, 1976), p. 55; Robert N. Essick, *The Separate Plates of William Blake* (Princeton: Princeton University Press, 1983), pp. 99–100. [5] Butlin 681. [6] *William Blake's Laocoön*, pp. 33–4.

FIG. 10. William Blake, *Laocoon*. Engraving for Rees's
Cyclopaedia, 1815.

FIG. 11. William Blake, free version of the *Laocoön*. Pencil,
pen, and watercolour, *c*.1825.

> He breaks his Bands, the fatal Altar flies,
> And with loud Bellowings breaks the yielding Skies.[7]

Blake may have begun this drawing in opposition to eighteenth-century aesthetic theories which, as we shall see, praise the *Laocoön* sculpture precisely because it did not express extreme pain or other violent emotion. He did not, for reasons unknown to us, complete his large drawing; but he had not yet done with the subject of the *Laocoön*.

Near the very end of his life Blake printed at least two examples of a large separate plate (Fig. 12) combining a reproductive engraving of the *Laocoön* group with a welter of aphorisms. His title for it begins **יהּ** *& his two Sons Satan & Adam*, יהּ (pronounced 'Yah') being a contraction of one of the names of God in the Old Testament.[8] This work may be considered a statement of his very late views on subjects of lifelong interest to him—art, the imagination, the divine and the human, and empire. It is in more than one respect an extraordinary work, even for Blake. Blake had of course created many works of composite art in which his words and designs interacted, but this is the only example of his featuring a substantial amount of his own text and an image not of his own invention.[9] Furthermore, the texts that Blake inscribed on this plate, unlike those of Blake's illuminated books, cannot be read in a linear fashion. In considering some of the issues of interpretation regarding this extraordinary work, we should consider the history of the sculptural group and its status as a cultural object before and during Blake's time.

The *locus classicus* for the discussion of the *Laocoön* in the eighteenth century was the Abbé J. J. Winckelmann's *Reflections on the*

---

[7] *The Works of John Dryden*, ed. Edward Niles Hooker and H. T. Swedenberg, Jr., vol. v, *The Works of Virgil in English* (Berkeley: University of California Press, 1987), pp. 386–7, ll. 280–303.

[8] Because the first word of the title is more prominent than the others, I print it in bold face. The engraving was once dated conjecturally *c.*1818–20, but Essick and Viscomi discovered the watermark 1826 on one of the two extant pulls (the other having no watermark). The watermarked pull is in the collection of Robert N. Essick, the other (formerly in the collection of Sir Geoffrey Keynes) is in the Fitzwilliam Museum. It would be, as Essick and Viscomi argue, extremely unlikely for Blake to go through the labour-intensive process of printing a single example of this work at one time and then to do it all over again in order to produce a second example of the same state. (This need not, of course, preclude his engraving the figures at one time and the texts at another.) See Essick and Viscomi, pp. 241–2.

[9] The second state of *Joseph of Arimathea Among the Rocks of Albion*, based on a figure by Michelangelo, has a brief text by Blake at its bottom.

FIG. 12. William Blake, יה *& his two Sons Satan & Adam.*
Engraving, c.1826.

Painting and Sculpture of the Greeks, first published in English in a translation by Henry Fuseli in 1765.[10] Blake is believed to have owned this book,[11] and he probably had Winckelmann's discussion of the *Laocoön* in mind when he wrote of one of his pictures in 1809: 'I understand that my Costume is incorrect, but in this I plead the authority of the ancients, who often deviated from the Habits, to preserve the Manners, as in the instance of Laocoon, who, though a priest, is represented naked.'[12] This is evidently an echo of Winckelmann, who wrote: 'Had Laocoon been covered with a garb becoming an antient sacrificer, his sufferings would have lost one half of their Expression.'[13] However, we must not imagine that this means that Blake would necessarily have agreed with Winckelmann in other respects. To the German scholar it was of the greatest importance that Laocoön did not give vent to his torment. It was, indeed, this sculpture that gave rise to the famous statement that 'The last and most eminent characteristic of the Greek works is a noble simplicity and sedate grandeur in Gesture and Expression'.[14] In a memorable simile, Winckelmann continued: 'As the bottom of the sea lies peaceful beneath a foaming surface, a great soul lies sedate beneath the strife of passions in Greek figures.' The purpose of great art is to reconcile the viewer with suffering through the transmutation of the suffering subject into an aesthetic object:

---

[10] Abbé J. J. Winckelmann, *Reflections on the Painting and Sculpture of the Greeks, Translated from the German Original by Henry Fusseli [sic], A.M.* (London: A. Millar, 1765).

[11] A copy of Fuseli's translation, once in the collection of Sir Geoffrey Keynes, bears the signature 'William Blake, Lincoln's Inn'. Although Blake was never, of course, at the Inns of Court, he did reside at 31 Lincoln's Inn Fields during his apprenticeship with James Basire. G. E. Bentley, Jr., appears to concur with Keynes's view that the signature is authentically Blake's. See Bentley, *Blake Books* (Oxford: Clarendon Press, 1977), p. 700.

[12] *A Descriptive Catalogue*, E 548. Where an author spells the name without a diaeresis over the last *o*, I follow the quotation as given.

[13] *Reflections*, p. 31. However, it should be noted that Jonathan Richardson the younger wrote 'of the Necessity there is Sometimes of venturing on Obvious Improprieties', and continued: 'How would the Low Criticks have Triumph'd on these Artists representing a Priest Naked, who was surpriz'd by this Terrible Accident just as he was Sacrificing! And yet who sees not that had This been Regarded, as it could not but be Foreseen, instead of the Finest piece of Sculpture in the World we must have had a very Indifferent One, or None at all?'—Jonathan Richardson, Sr., and Jonathan Richardson, Jr., *An Account of Some of the Statues, Bas-reliefs, Drawings and Pictures in Italy* (London: J. Knapton, 1722), p. 280.

[14] *Reflections*, p. 30.

'Tis in the face of Laocoon this soul shines with full lustre, not confined how-
ever to the face, amidst the most violent sufferings. Pangs piercing every
muscle, every labouring nerve; pangs which we almost feel ourselves, while
we consider—not the face, nor the most expressive parts—only the belly
contracted by excruciating pains: these however, I say, exert not themselves
with violence, either in the face or gesture. He pierces not heaven, like the
Laocoon of *Virgil*; his mouth is rather opened to discharge an anxious over-
loaded groan, as *Sadolet* says; the struggling body and the supporting mind
exert themselves with equal strength, nay balance all the frame.[15]

Winckelmann goes on to remark that 'Every action or gesture in
Greek figures, not stamped with this character of sage dignity, but
too violent, too passionate, was called "Parenthyrsos"', and that
such excess was at all costs to be avoided. 'In Laocoon,' he continues,
'sufferings alone had been Parenthyrsos; the artist therefore, in order
to reconcile the significative and ennobling qualities of his soul, put
him into a posture, allowing for the sufferings that were necessary,
the next to a state of tranquillity: a tranquillity however that is char-
acteristical: the soul will be herself—this individual—not the soul of
mankind; sedate, but active; calm, but not indifferent or drowsy.'[16] If
we think of the many expressions of suffering in Blake's works—the
howling face of Los on plate 7 of *The [First] Book of Urizen*,[17] for
example, or the anguished giant of *Jerusalem* 62, we can see that
Blake is unlikely to have shared this neo-classical view of the sublim-
ity of repressed suffering. Indeed, to Sir Joshua Reynolds's statement
that 'No one can deny that violent passions will naturally emit harsh
and disagreeable tones' Blake replied in his Annotations: 'Violent
Passions Emit the Real Good & Perfect Tones.'[18]

At an earlier time Blake may have been more sympathetic to
Winckelmann's views. He had been trained as an artist when neo-
classicism was at the cutting edge of art theory and practice, and as
late as 1799 he could declare that his aim as an artist was 'to renew
the lost Art of the Greeks'.[19] But in the early years of the nineteenth

---

[15] *Reflections*, pp. 30–1. On Sadolet (Cardinal Jacopo Sadoleto, 1477–1547), see
below.

[16] *Reflections*, p. 32.

[17] For illuminated books I follow the pagination in Bentley, *Blake Books*.

[18] Annotations to Reynolds's *Discourse* VII, E 660. This marginal note is cited by
James Bogan in connection with the large drawing; see Bogan, 'From Hackwork to
Prophetic Vision: William Blake's Delineation of the Laocoon Group', *Publications of
the Arkansas Philological Association*, 6 (1980): 49 (33–51).

[19] Letter to the Reverend Dr Trusler, 16 August 1799, E 701.

century, while living at Felpham and immediately after his return to London, Blake underwent a series of conversionary experiences that led him to embrace an immanent Christianity and to reject classical art and literature.[20] The artistic consequences of this can be seen in the letter that Blake wrote to William Hayley, on 23 October 1804, the day after visiting the Truchsessian picture gallery and finding himself 'again enlightened with the light I enjoyed in my youth':

For now! O Glory! and O Delight! I have entirely reduced that spectrous Fiend to his station, whose annoyance has been the ruin of my labours for the last passed twenty years of my life. He is the enemy of conjugal love and is the Jupiter of the Greeks, an iron-hearted tyrant, the ruiner of ancient Greece.[21]

Blake began his *Milton a Poem* with a prose address contrasting 'The Stolen and Perverted Writings of Homer and Ovid: of Plato & Cicero. which all Men ought to contemn' with 'the Sublime of the Bible'; and he concluded: 'We do not want either Greek & Roman Models if we are but just & true to our own Imaginations, those Worlds of Eternity in which we shall live for ever; in Jesus our Lord' (E 95). Passages such as these, along with the denunciation of classical literature in the single plate *On Homers Poetry | On Virgil*, provide a background for the aphorisms with which Blake surrounded his engraving of the sculptural group that Winckelmann had taken as the paragon of classical sculpture.

The Winckelmannian approach to the *Laocoön* was continued in the *Encyclopédie* of Diderot and d'Alembert.[22] The Chevalier de Jaucourt's article on the group is, indeed, mostly a translation and paraphrase of the exposition in the *Reflections*. The expression of the figures is declared to be superior to the passage in Virgil. Laocoön does not utter terrible cries—the opening of his mouth shows this. His character is as firm as it is heroic. He sighs profoundly, as Sadolet describes him. The pain of his body and the grandeur of his soul combine. Laocoön suffers like the Philoctetes of Sophocles and

---

[20] See Jean H. Hagstrum, 'The Wrath of the Lamb: A Study of William Blake's Conversions', in *From Sensibility to Romanticism: Essays Presented to Frederick A. Pottle*, ed. Frederick W. Hilles and Harold Bloom (New York: Oxford University Press, 1965), pp. 311–30; and Morton D. Paley, *Energy and the Imagination* (Oxford: Clarendon Press, 1970), pp. 142–70.

[21] E 756. On Blake's Truchsessian Gallery experience, see M. D. Paley, 'The Truchsessian Gallery Revisited', *Studies in Romanticism*, 16 (1977): 165–77.

[22] *Encyclopédie, ou Dictionnaire raisonné des sciences, des arts, et des métiers* (17 vols., Neuchâtel, 1765), 'Laocoon, le', ix. 279–80; 'Sculpteurs modernes', xiv. 829.

we are moved to support misfortune as he does. 'The expression of a soul so sublime much surpasses the representation of nature.'[23] This approach, emphasizing Laocoön's superiority to his suffering in the statue as opposed to Virgil's passage, is continued in a book we can be confident that Blake read, William Hayley's *Essay on Sculpture* (addressed to John Flaxman), to which Blake contributed three engravings and which was published in the year that Blake moved to Felpham.[24] Hayley wrote:

> Hail, thou sublime resemblance of the sire,
> Excruciated to see his helpless sons expire!
> Though Fate's fierce serpent round thy manly frame
> Wind its vast volumes, and with deadly aim
> Dart its impetuous poison near the heart;
> Though thy shrunk shank announce the wounded part;
> To selfish pangs superior thou art seen,
> And suffering anguish, more intensely keen . . .[25]

Also heavily indebted to Winckelmann's discussion was that of August Wilhelm Schlegel, in *A Course of Lectures on Dramatic Art and Literature*, published in English in 1815 (as it happens, the year in which Blake drew the Royal Academy's cast). 'Beauty', Schlegel wrote, 'is the object of sculpture, and repose is most advantageous for the display of beauty.'[26] We do not know whether Blake ever read Schlegel on the *Laocoön*, but he at least had the opportunity to do so. Schlegel praised the statue for turning suffering into beauty:

> In Laocoön the conflicting sufferings and anguish of the body, and the resistance of the soul, are balanced with the most wonderful equilibrium. The children calling for help, tender objects of our compassion, and not of our admiration, draw us back to the appearance of the father, who seems to turn his eyes in vain to the gods. The convolving serpents exhibit to us the

---

[23] *Encyclopédie*, ix. 279–80. Sophocles' Philoctetes is discussed in chapter 4 of Lessing's *Laokoon*. In 1812 Blake painted *Philoctetes and Neoptolemus on Lemnos* (Butlin 676, Fogg Art Museum).

[24] William Hayley, *An Essay on Sculpture* (London: T. Cadell and W. Davies, 1800). The passage on the *Laocoön* is in Epistle the Third, pp. 74–5 (ll. 474–510) plus note xiii on pp. 289–91. The note includes the Latin poem of Jacobus Sadoletus, discussed below.

[25] *An Essay on Sculpture*, Epistle the Third, ll. 476–83.

[26] August Wilhelm Schlegel, *A Course of Lectures on Dramatic Art and Literature*, trans. John Black (2 vols., London: Baldwin, Craddock, and Joy, 1815), i. 57.

inevitable destiny which unites together the characters in so dreadful a manner. And yet the beauty of proportion, the delightful flow of the attitude, are not lost in this violent struggle; and a representation most frightful to the senses is yet treated with a degree of moderation, while a mild breath of sweetness is diffused over the whole.[27]

All these views take the *Laocoön* group as an exemplum of classical virtue. We know what Blake thought of such virtue. In *Milton* Los conducts spirits to Golgonooza, free of the four traditional classical virtues, 'from the four iron pillars of Satans Throne | (Temperance, Prudence, Justice, Fortitude, the four pillars of tyranny)' (29: 48–9, E 128). Blake's rejection of the classical virtues and of the idea of works of art as virtuous exemplars is of course part of his rejection of the classics as part of the culture of the British Empire.

There was at least one other contemporary view of the *Laocoön* with which Blake may very well have been familiar. It was that of a major literary figure with whom he has seldom been associated— Goethe. Nevertheless, Goethe's 'Observations on the Laocoon' appeared in English in the *Monthly Magazine in* 1799.[28] The venue is important, because it is one with which Blake had several associations. One was as an engraver: Blake contributed a portrait of Joseph Wright of Derby to the *Monthly's* issue for October 1797.[29] Another was as a correspondent. In 1800 Blake wrote a letter, beginning 'Your Magazine being so universally Read', to the *Monthly Magazine* supporting George Cumberland's plan for a national gallery. Blake's letter was not published, but has survived because Blake transcribed it for Cumberland.[30] In 1806 the periodical did publish a letter by Blake defending the art of Henry Fuseli, and Blake wrote yet another letter to the editor of the *Monthly* on 14 October 1807.[31] There is therefore a strong likelihood that Blake was familiar with Goethe's ideas about the statue. If that is so, he might well have found Goethe's attempt to universalize the subject interesting.

[27] Ibid., i. 86.

[28] 'Observations on the Laocoon', 1 June 1799, 349–52, 399–401.

[29] See Essick, *William Blake's Commercial Book Illustrations*, p. 75.

[30] Letter postmarked 1 September 1800. See Robert N. Essick and Morton D. Paley, ' "Dear Generous Cumberland": A Newly Discovered Letter and Poem by William Blake', *Blake*, 32 (1998): 4–13.

[31] Undated letter published in the *Monthly Magazine*, 21 (1 July 1806), 520–1, E 768–9; letter to Richard Phillips (editor of the *Monthly Magazine*), dated 14 October [1807], E 769.

'Laocoon', Goethe wrote, 'is only a simple name; the artists have taken from him his priesthood, all that is national and Trojan in him, all the poetical and mythological accessories; all in fact that mythology has made of him is done away. . . .' (p. 351). Blake might not have been sympathetic to Goethe's reduction of the situation to a domestic drama in which 'A father sleeps at the side of his two sons, they are inlaced by two serpents, and at the instant of waking, they strive to extricate themselves from this living cord' (p. 351), and he would most decidedly not have agreed with Goethe's attempt to explain the effects of the statue in terms of a quasi-Aristotelian view of tragedy. Fear, terror, and compassion, says Goethe, are aroused by the *Laocoön* group:

> In the group of the Laocoon, the sufferings of the father excite terror to the highest degree; sculpture has done in it all that it could do; but, either for the sake of running through the circle of all human sensations, or of moderating the violent impression of terror, it excites compassion for the situation of the youngest son, and fear for that of the eldest; leaving yet some hope for the last. It is thus that the ancients gave, by variety, a certain equilibrium to their works; that they diminished or strengthened an effect by other effects, and were enabled to finish an intellectual and sensible whole.[32]

This would not have struck a responsive chord in the Blake who in *Jerusalem* condemned Greek tragedy for what he regarded as its exploitation of pity and terror to the end of the satisfaction of the self: 'as at a trajic scene. | The soul drinks murder & revenge, & applauds its own holiness' (37: 29–30, E 183). Goethe's view, no less than Winckelmann's, is that the purpose of such art is to reconcile human beings to their suffering, something that we would especially expect Blake to reject when the perpetrators of the suffering were, as in the Laocoön story, divine beings. Blake would have been more likely to have agreed with Percy Bysshe Shelley, who noted of the *Laocoön*: 'Intense physical suffering, against which he pleads with an upraised countenance of despair, and appeals with a sense of its injustice, seems the predominant and overwhelming emotion, and yet there is a nobleness in the expression and a majesty that defies torture.'[33]

[32] 'Observations on the Laocoon', p. 400.
[33] 'Notes on Sculptures in Rome and Florence', in *Shelley's Prose*, ed. David Lee Clark (Albuquerque: University of New Mexico Press, 1954), p. 344. I am grateful to Morag Harris for drawing this passage to my attention.

What of Lessing's *Laokoon*, a work that bulks much larger in contemporary critical discourse than those to which reference has been made so far? While it is true that parts of Lessing's *Laokoon* began to appear in an English translation by Thomas De Quincey in 1826, this was almost certainly too late to have any influence on Blake's conception of the subject.[34] There is no evidence that Blake, who did not know German, was conversant with Lessing's theories, although it has been argued that he could have known about Lessing's ideas through Henry Fuseli.[35] Fuseli asserts the 'necessity of . . . Unity' and rejects 'pedantic subdivision'.[36] In a manner reminiscent of Winckelmann, he says, 'All such division diminishes, all such mixtures impair the simplicity and clearness of expression', and he continues in what seems at least in part a slap at Goethe:

in the group of the Laocoon the frigid ecstacies of German criticism have discovered pity like a vapour swimming in the father's eyes; he is seen to suppress in the groan for his children the shriek for himself—his nostrils are drawn upward to express indignation at unworthy sufferings, whilst he is said at the same time to implore celestial help. To these are added the winged effects of the serpent-poison, the writhings of the body, the spasms of the extremities.

Fuseli dismisses such complexity :

His figure is a class, it characterizes every beauty of virility verging on age; the prince, the priest, the father are visible, but absorbed in the man serve only to dignify the victim of *one* great expression . . . for us to apply the compass to the face of the Laocoon, is to measure the wave fluctuating in the storm: this tempestuous front, this contracted nose, the immersion of these eyes, and above all that longdrawn mouth, are, separate and united, seats of convulsion, features of nature struggling within the jaws of death.

---

[34] The first instalment of De Quincey's edited and abridged translation appeared as *Gallery of the German Prose Classics. By the English Opium Eater.* 'No I.—Lessing', in *Blackwood's Edinburgh Magazine*, 20 (1826): 728–44; the second instalment as 'No. II.—Lessing' in 21 (1827): 2–24. I am grateful to Grevel Lindop for this information, and also for calling my attention to the 1824 *Blackwood's* article on Lessing cited below.

[35] See Nancy Moore Goslee, *Uriel's Eye: Miltonic Stationing and Statuary in Blake, Keats, and Shelley* (Tuscaloosa, Ala.: University of Alabama Press, 1985), p. 58; and Julia M. Wright, 'The Medium, the Message, and the Line in William Blake's Laocoön', *Mosaic*, 33 (2000): 106 (101–24).

[36] *Lectures on Art Delivered at the Royal Academy March 1801* (London: J. Johnson, 1801), pp. 48–9.

Although Fuseli agrees with Winckelmann in the idea of simplicity of effect, it would be hard to reconcile the *Sturm und Drang* of the last quoted sentence with Winckelmann's 'noble simplicity and sedate grandeur'; indeed, it seems more like 'Parenthyrsos'. Fuseli's view of the sculptural group is neither Winckelmann's nor Lessing's but his own.

There was, however, a short article from which Blake could have learned something about Lessing's *Laokoon* published in *Blackwood's* in 1824, though there is no evidence that Blake read it. The beginning of the article, far from opposing Winckelmann's view, is entirely congruent with it. The anonymous author, who has been identified as Robert Ferguson, quotes with approval Winckelmann's '*noble simplicity* and *calm magnanimity*', prints four paragraphs of Winckelmann on the *Laocoön*, and goes on to apply Lessing's statement about Beauty in Greek art to it.[37] The sculptor, he writes, had to soften Laocoön's suffering 'because the symmetry of the face would have been totally annihilated by it in the most disgusting manner'. This is a view which, as we have seen in discussing Winckelmann, Blake would have opposed. Lessing himself does not question the propriety of avoiding the representation of extreme suffering:

> The master aimed at the highest beauty compatible with the adopted circumstances of bodily pain. The latter, in all its disfiguring violence, could not be combined with the former; therefore he must reduce it; he must soften shrieks into sighs, not because a shriek would have betrayed an ignoble soul, but because it would have produced a hideous contortion of the countenance.[38]

The reason, then, is in the medium. Virgil could describe the injured Laocoön as bellowing like a bull, but the sculptor, limited to a single moment, had to leave to the viewer's imagination the highest intensity of physical expression. 'Thus if Laokoon sighs, the imagination can hear him shriek; but if he shrieks, it can neither rise a step higher nor descend a step below this representation, without seeing him in a condition which, as it will be more endurable, becomes less interesting.'[39] This is of course part of Lessing's general argument that the

---

[37] 'Horae Germanicae (No. XVIII): Lessing's *Laocoon*', *Blackwood's Edinburgh Magazine*, 16 (September 1824): 312–16. The anonymous author is identified as Robert Ferguson by the *Wellesley Index to Victorian Periodicals*.

[38] G. E. Lessing, *Laokoon and How the Ancients Represented Death* (London: G. Bell & Sons, 1914), p. 17. The translation is based upon that of E. C. Beasley.

[39] Ibid., p. 20.

medium of expression determines the criteria for judging works of art and poetry. Blake might well have preferred W. J. T. Mitchell's argument (made without reference to Blake) that 'the tendency to breach the supposed boundaries between temporal and spatial arts is not a marginal or exceptional practice, but a fundamental impulse in both the theory and practice of the arts . . .'.[40] It is, after all, what Blake had been doing all his life.

2

As Blake perceived in his Preface to *Milton*, in early nineteenth-century Britain the rhetoric and values of classicism imbued the rhetoric and values of empire. The same could be said to a certain extent of classical works of art, and especially, if we take a Blake's-eye view of the subject, of the *Laocoön*. Let us begin with Pliny's famous account, which Blake certainly knew by the time he read Flaxman's 'Sculpture' articles, for Flaxman quoted extensively from Pliny. It reads in its entirety:

The reputation of some [sculptors], distinguished though their work may be, has been obscured by the number of artists engaged with them on a single task, because no individual monopolizes the credit nor again can several of them be named on equal terms. This is the case with the Laocoon in the palace of the emperor Titus, a work superior to any painting and any bronze. Laocoon, his children, and the wonderful clasping coils of the snakes were carved from a single block in accordance with an agreed plan by those eminent craftsmen Hagesander, Polydoros, and Athenodoros, all of Rhodes.[41]

According to Pliny's account, the statue was placed in the house of the emperor who as a general had commanded the Roman forces that captured and destroyed Jerusalem and its temple, and who had an arch built commemorating that event.[42] In Blake's *Jerusalem* Titus

---

[40] Mitchell, *Iconology: Image, Text, Ideology* (Chicago and London: University of Chicago Press, 1986), p. 98.

[41] Pliny, *Natural History*, trans. D. E. Eicholz (Cambridge, Mass.: Harvard University Press, 1962) x. 29–31. The translator notes that there are actually five blocks, but Filippo Magi, the scholar responsible for the restoration of the statue as we now know it, found there were eight blocks. See Margaret Bieber, *Laocoon: The Influence of the Group Since Its Rediscovery* (rev. edn., Detroit: Wayne State University Press, 1967), p. 38.

[42] Although there is controversy among classical archaeologists as to where the statue was actually found, that need not concern us here.

appears as one of the three embodiments of world empire—'Titus! Constantine! Charlemaine'—whose 'Roman Sword' vainly attacks the image of the Lord.[43] Furthermore, after being unearthed in 1506, the *Laocoön* became a possession of Blake's 'Patriarch Druid'[44] the pope. Jacopo Sadoleto, friend of Bembo and future secretary to Pope Leo X, was quick to note the parallel between the ancient imperium and the modern one in his Latin poem 'Upon the Statue of the *Laocoön*' (*De Laocoontis Statua*):

> lo! time once more
> Has brought Laocoon home, who stood of old
> In princely palaces and graced thy halls,
> Imperial Titus. Wrought by skill divine
> (Even learned ancients saw no nobler work),
> The statue now from darkness saved returns
> To see the stronghold of Rome's second life.[45]

If, as I have suggested, Blake read Sadoleto's Latin poem as reprinted in William Hayley's *Essay on Sculpture* (1800), we know what he would have thought of 'Rome's second life'. Exhibited in the Belvedere of the Vatican,[46] where it is today, the sculpture underwent one dramatic change of venue in Blake's time. The *Laocoön* was one of about a hundred works of art ceded to France by the pope in 1796 after Napoleon's victories in Italy, according to the terms of the Armistice of Bologna.[47] Most of the eighty-seven statues and seven-

---

[43] *Jerusalem* 52: 21, E 202.
[44] Cf. *Jerusalem* 61: 50–1, E 212: 'Wilt thou make Rome thy Patriarch Druid & the Kings of Europe his | Horsemen?'
[45] Trans. H. S. Wilkinson, in Bieber, *Laocoon*, p. 13.
[46] For a comprehensive discussion of the installation, see Hans Henrik Brummer, *The Statue Court in the Vatican Belvedere*, Acta Universitatis Stockholmiensis/Stockholm Studies in History of Art, No. 20 (Stockholm: Almqvist & Wiksell, 1970), pp. 75–119.
[47] These provisions were reaffirmed in the Treaty of Tolentino on 19 February 1797. See M.-L. Blumer, 'La Commission pour la recherche des objets de sciences et arts en Italie (1796–1797)', *La Révolution Française*, 86 (1933): 62–88, 124–50, 222–5; and Eugène Müntz, 'Les Annexations de collections d'art ou de bibliothèques', *Revue d'histoire diplomatique*, 10 (1896): 484 (481–508). Interestingly this was not the first French attempt to obtain the *Laocoön*. King Francis I, through ambassadors at the Vatican, made it known that the gift of the statue would be very acceptable but was eventually fobbed off with plaster casts; see Leonard Barkan, *Unearthing the Past: Archaeology and Aesthetics in the Making of Renaissance Culture* (New Haven and London: Yale University Press, 1999), p. 10. A foreshadowing of things to come was rendered in an address given by the Abbé Henri Grégoire in 1794: 'It was Greece',

teen paintings left Rome in four convoys of wagons in 1797, soon to
be followed to Paris by other art treasures looted by treaty. On 27
July 1798 a great fête began: the captured works of art were paraded
before crowds through the boulevards to the Champ de Mars,
accompanied by the recitation of poetry and musical performances.
On 31 July the masterpieces were received by what was then called
the Museum central des Arts. They remained unexhibited while
restoration and repairs took place. (Goethe alludes to this in the
essay printed in the *Monthly Review*, and expresses concern about
possible damage in transit.) On 9 November 1800 a new gallery of
antiques was inaugurated in what was now called the Musée
Napoleon, in the Louvre.[48] Among the features of this gallery was a
Salle du *Laocoön*, which was the subject of a bronze medal by
Bertrand Andrieu, and this and an engraving made *c.*1810 show the
statue displayed in an apse-like niche very much like the one it had
occupied in the Belvedere.[49] A representation of the sculpture was of
course included among Tommaso Piroli's 240 engravings for the
Musée Napoleon published in Paris in 1804.[50] These events did not
of course go unnoticed in England. For example, as Essick and
Viscomi point out, in 1809 the Royal Academician Martin Archer
Shee expressed regret that the British had not marched on Paris to
liberate the masterpieces in the Louvre and taken them to London.[51]
As it turned out, the *Laocoön* resided in Paris only as long as the
emperor did. After the Congress of Vienna, it was returned with most
of the other stolen art treasures, arriving in Rome in January 1816.
Blake can hardly have been unaware of these highly dramatic events

said Grégoire, 'that decorated Rome; but should the masterpieces of the Greek
republics decorate the land of slaves? The French Republic should be their last home.'
*Rapport sur les destructions opérées par le Vandalisme, et sur les moyens de le
réprimer* (Paris, 1794), p. 27 (translation mine).

[48] See Francis Haskell and Nicholas Penny, *Taste and the Antique: The Lure
of Classical Sculpture, 1500–1900* (New Haven: Yale University Press, 1981),
pp. 243–7.

[49] The medal is reproduced by Haskell and Penny, *Taste and the Antique*, fig. 63; a
detail of the engraving in *D'après l'antique* [musée du Louvre exhibition catalogue],
ed. Jean-Pierre Cuzin, Jean-René Gaborit, and Alain Pasquier (Paris: Réunion des
Musées, 2000), fig. 71a (p. 233). In 1813 a Sèvres porcelain vase was created showing
the arrival of the *Laocoön* at the Louvre among other works 'acquises à l'issue de la
campagne d'Italie'. See *D'après l'antique*, p. 230, fig. 12.

[50] *Les Monumens antiques du Musée Napoléon* (4 vols., Paris, 1804).

[51] *Milton a Poem*, pp. 274–5, citing Shee's *Elements of Art*, ii. 223 n.

in which the *Laocoön* had become a trophy of war and empire. The masterpieces removed by the 'Spoilers', as Blake would call them, were returned to the 'Patriarch Druid' by 'his Horsemen', the 'Kings of Europe'.

In approaching Blake's engraving itself, a fundamental question must be asked. Why did he do it? If Essick and Viscomi are correct, as appears likely, in dating the print *c.*1826–7, it was executed while Blake was working on his last great artistic project: the illustrations for Dante's *Divine Comedy*, begun on John Linnell's commission in 1824 and ongoing at the time of Blake's final illness. For this great work he executed 102 large and several smaller drawings in various states of completion, and seven engravings. The time taken to engrave a large separate plate, a labour perhaps of months, would necessarily have been taken from the Dante series, unless Blake found a window of opportunity between proofing the *Job* engravings in 1825 and starting on the Dante engravings.[52] Even so, it would have come at a very busy time for Blake.

It is one thing to verbally condemn 'the silly Greek and Latin slaves of the Sword' as Blake did in his *Milton* (E 95); it is quite another to expend a considerable amount of time and labour in rendering a faithful copy of one of their sculptural works. If Blake wanted an image to surround with his aphorisms on art, money, true Christianity, and empire, why did he not render one of those 'wonderful originals' (*Descriptive Catalogue*, E 531) he had seen in vision rather than the debased version of three Rhodians? The answer to these questions may lie in the realm of, to use a Blakean distinction, the Corporeal rather than the Mental. I suggest that the origin of this plate lay in a commission to do a reproductive engraving of the *Laocoön* group for commercial purposes, that Blake completed the figures and might have proceeded to add an architectural background as in Marco Dente's *Laocoön* engraving (Fig. 13), but that the work was never published.

If the engraving of the *Laocoön* group was a rejected commission, as appears possible, it would not have been the first one in Blake's career. In 1799 his watercolour *Malevolence* was returned by Dr John Trusler (author of *The Way to be Rich and Respectable*). Trusler objected that 'Your *Fancy* . . . seems to be in the other world,

---

[52] See Essick and Viscomi, p. 242.

FIG. 13. Marco Dente, *Laocoön*. Engraving published in
A. Lafreri, *Speculum Romanae Magnificentiae*, c.1544–7.

or the World of Spirits'.[53] Blake aggressively defended his art. 'I really am sorry that you are falln out with the Spiritual World,' he began, and continued: 'That which can be made Explicit to the Idiot is not worth my care. The wisest of the Ancients considerd what is not too Explicit as the fittest for Instruction because it rouzes the faculties to act.'[54] It is the jaunty, self-confident retort of an artist who still thought he would achieve the recognition he deserved, and who knew he had a commission from Thomas Butts for fifty small paintings of biblical subjects.[55] Much different was Blake's reaction to his rejection as the engraver of his own designs for Robert Blair's *The Grave*. The story of this is well known. Blake's great white-line relief etching *Deaths Door*, deliberately executed in the style of early Italian engravers, failed to please the publisher R. H. Cromek, and in November 1805 Cromek transferred the commission for engraving Blake's designs to the more fashionable stipple engraver Louis Schiavonetti.[56] This time Blake, knowing himself increasingly marginalized in his profession, reacted by writing bitter verses in his Notebook, like:

> Cr—— loves artists as he loves his Meat
> He loves the Art but tis the Art to Cheat
>
> (E 509)

and satirizing Cromek's supposed opinions in an epigram entitled 'English Encouragement of Art' (E 510).[57] In these instances, Blake defended himself by writing vehemently against the aspersion to his art involved in the rejection. In the instance of the engraving he entitled יה & his two Sons, Blake would have found himself with a plate presenting large empty areas inviting the addition of text. What better use to make of this opportunity than to inscribe a series of aphorisms defending true art and attacking its 'Spoilers'—money, war, and empire?

---

[53] See Blake's letter to George Cumberland dated 26 August 1799, E 704.

[54] See letter dated 23 August 1799, E 702.

[55] See Blake's letter to Cumberland of 26 August 1799, E 704; and Martin Butlin, *William Blake* (London: Tate Gallery, 1978), p. 78.

[56] See Robert N. Essick and Morton D. Paley, *Robert Blair's* The Grave, *Illustrated by William Blake* (London: Scolar Press, 1982), p. 69.

[57] Another crisis of reception seems to have prompted Blake's assault on the third plate of *Jerusalem* some time after it was etched, literally gouging out words indicating a close rapport with his reader. See Blake, *Jerusalem*, ed. Morton D. Paley (London: William Blake Trust/Tate Gallery, 1991), pp. 10–11.

In engraving his image of the *Laocoön* group, Blake was, as ever, aware of the tradition of engraving to which he belonged. Seldom has a graphic artist been more conscious of his affinities and his dyspathies. The engravings of the *Laocoön* group are so many that it would be impossible to discuss even the principal ones here, but a brief glance at a representative selection may show something of what Blake was aiming at, and what he wished to avoid. As William F. Ivins has remarked in considering a group of *Laocoön* reproductions ranging over four centuries, 'Each bears the distinct marks of its time and of the nationality of its maker', and he intriguingly suggests that 'the particular piece of sculpture represented in our engravings was actually different for each of the men who made a picture of it'.[58] Blake, whose interest in the history of his craft was so acute, was of course familiar with the way some of his predecessors had seen and presented the statue. Among earlier reproductions of the *Laocoön* were an engraving by Giovanni Antonio da Brescia thought to be the first to show the group after its exhumation;[59] an engraving after Bartolomeo Marliani that served as the first illustration in *Urbis Romae topographia* (Rome, 1544);[60] two engravings by Nicolas Beatrizet;[61] etchings by Sisto Badalocchio (1606) and by Franciscus Perrier (1638) departing from the more typical front view;[62] an engraving (*c.*1532–7) attributed to Hendrick Goltzius, who executed a highly finished drawing of the subject;[63] an engraving by Johann Jakob Thurneysen for Joachim von Sandrart's *Sculpturae veteris admiranda* (Nuremberg, 1680), and many others. Among these, several are especially appropriate to compare with Blake's either for their representative importance, or because he probably

[58] William F. Ivins, 'Ignorance, the End', *Bulletin of the Metropolitan Museum of Art*, NS 2 (1943): 3, 4 (3–10).
[59] See Adam Bartsch, *Le Peintre Graveur* (Vienna: 1803–21), xiii. 326, 15; Brummer, *The Statue Court in the Vatican Belvedere*, p. 82 and fig. 68.
[60] Reproduced in Barkan, *Unearthing the Past*, p. 8, fig. 1.2. The muscles are brought out much more prominently than in the statue or other engravings of it, in a manner that also frequently characterizes Blake's treatment of the male nude body.
[61] See Bartsch, *Le Peintre Graveur*, xv. 264, 90 and 265, 91. For reproductions see Brummer, *The Statue Court in the Vatican Belvedere*, figs. 81–2. John Beer suggests that one of these may have prompted Blake 'to depict the one son as beautiful, the other with the curled hair that is for him a sign of dominant energy'.—Beer, *Blake's Visionary Universe* (Manchester: Manchester University Press, 1969), pp. 47–50.
[62] See Bieber, *Laocoon*, p. 17.
[63] See Guzin, Gaborit, and Pasquier, eds., *D'après l'antique*, p. 230, fig. 7 and pp. 244–5, no. 78.

knew them, or both. He could have felt an affinity with one by Marco Dente, a pupil of Marcantonio Raimondi, published in A. Lafreri's *Speculum Romanae Magnificentiae* (c.1544–7), for stylistically Dente's engraving style has much in common with Blake's. It was this style that Blake recalled George Michael Moser, Keeper at the Royal Academy when Blake was a student, condemning as 'old Hard Stiff & Dry',[64] and it is precisely these qualities that Blake admired. Although Blake does not mention Dente in his writings, he ranks Dente's teacher, Marcantonio Raimondi, among the greatest printmakers. Ironically addressing English engravers, he writes: 'Ye English Engravers must come down from your high flights ye must condescend to study Marc Antonio & Albert Durer.'[65] Dente's detailed delineation of the figures' musculature also would have appealed to Blake, always interested in the lineaments of the human form. The ruin in the background contributes to the gloomy cast of Dente's print, as do the omission of the central figure's restored right arm, and of the elder son's restored four fingers. Blake may well have had some kind of architectural background in mind before he inscribed the textual surround of his own engraving.

In an entirely different vein is Nicolò Boldrini's deliberately grotesque woodcut (c.1566) after Titian's caricature showing the three figures (reversed) as apes. Blake is very likely to have known this print, as it appears in George Cumberland's catalogue of Italian prints.[66] Though not published until 1827, Cumberland's work was circulated in manuscript among Cumberland's friends, and Blake is known to have borrowed it in November 1823.[67] Two things about it might have caught his interest. The arms of the central figure and of the son to his left are not stretched out and upwards, as in the Royal Academy cast of the first restoration, but are bent back at the elbows. Blake would follow this for the son but not for the father. More generally, the print gives a precedent for using the *Laocoön* as a vehicle for commentary upon art. In Leonard Barkan's words, the

---

[64] Annotations to Reynolds's *Discourses*, E 639. Blake says Moser made this remark while 'I was looking over the Prints from Rafael & Michael Angelo in the library of the Royal Academy'. Some of these prints must have been by Marcantonio Raimondi after Raphael.

[65] '[Public Address]', E 573.

[66] Cumberland, *An Essay on the Utility of Collecting the Best Works of the Italian School; Accompanied by a Critical Catalogue* (London, 1827), pp. 391–2. I thank Robert N. Essick for this reference.

[67] See Sir Geoffrey Keynes, 'George Cumberland and William Blake', in *Blake Studies* (2nd edn., Oxford: Clarendon Press, 1971), p. 247 (pp. 230–52).

subject includes 'ancient sculpture, modern painterliness, and—
most important—the process of imitation-emulation-assimilation—
read *aping*—that occupies the space between',[68] but Blake could of
course provide his own issues, and in his own way.

As a student Blake must have seen Jan de Bisschop's *Signorum
Veterum Icones*, as this collection of images of ancient sculpture, first
published in 1668–9, was very well known.[69] The *Icones* includes the
two etchings of the group (reversed) after very similar drawings by
P. Doncker and W. Doudijns (Fig. 14), each of whom spent some time
in Rome during the mid-seventeenth century. As Bieber remarks, 'the
strong Baroque character' is very much stressed here.[70] The massive-
ness and sheer brawn of the central figures have much in common with
Rubens's drawings of Laocoön early in the seventeenth century. Blake
accused Rubens of making Christ look like 'a Brewers Servant',[71] and
if we examine the immense right thighs in the etchings after Doudijns
and Doncker in comparison with those in Blake's and Dente's engrav-
ings, we can see that he would have had the same objection here.

As I have argued elsewhere,[72] Blake appears to have been familiar
with some of the images in Bernard de Montfaucon's great
work *L'Antiquité expliquée et représentée en figures,* and in the
Supplément to that work there appears a plate of the *Laocoön,*[73] an
anonymous stipple engraving (Fig. 15). The engraver or the artist on

[68] See *Unearthing the Past,* p. 14. The print is reproduced as fig. 1.9, p. 14. For an
extensive discussion of its possible meaning, see H. W. Janson, 'Titian's Laocoön
Caricature and the Vesalian–Galenist Controversy', *Art Bulletin,* 28 (1946): 49–53.

[69] In 'Wonderful Originals', I mistakenly identified the source as the *Paradigmata
Graphices Variorum* (Amsterdam, 1671), another collection by Jan de Bisschop,
referred to by Sir Joshua Reynolds as 'a book which is in every young Artist's hands;—
Bisshops Ancient Statues' (*Discourses on Art,* ed. Robert Wark, p. 274 and n.). The
Icones was also widely known; Reynolds had his own proof copy bound together with
a copy of the *Paradigmata* (see Jan G. van Gelder and Ingrid Jost, *Jan de Bisschop and
His Icones & Paradigmata: Classical Antiquities and Italian Drawings for Artistic
Instruction in Seventeenth Century Holland* (2 vols., Doornspijk, Netherlands:
Davaco, 1985), i. 62 n.).

[70] See Bieber, *Laocoon,* p. 17.

[71] 'To English Connoisseurs', E 513.

[72] See M. D. Paley, ' "Wonderful Originals": Blake and Ancient Sculpture', in *Blake
in His Time,* ed. Robert N. Essick and Donald Pearce (Bloomington and London:
Indiana University Press, 1978), pp. 170–97.

[73] *Supplément au Livre de L'Antiquité expliquée et représentée en figures* (5 vols.,
Paris, 1724), vol. i, between pages 244 and 245. This work was published in an
English translation by David Humphreys the following year as *The Supplement
to Antiquity Explained, and Represented in Sculptures, By the learned Father
Montfaucon, Translated into English by David Humphreys* (5 vols., London:
J. Tonson and J. Watts, 1725).

FIG. 14. Jan de Bisschop, *Laocoön*. Etching after a drawing
by W. Doudjins, *Signorum Veterum Icones*, 1668–9.

FIG. 15. Anonymous, *Laocoön*. Engraving for Bernard de
Montfaucon, *Supplément au livre de L'Antiquité expliquée et
représentée en figures*, 1724.

whose drawing the engraving was based allowed himself consider-
able liberty of representation, bending the right arms of both the
father and the younger son at the elbows, though in the case of the fa-
ther not as far as would be done in the second restoration. The fa-
ther's head is turned away from his dying younger son to face right
and upwards. The older son is missing three fingers of his upraised
right hand, and the head of the serpent grasped by the father's left
hand is missing; presumably this is in order to eliminate restored
parts, yet the left arm of Laocoön is included. Also, even Marco
Dente included the head of the serpent to our right. Although the out-
lines of the figures are firm, they are modelled in a mechanical man-
ner that Blake was capable of in his commercial work but that he
eschewed in his own plate of the subject. Another striking feature is
the omission of the genitalia of all three figures, not by the use of fig
leaves but by viewing the sculptural group from an angle low and to
the left, so that visual impediments intervene. This is something we
know Blake would have condemned, since, as he stated on his own
engraving of Laocoön and his sons, 'Art can never exist without
Naked Beauty displayed' (E 275).

Another rendition we may assume Blake disliked, but for a
different reason, is to be found among the plates illustrating the
Encyclopédie. The eleven volumes published as *Recueil de planches
sur les sciences et les arts* (1763) constitute a great example of the arts
of engraving and book production, and were consequently well
known in Blake's profession. Among the plates illustrating the sub-
ject of 'Design' is one signed 'Defehrt Fecit' and captioned *Dessein, |
Proportions de la Statue de Laocoon* (Fig. 16).[74] It is not so much a
reproductive representation as a diagram. The father and the older
son are shown (reversed) separately, the latter seen from two differ-
ent positions, with a multitude of numerical measurements illustrat-
ing the proportions of the statue in minute detail. The purpose here
is to exemplify the notions that the *Laocoön* and the other classical
statues illustrated in the 'Dessein' section are a means of knowing 'les
belles formes et l'élégance des proportions', and that the authors of
these masterpieces corrected the faults of common nature, making
beautiful choices from it, assembling these so as to create elegance
and grace impossible to find united in a single subject.[75] The student

[74] *Recueil de planches sur les sciences et les arts* (11 vols., Paris, 1763), vol. iii, plate
XXXVI of series.
[75] pp. 2–3 of section.

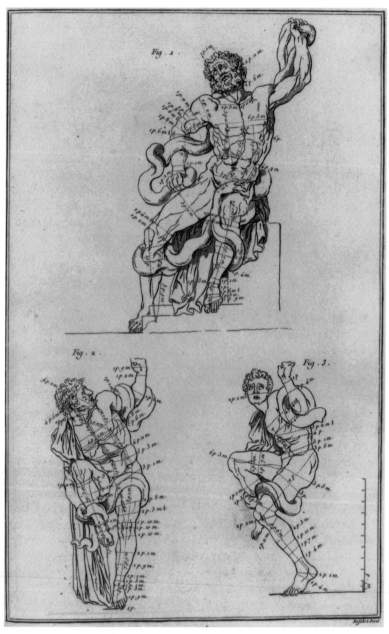

FIG. 16. A.-J. Defehrt, *Dessein, Proportions de la Statue de Laocoon.*
Engraving, for *Recueil de planches sur les sciences et les arts,* 1763.

would design separate parts, like heads, feet, and hands; after that he would put these together to do the whole figure. Blake, who despite his academic training (which of course began with drawing after casts of antique sculpture) often exaggerates the proportions of the human body for his own purposes, would surely have found such a mechanical procedure an example of what he called 'Mathematic Form' as opposed to 'Living Form' in *On Virgil* (E 270).

An engraver whose work Blake would once have found of interest was Tommaso Piroli, who engraved the *Laocoön* among many other works then in the Musée Napoléon.[76] It was Piroli who engraved Flaxman's line drawings illustrating *The Iliad*, *The Odyssey*, and *The Divine Comedy*, all published at Rome in 1793, followed by Flaxman's designs for the tragedies of Aeschylus in 1795.[77] These works, as is widely recognized, have much in common with the linearism of the George Cumberland–Blake collaboration of 1796, *Thoughts on Outline*. Furthermore, Blake contributed three additional engravings to the edition of Flaxman's *Iliad* published in London in 1805.[78] But despite their mutual participation in what Robert Rosenblum has termed the 'abstract linearism'[79] of the 1790s, Blake is unlikely to have found Piroli's rendition of the *Laocoön* (Fig. 17) of great interest. Perhaps it is because Piroli had to engrave 240 works of art for the *Monumens antiques du Musée Napoléon* that they have a sense of mechanical sameness. In this instance Piroli conveys none of the dynamism of the original, something that Blake would be especially successful in capturing in his own version.

Blake's own engraving of the Greek sculptural group displays a number of the characteristics of some of his other late engravings. It eschews the stipple technique of the Rees *Cyclopaedia* illustration and instead features the strong sense of line that Blake learned from his master James Basire. Crosshatching is used to supply volume, and, as Essick points out, the use of the burnisher provides highlights

[76] *Les Monumens antiques du Musée Napoléon dessinés et gravés par Thomas Piroli*, facing ii. 131.

[77] See Detlef W. Dörrbecker, 'A Survey of Engravings After Flaxman's Outline Compositions', in *John Flaxman, R.A.*, ed. David Bindman (London: Royal Academy, 1979), pp. 184–5.

[78] See Bentley, *Blake Books*, pp. 660–4.

[79] Rosenblum, *The International Style of 1800: A Study in Linear Abstraction* (New York: Garland, 1976).

FIG. 17. Tommaso Piroli, *Laocoön*. Engraving, for *Les Monumens antiques du Musée Napoléon dessinés et gravés par Thomas Piroli*, 1804.

to certain parts of the figures, and this adds to the sense of three-dimensionality.[80] In this representation of Laocoön the abdominal muscles are even more contracted than previously, and this could have something to do with the 1824 *Blackwood's* article on Lessing cited earlier. There the author refers to Goethe's discussion of Laocoön's expression: 'Goethe . . . said, that he *could* not cry out because of the contractions of the muscles of the abdomen.'[81] The author has been told by a medical friend that 'when we make any vio-

[80] Essick, *William Blake, Printmaker*, p. 185. Essick adds that Blake's crossing of his heavy strokes at right angles adds to the effect of stone in the engraving. See also Essick, *Separate Plates*, pp. 98–101.

[81] [Robert Ferguson], 'Horae Germanicae (No. XVIII): Lessing's *Laocoon*', pp. 312–16.

lent effort with the chest, we are obliged to fix the arms' so the mus-
cles in the arms can act on the chest. 'The chest is large and convex,
and the muscles of the abdomen drawn in, and it is now that the
effort [i.e. to disengage himself] can be made with any hope of suc-
cess, but during the effort, it is impossible for him to cry . . .'. This
explains the necessity of Laocoön's half-closed lip, and the convul-
sive efforts of his mouth. Whether or not Blake knew of this expla-
nation, or of Lessing's views, the engraving that he produced is a
powerful reproduction of one of the most celebrated sculptural
works of classical antiquity. Blake then went on to undermine its
authority in a series of aphorisms and apophthegms of his own
making, beginning with the title.

3

The title of the separate plate Blake created is not *The Laocoön*, a
name which appears nowhere in its text. The title is plainly given,
though editors have not seen fit to adopt it. Why is this important?
First, because ever since Martin Butlin retitled or un-titled numerous
Blake paintings and drawings in his great catalogue, we have become
accustomed to calling Blake's works, as we do those of other artists,
by the titles the artist gave them. It really does make a difference, for
example, whether we refer to a colour-printed drawing as *Elijah in
the Fiery Chariot*, as it was once called, or as *God Judging Adam* (or
possibly *God speaking to Adam*), which is the inscription by Blake
that Butlin found below the Tate Gallery impression (Butlin 294),
concealed by the mount. We should refer to Blake's works by the
titles he gave them. The title of the work at hand is, then: יה & his
two Sons Satan & Adam as they were copied from the Cherubim of
Solomons Temple by three Rhodians & applied to Natural Fact or
History of Ilium* or in short יה & his two Sons*. It is with this title that
our discussion of Blake's text begins.

Blake's statement that 'יה & his two Sons' were 'copied from the
Cherubim of Solomons Temple' is intimately connected with his idea
of the Hebrew origins of classical art. In his *Descriptive Catalogue* of
1809 (in which Blake makes one of his two allusions to Laocoön, the
other being in *On Homers Poetry*), Blake speaks of having been
taken in vision to see the 'stupendous originals' that lie behind later
art: 'Those wonderful originals seen in my visions, were some of

them one hundred feet in height; some were painted as pictures, and some carved as basso relievos, and some as groupes of statues, all containing mythological and recondite meaning, where more is meant than meets the eye' (E 531). The three Rhodian sculptors did not invent their subject but copied it from one of these sites, specifically 'from the Cherubim of Solomons Temple'. This idea would have been reinforced by Flaxman's discussion of Hebrew sculpture in Rees's *Cyclopaedia*. Flaxman began with that subject 'As the bible is the most ancient history we possess', and he went on to say that Bezaleel and Aholiab were inspired by the spirit of God, in the words of Exod. 31: 4–5 'to devise cunning works in gold, and silver, and in brass, and in the cutting of stones, and in carving of timber to work all kinds of workmanship'[82] for the Tabernacle and the Ark of the Covenant. Years earlier, Blake had written verses in his Notebook asserting the primacy of Bezaleel's and Aholiab's work:

And if Bezaleel & Aholiab drew
What the Finger of God pointed to their View
Shall we suffer the Roman & Grecian Rods
To compell us to worship them as Gods
They stole them from the Temple of the Lord
And Worshippd them that they might make Inspired Art Abhorrd[83]

The view of the cherubim that Blake expressed in his *Descriptive Catalogue* of 1809 also has much in common with Flaxman's. As early as 1807, Flaxman had pointed to the cherubim as instances of the divine sanction of sculpture, writing that 'divine precept directed images of cherubim to be made',[84] and Flaxman and Blake may have conversed about such ideas much earlier. In his *Cyclopaedia* article, Flaxman writes of the two cherubim on the holy of holies: 'of colossal dimensions: they covered the place of the ark with their wings; the height of each was ten cubits . . . A figure five yards high is capable of the greatest effects at perfection in art, and this no doubt they had, being done by divine command for purposes whose importance

---

[82] The Rees volume is not paginated. The wording of the Authorized Version differs from Flaxman's quotation in some details.

[83] E 501, from the Notebook.

[84] John Flaxman, 'Cursory Strictures on Modern Art', in *The Artist*, ed. Prince Hoare (London, 1810), p. 10 (1–16). This is reprinted from the issue of *The Artist* originally dated 30 May 1807.

reaches to the end of time.' Like Blake, Flaxman tended to allegorize
biblical statements, including those about sculpture—a similarity
perhaps owing to the influence of Swedenborg's ideas on both.
Flaxman calls the making of the golden calf 'this dreadful attempt to
annihilate inspired art at its birth', and he equates art and freedom in
a manner very similar to Blake's: according to Flaxman, 'The neces-
sity of such inspired sculptures and other inspired works of art is
explained sufficiently in the deliverance of Israel from the idolatry of
Egypt'; 'Israel deliverd from Egypt is Art deliverd from Nature &
Imitation' says Blake in ה׳ & his two Sons, adding a further dimen-
sion by making mimesis a form of bondage. However, Flaxman,
although he condemned Roman sculpture and the imperial culture
that produced it, admired the art of ancient Greece. For him the
Laocoön is one of those 'precious monuments' of art 'in which we see
the sentiment, heroism, beauty, and sublimity of Greece, existing
before us'. He does not suggest that the sculpture could be a copy of
anything else, though he does suggest that 'it was not ancient' in
Pliny's time.

In the case of the Laocoön, Blake was probably aware that there
was a literal side to the question of copy vs. original. Richard
Brilliant writes of 'the thorny question' of the Laocoön's originality
as much discussed among classical archaeologists today,[85] but it was
also discussed in the eighteenth and early nineteenth centuries, as
Blake could easily have known. The first to deny that the statue in the
Belvedere was the true original were the sixteenth-century antiquar-
ians Pirro Ligorio and Fulvio Orsini,[86] whose views found their way
into print by the early eighteenth century, and in 1724 Bernard de

---

[85] Richard Brilliant, *My Laocoön: Alternative Claims in the Interpretation of
Artworks* (Berkeley: University of California Press, 2000), p. 42. Indeed, one modern
art historian argues that the Laocoön was copied from a bronze executed at Pergamon
c.140 BCE, while another suggests that all the known classical works of art taking
Laocoön as a subject go back to a common prototype of perhaps the 4th c. BCE and
that the sculpture may be 'an aesthetic transformation of a Greek painting'. See Alain
Pasquier, 'Laocoon et ses fils', in Cuzin, Gaborit and Pasquier, eds., *D'après l'antique*,
p. 229 and n. 6 (citing B. Andreae, *Laokoon und die Kunst von Pergamon* (Frankfurt,
1991)); and Leopold Ettlinger, 'Exemplum Doloris: Reflections on the Laocoön
Group', in *De Artibus Opuscula XL: Essays in Honor of Erwin Panofsky*, ed. Millard
Meiss (2 vols., New York: New York University Press, 1961), i. 121–6; ii. 37. The
other classical representations comprise two Pompeian wall paintings, three contor-
niates, and a miniature in a Virgil manuscript in the Vatican. All are reproduced by
Ettlinger, 'Exemplum Doloris', ii. 37.
[86] See van Gelder and Jost, *Jan de Bisschop and his Paradigmata*, i. 103.

Montfaucon brought up the question. Pliny had made a point of saying that the group had been modelled from a single block of stone, while the sculpture that had been unearthed in 1506 was made of more than one block.[87] Montfaucon's opinion was that if the statue in the papal collection were not the original, it must nevertheless be an ancient copy made around the same time and perhaps by the same workers. Jonathan Richardson the younger, who thought the sculpture dated back to *c*.400 BCE, shows an awareness of contemporary disputes about whether it was the original or a copy. His view was that ''tis altogether Inconceivable that there should have been Another, a Better than This, which is the Utmost Perfection of Antique *Greek* Sculpture'.[88] Nevertheless, raising the possibility of the *Laocoön* group's being a copy opens the possibility of an original not at all contemporary with it. Of course Blake would not have been interested in the comparatively minor redatings of a putative ur-*Laocoön*, but for him the literal easily became metaphorical. The idea that the statue unearthed in 1506 might not have been the original opens up the possibility of an almost infinite recession to 'the ancient republics, monarchies and patriarchates of Asia' where he had seen 'those wonderful originals called in the Sacred Scriptures the Cherubim' (E 531).

Like so many of Blake's later ideas, this is a double-edged concept. On the one hand, the outward form of the original is preserved, but on the other it is misunderstood. The Rhodians 'applied' the original conception 'to Natural Fact or History of Ilium', whereas the original had nothing to do with such literalism. Yet it is possible to access the true meaning of the original through the imagination, and this is what Blake undertakes through word and image in יה & *his two Sons*. The Rhodian sculptors thought they were representing an episode of the Trojan War in which a priest of Neptune and his two sons were killed by two enormous serpents, but Blake knows that the powerful patriarch they mistook for a Trojan priest is actually the repressive father-god of his 1795 colour-printed drawing *Elohim Creating Adam* (Butlin 279). The powerful central figure is also similar to Urizen entrapped in his own Net of Religion in *Urizen* 28. Images of serpent-entwined human figures recur in Blake's works: as, for example, in the three falling figures in some copies of *Urizen* 6 and in the *Paradise Lost* design *Satan Watching the Endearments of*

---

[87] See n. 41 above.   [88] *An Account of Some of the Statues*, p. 278.

Adam and Eve (Butlin 529.5, Huntington Library and Art Gallery). The suggestion inescapably is that the serpent and human forms are aspects of the same being, which is also the subject of Dante illustration 55, showing Agnello Brunelleschi transformed into a serpent. (These serpents can also be associated with rationality, and in *Jerusalem* Blake presents himself as their Laocoön-like victim: 'Reasonings like vast Serpents | Infold around my limbs, bruising my minute articulations'—15: 12–13, E 159). The 'יה' who created the material world and is now entwined in it both is and is not the Jehovah of the Old Testament. It is true that at times Blake could talk and write as if Jehovah were the Demiurge. Yet Jehovah also has a positive aspect in *The Death of Abel* as 'Elohim Jehovah' with his 'Covenant of the Forgiveness of Sins' (29–30). יה is a common name for the Deity in the Hebrew Bible, as Blake would have known.[89]

Near the right side of יה's face and parallel to it is inscribed in Greek the name 'Ophiuchus', the constellation next to Serpens (which in Job 26: 13 is called 'the crooked serpent' formed by the hand of God). This is an ironical touch, for *Ophiuchus* means 'serpent holder', and יה is very much a serpent holder against his will. The irony deepens if we consider a possible reference to Mark 16: 15–18,[90] where Jesus appears to the apostles after the Resurrection and says:

Go ye into all the world, and preach the gospel to every creature.
He that believeth and is baptized shall be saved; but he that believeth not shall be damned.
And these signs shall follow them that believe; In my name shall they cast out devils; they shall speak with new tongues;
They shall take up serpents; and if they drink any deadly thing, it shall not hurt them; they shall lay hands on the sick, and they shall recover.

The serpents themselves are identified with words engraved over their heads as 'Evil' and 'Good', in accordance with the later Blake's belief that these moral categories partake of the same elemental error, bifurcating the unity of experience. In the Notebook essay known as 'A Vision of the Last Judgment' Blake refers to 'States of the Sleep which the Soul may fall into in its Deadly Dreams of Good

---

[89] I am grateful to Robert Alter for advice on this subject. For the argument that 'יה' involves a deliberate foreshortening of the Tetragrammaton, 'reflecting the degeneration from the original inspiration of "the Cherubim of Solomons Temple"', see Sheila Spector, 'Blake's Graphic Use of Hebrew', forthcoming in *Blake: An Illustrated Quarterly*.

[90] See Essick and Viscomi, p. 272.

& Evil when it leaves Paradise' (E 563). Here is one of those deadly dreams. Good and evil appear identical; they are reverse images of each other, and equally poisonous.

Also entwined by the serpents are the 'two Sons' of יה. At first this appellation may seem odd, but for one who, like Blake, reads *Paradise Lost* night and day, Satan and Adam really are Jehovah's two sons. Both were created by God directly, without the mediation of woman, and Satan's sibling rivalry is a prime motive for his decision to destroy Adam:

> 'him who next
> Provokes my envy, this new favourite
> Of Heaven, this man of clay, son of despite,
> Whom us, the more to spite, his Maker raised
> From dust: spite then with spite is best repaid.'
>
> (9: 174–8)

Presumably Adam is the younger son expiring from the serpent's poison at the right, while Satan, the elder, may be about to make his escape.[91] Together the two have a symbolic meaning to be found in Blake's later works, representing the limits of Contraction and Opakeness:

> And first he [the Saviour] found the Limit of Opacity & namd it Satan
> In Albions bosom for in every human bosom these limits stand
> And next he found the Limit of Contraction & namd it Adam
> While yet those beings were not born nor knew of good or Evil
>
> (*The Four Zoas* 56: 19–22, E 338)

> There is a limit of Opakeness, and a limit of Contraction;
> In every Individual Man, and the limit of Opakeness,
> Is named Satan: and the limit of Contraction is named Adam.
>
> (*Jerusalem* 42: 29–31, E 189)

In *Milton* 32 a diagram shows Milton's Track through the fiery world of the four fallen Zoas and into the mundane Egg, the ends of

---

[91] As we have seen, Goethe thought there was hope for the older son. Interestingly, in the Magi restoration (see n. 41) it was decided that the right foot of the elder son was originally farther from the left foot of his father; Brummer comments that 'As a result the dramatic content becomes more emphasized: the final escape of the elder son is now clearer than before' (*The Statue Court in the Vatican Belvedere*, p. 78).

which are inscribed 'Satan' and 'Adam'.[92] The assumption of these
limits shows how Milton takes upon himself the limits that define
human identity in the course of his redemptive descent. In the
Jerusalem passage too there is a positive aspect to these limits, exem-
plified by the creation of Eve:

> But when Man sleeps in Beulah, the Saviour in mercy takes
> Contractions Limit, and of that limit he forms Woman: That
> Himself may in process of time be born Man to redeem
> But there is no Limit of Expansion! there is no Limit of Translucence.
> In the bosom of Man for ever from eternity to eternity.
>
> (42: 32–6, E 189)

This possibility of the transformation of Limit to Limitless is absent
from the text of יה *& his two Sons*, where redemption is seen as com-
ing through Art and Art alone.

After reading the title of Blake's engraving and some words refer-
ring directly to it, we enter the area of the textual surround. It must
be said that there is nothing even in Blake like it. One can of course
find partial precedents and parallels. Visual art employed written
words long before Blake—only think of those scripts emerging from
angels' mouths in some Annunciation pictures. Hogarth's paintings
and prints often give prominence to textual elements, often displayed
on signs or on handbills. An even greater prominence is given to
textual elements in the works of caricaturists like James Gillray.
Furthermore, as David Bindman points out, such caricatures use
scripted text much more than they do printed text, and they charac-

---

[92] David Sten Herrstrom attempts to apply the symbolism of the cardinal points in
the diagram to the four quarters of the plate at hand, but Blake's symbolism resists
mechanical transference from one context to the other, and the result is, despite many
fruitful insights, an unsustainable overall interpretation, according to which what is
portrayed in the engraving is the moment of 'Jehovah's choice', that the central figure
is 'a god faced with the decision of whether to become a true God or not', and that as
a consequence 'God himself is redeemed'. See Herrstrom, 'Blake's Redemption of God
in the *Laocoön*', *Bucknell Review*, 30 (1986): 37–71. This is similar to the view
offered by David James, who asserts that 'The event represented . . . is the initiation of
the reversal of the fall, as specifically figured in the setting of the "Limit of Opacity"
and the "Limit of Contraction" ', and continuing with this optimistic interpretation,
identifies 'Jah' as 'imagination-God-Jesus'.—James, 'Blake's *Laocoön*: A Degree Zero
of Literary Production', *PMLA* 98 (1983): 226–36. In addition to ignoring the fact
that the letters *yod* and *heh* do not constitute the Tetragrammaton but only the first
two letters of it, these views ignore the fact that the central figure is clearly doomed,
both in the original statue and in Blake's representation of it.

teristically employ several different registers of text, rendering 'a sense of words as visual facts in themselves'.[93] Another parallel may be found in an engraving of 1793 by Garnet Terry, in which the Great Image of the Book of Daniel is displayed as what Terry calls 'an hieroglyphic print', accompanied by a prophetic pamphlet.[94] However, Terry's engraved image and texts emblematize meanings rather than expressing them in artistic terms and rousing the faculties to act. Blake himself provides a parallel in the *Job* engravings with their marginal texts in several registers and typographical styles, including the Gothic. Even so, the differences between יהוה & his two Sons and all these are far greater than the similarities. Paintings whether by Hogarth or Stuart Davis or R. B. Kitaj tend to relegate whatever textual content they may have to a subordinate status, while in יהוה & his two Sons they are of equal importance. Even Blake's *Job* engravings limit their verbal elements to quotations from the Bible and separate them from their main images by what Frederick Burwick aptly calls a 'mediating frame'.[95] This barrier is broken down in יהוה & his two Sons,[96] and the texts are very much Blake's own, employing a mode that he had utilized from an early point in his career—the aphorism. Blake was engaged with aphorisms early on, in annotating Lavater's *Aphorisms on Man* c.1788 and in making his own marginal attempts there. These, like Lavater's, are straightforward—the endeavour is to make an impression through direct statement: 'Active Evil is better than Passive Good' (E 592); 'Great ends never look at means but produce them

---

[93] See Bindman, 'Text as Design in Gillray's Caricature', in *Icons—Texts—Iconotexts: Essays on Ekphrasis and Intermediality*, ed. Peter Wagner (Berlin and New York: Walter de Gruyter, 1996), pp. 309–23.

[94] The only known example of this engraving is, with its accompanying pamphlet, in the collection of Robert N. Essick. See David Bindman, 'William Blake and Popular Religious Imagery', *The Burlington Magazine*, 128 (1986): 717 and fig. 13 (712–18); Jon Mee, *Dangerous Enthusiasm: William Blake and the Culture of Radicalism in the 1790s* (Oxford: Clarendon Press, 1992), pp. 63–7; catalogue entry by David Bindman in Frances Carey, ed., *Apocalypse and the Shape of Things to Come* (London: British Museum, 1999), p. 245, no. 16.

[95] Burwick, 'Blake's *Laocoön* and *Job*: or, On the Boundaries of Painting and Poetry', in *The Romantic Imagination*, ed. Frederick Burwick and Jürgen Klein (Amsterdam and Atlanta: Rodopi, 1996), p. 134 (pp. 125–55).

[96] Irene Tayler comments on the contrast between the 'three-dimensionality' of the representation of the statue and the contrasting 'crowded clutter of two-dimensional symbols' that are the words of the text—'Blake's *Laocoön*', *Blake*, 10 (1976–7): 72 (72–81). Nancy Moore Goslee makes a similar point in *Uriel's Eye: Miltonic Stationing and Statuary in Blake, Keats, and Shelley*, pp. 55, 60–1.

spontaneously' (E 595). In *The Marriage of Heaven and Hell* there are also some such straightforward maxims—'To create a little flower is the labour of ages' (E 27)—but there are others which, to adapt Blake's words from another context, rouse the faculties to act. 'Drive your cart and your plow over the bones of the dead' (E 35) and 'Sooner murder an infant in its cradle than nurse unacted desires' (E 38) move from the literal to the figurative, but a common basis of understanding with the reader is assumed. We can find examples of both these types in the texts Blake wrote on his last separate plate. 'Art can never exist without Naked Beauty displayed'[97] is self-evident in meaning, and 'The outward Ceremony is Antichrist' is metaphorically intelligible to anyone familiar with antinomian Protestantism. However, some of the aphorisms employ a gnomic vocabulary that demands a knowledge of Blake's later thought, and these require special attention. There are also the questions of how (some might say 'whether') the text of יה & *his two Sons* should be presented typographically and of the order in which the aphorisms may most fruitfully be discussed.

4

The unique nature of יה & *his two Sons* has given editors of Blake's works some special problems. On the whole their editions have fallen into two groups. Those of Sloss and Wallis and of David V. Erdman present the text in topical or thematic groups; those of Keynes and of Essick and Viscomi[98] attempt to follow the arrangement on the page, although it is of course impossible to do this in every respect typographically. In one way, this could be declared a non-problem. Since this work exists on a single sheet, it can simply be reproduced instead of being typeset. If ever a work cried out for a presentation as close as possible to Blake's own, it is יה *and his two Sons*. How important this is can be shown by a short examination of the arrangement in Erdman's edition. In beginning such a discussion,

---

[97] For reasons that will become clear in the following discussion, I do not refer to Erdman's text (E 270–2) here but transcribe directly from the engraving.

[98] *The Prophetic Writings of William Blake*, ed. D. J. Sloss and J. P. R. Wallis (2 vols., Oxford: Clarendon Press, 1926); E 273–5; *The Complete Writings of William Blake*, ed. Sir Geoffrey Keynes (London: Oxford University Press, rev. edn. 1972), pp. 775–7; Essick and Viscomi, pp. 268–71.

we should note that Erdman's *Complete Poetry and Prose* has justly become the most widely used typographical edition of Blake's writings, and also that Erdman himself writes of the inscriptions that 'There is no right way' to read them 'except all at once' (E 814). Nevertheless, it is important to point out the result of following what Erdman terms a 'more or less coherent thematic sequence' as an editorial arrangement, taking one part of the plate as an example. In the left-hand margin of the sheet there are four 'columns' of aphorisms. When the page is rotated ninety degrees these read:

[1] Spiritual War
Israel deliverd from Egypt
is Art deliverd from
Nature & Imitation

[2] A Poet a Painter a Musician an Architect: the Man
Or Woman who is not one of these is not a Christian
You must leave Fathers & Mothers & Houses & Lands if they stand
in the way of Art

[3] Prayer is the Study of Art
Praise is the Practise of Art

[4] Fasting &c. all relate to Art
The outward Ceremony is Antichrist

In *The Complete Poetry and Prose* these are arranged as part of a twelve-line sequence. [1] comprises the first two lines. But this is followed by an aphorism from the other side of the plate, occupying the third and fourth lines down from the right margin, parallel to the lower part of the body of the older son:

What we call Antique Gems | are the Gems of Aarons Breast Plate

The next lines are not those of column [2] but those of columns [3] and [4]. Then comes a line that is, again, far from the others. It is part of the text curving around Laocoön's upraised right hand and forearm. This section reads in its entirety:

The Gods of Priam are the Cherubim of Moses & Solomon The Hosts |
of Heaven
Without Unceasing Practise nothing can be done Practise is Art
If you leave off you are Lost

Erdman prints as the eighth line of the passage 'Without Unceasing

Practise nothing can be done', and after a section comprising five lines of text and two one-line gaps, he prints 'Practise is Art If you leave off you are Lost'. But although it's just possible that Blake might have written 'Practise is Art | If you leave off you are Lost' just after what immediately precedes it in Erdman's text, we don't know that for a fact, and this arrangement falsifies what Blake presents on the page. The material in column [2] then appears after a one-line space following 'Without Unceasing Practise nothing can be done'; and this is followed by: 'The unproductive Man is not a Christian much less the Destroyer'. Once more these words come from a different part of the plate, the second line of the lower part of the right margin. A one-line gap follows.

This, then, is an example of what Erdman means by 'coherent thematic sequence'. But aren't the four columns as Blake wrote them a coherent thematic sequence? Isn't that the way that he wanted us to read them, and isn't it the way in which we do read them? Furthermore: below columns [2]–[4] is inscribed in a larger register: 'The Eternal Body of Man is The Imagination, that is God himself' (the lettering of 'Imagination' is a bit larger than the rest; and it is more heavily inked). These words are followed by a continuation to the right and then below. This material appears considerably earlier in Erdman's text than the four columns above and (in the case of column [1]) to the left of it. The reader of the printed text of E alone would see no particular link between these two sections of text. Yet Blake has arranged things so that there is decidedly a very close connection, one which is visible in Essick and Viscomi's edition. In their own words: 'we have recorded the captions below the sculpture first, then the inscriptions immediately contiguous to the outline of the pictorial image (moving from left to right), and finally the outermost inscriptions, beginning in the bottom left corner and proceeding clockwise around the left side, top, and right side of the print.'[99] This is a sensible procedure, following as it does the way in which the reader would normally look at the text for the first time.

Fortunately, the nature of the יהּ *& his two Sons* plate is such that, comprising a single monochrome page, it can easily be reproduced, allowing the reader to choose his or her order of reading and rereading its text. For purposes of discussion, however, a sequence must be adopted by the critic or scholar. Needless to say, more than one

[99] p. 231 n. 15.

sequence is possible. An appealing possibility might be to try to reconstruct the texts in the order in which Blake inscribed them. It is possible that at some point in its composition this plate presented a much more obviously balanced visual arrangement than it later assumed. The 'four columns' just discussed provide one example of this. Another comprises the lines inscribed horizontally from the upper right down to just below the middle right. David Sten Herrstrom astutely points out that, reading down, you encounter four sets of inscriptions, each of which is followed by a command to read another text: 'Read Matthew C X. 9 & 10 v', 'See Plato's Works', 'See Virgils Eneid. Lib. VI. v 848', and 'See Luke Ch 2 v I'.[100] These may be vestiges of some earlier, more clearly organized state of the text before further alterations were made. One might also assume that the large-sized inscriptions reading from left to right were written first. Conversely, the tiny lettering of 'If Morality was Christianity Socrates was the Saviour' appears to have been squeezed in between the plinth and the lettering of the title as an afterthought. Having said this, though, we have pretty much exhausted the possibilities of this approach. We simply do not know, for example, whether Blake first turned the plate to the left or to the right to make inscriptions at an angle of 90 degrees to the original ones. And, though we can see that the words that curve so wonderfully along the upper arms and heads of the three figures were put there after the design was engraved, we have no way of telling whether they preceded or followed the writing nearest them. The best way of discussing the verbal aspect of יה & his two Sons is to explore three closely related themes: money, empire, and tax; the nature of art; and God, man, and the imagination. Because they are so closely related, any of these could be discussed first, but we may begin with the last named because of the prominence of two Hebrew words—in lettering larger than that of the title—in the upper centre of the plate.

As we look at the text of יה & his two Sons we are likely to notice two Hebrew words placed not far above Laocoön's head, and then 'The Angel of the Divine Presence', meaning close to the same thing in English, below them. Although these precise English words do not occur in the Authorized Version, there are two close parallels. In Isaiah 63: 9 it is said of God and the house of Israel that 'In their affliction he was afflicted, and the angel of his presence saved

---

[100] Herrstrom, 'Blake's Redemption of God in the *Laocoön*', p. 58.

them'. And in Luke 1: 19 the news that Elisabeth would conceive and give birth to the future John the Baptist is delivered to Zacharias by an angel who says: 'I am Gabriel, that stand in the presence of God.' These are both positively charged statements, yet we know that Blake was capable of revalorizing biblical phrases, or of rendering them ambiguous. In the watercolour 'The Angel of the Divine Presence Clothing Adam and Eve with Coats of Skins' (Butlin 436, Fitzwilliam Museum),[101] a gigantic bearded patriarch towers disquietingly over the meekly prayerful couple, and the bared left foot protruding from his gown is reminiscent of Urizen's in *The [First] Book of Urizen*, plate 28.[102] He is enfolding Adam and Eve in the clothing of sexual shame, in direct contradiction to Blake's aphorism on this plate that 'Art can never exist without Naked Beauty displayed'. Yet Blake also shows an indubitably positive version of this figure bringing Eve to Adam in *The Creation of Eve: 'And She Shall be Called Woman'* (Butlin 336, Metropolitan Museum of Art). A similarly two-sided presentation is found in Blake's *Milton*, where the Seven Angels instructing 'Hillel who is Lucifer' say:

> We are not Individuals but States: Combinations of Individuals
> We were Angels of the Divine Presence: & were Druids in Annandale
> Compelld to combine into Form by Satan, the Spectre of Albion,
> Who made himself a God &, destroyed the Human Form Divine[103]
>
> (32: 10–13, E 131)

But they immediately add:

> But the Divine Humanity & Mercy gave us a Human Form
> Because we were combind in Freedom & holy Brotherhood
>
> (14–15)

These Angels of the Divine Presence may be either positive or negative presences, depending on whether they are in Druid Form or Human Form. Also ambiguous is Blake's identification of a figure in his *Last Judgment* picture:

---

[101] The title is given in Blake's letter of 6 July 1803 to Thomas Butts (E 729), in which Blake says this is one of the pictures he has 'on the Stocks'.

[102] It has been pointed out by Mary Lynn Johnson that in the watercolour the Angel has six toes, which may link him with the six-toed Philistine giant of 2 Sam. 21: 20 (see Butlin 436, i. 337).

[103] On the complexities of the three Hebrew words that are inscribed in the margin here, see Essick and Viscomi, pp. 188–9.

The Aged Figure with Wings having a writing tablet & taking account of the numbers who arise is That Angel of the Divine Presence mentiond in Exodus XIVc 19v & in other Places this Angel is frequently calld by the name of Jehovah Elohim the I am of the Oaks of Albion[104]

In Exodus 14: 19 the angel of God ('of the Divine Presence' is added by Blake) casts darkness before the Egyptians as they pursue the Israelites toward the Red Sea, but the God who identified himself to Moses from the burning bush has here been moved among Druid Oaks. Although this figure is on the viewer's left, and so is among those rising, he himself is not rising but counting, and writing numbers down on a tablet seems a suspicious activity in the Blakean universe. Once more there is something dubious about the Angel of the Divine Presence. This dubiety extends to the two Hebrew words below the English. Except for one detail they would mean 'Messenger' or 'Angel' of 'God'. However, the *alef* in the first Hebrew word is reversed, and Spector argues that *alef* meant 'the supernal man' in the Kabbala, and that the reversed *alef* reflects 'materialism' resulting in 'an inverted concept of God'.[105] Similarly, above the centre of the framing line of *Job* engraving 2 appear the words 'The Angel of the Divine Presence', and immediately below them two Hebrew words meaning 'King Jehovah' (rather than 'Messenger/Angel [of] Jehovah') because the *alef* of the first word is absent entirely.[106] In יה & his two Sons the presentation of the divine, except where it is associated with art, is ambiguous where it is not negative.

In line with such a view of the ambiguity of the divine, or at least of human conceptions of the divine, is the statement in a large register near the top centre, and thus prominently featured: 'He repented that he had made Adam | (of the Female, the Adamah) | & it grieved him at his heart'. The initial reference is to Genesis 6, where God sees the great wickedness of man on earth, 'And it repented the Lord that

---

[104] *Vision of the Last Judgment*, E 559. Of the extant Blake Last Judgments, this winged figure appears only in the drawing in the National Gallery of Art, Washington, DC (Butlin 645), and in the tracing Blake made from it (Butlin 646, collection of Robert N. Essick).

[105] Spector, 'Blake's Graphic Use of Hebrew'. It is of course possible that the reversal of the *alef* was a mistake made by an engraver not used to rendering Hebrew letters with their necessary reversals on the copperplate.

[106] See E 687 and Essick and Viscomi, p. 272.

he had made man on the earth, and it grieved him at his heart' (6: 6). This is followed by God's decision to send the Deluge. The second part comes from Gen. 2: 7: 'And the Lord God formed man of the dust of the ground, and breathed into his nostrils the breath of life; and man became a living soul.' Four chapters later, God repents of his creation. But why does Blake change 'the dust of the ground' to 'of the Female, the Adamah'? This is a very deliberate change, for in the text of the illustrated Genesis manuscript (Huntington Library) that he produced *c.*1826–7, Blake frequently adds the word 'Adamah' as a gloss on the biblical word 'ground'[107] (see Chapter 4). 'Adamah' does mean 'earth' in Hebrew, but at first 'of the Female' may seem as arbitrary as 'his two Sons Satan & Adam' does at first. However, there is once more a precedent for this: in Jewish tradition, the Earth, in the words of Raphael Patai, is 'considered in a literal sense the mother of all living'.[108] We do not know how much Blake knew of such traditions, especially of the Kabbala; but that he knew something is attested by the appearance of the Hebrew name *Lilith* in the heart-shaped space between יה and Satan. This is a name that appears only once in the Bible, in Isaiah 34: 14, where it is said of the desolate wilderness: 'Yea, Lilith shall repose there And find her a place of rest'[109]—but not in the Authorized Version, where *Lilith* is rendered as 'screech owl'. Since the only biblical reference to Lilith is of such minor importance, Blake may have derived from some Kabbalistic or other Jewish source the notion that Lilith was Adam's wife prior to the creation of Eve, and that she became (or always was) a demonic being.[110] However, while in Jewish thought there are powerful positive female presences, especially the Shekhina, to counterbalance Lilith, and there the Adamah is a positively charged figure, that is not true of Blake's text, where 'of the Female' has a negative meaning. The third female mentioned is

[107] See C. H. Collins Baker, *Catalogue of William Blake's Drawings and Paintings in the Huntington Library*, enlarged and rev. R. R. Wark (San Marino, Calif.: Huntington Library, 1957), pp. 40–2; Robert N. Essick, *The Works of William Blake in the Huntington Collections* (San Marino, Calif.: Huntington Library, 1985), pp. 112–15.

[108] Patai, *The Hebrew Goddess* (3rd edn., Detroit: Wayne State University Press, 1990), p. 277.

[109] See S. Foster Damon, *A Blake Dictionary* (rev. edn., Hanover and London: University Press of New England, 1988), p. 240; translation from Patai, *The Hebrew Goddess*, p. 223.

[110] See Patai, *The Hebrew Goddess*, pp. 223–54.

'Satans Wife The Goddess Nature', who is equated with 'War & Misery'. This presentation of the negative female component of human identity, which would have been represented in *Jerusalem* by Vala and Rahab, without any counterpoise, such as Erin and Jerusalem herself, is but one aspect of the fiercely polarizing tendency of this text as a whole.

Other instances of the ambiguity of the divine are Blake's ideas of the Greek, Egyptian, and Trojan divinities. When Blake writes 'The Gods of Greece & Egypt were Mathematical Diagrams See Plato's Works', he is probably alluding to Thomas Taylor's edition, which abounds in statements like 'If it be necessary to mention the doctrine delivered through the mathematical disciplines . . . many may be contemplated in the *Timæus*', and 'the figures of the five elements, delivered in geometrical proportion in the *Timæus*, represent in images the idioms of the gods who preside over the parts of the universe'.[111] We can interpret Blake's statement as an implied contrast between what he calls 'Mathematic Form' and what he calls 'Living Form' in *On Virgil* (E 270), the first being 'Grecian' and the second 'Gothic'. Again, when Blake writes 'The Gods of Priam are the Cherubim of Moses & Solomon The Hosts of Heaven', he is asserting that just as the *Laocoön* sculpture is a debased version of 'the Cherubim of Solomons Temple', the Gods of Priam (whom of course Laocoön, a priest of Neptune, served) are debased versions of the Cherubim, identified with the 'multitude of the heavenly host praising God' that appeared to the shepherds near Bethlehem in Luke 2: 13. The conventionally opposed moral categories 'Evil' and 'Good' are here seen as identical, relegated to inscriptions over the heads of the two serpents in keeping with Blake's belief that 'the Soul may fall into . . . Deadly Dreams of Good & Evil when it leaves Paradise'.[112] Nevertheless, the inscriptions do affirm a positive aspect of the divinity. Although 'Adam is only The Natural Man & not the Soul or Imagination', the Imagination is affirmed as divine: 'The Eternal Body of Man is The Imagination, that is God himself | The Divine

---

[111] *Works of Plato* (5 vols., Frome, Somerset: Prometheus Trust, 1995–6 (London, 1804)), 'General Introduction', i. 25. George Mills Harper links Blake's statement to what he calls 'the mathematical bias of parts of Taylor's edition, notably the *Timæus*'. See George Mills Harper, *The Neoplatonism of William Blake* (Chapel Hill, NC: University of North Carolina Press, 1961), pp. 54–5. It may be noted that in Taylor's edition the *Meno* is illustrated by eighteen geometrical diagrams (v. 51–61), though not of gods, taken over from Floyer Sydenhams's earlier edition.

[112] *A Vision of the Last Judgment*, E 563.

Body', and this is followed by what appears to be the Hebrew name of Jesus,[113] and then 'we are his Members'. As previously mentioned, 'Imagination' is here inscribed in a large register and thicker letters, emphasizing its importance. And the lines below go on: 'It manifests itself in his Works of Art (In Eternity All is Vision)'. This is of course a persistent theme in Blake's later works, but what distinguishes its presentation here is its vehemence and exclusiveness.

Overlapping with the theme of the Imagination as 'God himself' is that of the divine nature of the productions of the Imagination—works of art. Blake's view of the redemptive nature of art and art alone is uncompromising here:

> A Poet a Painter a Musician an Architect: the Man
> Or Woman who is not one of these is not a Christian
> You must leave Fathers & Mothers & Houses & Lands if they stand in
> the way of Art

This plays on Jesus' injunction to leave family and follow him (Luke 14: 26–33), but while it may support the situation of a Paul Morel or of a Stephen Daedalus struggling to realize his artistic destiny, it has little to say to common humanity. The same transposition of religion to art occurs in a series of statements to the right of these:

> Prayer is the Study of Art
> Praise is the Practise of Art
>
> Fasting &c. all relate to Art

Blake carries this to its furthest extreme in writing: 'Jesus & his Apostles & Disciples were all Artists Their Works were destroyd by the Seven Angels of the Seven Churches in Asia. Antichrist Science'. In this categorical condemnation of science, Blake departs from his earlier view that, although there was indeed a 'self-destroying beast formd Science', there was also a 'sweet Science' related to the whole human identity (at the end of *The Four Zoas* 'The dark Religions are departed & sweet Science reigns').[114] In the world of *יה & his two Sons*, there is no positive Science. 'ﬣebrew Art is called Sin by the

[113] Spector ('Blake's Graphic Use of Hebrew') observes that the Hebrew name for Jesus should read ישׁוע but that here the *ayin* is reversed and the *vav* omitted, suggesting 'that the conventional interpretation of Jesus is a corruption that ignores true Christological vision'. This would of course make even the seemingly positive statement ambiguous, but perhaps Blake's knowledge of Hebrew is at fault here.

[114] *The Four Zoas*, Night IX, 120: 40, E 390; Night IV, 51: 30, E 334; Night IX, 139: 10, E 407.

Deist Science', and Art and Science are bluntly juxtaposed in the
neighbouring statements: 'Art is the Tree of Life GOD is Jesus', and
'Science is the Tree of Death'. As Morris Eaves has remarked,
'metaphors arranged in oppositions' are characteristic of this text,[115]
and it may be added that in these oppositions there is no 'true
Friendship' as in *The Marriage of Heaven and Hell* (E 42), no
possible marriage of Contraries. Such antitheses express the fiercely
antinomian and Gnostic spirit of the inscriptions as a whole. Blake
doesn't consider it part of his concern to explain how the non-artist
shall participate in his vision. 'The whole Business of Man Is The
Arts & All Things Common', he writes, referring to the practice of
the early Christian communities described in Acts 4: 32: 'And the
multitude of them that believed were of one heart and of one soul:
neither said any of them that ought of the things which he possessed
was his own; but they had all things common.' This communitarian-
ism is in contrast to the cash nexus that is denounced in the apho-
risms and linked to empire.

'Christianity is Art | & not Money | Money is its Curse': this highly
unequivocal statement contrasts with the professionalism about his
work that Blake exhibits elsewhere, as in the price lists for illumi-
nated books that he sent to Dawson Turner in 1818 and to George
Cumberland as late as 1827.[116] It is true that in these two letters
Blake shows his awareness of how high these prices appear and the
consequent unlikelihood of his finding customers, but my point is
that he also shows an awareness of the value of his time in monetary
terms. In יה & his two Sons there is no room even for the modest
price lists that Blake supplied. Here 'Where any view of Money exists
Art cannot be carried on, but War only', and Blake cites Matt. 10:
9–10, where Jesus tells the Apostles: 'Provide neither gold, nor silver,
nor brass in your purses, Nor scrip for your journey, neither two
coats, neither shoes, nor yet staves: for the workman is worthy of his
meat.' The question Blake posed is not so much how we are to live
like this but rather how Christianity, founded by a pacifist and origi-
nally practised by communities holding all things common, could
become the legitimizer and sanctifier of riches, war, and empire. The
charity condemned as early as 'The Human Abstract' of *Songs of*

---

[115] Eaves, *The Counter-Arts Conspiracy: Art and Industry in the Age of Blake*
(Ithaca, NY, and London: Cornell University Press, 1992), p. 134.
[116] 9 June 1818 (E 771) and 12 April 1827 (E 784).

Experience ('Pity would be no more | If we did not make somebody Poor', E 27) is seen as a product of the moral categories inscribed over the heads of the two serpents—'Good & Evil are Riches & Poverty a Tree of Misery propagating Generation & Death'. Money is mordantly characterized as 'the lifes blood of Poor Families' and even when given as charity is condemned as 'Caesar or Empire or Natural Religion'. Linking money with 'Caesar or Empire' plays on the reader's associations with Jesus' question in Luke 20: 24 and its answer: 'Shew me a penny. Whose image and superscription hath it? They answered and said, Caesar's.' Far from relegating what is Caesar's to a separate realm, Blake declares 'Empire against Art See Virgils Eneid. Lib. VI. v 848'. This reference is to the prophecy of Anchises to Aeneas in the underworld: 'Others, I doubt not, shall beat out the breathing bronze with softer lines; shall from marble draw forth the features of life; shall plead their causes better; with the rod shall trace the paths of heaven and tell the rising of the stars: remember thou, O Roman, to rule the nations with thy sway—these shall be thine arts—to crown Peace with Law, to spare the humbled; and to tame in war the proud!'[117] In *On Virgil* Blake tersely glosses this same passage as: 'Let others study Art: Rome has somewhat better to do, namely War & Dominion' (E 270).

The Roman practitioners of empire were the successors to the 'Spoilers' of the Old Testament. 'And the spoiler shall come upon every city, and no city shall escape: the valley also shall perish, and the plain shall be destroyed, as the LORD hath spoken.'[118]

Divine Union | Deriding | And Denying Immediate | Communion with God | The Spoilers say | Where are his Works | That he did in the Wilderness | Lo what are these | Whence came they | These are not the Works | Of Egypt nor Babylon | Whose Gods are the Powers | Of this World. Goddess, Nature. | Who first spoil & then destroy | Imaginative Art | For their Glory is | War and Dominion

The archetypal spoiler was Titus, in whose palace the *Laocoön* supposedly stood. His modern successors transported the statue from

---

[117] *Virgil*, with an English translation by H. Rushton Fairclough (Cambridge, Mass.: Harvard University Press, 1960), p. 567.

[118] Jeremiah 48: 8. Isaiah 16: 4 prophesies a time when the spoilers will be driven out: 'Let mine outcasts dwell with thee, Moab; be thou a covert to them from the face of the spoiler: for the extortioner is at an end, the spoiler ceaseth, the oppressors are consumed out of the land.'

Rome to Paris and back to Rome again. Blake sees nothing to choose from between the Greek and Trojan or the British and French empires. One special feature of empire, especially important to Blake at this time, is its power to tax universally, to reach into the poorest families and squeeze out their 'lifes blood'. This preoccupation with tax is characteristic of only the later Blake: the word and its cognates appear no earlier than two contexts in *Jerusalem*. In 64: 33–4, 'Human Miseries turnd fierce with the Lives of Men along the Valley | As Reuben fled before the Daughters of Albion Taxing the Nations' (E 215); and at the apocalyptic End, among the relics of the fallen world that are no more (including 'the Covenant of Priam', 98: 46), is the time when 'the Triple Headed Gog-Magog Giant | Of Albion Taxed the Nations into Desolation & then gave the Spectrous Oath' (98: 53; E 258). Both allude to the passage Blake cites in Luke 2, where 'there went out a decree from Caesar Augustus, that all the world should be taxed'. The power of empire to tax the world is true of course not only of Greece and Rome but also of Britain. And of course it is not only in the empires of Greece and Rome that visionary men like William Blake are accounted madmen.

In יהּ & his two Sons Satan & Adam Blake attacks empire by subverting one of its own artistic icons. Regarded by Blake as a copy of a Hebrew original that its adapters did not even understand, the *Laocoön* represents the inauthenticity of imperial culture, whether that of Troy, Greece, Rome, France, or Britain. Blake transforms it into יהּ & his two Sons Satan & Adam by surrounding it with texts denouncing money, war, and empire and affirming the ultimate value of art, texts representing the late Blake at his most uncompromising. They should not, of course, be read and interpreted in isolation from the image of the sculpture on the same page. The aphorisms establish a complex series of tensions with that image, involving both what it meant to Blake and what he knew it meant to critics, connoisseurs, and statesmen. In coming to terms with a work that is perhaps Blake's most vehement condemnation of the society in which he lived, we must bring to it an understanding of the cultural history both of antiquity and of his own time.

3 'In Equivocal Worlds Up & Down are Equivocal': Illustrations to *The Divine Comedy*

I

THE LITERARY REPUTATION of Dante was at a low point in England during much of the eighteenth century. This attitude was expressed in its most extreme form by Horace Walpole in a letter to William Mason dated 25 June 1782: 'Dante was extravagant, absurd, disgusting, in short a Methodist parson in Bedlam.'[1] Yet a counter movement was under way almost throughout the century, and it initially took the form of the appreciation of the episode of Count Ugolino in the *Inferno*. This was translated into English for the first time by Jonathan Richardson in the second of his *Two Discourses* of 1719. Joseph Warton in 1756 retold the story of Ugolino and commented: 'Perhaps the Inferno of Dante, is the next composition to the Iliad, in point of originality and sublimity. And with regard to the Pathetic, let this tale stand as testimony of his abilities: for my own part, I truly believe it was never carried to a greater height.'[2] Numerous other translations of this section appeared before the entire *Inferno* was first published in Henry Boyd's verse translation of 1785.[3] As in translation and criticism, so in art. In 1773 Sir Joshua Reynolds was the first to exhibit a painting after

---

[1] Paget Toynbee, *Dante in English Literature from Chaucer to Cary* (2 vols., New York: Macmillan, 1909), i. 340. My discussion of Dante's reception history is largely based on this book, hereafter cited as *DEL*; and on V. Tinkler-Villani, *Visions of Dante in English Poetry: Translations of the Commedia from Jonathan Richardson to William Blake* (Amsterdam: Rodopi, 1989).

[2] *An Essay on the Genius and Writings of Pope*, in *DEL* i. 266.

[3] For a list, see *DEL* i, pp. vi–vii.

Dante at the Royal Academy, with his *Count Hugolino and His Children in the Dungeon, as described by Dante in the thirty-third canto of the Inferno,* bought by the Duke of Dorset and hung at Knole Park, where it remains. It became widely known through a mezzotint engraving by John Dixon (1774) and, later, a line engraving by H. Raimbach (1811).[4] Reynolds's design was based on a relief sculpture then thought to be the work of Michelangelo but now attributed to Pierino da Vinci. Dixon's mezzotint[5] exploits the capacities of the medium for contrasting light and darkness, showing some features of Ugolino and his sons in light against the black background of the cell with its barred window. A little boy leans on the old man's right knee and looks imploringly up at him while he stares vacantly into space; to the left another little boy faints into the arms of an older one, while in the darkness a second older boy covers his face in despair. Reynolds's picture presents its subject as an object of domestic pathos, and it was for this reason very popular; Horace Walpole wrote: 'The prints after the Works of Sir Joshua Reynolds have spread his fame to Italy. In what age were paternal despair and the horrors of death pronounced with more expressive accents than in his picture of Count Ugolino.'[6] It was, however, later attacked by William Hazlitt for its lack of sublimity:

He had, it seems, painted a study of an old beggar-man's head; and some person . . . persuaded the unsuspecting artist that it was the exact expression of the Dante's Count Ugolino, one of the most grand, terrific and appalling characters in modern fiction. . . . There is all the difference between what the picture is and what it ought to be, that there is between Crabbe and Dante. The imagination of the painter took refuge in a parish workhouse, instead of ascending the steps of the Tower of Famine. . . . The subject of the *Laocoon* is scarcely equal to that described by Dante. The horror *there* is physical; in the other, the imagination fills up the long, obscure, dreary void of despair, and joins its unutterable pangs to the loud cries of nature. What is there in

⁴ See Paget Toynbee, *Dante in English Art* (Boston: Ginn & Co. [for the Dante Society], 1921), pp. 2–3; Frances A. Yates, 'Transformations of Dante's Ugolino', *Journal of the Warburg and Courtauld Institutes,* 14 (1951): 92–117; and Nicholas Penny, *Reynolds* (London: Royal Academy, 1986), no. 82, pp. 251–3.
⁵ For a reproduction, see John Beer, 'Influence and Independence in Blake', in *Interpreting Blake,* ed. Michael Phillips (Cambridge: Cambridge University Press, 1978), p. 208; and Penny, *Reynolds,* fig. 83, p. 253.
⁶ Quoted by Yates, 'Transformations', p. 116, from *Anecdotes of Painting,* ed. Ralph Wornum (1849), i, p. xvii.

the picture to convey the ghastly horrors of the scene, or the mighty energy of soul with which they are borne?[7]

A generation before Hazlitt's remarks, a sublime alternative to Reynolds's treatment of the subject had been exhibited by Henry Fuseli in a painting for which Blake publicly expressed his admiration. Writing of Reynolds's painting, Fuseli had criticized the composition and some details such as the muscularity of the children, and had complained that the da Vinci sculpture did not represent 'the fierce Gothic chief, deprived of revenge, brooding over despair in the stony cage . . .'.[8] Fuseli himself had done an ink drawing of Ugolino and his sons, along with a number of other Dante subjects, as early as the 1770s;[9] and in 1806 he exhibited his *Count Ugolino* at the Royal Academy, with the catalogue entry: 'Count Ugolino, chief of the Guelphs at Pisa, locked up by the opposite party with his four sons, and starved to death in the tower, from which that event, acquired the name of the *Torre della Fame*. See the *Inferno*, of Dante, Canto xxxiii.'[10] Now known only through an engraving by Moses Haughton, Fuseli's design indeed shows a 'fierce Gothic chief' glaring out at the viewer, his casque and one mailed glove on the floor in the left foreground. A wall of massive blocks and a heavy chain descending from above emphasize the finality of his imprisonment. One of his four sons (historically two sons and two grandsons) sits bent over in despair to his left; one slouches despondently to his left; one is represented only by a hand feebly emerging from the left margin; and one lies unconscious, draped over Ugolino's lap. It was especially this figure that drew the sarcasm of a reviewer in *Bell's Weekly*

[7] Quoted in *DEL* ii. 182–3, from Hazlitt's article 'On the Fine Arts' (1824) contributed to the *Encyclopaedia Britannica*. Hazlitt got his account of the origin of Reynolds's picture from James Northcote, who had posed for one of the children and said the person who suggested making the head into part of a historical painting was either Burke or Goldsmith. See Toynbee, *DEL* ii. 134–5, citing Northcote's *Memoirs of Sir Joshua Reynolds* (1813). For the name of the sitter and other details, see Penny, *Reynolds*, p. 252.

[8] Toynbee, *DEL* i. 427, from John Knowles, *The Life and Writings of Henry Fuseli* (2 vols., London, 1831), ii. 166. Fuseli first commented on the subject in his *Third Lecture on Painting* (London, 1801).

[9] See Gert Schiff, *Johann Heinrich Füssli 1741–1825: Text und Oeuvrekatalog* (2 vols., Zurich: Verlag Berichthaus, Munich: Prestel-Verlag, 1973), no. 427. The pictures catalogued in volume i are reproduced in volume ii with the catalogue numbers. This work is hereafter cited as Schiff.

[10] Toynbee, *Dante in English Art*, p. 10. See Schiff no. 1200.

Messenger, which drew in turn an irate response from William Blake. The anonymous critic says:

In the present groupe, Ugolino has the appearance of a man who, having in a fit of phrenzy destroyed the young female who lies across his knees, has just returned to a sense of reason and remorse at the act which he has perpetrated. By this material error, that of the professed story, as it were, being not only imperfectly narrated, but absolutely untold, the artist has entirely lost the passion he must have intended to enforce: he has substituted horror for pathos, and depicted ferocity instead of sympathy.[11]

The writer goes on to criticize the depiction of 'The figure of the daughter', which 'conveys more the idea of a drowned figure, just taken from the waters, than that of a female emaciated and contracted by famine. . . . The body is too short; in fact there is scarcely any body at all; the whole figure is arms and legs.' He also condemns the darkness of the picture—'tints that are black and heavy'. Blake responded in a letter to the *Monthly Magazine*, in which he says in effect that *Bell's* critic has looked for pathos where he ought to have looked for sublimity:

Mr. Fuseli's Count Ugolino is the father of sons of feeling and dignity, who would not sit looking in their parent's face in the moment of his agony, but would rather retire and die in secret, while they suffer him to indulge his passionate and innocent grief, his innocent and venerable madness, and insanity, and fury, and whatever paltry cold hearted critics cannot, because they dare not, look upon. Fuseli's Count Ugolino is a man of wonder and admiration, of resentment against man and devil, and of humiliation before God; prayer and parental affection fills the figure from head to foot. The child in his arms, whether boy or girl signifies not, (but the critic must be a fool who has not read Dante, and who does not know a boy from a girl); I say, the child is as beautifully drawn as it is coloured—in both, inimitable! and the effect of the whole is truly sublime, on account of that very colouring which our critic calls black and heavy. The German flute colour, which was used by the Flemings, (they call it burnt bone), has possessed the eye of certain connoisseurs, that they cannot see appropriate colouring, and are blind to the gloom of a real terror.[12]

Blake's impassioned defence is eloquent, but in one respect a bit disingenuous. He is of course correct in saying that the child referred to as a girl by the reviewer is a boy in Dante's text, but it must be said

[11] Toynbee, *DEL* ii. 30–1, from *Bell's Weekly Messenger* for 25 May 1806.
[12] E 768, from the *Monthly Magazine*, 21 (1 July 1806): 520–1.

that the figure as rendered in Haughton's engraving is decidedly ambiguous, and that its posture and its being bathed in white light are reminiscent of the woman in Fuseli's famous *The Nightmare*[13] (1781, Detroit Institute of Arts). Fuseli's friend John Knowles gave a more balanced view when he wrote 'This picture . . . is as superior in drawing, in truth to nature placed in such circumstances, and to the story, as Sir Joshua's soars above it in colour, in manual dexerity, and in chiaroscuro.'[14] However, Blake's aim in this letter is not to be even-handed but to defend not only his friend but also the ideas about sublime history painting that they shared.

It must be said that Blake's own earliest finished treatment of the Ugolino subject,[15] executed long before Fuseli's painting, was far from sublime. It is the design at the top of plate 16 of *The Marriage of Heaven and Hell* (1790). Although the Ugolino episode is not referred to in the text, it would be obvious to the educated reader/viewer that Blake has chosen it to represent his opening statement about 'The Giants who formed this world into its sensual existence and now seem to live in it in chains . . .' (E 40). Indeed, the scene is as much one of domestic pathos as is Reynolds's: two boys[16] are seated on the ground on each side of the white-bearded father-figure, and they bend towards him as he raises his eyes in despair. The composition of Blake's next version of this theme, for plate 12 of the emblem book *For Children: The Gates of Paradise* (1793),[17] which has been discussed in its later form in the Introduction, differs from the one in *The Marriage* in several ways. The walls of the small cell now consist of thick, heavy blocks, creating a claustrophobic feeling. As in both of Blake's early drawings, the two older boys are in the foreground, their backs to opposite walls and their legs extended, with the younger ones on either side of the old man. As in Butlin 208 alone, the father looks crazed with his hair standing

[13] On this point see Jeremy Tambling, 'Dante and Blake: Allegorizing the Event', in Nick Havely, ed., *Dante's Modern Afterlife: Reception and Response from Blake to Heaney* (New York, St Martin's Press, 1998), pp. 40–1.

[14] *The Life and Writings of Henry Fuseli*, i. 290.

[15] In the early 1780s Blake had made two pencil sketches on the subject: Butlin 207 (Victoria and Albert Museum) and 208 (Hamburg, Kunsthalle).

[16] David V. Erdman sees the two figures nearest the old man as female. See *The Illuminated Blake*, p. 113.

[17] Blake made a pencil drawing for this engraving in his Notebook: see *The Notebook of William Blake*, p. N59. In this drawing but not in the engraving there appears to be a window behind and above Ugolino.

on end, and one boy looks beseechingly up at him, much as in Reynolds's picture.[18] The children look emaciated, which is not the case in *The Marriage.* An additional dimension of meaning is given by Blake's inscription 'Does thy God O Priest take such vengeance as this?'

The Priest to whom Blake alludes is, as we have seen, Ugolino's enemy Archbishop Ruggieri, who imprisoned Ugolino and his sons and grandsons and starved them to death. This brings us to a feature shared by all the pictures discussed so far—Reynolds's, Blake's, and Fuseli's—and by the written remarks of the two latter artists. In all of them Ugolino is regarded only as a victim. He is a victim who may move the viewer by the pathos of his situation or by the sublimity of his heroic fortitude, but the reason for his presence in the *Inferno* is not part of the subject. This missing element was supplied by Hazlitt when he wrote: 'The hero of Dante is a lofty, high-minded and unprincipled Italian nobleman, who had betrayed his country to the enemy, and who, as a punishment for his crime, is shut up with his four sons in the dungeon of the citadel, where he shortly finds the doors barred upon him and food withheld.'[19] However, Hazlitt was writing in 1824, and the views of Blake and his contemporaries are typical of an earlier generation. At that time, Ugolino was seen as a victim of clerical and political tyranny, Bastilled in the Hunger Tower like more recent victims.[20] Blake would treat the subject in a somewhat different (though not opposite) way when he came to execute his illustrations to the *Comedy.* Before that he would execute one more picture on a Dante subject, and the Ugolino episode would form part of it.

In 1800, shortly after Blake had moved to Felpham, William Hayley commissioned him to produce eighteen heads of poets (all now in the Manchester City Art Gallery), and one of these was a head of Dante (Butlin 343.4). The ultimate source of Dante in profile here was the portrait in Raphael's *Disputa*, but Blake would have had to know this through an engraving, and it has been convincingly sug-

[18] See Beer, 'Influence and Independence in Blake', p. 210.

[19] Hazlitt, 'On the Fine Arts', in *DEL* ii. 182–3.

[20] On this point, see Yates, 'Transformations', pp. 108–10. Yates interestingly discusses a passage from G. Baretti, *Easy Phraseology for the Use of Young Ladies* (1775), in which Reynolds's painting is linked with Liberty and with the cause of the Americans.

gested that his model was one by Paolo Fidanza (1757).[21] As in the other Heads of the Poets, a wreath is placed around the subject's head, in this instance a rich one of bay leaves. To our right, as if this were the single most memorable episode of the *Comedy*, are placed Ugolino and the four boys. Two are on each side of him, but the symmetrical arrangement of the earlier designs has been abandoned. Ugolino, who seems perturbed but not anguished, is shown in profile, staring ahead beneath an arch of massive stones. A heavy chain goes down to the floor from his left arm, disappears 'below' to emerge at our left (behind Dante's head), attached by a ring to the wall, which is also made of massive stones. The situation of the chained prisoner is a recurrent one in Blake (cf. *America* 1 and the colour-printed drawing *The Chaining of Orc* (Rosenwald Collection, National Gallery of Art), in both of which it is the spirit of revolutionary energy who is chained, and *Europe* 13). Palm fronds, which may be associated with the victims,[22] are glimpsed at the upper right and upper left. Thus we see that in 1800 the prime Dante subject for Blake was still Ugolino, and that he presented this subject in a visual context associated in his time with the repression of liberty.

2

How much of Dante had Blake read before the idea of illustrating the entire *Comedy* was broached, and what was Blake's attitude towards him? The first question is difficult to answer. In *The Marriage of Heaven and Hell* Blake links Dante with Shakespeare (21, E 43), but before 1800 he had probably read only one of the separate translations of the Ugolino episodes previously mentioned. It was probably William Hayley, who himself published a translation of cantos 1–3 in 1782,[23] who gave Blake the first English translation

---

[21] See William Wells, *William Blake's 'Heads of the Poets'* (Manchester: Manchester City Art Gallery, 1969), pp. 17–18, 32, 40 fig. 6.

[22] As Tinkler-Villani, *Visions of Dante*, p. 255, suggests.

[23] In the notes to Hayley's *Essay on Epic Poetry* (London: J. Dodsley, 1782). For the strengths and weaknesses of Hayley's translation, see Tinkler-Villani, *Visions of Dante*, pp. 93–106.

of the *Inferno*, that of Henry Boyd.[24] We do not know whether Blake read Boyd's translation, which is in jingly six-line stanzas rhyming aab ccb, but he made some vigorous annotations to Boyd's extensive introduction, probably soon after receiving the book.[25] As Blake does in *The Marriage*, Boyd links Dante and Shakespeare, declaring 'Like Shakespear, the poetry of Dante, unfettered by rules, is distinguished by bold original strokes of sublimity, and pathos . . .'.[26] Blake makes no rejoinder to this, nor even to Boyd's statement (i. 28) that Dante is more sublime than Milton. Blake's quarrel with the first part of Boyd's disquisition has to do with the compatibility of morality and art, which Boyd affirms and Blake vehemently denies. In opposition to Boyd's argument that we learn more about right and wrong from Shakespeare's tragedies than 'from all the moralists that ever wrote' (i. 46), Blake memorably asserts 'the grandest Poetry is Immoral the Grandest characters Wicked. Very Satan. Othello a murderer. Prometheus. Jupiter. Jehovah, Jesus a wine bibber' (E 634). The other area of Blake's interest in these annotations has to do with politics. Boyd criticizes Dante's attempt, while a Prior of Florence, to reconcile the Black and White Guelphs as *'ruinous to himself*, and *pernicious to his native country'* (i. 118 and E 634, with italics indicating Blake's underlinings). Blake's note appears to agree with Boyd's view and at the same time to condemn his integrity:

†Dante was a Fool or his Translator was Not That is Dante was Hired or Tr was Not

It appears to Me that Men are hired to Run down Men of Genius under

---

[24] Henry Boyd, *A Translation of the Inferno of Dante Alighieri in English Verse* (2 vols., Dublin, 1785). Geoffrey Keynes suggests, following A. H. Palmer (whose father, Samuel Palmer, owned the book after Blake's death), that around 1800 Hayley gave Blake one of the seven copies for which Hayley had subscribed. (Blake's annotated copy is now in the Cambridge University Library.) See Keynes, 'Blake's Copy of Dante's *Inferno*', in Keynes, ed., *Blake Studies*, p. 150. This would more or less coincide with Blake's work on the Heads of the Poets for Hayley. Boyd, for his part, admired Hayley's translation (i. 6) and also noted that in his edition 'Many biographical particulars of Dante, are taken from Mr. Hayley's Notes to his Essay on Epic Poetry' (i. 151).

[25] As Keynes, 'Blake's Copy of Dante's *Inferno*', p. 150, postulates. G. E. Bentley, Jr. agrees in his edition of *William Blake's Writings* (2 vols., Oxford: Clarendon Press, 1978), ii. 276.

[26] Boyd, *Inferno*, i. 28. Further references to Boyd will be given parenthetically in the text.

the Mask of Translators, but Dante gives too much Caesar he is not a
Republican
 Dante was an Emperors ⟨a Caesars⟩ Man Luther also left the Priest &
joind the Soldier

                (E 634)

Blake appears to simultaneously declare that Boyd has been sub-
orned by the powers that be ('Hired') to run down men of genius like
Dante, and that Dante was wrong to see in the emperor a political
saviour who would end the internecine wars of Italy. In regarding
Dante's (later) support of the emperor as a form of Caesarism, Blake
takes an ahistorical view that transposes the roles of figures from one
era to another without regard for historical context. This had per-
haps been a typical view of Dante a century or so earlier, but it was
retrograde by the time Blake wrote, when at least some critics could
understand Dante's view of the empire as a potential European gov-
ernment and a force of opposition to the papacy, or could simply put
aside Dante's beliefs and concentrate on his poetry. Hayley, a Whig,
translated and (in *The Triumphs of Temper*, 1781) imitated Dante;
and the philosophical anarchist William Godwin wrote in his *Life of
Chaucer* (1803):

> Dark as was the age in which he studied and wrote, unfixed and fluctuating
> as were then the half-formed languages of modern nations, he trampled
> upon those disadvantages, and presents us with sallies of imagination and
> energies of composition, which no past age of literature has excelled, and no
> future can ever hope to excel.[27]

In general Blake's annotations to Boyd are typical of his convictions
of the 1790s, affirming liberty in every possible way. His political
criticism of Dante is that Dante was 'not a Republican', not that
Dante concerned himself with politics at all. When Boyd asserts that
toleration was a mark of decadence in the ancient world and con-
demns 'the times of universal toleration, when every pollution, from
every clime, flowed to Rome', Blake memorably replies: 'What is
Liberty without Universal Toleration?' (i. 133, E 635). Only one of
Blake's notes has to do with a religious subject. To Boyd's statement
that '*nature teaches* [his emphasis] . . . that there is a future life'
Blake rejoins 'Nature teaches nothing of Spiritual Life but only of
Natural Life' (i. 56–7, E 634). Objections of this kind would become

---

[27] Toynbee, *DEL* i. 642.

more frequent and more vehement in Blake's later notes on Dante.

3

The commission for the Dante illustrations was given to Blake in 1824.[28] It is interesting that Linnell, a Baptist,[29] should evidently see no anomaly about his interest in the *Comedy*. Linnell gave Blake a folio volume of drawing paper for the purpose. The drawings were done in this volume, which Samuel Palmer found Blake working on in bed:

On Saturday, 9th October 1824, Mr. Linnell called and went with me to Mr. Blake. We found him lame in bed, of a scalded foot (or leg). There, not inactive, though sixty-seven years old, but hard working on a bed covered with books sat he up like one of the Antique patriarchs, or a dying Michael Angelo. Thus and there was he making in the leaves of a great book (folio) the sublimest designs from his (not superior) Dante.[30]

Blake does not appear to have executed the designs in any preconceived sequence, as for the various parts of the *Comedy* there exist some drawings that are pencil sketches and others that are completely finished watercolours. His technique for the latter has been well described by Anthony Blunt:

[28] According to Gilchrist, *Life*, p. 328. However, A. H. Palmer says in notes written in his father's copy of the 1863 Gilchrist biography (Henry E. Huntington Library) that it is 'entirely wrong' that Blake worked on the Dante drawings while still engraving the *Job*. He writes: 'The *Job* was finished before the Dante was begun', giving John Linnell Jr.'s copy of the manuscript *Life of John Linnell* as his source. This would, if correct, put the date back to 1825, a date supported by Alfred T. Story, *The Life of John Linnell* (2 vols., London: Richard Bentley & Son, 1892), i. 231. However, if Samuel Palmer's memory was correct, he found Blake working on the Dante illustrations in October 1824 (see below).

[29] Linnell was baptized into the Baptist Church on 21 January 1812. He came to it through the influence of his fellow artist and friend Cornelius Varley. He and his wife attended the Keppel Street Chapel. They were later (1828? 1830?) expelled for non-attendance, though Linnell pleaded illness. Linnell considered becoming a Quaker and corresponded with Bernard Barton, but they both concluded he ought not to do so. He remained outside the established Church. See David Linnell, *Blake, Palmer, Linnell and Co.: The Life of John Linnell* (Sussex: The Book Guild, 1994), pp. 26, 122–5.

[30] See Todd's note in Gilchrist, *Life*, p. 391, from A. H. Palmer's *Life and Letters of Samuel Palmer* (1892). Blake, b. 28 November 1757, was not quite 67 at the time.

He began by laying in the main design in the broad washes which are traditional in the medium, and which he had employed in the Biblical watercolours for Butts, but he then worked over the whole surface in a series of small touches, almost as if he was painting in tempera, frequently going over the same area many times. The result is an effect of greater richness than in the earlier works in the medium, but the miracle is that Blake manages to avoid the messiness which normally comes with working over the same part several times in water-colour. The different touches are superimposed, so that the upper ones do not disturb the freshness of the lower layers. The artist must have taken the greatest care not to add one touch until the lower layer had completely dried, and he probably used his paint as dry as possible. The effect is one rarely to be seen in water-colour, though it has, curiously enough, a close parallel in the later water-colours of Cézanne.[31]

Even during the last years of his life, Blake was extending his extraordinary technical mastery.

For his English text Blake used the translation of the Revd Henry Frances Cary, which had become the standard one by this time, thanks to the favourable attention given it by Samuel Taylor Coleridge and by Ugo Foscolo.[32] Henry Crabb Robinson noted that Blake was using the Cary translation in 1825, and John Thomas Smith in *Nollekens and His Times* wrote that Blake thought Cary's translation 'superior to all others'.[33] The other edition Blake is known to have consulted—though to what degree we do not know— was in Italian and is identified in the *Literary Gazette* obituary as one of Alessandro Vellutello's.[34] Blake had not known Italian previously

---

[31] *The Art of William Blake* (New York: Columbia University Press, 1959), p. 89.

[32] Cary's *Inferno* was published in 1805–6, and his translation of the entire poem (3 vols.) in 1814: *The Vision; or Hell, Purgatory, and Paradise, of Dante Alighieri*. These aroused little attention until Cary's work was brought to public notice in Coleridge's lectures of 1818 and 1819 (see R. A. Foakes, Introduction to Samuel Taylor Coleridge, *Lectures 1808–1819 On Literature* (2 vols., Princeton: Princeton University Press, 1987), i. 33; ii. 185–6). Coleridge arranged with Taylor and Hessey to reissue the remaining copies of the 1814 edition, and in 1819 a new, revised edition of the three-volume translation was published. Also contributing to the success of Cary's *Vision* was Foscolo's review of the 1814 edition, calling Cary's 'the most successful' English translation of Dante, in the *Edinburgh Review* for February 1818: 'Biagoli's Edition of the Divina Commedia.—Cary's Vision of Dante' (reprinted in Toynbee, *DEL* ii. 161–2).

[33] See Gilchrist, *Life*, p. 336; and *BR*, p. 475. Cary's translation is also mentioned as being on Blake's table at Fountain Court in the very knowledgeable obituary published anonymously in the *Literary Gazette* on 18 August 1827 (*BR*, p. 349). Blake became personally acquainted with Cary, and after Blake's death Cary purchased Blake's watercolour *Oberon, Titania, and Puck with Fairies Dancing* (Butlin 161, Tate Gallery) for the benefit of Mrs Blake.

[34] At least six editions of Vellutello's Dante were published between 1544 and 1596. Of these, four—1564, 1571, 1578, and 1596—are folio-sized.

and is said to have learned it in 'a few weeks' time' for the purpose of illustrating Dante.[35] One wonders how much of Dante's Italian, difficult even for modern readers of the language, Blake could have learned in such a short period.[36] He no doubt consulted Vellutello from time to time, but his main source must have been the Cary translation.

Before Blake undertook his project, there had been at least three sets of illustrations to the complete *Commedia*. Sandro Botticelli's great drawings were, as it happens, in Britain in the early nineteenth century.[37] The Vellutello editions included an anonymous engraving for each canto, plus some additional illustrations; and John Flaxman's drawings, engraved by Tommaso Piroli, were first published in Rome in 1793 and reissued in England in 1807.[38] We know that Blake possessed a Vellutello, and, as we shall see, it may be that one of the engravings in it provided the germ of one of Blake's best-known designs. That Blake knew Flaxman's illustrations is manifest from Blake's charge that Flaxman had plagiarized from him in them, writing *c*.1809–10 'how much of his Homer & Dante he will allow to be mine I do not know as he went far enough off to publish them even to Italy. but the Public will know & Posterity will know'.[39] Though it has been suggested that Henry Fuseli saw the Botticelli drawings and that his *Dante and Virgil on the Ice of Cocytus* (Schiff

---

[35] Story, *The Life of John Linnell*, i. 231; and Gilchrist, *Life*, p. 328. Also, John Thomas Smith in *Nollekens and His Times* says that 'at the age of sixty-three years, he learned the Italian language purposely to enjoy Dante in the highest possible way' (*BR*, p. 475; as Bentley points out, this would have been in 1820, years before the Dante commission); and Frederick Tatham wrote in his manuscript biography of Blake that 'He read Dante when he was past 60, altho' before he never knew a word of Italian' (*BR*, p. 527).

[36] Tinkler-Villani discusses Blake's knowledge of Italian but does not reach a firm conclusion; see *Visions of Dante*, p. 344 n. 27. It should be noted that the pages of Vellutello's edition comprise a relatively small portion of Dante's text surrounded by a much greater amount of commentary.

[37] They were in the collection of the Duke of Hamilton by 1819. See G. F. Waagen, *Treasures of Art in Great Britain* (London, 1854), iii. 107; Ursula Hoff, *William Blake's Illustrations to Dante's Divine Comedy* (Melbourne: National Gallery of Victoria, 1961), p. 3 n. 28; Hein.-Th. Schulze Altcappenberg, Introduction to Sandro Botticelli, *The Drawings for Dante's Divine Comedy* (London: Royal Academy, 2000), p. 12. The drawings are now in Berlin and in the Vatican Library.

[38] *Compositions by John Flaxman, Sculptor, R.A., from the Divine Poem of Dante Alighieri, Containing Hell, Purgatory, and Paradise* (London: Longman, Hurst, Rees & Orme, 1807).

[39] ['Public Address'], E 572. This statement, written in Blake's Notebook, would not of course have been known to Flaxman.

425, Zurich Kunsthaus) was influenced by one of them,[40] Blake would have had neither the means nor the social standing to gain admission to them at the Duke of Hamilton's collection in Scotland. Nevertheless, it will at times be interesting to compare or to contrast Blake's treatment of certain themes with Botticelli's.[41]

As we may well imagine, the subject that Linnell assigned Blake was far from entirely congenial to him. Indeed, his comments on Dante at this time are even more vituperative than those he wrote in Boyd's *Inferno*. Henry Crabb Robinson recorded Blake as saying on 17 December 1825:

Our conversation began abt Dante[.] 'He was an atheist—a mere politician busied abt this world as Milton was till in his old age he returned back to God whom he had had in his childhood.—' I tried to get out of B; that he meant this charge only in a higher sense And not using the word atheism in its popular meaning[,] but he wod not allow this—[42]

In addition to Dante's politics, Dante's theodicy is now a subject of his abhorrence. On design 7 of the series, *Homer Bearing the Sword, and His Companions* (Fogg Art Museum), Blake wrote:

Every thing in Dantes Comedia shews That for Tyrannical Purposes he has made This World the Foundation of All & the Goddess Nature & not the Holy Ghost as Poor Churchill said Nature thou art my Goddess (E 689)

The reference to Charles Churchill (1731–64) is to 'The Prophecy of Famine. A Scots Pastoral Inscribed to John Wilkes, Esq.', lines 93–6:

---

[40] Hoff, *William Blake's Illustrations to Dante's Divine Comedy*, p. 4 n. 28.

[41] Nor is Blake likely to have seen the *Comento di Christophoro Landino Fiorentinto sopra la Comedia di Danthe Alighieri* (Florence, 1481) with its engravings for part of the *Inferno*, attributed to Bacco Baldini and his assistants after a different series of Botticelli drawings. Unlike the Vellutello editions, the 1481 Landino *Comento* was a very rare book, and in any event, Blake could have seen a list of these small engravings and a reproduction of one of them in William Young Ottley's *Inquiry into the Origin and Early History of Engraving* (2 vols., London, 1816), i. 420, but neither the one reproduced, showing the centaur archers of canto 12, nor any of the others present any parallel to Blake's designs. On these engravings, see Peter Keller, 'The Engravings in the 1481 Edition of the *Divine Comedy*', in Sandro Botticelli, *The Drawings for Dante's Divine Comedy*, ed. Hein.-Th. Schulze Altcappenberg, pp. 326–33.

[42] *BR*, p. 316. This is the same entry, quoted in the Introduction, in which Robinson asserts that Blake assented to his remark about 'the Manichaean doctrine . . .'.

> Thou, Nature, art my goddess—to thy law
> Myself I dedicate—hence, slavish awe,
> Which bends to fashion, and obeys the rules
> Imposed at first, and since observed by fools![43]

The opening words are of course more familiar to us—and no doubt to Blake—from *King Lear*, where Edmund begins his first speech 'Thou, Nature, art my goddess; to thy law | My services are bound.'[44] Edmund then goes on to reveal his plan to displace his older brother in an intrigue that will result in the blinding and ultimate death of his own father. Such, to Blake's mind, was the result of Nature-worship. Churchill is 'Poor Churchill' because (perhaps unconsciously) he naively appropriated Edmund's line without realizing the consequences of such an attitude.[45] In his annotations to Boyd, Blake had denied that natural life could teach anything about spiritual life, but that was only one sentence among many, and it lacks the vehement, thoroughgoing rejection of Nature in the rest of Blake's note:

> ... & the Goddess Nature ⟨Memory⟩ ⟨is his Inspirer⟩ & not ⟨Imagination⟩ the Holy Ghost. ...
>
> Round Purgatory is Paradise & round Paradise is Vacuum or Limbo. so that Homer is the Center of All I mean the Poetry of the Heathen Stolen & Perverted from the Bible not by Chance but by design by the Kings of Persia and their Generals The Greek Heroes & lastly by The Romans
>
> Swedenborg does the same in saying that in this World is the Ultimate of Heaven
>
> This is the most damnable Falshood of Satan & his Antichrist (E 689)

This yoking of Nature and the classics had been going on in Blake's works at least since the revision of *Vala* into *The Four Zoas* and had been continued in *Milton*. Indeed, probably because he associated Dante with classical values, Blake struck out what would have been a favourable reference to Dante in *Jerusalem*, in a passage where

---

[43] As first pointed out by Keynes, *Complete Writings*, p. 925. See *The Poetical Works of Charles Churchill* (2 vols., London: Bell & Daldy, 1866), i. 100. 'The Prophecy of Famine' was one of the poems by Churchill included in *The Works of the British Poets*, ed. Robert Anderson (London, 1795), x. 472–7.

[44] *King Lear*, ed. Kenneth Muir (Cambridge, Mass.: Harvard University Press, 1959), I. ii. 1–2 (p. 24).

[45] 'Poor' may be reinforced by the fact that Churchill died at age 33 and had a reputation for dissipation.

. . . Los creates
Adam Noah Abraham Moses Samuel David Ezekiel
[*Pythagoras Socrates Euripedes Virgil Dante Milton*]
Dissipating the rocky forms of Death, by his thunderous Hammer

(73: 41–3, E 229)

As in Blake's late works there can be no reconciliation between the natural and the spiritual, so there can be none between the classical tradition and the Bible read in its spiritual sense. This no doubt explains why what would be Blake's last written reference to Swedenborg is a negative one, since the Swedish visionary tended to describe his Heavens in terms of earthly cities.[46]

Despite Blake's critical attitude toward Dante, we should not assume that he approached his subject primarily in a spirit of resentment. For the Dante series Blake produced 102 drawings in various stages of completion and seven engravings (none of them quite completed). Many of these are of extraordinarily high artistic quality, and it is clear from this and from the quantity of these designs, as well as from statements Blake made in his correspondence, that he approached his subject with zest, taking full advantage of the pictorial opportunties Dante offered. The fact that the great majority of his subjects are from the *Inferno*—seventy-two drawings and all seven engravings, versus twenty drawings for the *Purgatorio* and ten for the *Paradiso*, may be significant, if only because Blake equated Dante's Hell with the material world. Beyond this, criticism is divided on how far to go in considering Blake's illustrations as conveying his own views through his own symbolism. Interpretation was long dominated by Albert S. Roe's learned monograph of 1953, *Blake's Illustrations to The Divine Comedy*,[47] in which the interpretation is keyed to 'Blakean' concepts. For example, Roe can declare of the figures of Dante and Virgil in design 7,[48] *Homer Bearing the*

[46] See the section headed 'The Material Character of Heaven', in Colleen McDannell and Bernhard Lang, *Heaven: A History* (New Haven and London: Yale University Press, 1988), pp. 191–9. On Blake's shifting attitudes toward Swedenborg, see Morton D. Paley, ' "A New Heaven Is Begun": Blake and Swedenborgianism', *Blake*, 13 (1979): 64–90.

[47] Princeton: Princeton University Press, 1953. This work is hereafter cited as Roe.

[48] My numbering and titles are those of the facsimile *Illustrations to the Divine Comedy of Dante by William Blake* (London: National Art-Collections Fund, 1922), which in turn are followed by Martin Butlin in *The Paintings and Drawings of William Blake*. Butlin's number for the whole Dante series is 812, followed by the number of the particular drawing; I give the latter numbers (in boldface) only, as they are sufficient for this discussion. For other systems of numbering, see the Appendix to this chapter.

Sword, and His Companions (Fogg Art Museum), 'The group which seems to represent Dante and Virgil in the upper left, in reality shows the Fallen Albion asleep upon the rock of his eternal life, guarded over by his emanation, Jerusalem.'[49] Milton Klonsky's study of 1980[50] largely followed Roe's approach. Roe's premises were first seriously questioned in an important article by David Fuller that appeared in 1988,[51] in which Roe's method is attacked as over-schematizing, as ignoring context, and as making Blake 'seem a more formulaic artist, and a more formulaic thinker, than he actually is'.[52] V. Tinkler-Villani in 1989 took a middle position, accepting Roe's interpretations in some instances and in others pointing out the importance of considering the details of Dante's text more closely.[53] The hermeneutics of the Dante series is, as we can see, a contested subject, and, as we will see, no single approach will do for interpreting all the Dante pictures. In discussing the individual designs in the series, we must at times ask to what extent they are straightforward illustrations, to what extent they may depend upon a knowledge of the symbolism of some of Blake's other works, and whether some of them may be subversive of Dante's meaning.

4

The structure of Dante's Hell as Blake understood it, is indicated in a diagram (Fig. 18) he drew, with annotations, in design 101, *The Circles of Hell* (British Museum), which despite its number is generally recognized as coming fairly early in the *Inferno*.[54] Here Blake drew a series of ellipses spiralling downward from or upward toward the figure of an angel (for, as Blake wrote on this page, 'In Equivocal Worlds Up & Down are Equivocal'). The ellipses correspond to the nine circles of Dante's Hell, and within them Blake has written the names of the figures he evidently considered most important, along with some other notes, as follows, reading from the bottom up:

---

[49] Roe, p. 57.

[50] Milton Klonsky, *Blake's Dante: The Complete Illustrations to* The Divine Comedy (New York: Harmony Books, 1980), hereafter cited as Klonsky.

[51] David Fuller, 'Blake and Dante', *Art History*, 11 (1988): 349–73. This article is hereafter cited as Fuller.

[52] Fuller, pp. 350–1.   [53]*Visions of Dante*, p. 263.

[54] On the numbering of the illustrations, see the Appendix to this chapter.

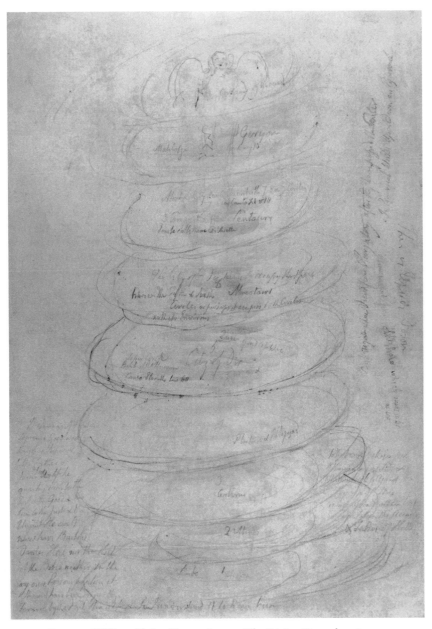

FIG. 18. William Blake, Illustrations to *The Divine Comedy*, 1824–7.
Inferno, canto 11[?]: *The Circles of Hell*. Watercolour over pencil.

Limbo 1 Charon
2 Minos
3 Cerberus
4 Plutus & Phlegyas
5 City of Dis furies & Queen of Endless Woe Lesser Circle Point of the Universe Canto Eleventh line 68
6 Minotaurs The City of Dis seems to occupy the Space between the Fifth & Sixth Circles or perhaps it occupies both Circles with its Environs
7 Centaurs Most likely Dante describes the 7 8 & 9 Circles in Canto XI v 18 3 Compartments Dante calls them Cerchietti
8 Geryon Malebolge Containing 10 Gulphs
9 Lucifer Containing 9 Round[55]

On the right side of the drawing Blake wrote some notes that will later help us understand his view of the transition from Hell to Purgatory, while below his diagram, on the left and right sides of the page, he continued his attack on Dante's system:

It seems as if Dantes supreme Good was something Superior to the Father or Jesus [as] ⟨for⟩ if he gives his rain to the Evil & the Good & his Sun to the just & the Unjust He could never have Builded Dantes Hell nor the Hell of the Bible neither in the way our Parsons explain it It must have been originally Formed by the devil Him self & So I understand it to have been

Whatever Book is for Vengeance for Sin & whatever Book is Against the Forgiveness of Sins is not of the Father but of Satan the Accuser & Father of Hell

Again we see how Blake felt the need to dissociate himself from the system of the poet he was illustrating—and yet the diagram with its comments shows how seriously Blake studied that system, and it will indicate some key points to consider as we explore his rendition of it.

In *Dante Running from the Three Beasts* (1, National Gallery of Victoria), the scene at first seems much as one would expect in an

---

[55] The transcription of the texts on design 101 is my own (not preserving line breaks) from the original in the British Museum and differs in some minor respects from that of E 690. It has also been compared with those of Keynes (*Complete Writings*, pp. 785–6), Bentley (*Writings*, ii. 1243–4), and Butlin. Blake's '9 Lucifer Containing 9 Round' must be a slip, as the ninth circle has four subdivisions.

illustration of the canto in which Dante, astray 'in a gloomy wood',[56] flees from a panther, a lion, and a she-wolf, and encounters Virgil, who becomes his guide (1: 30–81). Blake would have known that Cary's notes identify the panther as 'pleasure in luxury', the lion as 'pride or ambition', and the she-wolf as 'avarice', and that Cary suggests a source in Jer. 5: 6: 'Wherefore a lion out of the forest shall slay them, and a wolf of the evenings shall spoil them, a leopard shall watch over their cities.' Nevertheless, the three beasts are hardly fearsome but are rather stylized in the direction of the grotesque, as, indeed, are most of Blake's other monsters (cf. Leviathan and Behemoth in *Job* engraving 15). The she-wolf with enormous teats is based, as is widely recognized, on the famous bronze in the Capitoline (or an engraving of it), while sources in the Townley Collection of the British Museum have been suggested for the lion's head.[57] 'Aloft the sun ascended with those stars', as in the text, but it rises over the sea, not mentioned in canto 1, bathing the mid-ground in colour. This detail may be regarded as having metaphorical extension,[58] but it is incorporated into a believable landscape. The dangers of the gloomy wood are represented not so much by its trees—only four can be seen—as by the nasty-looking thorns stretched across the foreground and the poisonous mistletoe[59] growing near the centre of the picture space.

Any artist who illustrates the *Comedy* has the problem of differentiating between Dante and Virgil. Flaxman solved this by giving Dante the aquiline nose of traditional portraits. As a result he did not need to give Virgil any identifying feature, though at times his rendition of the Roman poet oddly resembles some representations of

---

[56] English quotations from Dante are, unless otherwise indicated, from the 1819 edition of Cary's translation. Line numbers will be supplied where relevant. As Cary's notes are at the foot of each page, I have not cited page references for these unless there was a particular reason for doing so.

[57] See Roe, p. 41 n.; and Joseph Burke, 'The Eidetic and the Borrowed Image: An Interpretation of Blake's Theory and Practice of Art', in Essick, ed., *The Visionary Hand*, pp. 287 and 291, figs. 95 and 96.

[58] Tinkler-Villani, *Visions of Dante*, p. 264 remarks: 'Blake's addition of the sea in fact makes of this first drawing a complete icon of the spirit and its possible Destiny in Dante's terms: man falling, at the moment of danger and approaching death, from a high place, down into a valley, towards the sea. The landscape, therefore, is spiritual and internalized. Most of Blake's illustrations are of this kind: they create an aesthetic object which can be read in terms of both systems, Dante's and Blake's.'

[59] See Klonsky, p. 137, who points out it is a plant 'once venerated by the ancient Druids'.

Napoleon Bonaparte. Although in Blake's first design Dante's nose is rather pointed, this is not carried further. Instead, having the advantage of colour, Blake uses complementary blue and red for Virgil and Dante respectively. Sky blue is appropriate to an extramundane visitant, red to a man of flesh and blood.[60] In *Dante Running from the Three Beasts*, but not elsewhere, this contrast is reinforced by having Virgil in his first appearance levitate about a foot above the ground, a detail not in the text. His arms down with a palms-out gesture express reassurance, in contrast to Dante's arms outflung in fear as he runs from the three beasts. Otherwise, here and elsewhere, the two poets, each long-haired and bareheaded and wearing loose, limb-revealing gowns, are almost identical. This picture introduces, as we have seen, certain stylistic elements characteristic of Blake, and it introduces one pictorial element—the sea—not in the text, but as a whole it illustrates the basic situation of canto 1. *Dante and Virgil Penetrating the Forest* (2, Tate Gallery) does the same for canto 2: 140–1, in which Dante leads Virgil through the gloomy wood. Both these designs are good examples of Blake as a literal illustrator of Dante.

The same cannot be said of design 3 (Birmingham City Museum), *The Mission of Virgil* (Fig. 19). The lower centre contains details from the preceding design, seen through an arch of fire and smoke, the vertical component of which comprises two naked giants in flames. The one to our right is youthful and chained, reminding us of the chained embodiment of energy, Orc, in Blake's earlier works. The other, in a blue flame, bears some resemblance to Skofeld, one of Albion's giant sons, pictured in *Jerusalem* 51 with his head shaven like a lunatic's or a convict's. Both wear expressions of torment and despair; neither is mentioned in Dante's text. Between and beyond these giants, we see a variant of the previous scene, with Virgil addressing Dante, Dante recoiling in fear, and the heads of the three beasts peering out from behind the blue flame. Seen from this perspective, they appear no more dangerous than stuffed toys, and the lion in particular seems as quizzical as Blake's famous puzzled-looking Tyger. The smoke that forms the horizontal part of the arch is inhabited by three female figures, with a fourth, somewhat above them to our left, seated by a spinning wheel in a leafy bower. These are doubtless the ones who figure in Virgil's account of how he came

[60] In engravings 4, 5, and 7 Blake attempts an equivalent of this by the dark shading of Dante's garment.

FIG. 19. William Blake, Illustrations to *The Divine Comedy*, 1824–7.
Inferno, canto 2: *The Mission of Virgil*. Pen and watercolour over pencil.

to save Dante (lines 51–119): the Virgin dispatched Lucia to Beatrice, who was seated beside Rachel, to summon the 'courteous shade of Mantua' and send him on his mission to Dante.[61] The upper half of the picture, however, cannot be identified with the text of canto 2 in any such way. A man clothed in an ornate costume decorated with fleurs-de-lis, castles, and a large Maltese cross, and wearing a spiked crown that seems to grow out of his head, kneels before a plinth above which a doleful-looking patriarch is seated. With his left index finger the supplicant points to the world below, and his right hand swings a censer from which fumes of incense arise. In pencilled inscriptions, Blake identifies the bearded one as 'The Angry God of This World', and the one whose robe bears symbols of the ancient order of Europe as 'Caesar'. From the Angry God's outspread arms descend serpentine thunderbolts, and his left foot extends out from under his robe to reveal an enormous cloven hoof, like that of the nightmare figure of *Job* 11, 'With dreams upon my bed thou scarest me & affrightest me with Visions'.[62] Ranged on either side of this ogre father are sketchy indications of what may be meant as the four and twenty elders of Rev. 4: 4, who are the subject of Blake's water-colour *The Four and Twenty Elders Casting Their Crowns Before the Divine Throne* (Butlin 515, Tate Gallery). The situation is one in which God allows the spirit of empire to assume control of our world. While comparisons with some of Blake's other works and reference to his inscriptions may support this interpretation, it should be emphasized that these are hardly necessary. The configuration speaks for itself, and it exemplifies the extraordinary freedom with which Blake could approach his subject.

In *The Mission of Virgil* Blake shows his implacable opposition to both Church and State. This is of course not true of Dante. Dante could put popes in Hell and could denounce the politics of Florence, but he nevertheless believed that a better state of things could be attained. In canto 1 Virgil prophesies the destruction of the wolf, now representing the papal alliances, by a political saviour:

> So bad and so accursèd is her kind,
> That never sated is her ravenous will,
> Still after food more craving than before.

---

[61] S. Foster Damon, *William Blake: His Philosophy and Symbols*, p. 219, names the woman in the bower Beatrice, while Butlin identifies her as the Virgin and the woman in the cloud at the right as Beatrice.

[62] As pointed out by Roe, p. 51, who also compares the hopeless expression on God's face in *Job* 5, and that of Urizen on plate 15 of *Milton*.

> To many an animal in wedlock vile
> She fastens, and shall yet to many more,
> Until that greyhound come, who shall destroy
> Her with sharp pain. He will not life support
> By earth nor its base metals, but by love,
> Wisdom and virtue; and his land shall be
> The land 'twixt either Feltro.
>
> (93–102)

The specific identity of the greyhound, much discussed by Dante scholars, need not concern us here; what is important is that Dante did have such a hope, which is why Blake calls him 'an Emperors ⟨a Caesars⟩ Man' in the Boyd annotations (E 624). As for Dante's religion, we have already seen Blake's view in his comment pencilled on design 101, a statement consistent with the uncompromising 'Manichaeanism' of Blake's later years. There is an unbridgeable gap between such views and Dante's, but this did not prevent Blake from exploiting situations in the *Comedy* as subject matter for some of his most memorable designs.

Dante and Virgil cross the portal of the underworld in 4 (Tate Gallery), with the inscription over its gate translated by Blake as 'Leave every Hope you who in Enter.'[63] With 5, *The Vestibule of Hell and the Souls Mustering to Cross the Acheron* (National Gallery of Victoria), we have the first scene entirely within Hell. This magnificently realized picture is a good example of the combination of freedom and literal accuracy that Blake could bring to his subject. The souls congregating on the shore are condemned because they took no active part in either good or evil; in the text they

> Went on in nakedness, and sorely stung
> By wasps and hornets, which bedewed their cheeks,
> With blood, that, mixed with tears, dropped to their feet,
> And by disgustful worms was gathered there.
>
> (3: 61–4)

Blake includes winged insects and worms, though no blood is visible, but he renders the spirits as clothed,[64] probably in order to give them some accoutrements indicating status—a crowned queen being among them, and a Whore of Babylon figure wearing a diadem, bracelets, and necklace (cf. *The Whore of Babylon*, Butlin 549,

---

[63] E 689. Cary 3: 9 reads: ' "All hope abandon, ye who enter here." '
[64] As Roe, p. 55, points out.

British Museum). Lamenting in a row at the top of the picture are figures identified by William Michael Rossetti as the 'companion-angels'[65] to those below, a view supported by Virgil's words to Dante in 3: 35–7. The Acheron is dark and billowy, and on its opposite shore we see a kind of concentration camp guarded by two demons with a file of prisoners walking up into it. Rowing away from them, Charon plies the oars of a small boat—it's clearly going to take a very long time to get all the souls on the near shore across the river. The design is strikingly vivid, one of the most accomplished in the entire series.[66]

We next see Charon at the quayside in *Charon and the Condemned Souls* (6, Fogg Art Museum). The boat, though retaining the same shape, has become considerably larger, and in accordance with the text the boatman becomes 'Charon, demoniac form, | With eyes of burning coal' (3: 100–1). Where Flaxman in 'Charon's Boat' (3) shows Charon as a heroic-looking muscular figure, Blake presents him as powerful but grotesque, with eyes bulging like a fish's. William Michael Rossetti evidently regarded this as a failure on Blake's part, remarking 'Charon is very grotesque—almost ludicrous.'[67] However, the grotesque has an important role to play in Blake's pictorial vocabulary. As we have already seen, the three beasts of 1 and 2 are grotesque, and we will shortly see a grotesque Cerberus and, later, a grotesque Geryon. As I have argued elsewhere, pushing the apocalyptic beyond a certain point of stylization moves it from the sublime to the grotesque,[68] and this is typically Blake's practice in presenting monstrous beings. As Tinkler-Villani remarks, 'While Cary and Coleridge used definite personal preferences as the standard for value judgment, deciding that the Miltonic sublime was "good" style but the grotesque was "bad" style, Blake simply takes whatever style is most appropriate for creating the desired effect.'[69]

---

[65] Gilchrist, *Life* (1880), ii. 227.

[66] The influence of 'a woodcut of the same scene in the edition of the Divine Comedy by Benalius and Capcasa, Venice, 1491' has been suggested by Ursula Hoff in *William Blake's Illustrations to Dante's Divine Comedy*, p. 2. I have examined that edition at the Huntington Library and find the slight resemblance entirely owing to the subject: Charon is rowing a boat and there is a suggestion of a crowd on the shore with others on the other bank.

[67] Gilchrist, *Life* (1880), ii. 227.

[68] See Morton D. Paley, *The Apocalyptic Sublime* (New Haven and London: Yale University Press, 1986), pp. 184–6.

[69] Tinkler-Villani, *Visions of Dante*, p. 272.

In the first (bottom) ellipse of his diagram on 101, Blake evidently wrote '1 Charon' first and then Limbo to the left of it, after realizing that Limbo came after Charon and not before, and that the first circle of hell is actually Limbo. We enter it in 7, where of a number of possible subjects in canto 4—Flaxman chose Christ liberating the Old Testament patriarchs (lines 50–60)—Blake centred upon one he hated: *Homer Bearing the Sword, and His Companions* (Fogg Art Museum). Blake had already stated his view of Homer and his influence in *On Homers Poetry*: 'The Classics! It is the Classics! & not Goths nor Monks, that desolate Europe with Wars' (E 270). Accordingly he shows Homer grasping a large broadsword in his right hand, a detail not supplied by the text, and he wrote 'Satan' between Homer's head and the sword. As we have already seen, Blake also wrote inscriptions on this drawing in which he equated classical poetry with mere Nature. In another visual gloss of this part of canto 4, *Homer and the Ancient Poets* (8, Tate Gallery), Blake depicts Homer, still bearing the sword, with three other poets named as Horace, Ovid, and Lucan, with a fourth, unnamed one on the far right.

> So I beheld united the bright school
> Of him the monarch of sublimest song . . .
>
> (89–90)

But far from dominating the scene, these poets are tucked away in the lower left-hand corner, with the foliage of a laurel grove low over them. If these classical trees were not enough to close off their vision, that function would be accomplished by a layer of thick cloud that goes from the upper left-hand corner to the middle of the right margin. In the sky between the treetops and the cloud, fly the souls of the unbaptized, 'multitudes, many and vast, | Of men, women and infants'.[70] The two figures, one of them playing a pipe, under a tree at the right may represent Blake's idea of the pastoral as the positive aspect of classical poetry,[71] yet these too are under the thick cloud. Also subject to interpretation is the bearded figure standing before the flame of an altar over the heads of the assembled poets; altars may have positive or negative associations for Blake, but here again

---

[70] As identified by Tinkler-Villani, *Visions of Dante*, p. 274, who points out that Roe's calling them 'the graceful, flying forms of imagination' (p. 60) illustrates 'the danger of scanning Blake's works, without referring to Dante's text'.

[71] See ibid., p. 274.

the dark cloud directly above the priest suggests the occlusion of vision.[72] As we see, both these pictures give visual clues, in addition to Blake's written remarks on the first of them (which would of course have been painted over or erased had the watercolour been completed), showing Blake's antipathy to their subjects.

The second circle, as Blake indicates in his diagram, begins with *Minos* (9, National Gallery of Victoria). This 'judge severe | Of sins' (5: 10–11) sweeps with his tail the souls of sinners to their assigned circle of hell. However, Dante specifies only carnal sinners here, and Blake follows him in this. We know what Blake thought, early and late, of judges severe of sins, and so it is no surprise that Minos is depicted as a monstrous crowned tyrant clutching a heavy spear, with a white beard and long white hair cascading down behind him. Four faces peer out of discs on either side of Minos; Rossetti suggests these are 'Terrible retributive angel heads',[73] but their expressions are bland or at the most glum. They could be the four Evangelists helplessly witnessing how the Gospel has been perverted. For Blake there was, however, a distinction, as Jesus puts it to Mary Magdalene in *The Everlasting Gospel*, between 'love or Dark Deceit' (f: 58, E 522), and the couples in the picture are hardly practising love: the members of one pair prostrate themselves before Minos, while three other couples behave more like cruel antagonists than lovers.[74] This is not, however, true of Dante's—and Blake's—most famous pair of lovers in 10, *The Circle of the Lustful: Francesca da Rimini* or *The Whirlwind of Lovers* (Birmingham City Museum).[75] Blake devised a brilliant composition for this subject, taking Dante as a starting point:

> Bellowing there groaned
> A noise, as of a sea, in tempest torn
> By warring winds. The stormy blast of hell

[72] Roe (p. 61) says 'A figure tends the sacred flame of Poetic Genius', but the cloud and the two massive slabs upon which the figure stands tend to support a negative interpretation, such as Klonsky's (*Blake's Dante*, p. 138).

[73] Gilchrist, *Life* (1880), ii. 228.

[74] Butlin suggests that the couple in the right mid-ground is based on 'an Antique or Renaissance sculptural group of "Apollo and Daphne" or "The Rape of the Sabine Women"'.

[75] The first title has, as most of the rest of the series, its basis in Rossetti's catalogue (see Appendix to this chapter). Blake inscribed 'The Whirlwind of Lovers from Dantes Inferno Canto V' in mirror writing on the engraving he executed after this drawing, and on the verso of a different drawing (56), where he made a sketch for the present picture, he wrote: 'One of the Whirlwinds of Love | Hell Canto 5 Paulo & Francesca' (E 689).

With restless fury drives the spirits on,
Whirled round and dashed amain with sore annoy.
When they arrive before the ruinous sweep,
There shrieks are heard . . .

(5: 30–6)

Blake creates a whirlwind of naked bodies that corkscrews powerfully out of a flame-tinged sea into the air and out of the picture space at the upper right.[76] Their features more precisely individualized in the striking print (Fig. 20) Blake engraved after his watercolour, Paolo and Francesca rise in their own separate flame as Francesca tells their story. To the right in a radiant disc is pictured the moment when

he, who ne'er
From me shall separate, at once my lips
All trembling kissed.

(131–3)

As in the text, Dante faints away in compassion.

The germ of Blake's idea for this design may have come from the third illustration (Fig. 21) in Vellutello's Dante.[77] There a throng of naked figures sweeps counter-clockwise (in distinction from the clockwise movement Blake gives them), making gestures as if swimming, with clouds around them. At the upper left a male and a female figure with limbs intertwined are seen in a cloud. The woman leans out of the cloud with her right arm extended, her hand pointing toward Dante. Although Blake drew upon a number of sources in executing this series, 10 is one of the few instances in which he may have been indebted to another illustrator of Dante. This design also reminds us that some of Blake's greatest achievements are as a

[76] Kenneth Clark compares 'the so-called Celtic rhythm'; see *The Romantic Rebellion: Romantic versus Classic Art* (New York: Harper & Row, 1973), p. 174. Anthony Blunt suggests a parallel in 'the swirling design' of Thomas Banks's relief sculpture *Thetis and Her Nymphs Rising from the Sea to Console Achilles for the Loss of Patroclus* (Victoria and Albert Museum). See 'Blake's Pictorial Imagination', *Journal of the Warburg and Courtauld Institutes*, 6 (1943): 211.

[77] *Dante con l'espositione di Christoforo Landino, et di Alessandro Vellutello* (Venice, 1564), 'Carnali Cerchio Secondo', n.p. A comparison of the six 16th-c. editions of Vellutello in the British Library shows them all to have the same illustrations, with the exception of the tiny 1551. This one, like all the others, appears twice in the volume, with minor variations—first as part of Vellutello's description of Dante's Hell, then as the illustration to canto 5. The upper right-hand portion of the picture shows naked figures, some on their knees, imploring Minos, shown as a long-tailed demon.

FIG. 20. William Blake, Illustrations to *The Divine Comedy*, 1827.
Inferno, canto 5: *The Circle of the Lustful: Francesca da Rimini* or
The Whirlwind of Lovers. Engraving.

FIG. 21. Anon. artist, *Carnali Cerchio Secondo* from
'Descrittione de lo Inferno di M. Alessandro Vellutelli', *Dante
con l'espositione di Christoforo Landino, et di Alessandro
Vellutello*. Venice, 1564. Engraving.

straightforward illustrator, but one who interprets the text imaginatively and uses his own pictorial vocabulary.[78]

'Cerberus' is inscribed in Blake's third circle, and we first see the three-headed monster barking 'as a dog | Over the multitude immersed beneath' (6: 13–14) in *The Circle of the Gluttons, with Cerberus* (11, Fogg Art Museum). No. 12 (Tate Gallery) brings us close up to its three huge grotesque heads. Triple-headed monsters figure in *Jerusalem* (the giant Hand) and elsewhere in Blake, but this one is firmly grounded in Dante's text. Even more literal is Blake's second version (13, National Gallery of Victoria), where Virgil pacifies 'that great worm' by feeding it earth while Dante watches. They then proceed to the fourth circle, labelled 'Plutus & Phlegyas' by Blake, where in *Plutus* (14) they encounter the enraged demon with his right hand on a sack full of coins, and Virgil quells it with his words. Less literal is *The Goddess of Fortune* (16, National Gallery of Victoria), in which the subject of conversation between Dante and Virgil is represented as a naked woman sunk to the waist in a pit, with her arms behind her head in a seductive posture. Dante through Virgil propounds the characteristic medieval view that God deputed Fortuna 'Over the world's bright images to rule' (7: 78), credits her with divine foresight (88), and even goes so far as to say 'she is bléssèd' (97). Blake will have none of this sanguine view of distributive order. 'The hole of a Shit house', he wrote over the pit she stands in. 'The Goddess Fortune is the devils servant ready to Kiss any ones Arse' (E 689). Above her, coming from opposite sides of the picture, the souls of the Prodigal and of the Avaricious roll enormous weights against each other.

After passing the marsh depicted in *The Stygian Lake, with the Ireful Sinners Fighting* (15), a design Flaxmanesque in its symmetry, the two poets reach 'a tower's low base' (8: 34) in *Dante and Virgil about to Pass the Stygian Lake* (17, Fogg Art Museum). The tower is an interesting structure—a pharos made up of ascending slabs, with two crescent-moon-shaped lights emanating from a lantern at its top. A light answers from a tower on the other side.[79] Here is one instance in which Blake's drawing does resemble Botticelli's of the same subject: the Renaissance artist shows two towers, one of them at sea and rather similar to Blake's. (Flaxman's no. 9, 'The Pool of

---

[78] Butlin points out that the position of the lovers in the disc is that of the couple in plate 28 of *Jerusalem*.

[79] Butlin suggests that the two lights and the one answering from the opposite shore may 'have been suggested by Cary's translation of "fiamette" in 8: 4 as "cressets" '.

Envy', illustrates a later point, in which Dante and Virgil, rowed in a boat, approach the City of Dis, which Flaxman presents as an elaborate fortified structure, like a castle keep.) In this design, as in a number of others in the Dante series, there is a striking representation of an imaginary landscape. Tinkler-Villani perceptively remarks:

> As in many of Blake's illustrations, landscape is a tool for creating a complex picture and increasing its meaning. But here landscape also has a role of its own in that it creates a contradictory sense of space: it adds sublimity, but it limits it. The view . . . showing the Stygian lake, which takes up most of the drawing, is characteristically sublime, the huge expanse of the lake being delimited in the bottom part of the drawing by a strong tower, whose powerful structure dwarfs the little figures of the two poets. . . . There is a strong sense of space and the idea of the direction of the poets' journey, but the clouds covering the sky and the mountains on the opposite shore put a limit to the sublimity of the spacious, bright picture.[80]

Indeed, landscape plays a role in the Dante series that is far greater than we find in most of Blake's works. The many rock arches of the *Inferno* and its agitated, murky, or blood/flame-coloured waters are among the signifiers of power that produce a sense of helplessness, and in the *Purgatorio* images of the ascent of the rugged mountain and of the lush paradise at its top establish their own visual meanings. (As we would expect, there are no landscapes in the *Paradiso*.) In 17 we look with Dante and Virgil across the broad Stygian lake as Phlegyas in his boat, its sail white against the grey water, nears the base of the tower. Perhaps this is why Blake wrote 'Phlegyas' in the fourth circle, even though he properly belongs to the fifth, which comprises the marsh across which he takes his passengers to the gates of the city of Lucifer, in the course of which journey Virgil repels the wrathful Filippo Argenti from the boat (18).

Blake noted 'The City of Dis seems to occupy the Space between the Fifth & Sixth Circles or perhaps it occupies both Circles with its Environs'. Three designs are devoted to it: 19, in which the angel comes to get access for Dante and Virgil; 20, where the angel confronts the three Furies; and 21, showing Dante conversing with Farinata degli Uberti within the city. The three have a strong sense of narrative progression, and Blake includes many of the details of the Cary translation. For the approach of the huge angel he creates a deliberately ugly counterpart to the whirlwind of 10—a spiral of the ineffectually opposing damned in the dark water of the Styx:

---

[80] Tinkler-Villani, *Visions of Dante*, p. 269.

> As frogs
> Before their foe the serpent, through the wave
> Ply swiftly all, till at the ground each one
> Lies on a heap; more than a thousand spirits
> Destroyed, so saw I fleeing before one
> Who passed with unwet feet the Stygian ground.
>
> (9: 75–80)

In 20 there appear on the city's battlements the 'three hellish furies' who are the handmaids of the 'queen of endless woe' (a phrase Blake jotted down among the inscriptions in his fifth circle) a little earlier in the text (9: 39–54), and who call for Medusa, causing Virgil at the lower left to protectively hide Dante's face in order to shield him from the sight of the Gorgon. The angel stands before the portcullis and addresses the Furies.

> 'Outcasts of heaven! O abject race, and scorned!'
> Began he, on the horrid grunsel standing . . .
>
> (9: 90–1)

The English 'grunsel' can have either of two meanings. 'Grunsel' or 'groundsel' (*OED*, s.v.) can signify a common European weed or, alternatively, the lowest part of a structure. Blake was evidently unsure of the sense, because he shows the angel's left foot on the doorsill of the gate and his right on the ground near some strange-looking plants. The Italian *soglia* means 'threshold', and this instance may be an indication that Blake was not sure enough of his Italian to choose between the two meanings of Cary's word. Once inside the city, we are in the sixth circle among the tombs of the heretics. In a picture dominated by fiery colour, *Dante Conversing with Farinata degli Uberti* (21, British Museum), Blake shows in the background his version of Dante's imagery from the preceding canto:

> 'The minarets already, Sir!
> There, certes in the valley I descry,
> Gleaming vermilion, as they from fire
> Had issued'.
>
> (8: 68–71)

Farinata is shown conversing with Dante while to his left we see the head and hands of Cavalcante Cavalcanti, who will ask about his son Guido, Dante's friend. All three of these pictures are literal depictions of their subjects, imaginatively embellished.

At the entrance to the seventh circle (still one number ahead of Blake's diagram), the poets encounter the Minotaur (**22**, Fogg Art Museum), whose grotesque goggle eyes are reminiscent of those of Charon and Cerberus. He is shown, as described in the text (12: 21–5), rearing in impotent rage while Dante under Virgil's protection begins to descend to the river of blood. This is the subject of the unfinished **23** (Fogg Art Museum), in which centaurs pursue those who were violent tyrants. We are now at the point that Blake noted as: '7 Centaurs Most likely Dante describes the 7 8 & 9 Circles in Canto XI v 18 | 3 Compartments Dante calls them Cerchietti'.[81] These *cerchietti* are called by Virgil 'three close circles in gradation placed' in 11: 18, and in the second one, described in canto 13, are the violent against themselves. Wonderfully grotesque harpies with human faces except for their beaks, owl-like bodies with wings and claws, and female breasts perch in trees in both **24**, *The Wood of the Self-Murderers: The Harpies and the Suicides* (Tate Gallery), and **25**, *The Hell-Hounds Hunting Destroyers of Their Own Goods* (National Gallery of Victoria). They largely follow the description in 13: 14–16:

> Broad are their pennons, of the human form
> Their neck and countenance, armed with talons keen
> These sit and wail on the drear mystic wood.

In **24** the tree bleeding at the place from which Dante has plucked a branch has a man's face, personifying the voice of the suicide Pier delle Vigne, telling his story. Other trees have suggestions of human forms and faces embedded in them, an effective way of showing what they once were, though not presented as a physical detail by Dante.[82]

Before leaving the seventh circle, Dante and Virgil encounter a

---

[81] Why Blake wrote that 11: 18 'describes the 7 8 & 9 Circles' is puzzling, as he clearly knew that the second and third *cerchietti* are part of the seventh circle, with circles 8 and 9, as indicated by his diagram, to come after them.

[82] Tinkler-Villani discusses the similarities between **24** (which she numbers 25) and Flaxman's no. 14, 'Forest of Harpies', pointing out that there are two elements in both of these that are new to Dante illustrations: 'First, the suicides trapped within trees are pictured through the subtle and effective sketching of figures in tree-trunks, and, secondly, the harpies perched on the branches are here small, stocky birds, whose small bodies are dwarfed by their big heads, clawed feet, and large breasts' (*Visions of Dante*, p. 246). However, Flaxman's harpies do not have the strange combination of ludicrousness and menace that Blake's do, and Blake had depicted a tree trunk with a human face as early as 1790 in some copies of *The Marriage of Heaven and Hell*, plate 11.

figure that, like a number of others in Blake's Hell, derives from a classical source (or sources). In *Capaneus the Blasphemer* (27, National Gallery of Victoria) the 'huge spirit' (14: 43) killed by Jupiter's thunderbolt before the walls of Thebes is depicted in the reclining position of a Greek or Roman river god.[83] Struck by lightning from above and engulfed in flame, he yet displays the 'proud scorn' (14: 44) that Dante attributes to him. In the following design, several classical sources are involved. No. 28, *The Symbolic Figure of the Course of Human History Described by Virgil* (National Gallery of Victoria), with its crown of spiky rays, is in part based 'on some ancient statue of Helios', as Anthony Blunt points out, adding 'but here again Blake has transformed his model by giving it a terror quite contrary to the spirit of ancient sculpture'.[84] This time the subject is not one of the denizens of the Inferno but a figure described by Virgil as the Old Man of Crete (14: 101–9):

> Of finest gold
> His head is shaped, pure silver are the breast
> And arms, thence to the middle is of brass,
> And downward all beneath well-tempered steel,
> Save the right foot of potter's clay, on which
> Than on the other more erect he stands,
> Each part, except the gold, is rent throughout;
> And from the fissure tears distil, which joined
> Penetrate to that cave.

His tears become the three rivers of Hell—Acheron, Styx, and Phlegethon, which then flow down to form the lake Cocytus at the lowermost level. (This development is clearer in Flaxman's treatment of the subject, 'The Statue of Four Metals', in which the great bearded figure, arms outspread and one leg raised at the knee, also

---

[83] Joseph Burke, 'The Eidetic and the Borrowed Image', pp. 286–7, figs. 88 and 89, compares a statue in the Vatican, *Personification of the River Nile*. If Blake knew this particular figure, it would have to have been, as Burke suggests, through engravings. Ursula Hoff suggests the influence of Joseph Anton Koch's drawing of Capaneus. She writes that Koch's drawings were commissioned in Rome by the Revd George Nott, and 'were remarked upon in the *Monthly Magazine* of May, 1805 . . . which suggests that they may have been on view in London at that time . . .'. This supposition seems unnecessary, especially as Hoff says the resemblance is in 'the right arm outstretched, bearing the weight of the figure', and in Blake's picture the right arm, though indeed outstretched, bears no weight at all. See Hoff, *William Blake's Illustrations to Dante's Divine Comedy*, p. 2 and p. 4 n. 27.

[84] Blunt, 'Blake's Pictorial Imagination', 198.

has a striking resemblance to Blake's engraving after Fuseli, *The Fertilization of Egypt*.[85]) Blake adds the sinister-looking scales at the figure's middle and endows it with the crown, cross-surmounted orb, and trefoil sceptre of worldly power.[86] The four metals—gold, silver, brass, and iron (Cary's 'steel' for *ferro eletto*, 'chosen iron', is of course an anachronism)—are indicative of the descending stages of human society as described in Ovid's *Metamorphoses*, 1: 89 ff.; but for the foot of clay, and for the general significance of the figure Dante went to an even more important source, as Blake well knew. It is the 'great image' of Dan. 2: 32–3:

> This image's head was of fine gold, his breast and his arms of silver, his belly and his thighs of brass,
>   His legs of iron, his feet part of iron and part of clay.

In Nebuchadnezzar's dream 'Then was the iron, the clay, the brass, the silver, and the gold, broken to pieces together, and became like the chaff of the summer threshingfloors; and the wind carried them away, that no place was found for them: and the stone that smote the image became a great mountain, and filled the whole earth' (35). Daniel's interpretation to the king is that 'Thou art this head of gold', and that after the fall of his kingdom, successive kingdoms shall rise and fall until a distinctively different kingdom be established: 'And in the days of these kings shall the God of heaven set up a kingdom, which shall never be destroyed: and the kingdom shall not be left to other people, but it shall break in pieces and consume all these kingdoms, and it shall stand for ever' (44). This section of Daniel had a special importance to Blake and to some of his contemporaries, who applied its framework of apocalypse followed by millennium to their own time and the immediate future.[87] Perhaps the 'terror quite contrary to the spirit of ancient sculpture' seen by Blunt in Blake's image is a result of such apocalyptic consciousness.

After encountering the violent against nature and the violent against art, the subjects of 31 and 32, the two poets are conveyed by the monster Geryon, whose name Blake inscribed in the eighth circle

---

[85] For *The Botanic Garden* by Erasmus Darwin, 1791.

[86] See Butlin 812.28. Butlin also points out that Blake used his own drawing *Old Parr When Young* 'for the complete figure with only minor adjustments to the arms and his left leg'. The trefoil design is characteristically associated by Blake with the old order of Europe—cf. the wands held by the angels before the enthroned pope in *Europe* 10.

[87] On this subject, see Morton D. Paley, *Apocalypse and Millennium in English Romantic Poetry* (Oxford: Clarendon Press, 1999), pp. 5–9, 20, 38, 59, 75, 111, 215, 233, 279–80.

of his diagram. In *Geryon Conveying Dante and Virgil Down Towards Malebolge* (31, National Gallery of Victoria) this 'image vile of Fraud' (17: 7) is shown very much as Dante describes him.

> His face the semblance of a just man's wore,
> So kind and gracious was its outward cheer;
> The rest was serpent all; two shaggy claws
> Reached to the armpits; and the back and breast,
> And either side, were painted o'er with nodes
> And orbits.
>
> .   .   .   .
>
> In the void
> Glancing, his tail upturned its venemous fork,
> With sting like scorpion's armed.
>
> (17: 10–15, 24–6)

Once more, as Blake would have recognized, Dante had an apocalyptic model here: the giant locusts with their king Apollyon that come out of the bottomless pit in Rev. 9. Their faces 'were as the faces of men' (7), and 'they had tails like unto scorpions, and there were stings in their tails' (10). Blake pictures Dante and Virgil riding this gigantic apocalyptic beast in 'wheeling gyres' (17: 93) down to the eighth circle.

The eighth circle, as Blake noted in his diagram, is 'Malebolge Containing 10 Gulphs'. It is an enormous construction of chasms, cliffs, and archways; and what takes place in it comprises cantos 18–31—more than one-third of the *Inferno*—for which Blake made thirty-one illustrations.[88] Among these, two visual themes are especially prominent, and some individual designs are of particular importance.

Before we enter the eighth circle, demons or devils have made only one appearance, as small figures in the background of 5, guarding the souls who have already been ferried across the Acheron. In 32, *Demons Tormenting the Panders and Seducers in Malebolge* (Fogg Art Museum),

> Horned demons I beheld, with lashes huge,
> That on their back unmercifully smote.
>
> (18: 36–7)

---

[88] Assuming that 102, *The Punishment of the Thieves* (Tate Gallery), is part of this series, and not counting the remarkable *Antaeus Setting down Dante and Virgil in the Last Circle of Hell* (63, National Gallery of Victoria).

True to the text, Blake's demons are horned and armed with thongs, but he gives them a stylized version of bat wings, and they attack the panders and seducers from the air. Two of them, one male and one female, have winding tails instead of legs. Fantastic bat wings are displayed by many of Blake's monsters, such as the caricatured pope in *Europe* 10 and the Spectre of Los in *Jerusalem* 7, while the Great Red Dragon of Blake's illustrations to Revelation has bat wings and a winding tail.[89] In **34**, *The Devils Under the Bridge* (National Gallery of Victoria), we are under the bridge as a devil with a long hooked staff hooks a sinner in the gulf. (The natural bridge is formed of parts of human beings, a Blakean touch not in Dante's text.) Then, after the two succeeding drawings comes a series of seven pictures featuring demons or devils. A muscular, bat-winged one stands on a natural arch in **37**, *The Devils Carry the Lucchese Magistrate to the Boiling-Pitch Pool of Corrupt Officials* (National Gallery of Victoria), while two others look on. In the following designs, the devils are wonderfully individualized. First, in *Virgil Abashing the Devils* (**38**, British Museum), while Dante hides behind a rock, Virgil, pointing upward to heaven as the source of his power, faces down Malacoda—'so fell his pride, that he let drop | The instrument of torture at his feet' (21: 83–4). Consequently, the two poets are accompanied by a guard detail of ten devils, all holding their hooks (**39**, *The Devils Setting Out with Dante and Virgil*, National Gallery of Victoria). In the lead, smiling as if enjoying a good joke, is Barbariccia, who has the dark, muscular body, horns, bat wings, and tail of Blake's typical devil. Directly behind the poets is 'Fanged Ciarotto', with three others, two of them but lightly drawn, following. For their names we may choose among Scarmiglione, Alchino, Calcabrina, Libicocco, Draghignazzo, 'Graffiacane fierce, | And Farfarello, and mad Rubicant' (103, 116–21). The party then moves through a nightmarish landscape of criss-crossing arches, black pitch, and red flames in **40**, *The Devils with Dante and Virgil by the Side of the Pool* (Tate Gallery), with Barbariccia assuming the arms-raised posture of the central figure of Blake's painting of *c.*1805 *Satan Calling Up His Legions* (Butlin 662, Petworth House). In the black lake are the souls of barrators or peculators, and Barbariccia pulls one of them, Ciampolo, out by his hair. The

---

[89] For example: *The Great Red Dragon and the Woman Clothed with the Sun* (Butlin 519, Brooklyn Museum).

devil Libicocco 'darting forth a prong, seized on his arm, | And mangled bore away the sinewy part' (22: 70–1). This horrifying incident, the subject of *Ciampolo the Barrator Tormented by the Devils* (41, Fogg Art Museum), is made all the more terrible by the casual enjoyment on the faces of the devils, more like men gathered to enjoy a cockfight or some other cruel sport, rather than the tormentors of souls. However, Ciampolo outwits his captors and dives back under the pitch, causing the devils to become furious with one another, and in *The Baffled Devils Fighting* (42, Birmingham City Museum) Blake shows two of them attacking each other over the fiery pool while the others form an audience on one bank. Seeing the poets depart, they take off after them, but Virgil takes Dante in his arms and hurries with him into the next chasm (43, *Dante and Virgil Escaping from the Devils*, Fogg Art Museum).

Blake's devils are disturbing precisely because, unlike his grotesque monsters, they are not unbelievable. Their muscular, dark bodies display human proportions and their faces (when fully drawn) show human, though 'diabolical' expressions. In the engravings—Blake showed the importance he attached to this series by making two of them the subjects of the seven engravings he executed—this effect of reality is increased by the sense of contour. The devils fighting in engraving 3 (42) could be two louts in a bar-room brawl, except that they happen to be flying. In 2 (43), Blake has completed the fanged face of Ciarotto so as to increase the effect of his smile, and he has also given the demon at the left a look of rapt pleaure (as well as a long hook). These designs, both engravings and watercolours, illustrate human, not supernatural evil. 'Believe Christ & his Apostles', Blake wrote in his preface to *Milton*, 'that there is a Class of Men whose whole delight is in Destroying' (E 95).

The second group of designs closely aligned both in narrative and in theme has its basis in cantos 24 and 25 and involves reciprocal transformations of the serpent and the human. This topos had long interested Blake. His early symbol of revolution, Orc, has both human and serpent forms: he possesses both when he first names himself in *America* 8: 1 (E 54), and he begins as human in *The Four Zoas*, but in Night the Seventh of the latter he becomes a serpent entirely (81: 1–6) and never reverts to his former human identity. These transmutations have, at least on one level, a political significance involving the degeneration of France from Republic to Empire.[90] The subject of the relations of human and serpent forms continued to interest Blake after he ceased to attach political significance to these images, as we see in the watercolour *Satan Watching the Endearments of Adam and Eve*, the first version of which was executed in 1806 (Butlin 531, Fogg Art Museum), where the fallen angel's human form is entwined by his serpent identity. (Blake reworked this subject in 1808 (Butlin 536.4, Boston Museum of Fine Arts) and again for John Linnell in 1822 (Butlin 537.1, Tate Gallery).) In his designs for cantos 24 and 25 of the *Inferno*, Blake includes eight involving serpents and humans. In the seventh gulf of the eighth circle the thieves are tormented by serpents.

> With serpents were their hands behind them bound,
> Which through their reins infixed the tail and head,
> Twisted in folds before. And lo! On one
> Near to our side, darted, an adder up,
> And where the neck is on the shoulders tied,
> Transpierced him.
>
> (24: 93–8)

Blake illustrates this scene fairly literally, with a winged serpent flying to attack the figure on our left, but adds a distinctively Blakean serpent in the rear, one with a cobra head, female breasts, little bat wings, and a grotesque face, reminiscent of a drawing on page 26 of the *Four Zoas* manuscript.[91] More naked human figures are attacked by snakes in *The Punishment of the Thieves* (102, Tate Gallery), which probably belongs at this point in the sequence (see Appendix). In *The Serpent Attacking Vanni Fucci* (48, British Museum) the church robber is about to be bitten in the back of the neck, and he is then attacked by several snakes in 49 (*Vanni Fucci 'Making Figs' Against God*, National Gallery of Victoria). In these parts of the text, the human figures burn and turn into ashes after being bitten, after which they reassume the shapes they had before. Later in canto 25 occurs a different kind of transformation, which Blake made the subject of four extraordinary designs.

---

[90] On this subject see Morton D. Paley, *Energy and the Imagination: A Study of the Development of Blake's Thought* (Oxford: Clarendon Press, 1970), pp. 73–82, 102–20, 122–30, 154–6, 249–51.

[91] Reproduced in *The Four Zoas* by William Blake, ed. Cettina Tramontano Magno and David V. Erdman (Lewisburg, Pa.: Bucknell University Press, 1987), p. 140.

Still among the thieves in canto 25, the poets see the Florentine Agnello Brunelleschi attacked by 'a serpent with six feet' (25: 45) who turns out to be his compatriot Cianfa di Donati. What happens is represented in 51, *The Six-Footed Serpent Attacking Agnello Brunelleschi* (National Gallery of Victoria):

> lo! a serpent with six feet
> Springs forth on one, and fastens full upon him:
> His midmost grasped the belly, a forefoot
> Seized on each arm (while deep in either cheek
> He fleshed his fangs); the hinder on the thighs
> Were spread, 'twixt which the tail inserted curled
> Upon the reins behind.

(25: 45–51)

Their physical interconnection is so close in Blake's picture that they appear a composite being, and the wings and the six legs of the serpent make it appear at the same time some horrifyingly gigantic insect. There are at least two possible visual sources for this picture. One, suggested by Ursula Hoff, is Hendrik Goltzius's engraving *The Dragon Devouring the Fellows of Cadmus*.[92] The other is in volume I of *The Antiquities of Athens* by James Stuart and Nicholas Revett,[93] where plates XVI and XIX, engraved by Blake's master James Basire, show pirates turning into dolphins. Nevertheless, Blake's water-colour and the engraving (4, Fig. 22) that he made after it,[94] convey a unique sense of terror.

In *Agnello Brunelleschi Half Transformed by the Serpent* (52, Fogg Art Museum) we see the two identities:

> The two heads now became
> One, and two figures blended in one form
> Appeared, where both were lost. Of the four lengths

---

[92] *William Blake's Illustrations to Dante's Divine Comedy*, p. 2. As Hoff points out, the literary prototype of this subject in Ovid's *Metamorphoses* is mentioned by Dante in ll. 87–90. Goltzius's engraving, after C. van Haarlem, is reproduced by F. W. H. Hollstein in *Dutch and Flemish Etchings, Engravings, and Woodcuts ca. 1450–1700* (Amsterdam: Menno Hertzberger, 1949–), viii. 104. The dragon's jaws around the face of one of the men could be perceived by the viewer as one head combining human and dragon features.

[93] London, 1762.

[94] In the engraving it is clear that the androgynous-looking figure to Agnello's left is male. A drawing in the Henry E. Huntington Library and Art Gallery appears to have been done after the watercolour and before the engraving—see Robert N. Essick, *The Works of William Blake in the Huntington Collections* (San Marino, Calif.: Huntington Library, 1985), p. 130.

Two arms were made: the belly and the chest,
The thighs and legs, into such members changed
As never eye hath seen.

(25: 62–7)

Brunelleschi's serpent portion extrudes from his back, with its head near its feet, and he displays scales and fangs but is otherwise a deformed human. Three snakes look on, one of them hooded and another goggle-eyed. Of all the human-serpent pictures, this is the only one that could be called grotesque rather than horrifying. The element of genuine horror returns with 53, *The Serpent Attacking Buoso Donati* (Tate Gallery, Fig. 23), and 54, *Buoso Donati Transformed into a Serpent; Francesco De' Cavalcanti Transformed from a Serpent into a Man* (Fogg Art Museum). First, 'an adder all on fire' (75), who turns out to be Guercio de' Cavalcanti, pierces Buoso Donati; then Guercio rises in human form, identical with the former one of his victim. No. 53 is also the subject of one of Blake's seven engravings (5), and there he gives Buoso scaly genitals and the serpent two front paws. Blake could also have chosen the details of metamorphosis described in lines 94–127 as a pictorial subject, but perhaps he thought this would involve a repetition of 51 and 52. As it was, he had devoted five pictures to the serpent/human subjects of cantos 24 and 25, comprising a whole spectrum of changes from human to serpent to human. Part of the motive for this was no doubt literal representation, in which Blake like Dante is concerned with the serpentine as representing duplicity (the thieves) and as associated with Satan in his role as the tempter and enemy of humankind. Blake may also have recalled Henry Boyd's view that Dante 'adapted the *Pythagorean* doctrine of the transmigration of souls', and that 'By this means he has contrived to blend the torments of the mind and body in one horrible description (25) where the sufferings of the victims are increased by their being (while still conscious of their superior nature) changed into detestable and portentous shapes'.[95]

The last appearance of devils in the series is in the sky of *The Hypocrites with Caiphas* (44, Tate Gallery), but the importance of

---

[95] Boyd, *Inferno*, i. 68. Boyd begins his translation of canto 25: 'Argument. The Poet . . . sees several strange transformations and transmigrations among four Florentines . . .' (ii. 193). Pythagoras was one of the names, including Dante's, that Blake first etched and then deleted in *Jerusalem* 73: 41.

FIG. 22. William Blake, Illustrations to *The Divine Comedy*, 1827. *Inferno*, canto 25: *The Six-Footed Serpent Attacking Agnello Brunelleschi*. Engraving.

FIG. 23. William Blake, Illustrations to *The Divine Comedy*, 1827. *Inferno*, canto 25: *The Serpent Attacking Buoso Donati*. Engraving.

this design lies in its brilliant presentation of the hooded hypocrites walking over Caiaphas crucified on the ground. Caiaphas is of course the high priest who said 'that it was expedient that one man should die for the people' (John 18: 14, echoed in Dante's lines 119–20). In 'A Vision of the Last Judgment' (1810), Blake terms Pilate and Caiaphas 'Two States where all those reside who Calumniate & Murder ⟨under Pretence of Holiness & Justice⟩' (E 558), and so he is very much with Dante in placing him among the hypocrites. Blake's rendition is similar to Flaxman's 25 ('Caiaphas and the Hypocrites'),[96] and that may be one of the Flaxman illustrations Blake had in mind when he accused Flaxman of stealing his ideas. Since Flaxman's Dante was published long before Blake's illustration was drawn—first in Italy in 1793, then in England in 1807—Flaxman could well have accused Blake of copying from *him*. However, a great deal of the resemblance may simply come from following Dante's description of the hypocrites and of the crucified Caiaphas:

> Caps they had on, with hoods that fell low down
> Before their eyes, in fashion like to those
> Worn by the monks in Cologne.
>
> (23: 61–3)

> 'He doth lie
> Transverse; nor any passes, but him first
> Behoves make feeling trial how each weighs.'
>
> (23: 120–2)

It may be worth noting that Botticelli's drawing for canto 23, which Blake almost certainly did not know, also shows hooded figures around Caiaphas, lying crucified on the ground.

Passing the giants who rim the pit between the eighth and the ninth circles, the poets enter the deepest circle of Hell. In *The Complaint of the Giant Nimrod* (61, Fogg Art Museum), Blake's choice of subject is important. Nimrod was included neither by Botticelli nor by Flaxman, but to Blake he had a special importance. The ultimate source is Gen. 10: 8–10:

And Cush begat Nimrod: he began to be a mighty one in the earth.

He was a mighty hunter before the LORD: wherefore it is said, Even as Nimrod the mighty hunter before the LORD.

[96] On this resemblance see Blunt, 'Blake's Pictorial Imagination', 211.

And the beginning of his kingdom was Babel, and Erech, and Accad, and Calneh, in the land of Shinar.

Although nothing is said here about the tower of Babel, which comes in Gen. 11 and is not linked with Nimrod, the tower (and with it the fragmentation of what was once a single language) became associated with him because the tower was 'called Babel' (11: 9). From this brief biblical mention a tradition grew up. In *Paradise Lost* (12: 24–62) Milton has Michael deliver a long prophecy of Nimrod, saying:

> one shall rise,
> Of proud, ambitious heart, who, not content
> With fair equality, fraternal state,
> Will arrogate dominion undeserved
> Over his brethren, and quite dispossess
> Concord and law of nature from the Earth—

Rebellious against God, Nimrod and his crew shall march from Eden towards the west, and find 'The plain wherein a black bituminous gurge | Boils out from under ground, the mouth of Hell'. Of this stuff and brick they will build the city and tower, until God prevents them from going further by sowing among them 'a jangling noise of words unknown'. Emanuel Swedenborg gives Nimrod a meaning in the life of the spirit, interpreting his name as signifying a religion of outward forms and ceremonies only. 'By Nimrod are signified those who made internal worship external. . . . By his being mighty in hunting before Jehovah, is signified that he pursuaded many . . .'.[97] According to Swedenborg, those who adhered to such worship separated faith from charity. And Jacob Bryant, whose *New System* Blake had a hand in illustrating, wrote: 'It is said of Nimrod . . . that the *beginning of his kingdom was Babel* . . . He is described as a gigantic, daring personage; a contemner of every thing divine'.[98]

Blake placed himself in this tradition of interpreting Nimrod, in both his pictorial art and his poetry. His personification of death in the *Night Thoughts* illustrations is clearly a Nimrod figure, though not named as such in Young's text ('Till death, that mighty hunter, earths them all', marked with an asterisk in the Edwards edition).[99]

[97] *Arcana Cœlestia, Now first translated from the original Latin . . . by a Society of Gentlemen* (13 vols., London: J. & E. Hodson, 1802–16), ii. 30, no. 1173.
[98] Bryant, *A New System* (3 vols., London, 1774–6), iii. 33–6.
[99] See Edward Young, *Night Thoughts* (London: R. Edwards, 1797), p. 30 and engraving 32. The watercolour (British Museum) is Butlin 330.117.

Writing to Thomas Butts about his *Riposo* (Butlin 405, unlocated) on 6 July 1803, Blake says: 'I have given in the background a building which may be supposed the ruin of a Part of Nimrods tower which I conjecture to have spread over many Countries for he ought to be reckond of the Giant brood' (E 729). Nimrod is named once in *The Four Zoas* and five times in *Jerusalem*, for example:

> Great is the cry of the Hounds of Nimrod along the Valley
> Of Vision, they scent the odor of War in the Valley of Vision.
>
> (22: 9, E 167)

In design **61** Blake follows some details of Dante's text and introduces others. Nimrod's mouth is open as if shouting the words in the no-language that Dante assigns him, and his horn hangs from a belt around his neck. With the other giants (to be seen in **62**) he is 'In the pit . . . immersed, | . . . from his navel downward . . .' (31: 28–9). Blake has given him a huge spiked crown and long, braided locks of hair. The latter may derive from an engraving of the Persepolis sculptures, as Anthony Blunt suggests.[100] There is brickwork behind him, and more to our left, perhaps 'a building which may be supposed the ruin of a Part of Nimrods tower', as quoted above. Within what appears to be an arched niche in the broken wall behind Dante and Virgil, is a bat-winged figure wearing a spiked crown like Nimrod's and holding an orb and a fleur-de-lis sceptre. This may be, as Roe suggests, 'Satan walled up in a blind niche in the Tower of Babel, wearing the panoply of earthly power'.[101]

Dante and Virgil exit from Malebolge with the aid of Antaeus, the giant who did not take part in the war against the Olympian gods. This transition involves a descent over a chasm to the ninth circle below, and Blake seizes the opportunity for a daringly literal representation. In *Antaeus Setting down Dante and Virgil in the Last Circle of Hell* (**63**, National Gallery of Victoria), the giant is shown gripping the rock behind him with his left hand as he bends at a right angle to release the poets from his right, far below. Blake's picture

---

[100] Blunt compares a head from a Persepolis engraving in the second volume of Sir William Ouseley's *Travels in Various Countries of the East* (3 vols., London: Bowdell & Martin, 1819–23), in which 'The figure has the same long, tight curls . . .' ('Blake's Pictorial Imagination', 205). Two of the plates, [XLIII] and XLIV, both engraved by H. Multow, show such heads; a note referring to the latter (254 n.) mentions 'the thick and numerous curls which adorn these heads'.

[101] Roe, p. 122. Fuller calls it 'a Miltonic republican addition which enforces the identification of Nimrod as an archetype of tyranny' (p. 379 n. 19).

captures the vertiginous effect of Dante's description, where the comparison is to a leaning tower in Bologna:

> As appears
> The tower of Casienda, from beneath
> Where it doth lean, if chance a passing cloud
> So sail across, that opposite it hangs;
> Such then Antaeus seemed, as at mine ease
> I marked him stooping. I were fain at times
> To have passed another way. Yet in the abyss,
> That Lucifer with Judas low ingulfs,
> Lightly he placed us; nor, there leaning, stayed;
> But rose, as in a bark the stately mast.

(31: 127–36)

We would not imagine Blake's poets going among the traitors of the ninth circle without a visit to Count Ugolino. Indeed, he figures in three designs, frozen in the same hole as his arch-enemy Ruggieri in two of them. The main subect of **66**, *Dante Tugging at Bocca's Hair* (Fogg Art Museum), is Bocca degi Abbati, who betrayed the Guelfs at the battle of Montaperti; but to our left behind Virgil, in a sort of igloo, we see Ugolino taking his revenge on his murderer.

> and as bread
> Is ravened up through hunger, the uppermost
> Did so apply his fangs to the other's brain,
> Where the spine joins it.

(32: 124–7)

The irony of Ruggieri, who caused Ugolino to starve to death, being gnawed at by his victim did not escape Blake, who made this subject the central one of *Ugolino Relating His Death* (**67**, Fogg Art Museum). Archbishop Ruggieri, bleeding profusely from his tormentor's bites, is hunched at the far left; part of his garment is coloured red, and a red broadbrimmed hat with a tassel (as if he were a cardinal) above him. His crozier lies in the foreground. The white-bearded Ugolino squats in a 'storytelling' position with his elbows close to his body and his hands palms-out, giving the account that we already know. This part of the subject, Ugolino's revenge in addition to his traitorousness, was avoided by other artists, no doubt because they preferred the sentimental or romantic idea of the sufferer and his sons in the tower. Blake himself does not ignore that aspect in the

Dante illustrations but indeed embellishes it in an unusual way. Lightly sketched in pencil, *Ugolino and His Sons in Prison* (**68**, British Museum) has the basic composition of Blake's *Gates of Paradise* engraving, with one significant difference. In the air over the central group hover two angels, very much like those in *Christ in the Sepulchre, Guarded by Angels* (Butlin 500, Victoria and Albert Museum), executed *c*.1805, except that the angel above Ugolino's right side has its hands to its face in a weeping gesture. As we have seen, the implications of Blake's early representations of Ugolino, with those of his contemporaries, were political; but those here are spiritual. These angels are present not only for the four innocent children (who, after all, are not present in Hell but only in Ugolino's narrative) but also for the traitor himself. Two angels also feature prominently in Blake's magnificent tempera of 1826 or 1827 *Count Ugolino and his Sons in Prison* (Fitzwilliam Museum), with light radiating from their heads and illuminating the prison cell. The theme they represent is that frequently found in Blake's later works—the forgiveness of sins. As we have seen, Blake's belief, as stated on design 101, is 'Whatever Book is for Vengeance for Sin & whatever Book is Against the Forgiveness of Sins is not of the Father but of Satan the Accuser & Father of Hell'. Blake can go from closely following Dante in one picture to undermining his meaning in the next.

In the inner circle of frozen Cocytus is Lucifer, whose name Blake wrote here as in the last circle of his diagram. Blake follows Dante's description of him fairly closely in *Lucifer* (**69**, National Gallery of Victoria), though he did not get to the point of colouring his faces:

> Upon his head three faces: one in front
> Of hue vermilion, the other two with this
> Midway each shoulder joined and at the crest;
>
> .   .   .   .
>
> . . . Under each shot forth
> Two mighty wings, enormous as became
> A bird so vast. . . .
>   No plumes had they,
> But were in texture like a bat . . .
>
> (34: 37–9, 43–5, 46–7)

To render this monstrous giant, Blake attaches a grotesque head to a muscular human body, adding two more sketchily pencilled heads on either side of it, and giving all three crowns. Each mouth is chewing a sinner's soul, although only the middle one is distinct. This one is identified by Virgil as Judas Iscariot, the other two as Brutus and Cassius (which no doubt reinforced Blake's belief that 'Dante was an Emperors ⟨a Caesars⟩ Man'). The forms of some other traitors may be seen through the ice below, 'transparent, as through glass | Pellucid the frail stem' (12–13). At least one figure tiny by comparison can be seen at the left with some suggestions of others; Blake may have intended to represent Dante and Virgil scrambling over the ice in the completed picture.[102] In the text Virgil leads Dante over Lucifer's thigh and through an opening in the rock so that, having traversed the centre of the earth, Dante looks back to see Lucifer 'with legs upward' (84). This caused Blake to inscribe on the right side of 101:

> This is Upside Down | when viewd from Hells Gate

Having read these words by turning the drawing lengthwise, the viewer must turn it 180 degrees to read the next line, which is written upside down below it:

> But right when viewd from Purgatory after they have passed the Center
> In Equivocal Worlds Up & Down are Equivocal

Dante's ingenious method of setting the poets on the way to Purgatory becomes for Blake a confirmation of the 'Equivocal' nature of Dante's vision, and he cleverly forces the viewer to re-enact the process in order to demonstrate its arbitrary nature.

5

The first three of the *Purgatorio* designs are situated on the shore east of Mount Purgatory, where the poets encounter the spirit of Cato. In Flaxman's illustration 'The Mountain of Probation', Cato is presented in an entirely positive way: as in Dante's text, his head is surmounted by four stars as he makes a gesture of benediction and Dante and Virgil incline their heads. Blake's *Dante, Virgil and Cato* (71, Fogg Art Museum) is more 'equivocal'. The severe-looking,

---

[102] Roe, p. 135, sees four figures at the left, 'suggested by the passage in which Dante and Virgil cross Satan's thigh and direction reverses'.

bearded Cato, standing in a cloud, points downward while Virgil gestures upward with his left hand and downward with his right. These gestures are evidently meant to convey Cato's questioning how they got out of Hell and Virgil's reply that he was directed by 'a dame from heaven' (1: 53). Cato orders Virgil to gird Dante's head with a reed, 'and his face | Lave till all sordid stain thou wipe from thence' (95–6). That is the subject of *Virgil Girding Dante's Brow with a Rush* (70, Tate Gallery), which, as Bindman remarks, 'is the first [picture] to show the different and clearer light that characterises Purgatory, with its suggestion of dawn and rebirth'.[103] Although most of the design is uncoloured, the sky is very blue, and the setting is for the most part as Dante describes it:

> The dawn had chased the matin hour of prime,
> Which fled before it, so that from afar
> I spied the trembling of the ocean stream.

One important detail, however, is not in Dante's text. More than half the sky is covered with heavy clouds, clouds that will appear in a number of Blake's scenes of Purgatory. The presence of these obscuring clouds may be Blake's way of saying that the very idea of Purgatory is a clouded one, the result of an imperfect vision. The clouds disappear temporarily in 72, no doubt dispersed by the angelic radiance in *The Angel in the Boat Departing After Wafting over the Souls for Purgation* (British Museum). The angel has ferried souls from the mouth of the Tiber to the bottom of the mountain. His yellow boat is shaped like the crescent moon-boat of *Jerusalem* 24 and is propelled by the force of his wings. Among the newly arrived souls is Dante's friend the musician Casella, and the two embrace. To the left is Cato, who at the end of the canto will chide them all for listening to Casella's song instead of getting on with the ascent of Purgatory. Behind the old man is a niche in the rock, perhaps a shrine for meditation, in which a lamp is burning.[104]

Design 74, *The Ascent of the Mountain of Purgatory* (National

---

[103] Blake, *The Divine Comedy*, ed. David Bindman (Paris: Bibliothèque de l'Image, 2000), p. 166.

[104] This detail is not in Dante's poem. According to Roe (p. 140) it is 'a burning lamp before what appears to be a painted shrine in form of a diptych'; but Tinkler-Villani (*Visions of Dante*, p. 278) calls it 'an enclosure in which idols are placed for worship . . .'.

Gallery of Victoria), initiates the sense of upward thrust that will dominate until Dante reaches the Earthly Paradise. The two poets, Virgil in the lead, are making their difficult way along the steeply inclined ledge that corkscrews up the mountain above the sea. Once more, Blake introduces a thick, dark cloud; it crosses the disc of the sun and also appears in the next design (73, *The Rest on the Mountain Leading to Purgatory*, Tate Gallery), in which the poets find a green space to sit on and look back. When they move on, they encounter the late-repentant (75) and then the negligent rulers. The latter inhabit a wooded glen in which Blake (but not Dante) has made the foliage screen from their sight two guardian angels in the sky bearing flaming swords (76, *The Lawn with the Kings and Angels*, National Gallery of Victoria). Blake also makes them unaware of a threat to their sheltered world:

> Along the side, where barrier none arose
> Around the little vale, a serpent lay,
> Such haply as gave Eve the bitter food.
> Between the grass and flowers, the evil snake
> Came on, reverting oft his lifted head;
> And, as a beast that smooths its polished coat,
> Licking his back.

> (8: 96–102)

Blake's serpent is very like the ones of his *Paradise Lost* illustrations—huge and crested. Although Blake does not show the moment of its expulsion, the angel on the right has already noticed the serpent, and the outcome is foreseeable. Also set in a temporary paradise, the next design (77, *Lucia Carrying Dante in His Sleep*, Fogg Art Museum) shows a beautiful lush landscape carpeted in green with strange plants growing, and the starry blue sky lit with the rays of approaching dawn. Against the disc of the full moon, we see a large female figure carrying the sleeping Dante up the slope, with Virgil following on foot. Blake has not changed the basic scene described by Dante, but he has yoked two parts of it. In the text Dante dreams that he has been seized by 'a golden-feathered eagle' (9: 18) and carried aloft. It is after he awakens in a new place that Virgil explains it was Lucia (who has previously figured in canto 2 as taking the Virgin's message to Beatrice) who bore him. The world of the picture is very much that of Beulah, associated with the moon, the starry night, and those who sleep;

but Blake does not let Dante linger there but has him borne from it as quickly as possible, to the entrance to Purgatory itself. *Dante and Virgil Approaching the Angel Who Guards the Entrance of Purgatory* (**78**, Tate Gallery) is one of the designs that has caused disagreement among the interpreters of Blake's Dante.

> I could descry
> A portal, and three steps beneath, that led
> For inlet there, of different colour each;
> And one who watched, but spake not yet a word,
> As more and more mine eye did stretch its view,
> I marked him seated on the highest step,
> In visage such, as passed my power to bear.
>
> (9: 68–74)

The poets are shown standing in prayerful positions on the green grass of an outcropping over the sea. The sun is hidden by thick, blood-red clouds, but its rays shine yellow on the water. The angel, with the head of an aged, white-bearded man, sits at the top of a flight of three steps, in a niche framed by a Gothic arch. A white nimbus surrounds him. The picture appears to send a mixed message. While the Gothic is positive for Blake, the clouds are surely negative, and the head of the angel calls to mind Blake's Urizen. (Not all white-bearded patriarchs are Urizens, but Blake makes a point of making the angel, who is not described at all in the text, a white-bearded patriarch).[105] The angel sits at the head of a staircase of three great slabs, coloured white, black, and red, which Cary's note explains as respectively signifying the sinner's distinctness of conscience, his contrition, and 'the fervour with which he resolves on the future pursuit of piety and virtue'. However, Blake's representation of them gives an oppressive feeling, as they are so out of proportion to the human footstep. Having ascended to the angel's cell in **79** (*The Angel Marking Dante with the Sevenfold 'P'* (Royal Institute of Cornwall, Truro), Dante kneels in an attitude of prayer while the angel uses the

---

[105] Roe, p. 149, thinks the angel is 'blind'; Klonsky, p. 17, thinks his eyelids are 'half-shut'. However, his eyes appear open and sorrowful, and because this part of the picture is unfinished we can only guess that Blake intended to do something further to make 'his visage such, as passed my power to bear'. Klonsky's view that Dante is shown entering the cave of Sleep is effectively refuted by Tinkler-Villani, *Visions of Dante*, p. 278, who warns against the danger of ignoring the details of Cary's translation. She is, however, uncertain as to whether the angel should be identified with Urizen.

point of his sword to inscribe seven Ps (*peccata*) on Dante's forehead—representing the seven deadly sins that are to be purged in the following cantos. Blake believed in the forgiveness of sins, not their purgation; and he seldom represents true worship as coming from a person kneeling with his hands in a prayerful position. In *Job* 1 most of Job's family is shown in such an attitude while their musical instruments hang on a tree; in *Job* 21 they stand and joyfully produce music (see Chapter 4). Yet the clouds in the sky have turned golden, perhaps suggesting that the sun is about to break through. Neither picture can be given an entirely unified interpretation, but in both there are some elements that contradict Dante's meaning.

The sense of upward thrust continues, with the next six pictures set on the terraces of Purgatory. Interestingly, the first sight the poets encounter is not of the dead purging their sins, which in fact is the subject of only two *Purgatory* designs, but of sculpture. Sculpture was important to Blake in part because of its historical and aesthetic connection with engraving (preserved in the use of the verb *sculpsit* after the engraver's signature), and in part because its extension into the third dimension suggests the archetypal, as in *Jerusalem*, where 'All things acted on Earth are seen in the bright Sculptures of | Los's Halls & every Age renews its powers from these Works' (16: 61–2, E 161).[106] *The Rock Sculptured with the Recovery of the Ark and the Annunciation* (80, Tate Gallery) shows the poets admiring two of the relief sculptures carved into the side of the mountain. In one of them the angel is making the annunciation to Mary, whom Blake chooses to show writing rather than reading (as is usually the case), the other David, 'girt in humble guise' (1: 59) dancing before the Ark, and Uzzah struck dead by the Lord for presuming to steady it. The humility of Mary in the first image is counterbalanced by the pride of Michal, who looks down from her window 'like a lady full of scorn | And sorrow' (10: 63–4). Significantly, Blake leaves out Dante's classical example of humility, involving the Emperor Trajan and a widow. These sculpted scenes introduce the penance for pride in 81, *The Proud under Their Enormous Loads* (Birmingham City Museum and Art Gallery), in which the proud struggle up a flight of

---

[106] On the subject of Blake and sculpture, see Morton D. Paley, ' "Wonderful Originals"—Blake and Ancient Sculpture', in *Blake in His Time*, ed. Essick and Pearce, pp. 66–80.

stairs cut in the rock with a waxing moon shining over the sea on the right. The loads under which the proud are bent are supplied by Blake, but in this instance to reinforce rather than undermine Dante's meaning. Sculpture once more provides the examples in *The Angel Descending at the Close of the Circle of the Proud* (82, British Museum). Among the figures carved on the ground we see the huge form of Satan upside-down, the many-headed Briareus (a Titan), Nimrod before his tower, a crowned king, and a female who may be Niobe in 'a trance of woe' (12: 33). At the top centre appears a very striking angel, huge wings spread in a crescent reminiscent of that of the angelic boat of 72, and conveying a wonderful sense of urgency to match his words: ' "Onward! the steps, behold, are near . . ." ' (85).

Blake has Dante proceed to the second cornice, with *The Terrace of Envious Souls* (83, Fogg Art Museum), a very rough pencil sketch. Once more, Blake's interest is not in penance for sin, and he leaves the next thirteen cantos unillustrated, resuming with *The Angel Inviting Dante to Enter the Fire* (84, National Gallery of Victoria), in which Dante once again labours to climb a staircase spiralling upward. An angel stands in flames on the stairs above, and cries ' "Go ye not farther, holy spirits!" . . . | Ere the fire pierce you . . .' (27: 12–13). Blake shows Dante wringing his hands in terror, Virgil gesturing upward with his right arm, and the poet Statius (who has been with them since canto 21) repeating Virgil's gesture with his left arm. Dante is still in the same terrified hands-clasped-over-the-head posture in the next drawing, even though Virgil has already preceded him into the flames. The extraordinarily beautiful *Dante at the Moment of Entering the Fire* (85, National Gallery of Victoria, Fig. 24) also shows the angel hovering over Virgil and four female figures dancing in the flames ahead. The presence of the angel may be inferred from the previous design, but there is nothing of the exuberant women in Dante's text, although a hint may have been provided by Virgil's mention of Beatrice as an incitement to enter the fire: ' "Her eyes," saith he, | "E'en now I seem to view" ' (27: 53–4). Perhaps the dancing women prefigure the joys of reunion with Beatrice, before which Dante must first undergo the test of passing through flame, a test of the kind Wagner's Siegfried would later undergo in order to reach Brünnhilde.

Immediately after the ordeal by fire comes repose. *Dante and Statius Sleeping, Virgil Watching* (86, Ashmolean Museum) shows

FIG. 24. William Blake, Illustrations to *The Divine Comedy*, 1824–7.
Purgatorio, canto 27: *Dante at the Moment of Entering the Fire*. Pen, ink,
and watercolour over pencil and black chalk.

each poet lying upon a step of the massive staircase lined by foliage on either side, a scene in which W. B. Yeats found 'a placid, marmoreal, tender, starry, rapture'.[107] There are only four stars in the night sky because an enormous, radiant full moon is shining over the sea, and in the disc of the moon Dante's dream of Leah and Rachel is represented. These two figures from Gen. 19 ff. were taken by Christian commentators as types of the active and contemplative life, represented by Mary and Martha in the New Testament. Leah, plucking flowers, says:

> '. . . for my brow to weave
> A garland, these fair hands unwearied ply.
> To please me at the crystal mirror, here
> I deck me. But my sister Rachel, she
> Before her glass abides the livelong day,
> Her radiant eyes beholding, charmed no less,
> Than I with this delightful task. Her joy
> In contemplation, as in labour mine.'
>
> (27: 102–9)

Cary's note (ii. 251 n.) says that the mirrors of Leah and Rachel are equated by Dante with God; i.e. that in looking into these mirrors they behold and admire the Supreme Being. It is difficult to believe that Blake could accept such a view. We have seen early on the danger of imposing a consistent 'Blakean' meaning upon the Dante illustrations, but there is also a danger in ignoring Blake's characteristic views and the images associated with them. Rachel and her mirror recall 'the Looking Glass of Enitharmon', representing the mere materiality of nature in *Jerusalem* 63: 21; and Leah says she will adorn her brow so that she too may admire herself in the mirror. As Roe points out, this negative view is reinforced by the fact that Leah is represented not walking, as in Dante's text, but seated.[108] Blake ignores whatever meaning Dante may have intended and presents both Rachel and Leah as images of narcissism.

The night scene of **86** effected a transition from the mountain slope to the gate of Purgatory. Similarly a transition takes place after

---

[107] 'William Blake's Illustrations to Dante', in *Essays and Introductions* (New York: Macmillan, 1961), p. 127. This essay was first published in 1897.

[108] Roe, p. 161. Roe also comments that 'The pale brilliance of the moonlight and the weirdly graceful foliage give the entire composition a mysterious unearthly quality as of the dream itself'.

the second night scene, from the winding stairs of Purgatory to the earthly Paradise where Dante roams a 'celestial forest',

> Along the champain leisurely my way
> Pursuing, o'er the ground, that on all sides
> Delicious odour breathed.
>
> (28: 1, 5–7)

The poet wanders until he reaches a stream and sees on the other side 'The tender may-bloom, flushed through many a hue, | In prodigal variety' (36–7), and a lady to whom he speaks, and who discourses to him of Paradise. All these features Blake incorporates in the foreground of *Beatrice on the Car, Matilda and Dante* (87, British Museum). Dante stands beneath overarching trees at the edge of the stream with Virgil and Statius, who are about to disappear from the narrative entirely, well behind him. On the opposite bank facing him is the lady who will turn out to be Matilda, a precursor of Beatrice. She makes an explanatory gesture with her left hand as she expounds the nature of Paradise to Dante, who makes a receptive gesture with both hands. From the right mid-ground and across the picture comes a procession of figures, mostly sketched in pencil, preceding and following a chariot. The parts of the drawing that are coloured, such as the variegated turf and the streaked sky, are, as Bindman says, 'of incomparable radiance'.[109]

   In conceiving this design, Blake may have been affected by a painting he saw in the collection of Karl and Elizabeth Aders, to whose weekly gatherings Blake was introduced by John Linnell.[110] The Aderses owned the most important collection of northern European painting then in London, and Blake felt an affinity for early northern painting, as shown by his recognizing a resemblance between one of the Aderses' pictures and a figure in his *Canterbury Pilgrims* engraving (*c.*1810).[111] Among the Aderses' treasures was a seventeenth-century copy of Hubert and Jan van Eyck's polyptych *Adoration of the Lamb*. This copy (now in the Museum voor Schone Kunsten, Antwerp) was especially important at the time because the wings of

[109] Blake, *The Divine Comedy*, p. 198.
[110] The first dated reference to Blake's presence at the Aderses is 10 December 1825, when Henry Crabb Robinson met Blake and Linnell there (*BR*, p. 309); but it is very possible that Linnell, always eager to advance his friend's interests, introduced him earlier.
[111] See Gilchrist (quoting Henry Crabb Robinson), *Life*, p. 333.

the original had been dispersed.[112] The Aderses delighted in showing their collection to their guests, and John Linnell made an engraving after one of the wings in 1826.[113] The van Eycks' magnificent composition features processions in a beautiful natural landscape, symbolic imagery from Revelation, and moving water—all elements of Blake's picture (in which there is, of course, only one procession). It may be that Blake found in the Aderses' copy of the Ghent altarpiece a stimulus for his own work.[114]

In his procession Blake largely follows Dante's description but also adds some important details. For the seven 'tapers of gold' (29: 49) at the head of the procession he substitutes a seven-branched candelabrum with the base of a palm tree, its candlesticks formed by angels and its lights 'of seven listed colours' (76) reflected in the water and streaming across the sky. Blake would of course have recognized Dante's allusion to the seven golden candlesticks of Rev. 1: 12, perhaps conflated with the seven lamps of Rev. 4: 5, and he rendered these in his own manner, adding on each side an angel carrying a book.[115] Next come, sketchily indicated by Blake, the 'four and twenty elders, | By two and two' (81–2) of Rev. 4: 4, standing for the books of the Old Testament. Then, in Dante's text

> . . . came after them
> Four animals, each crowned with verdurous leaf.
> With six wings each was plumed; the plumage full
> Of eyes . . .
>
> (29: 88–91)

The animals, who are of course the embodiments of the four Gospels, are not visible in this picture, except for their wings (translated by Cary as 'pennons'). Of these, Dante says:

> . . . But read
> Ezekiel; for he paints them, from the north

---

[112] See Johann David Passavant, *Tour of a German Artist in England* (2 vols., London: Sanders & Otley, 1836), i. 201–4. The wings were later reunited with the rest of the altarpiece (Sint-Baafskathedraal, Ghent), but the panel of the *Just Judges* was stolen in 1934 and has been replaced by a copy.

[113] Reproduced in David Bindman, *William Blake: His Art and Times* (London: Thames & Hudson, 1982), p. 188, fig. 120.

[114] Although Jan van Eyck used oil, which Blake condemned, as his medium, Blake (who calls him 'John of Bruges') appears to deny that he did. See *A Descriptive Catalogue*, E 530.

[115] Fuller points out that in Rev. 1: 20 the seven angels are 'the presiding geniuses of each of the churches'—'Blake and Dante', p. 352.

> How he beheld them come by Chebar's flood,
> In whirlwind, cloud, and fire; and even such
> As thou shalt find them charactered by him,
> Here were they; save, as to the pennons: there,
> From him departing, John accords with me.
>
> (29: 95–101)

The reference is to two of Blake's favourite texts, Ezek. 1: 4–14 and Rev. 4: 6–9, and Blake would of course have known that in Ezekiel the 'living creatures' have four wings while they have six in John. (Cary's note, ii. 267n., cites the commentary of P. Baldassarre Lombardi as saying: 'Ezekiel discovered in these animals only four wings, because his prophecy does not extend beyond the fourth age, beyond that is the end of the synagogue and the calling of the Gentiles: whereas Dante beholding them in the sixth age, saw them with six wings as did Saint John.') Blake shows the eyes in the wings' plumage reflected in the stream between Dante and Matilda.

The triumphal car itself is pictured as 'on two wheels . . . | Drawn at a Gryphon's neck' (103–4). The gryphon, with eagle head and body of a lion, is traditionally taken in Dante criticism, as in Cary's note to this passage, as a symbol of the combination of the human and divine in Christ; and more will be said about this in our discussion of the following picture. At the left chariot wheel, which is the one visible, dance 'a band quaternion' (125) of women personifying the four Cardinal Virtues. The flames that Blake shows emanating from the wheels are not in Dante's literal description, though he does say that the car is brighter 'than that chariot of the sun, | Erroneous, which in blazing ruin fell' (113–14). That part of the procession following begins with two grave old men. The first, a disciple of Hippocrates and therefore a physician, is, according to Cary, Saint Luke as the supposed writer of the Acts of the Apostles. The second, Saint Paul, is carrying a sword, possibly, says Cary, 'because of the power of his style'. However, the Temple Classics edition suggests a reference to Eph. 6: 17: 'the sword of the Spirit, which is the word of God', and also points out that because Paul was martyred with a sword he was traditionally represented with one.[116] Paul's spiritual sword is of course the Blakean contrary to the material sword carried

---

[116] *The Purgatorio of Dante Alighieri*, ed. Herman Oelsner, trans. Thomas Okey (London: J. M. Dent (Temple Classics), 1956 (1901)), p. 375.

by Homer in 7 and 8. After them come four men, identified by Landino and Vellutello, Cary points out, as 'the authors of the epistles, James, Peter, John, and Jude'. Last comes 'one single old man, sleeping as he came, | With a shrewd visage' (140–1)—John as the visionary author of Revelation.

Even Blake's deviations from Dante's text mentioned so far are not contrary to its spirit. He makes his own version of Dante's candlesticks, but Blake's candelabrum refers to Revelation as does Dante's, and it is a striking object for the head of a procession. The flames emanating from the car could be compared to those of the 'chariot of fire' that took Elijah to heaven in 2 Kings 2: 11, and that Blake himself called for in the famous poem prefixed to his *Milton* (1: 12, E 95). One detail, however, is not consistent with either Dante's description or its underlying meaning: the low-lying cloud that stretches from the bottom of the candelabrum along the entire length of the procession. It is as yet not in a position to obscure vision, but its very presence is ominous. As we will see, this cloud will rise in the next picture.

Perhaps the most discussed picture in the series, both for its striking beauty and for the problems of interpretation to which it gives rise, is *Beatrice Addressing Dante from the Car* (88, Tate Gallery, Fig. 25). Is this a beautiful illustration of the situation in the earthly Paradise as set down in cantos 29 and 30, or does it attempt to undermine Dante's meaning? Is it true, as Roe says, that 'Blake infuses it with a meaning of his own',[117] or that, in Fuller's words, 'The design means largely what this episode of the *Commedia* meant for Dante'?[118] Perhaps we can best arrive at its overall meaning by discussing its constituent parts.

In the foreground, on the same level as the listening Dante, stand three women, dressed (from left to right) in green, red, and white. These are of course, as in Dante's text, the colours of the three Theological Virtues—Hope, Charity, and Faith, characterized in canto 29:

> . . . Three nymphs
> At the right wheel, came circling in smooth dance:
> The one so ruddy, that her form had scarce
> Been known within a furnace of clear flame;

---

[117] *Blake's Illustrations to* The Divine Comedy, p. 171.
[118] 'Blake and Dante', 357.

FIG. 25. William Blake, Illustrations to *The Divine Comedy*, 1824–7.
Purgatorio, cantos 29–30: *Beatrice Addressing Dante from the Car*.
Pen and watercolour.

> The next did look, as if the flesh and bones
> Were emerald; snow new-fallen seemed the third.

> (116–21)

Blake gives his Caritas-figure her traditional attribute of accompa-
nying infants, while Faith points toward a book, also her traditional
accompaniment, with one hand, while with the other she indicates
the gryphon who draws the chariot of the Church. Her gesture is a
way of saying 'Behold the book!'[119] but there is something disquiet-
ing about the book here, as it rests on a cushion of cloud. As we have
seen, many of the *Purgatorio* designs feature clouds implying an
impediment to vision, and in 88 the cloud layer continues as a bow

---

[119] According to Byron, this was the reply of Bishop Watson, 'holding up the
Scripture' whenever the Fathers were quoted to him. See Preface to *Cain, A Mystery*,
in Byron, *The Complete Poetical Works*, vol. vi, ed. Jerome J. McGann and Barry
Weller (Oxford: Clarendon Press, 1991), p. 229.

over the head of the gryphon.[120] For Dante this beast, combining the bodies of a lion and an eagle, may, as Cary's note says, represent 'the union of the divine and the human nature in Jesus Christ'; but in Blake's depiction it looks stolid to the point of caricature, and Faith appears to be showing the relevance of a cloud-bound book to a stuffed animal.[121] The cloud above it branches out in the centre of the bow to arch over the figure of Beatrice standing on the car so as to include almost the entire picture in its visual significance.

Over the car are four discs, each containing a head with the iconic image of one of the four evangelists: John (eagle), Mark (lion), Luke (ox), and Matthew (man). As Dante tells us, the sources for this are Ezekiel (1: 4–14) and Revelation (4: 6–9):

> . . . Four animals, each crowned with verdurous leaf.
> With six wings each was plumed; the plumage full
> Of eyes; and the eyes of Argus would be such,
> Were they endued with life.
>
> (29: 89–92)

Ezekiel makes each creature a composite, while Blake (without any basis in Dante) differentiates them. He preserves the crown of leaves only for John, who looks not so much like an eagle as the mysterious creature engraved by Linnell after John Varley for Varley's *Zodiacal Physiognomy*, and captioned 'Gemini ("Cochabiel")' and 'The Genius Cochabiel'.[122] All four are doleful-looking, as if unhappy to find themselves there. The visible wheel of the chariot, not described in the text, is inspired by Ezekiel's description of 'their rings . . . full of eyes round about them four' (1: 18). Blake introduces three human faces in the wheel, and successfully imparts a sense of whirling motion to it. Thus we have elements drawn from Dante's text, from its sources in Ezekiel and Revelation, and from Blake's own imagination in these interrelated images. Some of these tend toward straightforward illustration while others suggest an underly-

---

[120] This gryphon resembles the one in the *Recueil d'Antiquités Égyptiennes, Étrusques, Grecques, et Romaines* (Paris, 1752–7) of Anne Claude Philippe de Tubières, Comte de Caylus. See M. D. Paley, ' "Wonderful Originals"—Blake and Ancient Sculpture', p. 177.

[121] Tinkler-Villani, *Visions of Dante*, p. 279, writes 'The seemingly blind, statuesque Griffin cannot be taken as an emblem of spiritual renewal and self-knowledge . . .'.

[122] See the plate of ten heads facing p. 58 of Varley's *Zodiacal Physiognomy* (London, 1828).

ing motive subversive of Dante's meaning. Our overall interpretation of this design must necessarily depend on the figure of Beatrice herself.

In the words of lines 31–3 of canto 30 the Cary translation, Beatrice appears 'in white veil with olive wreathed, | . . . beneath green mantle, robed in hue of living flame . . .'. These are, once more, the colours of the three Theological Virtues. Blake makes little attempt to follow this colour scheme. He shows the 'hue of living flame' only at the lower outside part of her mantle; the rest of it is blue, not mentioned at all by Dante and traditionally associated with the Virgin Mary. It falls from her head down behind her, while her form is clothed only in a semi-transparent veil, through which her body is visible, although Dante says:

> Towards me, across the stream, she bent her eyes;
> Though from her brow the veil descending, bound
> With foliage of Minerva, suffered not
> That I beheld her clearly . . .
>
> (30: 64–7)

However, in Blake's illustration Beatrice wears not Minerva's olive leaves but a golden crown. The fact that her face is visible may perhaps be explained by the suggestion that Blake is looking forward to the end of canto 31, where the Theological Virtues call upon Beatrice for Dante's sake to 'unveil to him thy cheeks' (138).[123] However, it should be noted that Flaxman, in his own illustration for canto 30, 'The Descent of Beatrice', pictures her wearing a body-length gown and a cowl but with her face unveiled. It may be that the detail of whether or not her face was visible did not interest either artist. In any event, there is nothing in Dante's text to justify the transparent veil/gown in Blake's drawing. Tinkler-Villani interestingly connects it with the gauzy costume of 'Ch—h' in Hayley's *Triumphs of Temper*, 'whose "charms amaz'd the public sight" when she appeared "in a veil so thin that the clear gauze was but a lighter skin"' (VI. 87–8).[124] Whatever Hayley may have meant by it, for Blake the teasing covering that hides but does not hide is the opposite of

---

[123] As argued by Fuller, p. 355. Fuller also suggests that Blake substitutes the crown for Minerva's olive leaves because he doesn't want to show in Beatrice 'the combination of classical and Christian virtues' (p. 356). Of course Blake could have chosen to leave Beatrice uncrowned.

[124] *Visions of Dante*, pp. 280–1.

the 'Naked Beauty displayed' without which 'Art can never exist' (E 275). Comparisons with Blake's symbol of the Veil of Vala are in this instance appropriate,[125] and Dante's obeisance before the elevated Beatrice is reminiscent of Albion's worship of Vala in *Jerusalem* 29 [33]:

> Albion spoke. Who art thou that appearest in gloomy pomp
> Involving the Divine Vision in colours of autumn ripeness
> I never saw thee till this time, nor beheld life abstracted
> Nor darkness immingled with light on my furrowd field
> Whence camest thou? who art thou O loveliest? the Divine Vision
> Is nothing before thee, faded is all life and joy.
>
> (39–44, E 175)

Beatrice in her multicoloured mantle is in this sense analogous to the light passing through Newton's prism, for Blake a symbol of the phenomenal world. The fact that she is presented under an overarching cloud, which breaks only because it reaches the limit of the picture space and then resumes, is also significant. Blake's Beatrice signifies the beauty of the realm of the senses, which Blake regards as delusive, as he regards Dante's submission to her as a betrayal of the Divine Vision. '. . . The Goddess Nature', as he says in an inscription on design 7 '⟨Memory⟩ ⟨is his Inspirer⟩ & not ⟨Imagination⟩ the Holy Ghost' (E 689). Like the ancient pictures and statues Blake reported as having seen in vision, *Beatrice Addressing Dante* is a work all containing mythological and recondite meaning, where 'more is meant than meets the eye'.[126]

In the following picture, *The Harlot and the Giant* (89, National Gallery of Victoria), Blake's vision virtually coincides with Dante's, although with somewhat different implications. In the text, Dante falls asleep and then awakens to find the scene transformed:

> The holy structure, through its several parts,
> Did put forth heads; three on the beam, and one
> On every side: the first like oxen horned;
> But with a single horn upon their front,
> The four. Like monster, sight hath never seen.
> O'er it methought there sat, secure as rock
> On mountain's lofty top, a shameless whore,
> Whose ken roved loosely round her. At her side,
> As 'twere that none might bear her off, I saw

---

[125] See Roe, pp. 165–6.   [126] *Descriptive Catalogue* (1809), E 531.

> A giant stand; and ever, and anon
> They mingled kisses.
>
> (32: 141–51)

Dante draws upon Rev. 12: 3 for the great red dragon with seven heads and upon Rev. 17: 3–5 for the woman seated on it 'having a golden cup in her hand full of abominations and filthiness of her fornication'. Blake had used this passage as the basis for a number of designs, among them *The Whore of Babylon* (Butlin 523, British Museum) and the striking title page for Night VIII of Edward Young's *Night Thoughts* (Butlin 330.345, British Museum), with the difference that here alone he makes the woman look genuinely seductive. For Dante the situation is the 'Babylonian captivity' of the Church at Avignon, with Pope Clement V dominated by the French king Philip the Fair. It is thus remediable, even if considered as representing the corrupt relations of Church and State in general. However, for Blake monarchy and state religion are in essence evil, as represented in Night VIII of *The Four Zoas*, where Rahab is analogous to the Whore and Urizen to the Beast:

> Rahab triumphs over all she took Jerusalem
> Captive A Willing Captive by delusive arts impelld
> To worship Urizens Dragon form to offer her own Children
> Upon the bloody Altar. John Saw these things Reveald in Heaven
> On Patmos Isle & heard the Souls cry out to be deliverd
> He saw the Harlot of the Kings of Earth & saw her Cup
> Of fornication . . .
>
> (111: 1–7, E 385–6)

A passage like this one reinforces our sense of Blake's meaning, but there are pictorial details in **89** that establish it as well. Dante says nothing about the headgear of the monster except for horns, but Blake gives them kingly crowns, warriors' helmets, and in the instance of the simian-looking head at the right a papal tiara. Dante then sees Beatrice seated on the ground at the root of a tree, 'as she had there been left | A guard upon the wain . . .' (93–4); but Blake shows her kneeling rather than seated, and making a powerless gesture with her hands. The text says 'The seven nymphs | Did make themselves a cloister round about her' (95–6), but Blake's picture shows only the three Theological Virtues; and they do not surround Beatrice protectively but rather stand off to the right, looking sad and subdued, and without the tapers that Dante describes them as carrying (97). Faith now holds her book closed. The tree, which Dante dreamed of as regenerate, is the familiar tree of the knowledge of good and evil of *Jerusalem 76* and the *Paradise Lost* design *The Judgment of Adam and Eve*[127]—leafless but heavy with fruit. Savage-looking thorns, not mentioned in the text and not seen in the Dante series since the *Inferno*, extend along the foreground. It is perhaps significant that Blake does not attempt to illustrate canto 33, in which Beatrice gives an optimistic long view of events in which Church and State will be purified, but rather plunges straight into Paradise.

<h1 style="text-align:center">6</h1>

For the *Paradiso*, Blake executed a total of only ten drawings. The reason for this cannot lie in the order in which he drew the pictures, as some of these watercolours are nearly finished, and among those are some of the most magnificent pictures in the series. The answer no doubt lies at least in part at the inescapable lack of substantiality of the imagery of Paradise, which Dante describes mostly in terms of light. Blake found his own way of overcoming this problem, which caused difficulties for both Botticelli and Flaxman, beginning with the first illustration in this group. Bypassing the first thirteen cantos, he begins with the image of Christ. In Dante's text, the light of the stars forms a cross and 'Christ | Beamed on that cross' (96–7) but there is no physical description. In *Dante Adoring Christ* (90, National Gallery of Victoria) Blake presents Christ's human body, in accordance with *Auguries of Innocence*:

> God Appears & God is Light
> To those poor Souls who dwell in Night
> But does a Human Form Display
> To those who Dwell in Realms of day
>
> (129–32, E 493)

And where Dante presents Christ crucified Blake shows the resurrected Jesus. His arms are indeed in a cruciform position, but his extended hands are on two discs, and he stands on a third. The light emanating from him swirls with energy, and he looks forward with a

---

[127] Butlin 529.10, Huntington Library; and Butlin 536.10, Houghton Library.

calm, penetrating gaze. Dante stands on his knees in the foreground, his arms outspread in the imitation of Christ. Thus we enter Blake's *Paradiso* with the worship of the Human Form Divine.

In the next picture the human form is anything but divine. The subject of *The Recording Angel* (92, Birmingham City Museum and Art Gallery) is, as Butlin points out, 'only hinted at' in Dante's text. The divine eagle who discourses to Dante of justice mentions a 'volume' in which the 'dispraise' of unjust kings 'is written' (19: 112–13), but there is no mention of a bearded, winged old man who points with his right index finger to something in the scroll on his lap. His exposed bare left foot makes us think of the white-bearded figure on the title page of *The [First] Book of Urizen*. He is seated so as to parallel the sitting judges of the *Inferno* and the *Purgatorio*— Minos (9) and the Angel guarding the gate of Purgatory (78). All three pictures subvert the ideas, accepted by Dante, of sin and judgement.

The place of *The Spiral Stairway* (91, British Museum) in the series has been a subject of disagreement (see Appendix), partly because of Blake's partially erased '19' at the upper right, but the passage illustrated is surely, as Butlin argues, in canto 21:

> . . . I saw reared up,
> In colour like to sun-illumined gold,
> A ladder, which my ken pursued in vain,
> So lofty was the summit; down whose steps
> I saw the splendours in such multitude
> Descending, every light in heaven, methought
> Was shed thence.
>
> (25–31)

Flaxman chose the same passage for a rather prosaic illustration. It is Blake who makes the shape spiral, an angelic counterpart to the spiralling circles of Hell in 101, and its similarity to the one in *Jacob's Dream* (Butlin 438, British Museum) is widely recognized. It is likely, as Fuller suggests, that the flaming figures on the second level of the staircase and the stars above are meant to suggest the 'glitterance' (*sfavillar*) that Dante sees.[128]

After these three independent pictures comes a series of closely linked ones, all of extraordinary beauty, and all including Dante and

---

[128] 'Blake and Dante', p. 371 n. 12.

Beatrice. In *Dante and Beatrice in the Constellation of Gemini and the Sphere of Flame* (93, Ashmolean Museum) they are alone in the eighth heaven, that of the fixed stars, except for the small, sketchily pencilled figures who rotate on the rims of the three intersecting spheres behind them. These are probably the members of the community of saints whom Beatrice asks to sprinkle Dante with their sacred dews:

> . . . Beatrice spake;
> And the rejoicing spirits, like to spheres
> On firm-set poles revolving trailed a blaze
> Of comet splendour: and as wheels, that wind
> Their circles in the horloge, so work
> The stated rounds, that to the observant eye
> The first seems still, and as it flew, the last:
> E'en thus their carols weaving variously,
> They, by the measure paced, or swift, or slow,
> Made me to rate the riches of their joy.
>
> (24: 10–19)

Two spheres, blue and pink, intersect, with a third, lavender one in front of them. Dante and Beatrice appear to be in conversation, their palms-out gestures almost identical. There is a sense of conversational intimacy, in contrast to the way in which Botticelli represents them in the spheres of Paradise. Botticelli shows Beatrice (most of the time larger in size than Dante) gesturing as if making a point. In some of them Dante gestures back as if getting the point, but there isn't the kind of reciprocity that we find in the corresponding Blake designs. Another important contrast is that the saints whom Blake pictures in **94**, **95**, and **96** are presented by Botticelli, following Dante's text, only as flames; Blake, who believed that 'Cloud Meteor & Star | Are Men Seen Afar',[129] gives them human faces and bodies in three splendid illustrations.

Saint Peter is alluded to as 'he . . . To whom the keys of glory were assigned' in the last two lines of canto 24. He is reintroduced in 25: 20–1 as 'that [spirit] which I did note in beauty most | Excelling'; Beatrice refers to his 'keys' in line 36. In *St. Peter Appears to Beatrice and Dante* (**94**, National Gallery of Victoria, Fig. 26) Peter, holding a great key, swoops down in a flame against the disc of the sun. Dante and Beatrice rise toward him in graceful complementary diagonals.

---

[129] From verses in a letter to Thomas Butts, 2 October 1800, E 712, ll. 30–1.

Their hands seem to speak a language. After Peter has examined Dante concerning Faith, St James of Compostela appears in *St. Peter and St. James with Dante and Beatrice* (95, National Gallery of Victoria, Fig. 27) to question him about Hope. The two saints, each in his own flame, appear to converse against the disc of the sun, with Dante and Beatrice's cursive bodies becoming almost mirror images of each other below. Peter holds up his right hand in benediction.

> Thus benediction uttering with song,
> Soon as my peace I held, compassed me thrice
> The apostolic radiance, whose behest
> Had oped my lips: so well their answer pleased.

> (25: 49–52)

Then a third saint appears in *St. Peter, St. James, Dante and Beatrice with St. John Also* (96, British Museum, Fig. 28) to examine the poet concerning Love. In keeping with the tradition that John was the 'beautiful apostle', the newcomer is pictured as a youth in contrast to the white-bearded Peter and James. Dante and Beatrice kneel together in the centre foreground, and Beatrice is for the first time without her crown. The five figures form what Rossetti called 'an irregular cinq-foiled composition',[130] and the saints in their discs have been compared to overlapping medieval roundels[131] and to the design of a trefoil window.[132] Eight stars, four on each side, are visible.[133] This radiantly coloured illustration is fittingly the climax of a series in which Dante and Beatrice draw closer and closer together, and in which a higher level of vision, as represented by the introduction of each saint, is attained in three steps.[134]

After the concentrated power of these four designs, it is a bit of an anticlimax to come to *The Vision of the Deity, from Whom Proceed the Nine Spheres* (97, Ashmolean Museum), illustrating the vision of the universe that Dante is vouchsafed in canto 28, and Beatrice's

---

[130] Gilchrist, *Life* (1880), ii. 234.

[131] Blunt, *The Art of William Blake*, p. 91 and pl. 64a. Blunt, pl. 64b, also compares an initial from a 13th-c. psalter showing figures in four discs.

[132] Clark, *The Romantic Rebellion*, p. 174.

[133] Butlin (*William Blake*, p. 154) notes that 'Behind, on each side, Blake originally drew four angels, as in the famous Job illustration "When the Morning Stars sang together" . . . but he later overpainted them and replaced them with eight stars, probably to represent Dante's eight Heavens, the region of the fixed stars, in which this scene occurs.'

[134] On this point see Tinkler-Villani, *Visions of Dante*, p. 282.

Fig. 26. William Blake, Illustrations to *The Divine Comedy*, 1824–7. *Paradiso*, canto 24: *St. Peter Appears to Beatrice and Dante*. Pen, ink, and watercolour over pencil and black chalk.

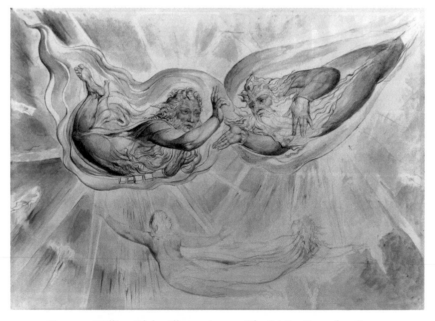

Fig. 27. William Blake, Illustrations to *The Divine Comedy*, 1824–7. *Paradiso*, canto 25: *St. Peter and St. James with Dante and Beatrice*. Pen and watercolour over pencil.

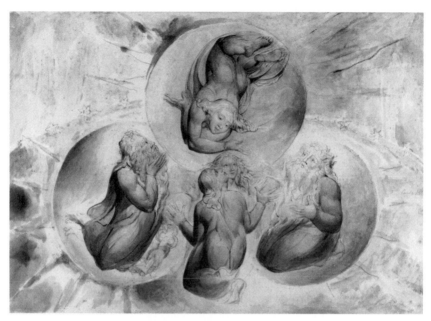

FIG. 28. William Blake, Illustrations to *The Divine Comedy*, 1824–7.
*Paradiso, canto 25: St. Peter, St. James, Dante and Beatrice with St. John
Also.* Pen and watercolour over pencil.

explanation of it, beginning with God, who in Dante is described in
insubstantial terms:

> . . . a point I saw, that darted light
> So sharp, no lid unclosing may bear up
> Against its keenness.

$$(28: 15-17)$$

Blake presents above the spheres an old man very similar to the one
who presides over *The Mission of Virgil* (save that he has no cloven
hoof), making a gesture of powerlessness. Below him are the nine
spheres with their winged angelic intelligences, as Beatrice explains
them to Dante, in descending order, in lines 92–120. In Blake's
representation, none of them look happy. They are:

9. Seraphim. These are only suggested at the sides of the Deity.
8. Cherubim. Two triads of youthful, possibly female faces, with
   two small standing figures between them.

7. Thrones. Two tired-looking old men.
6. Dominations. Two sad-looking bearded men.
5. Virtues. Two doleful, helmeted (the sphere is Mars) males.
4. Powers. Stoical-looking female faces.
3. 'Princedoms' (Principalities). Two attractive, long-haired female heads.
2. Archangels. Two young male heads with stylized disc haloes.
1. 'The band angelical'. Two young female faces. Below them the green disc of the earth.

The depressed looks of some of these angels again suggests Blake's disagreement with the orderly Ptolemaic universe described by Beatrice.[135]

A somewhat more positive view appears in 98, *Dante in the Empyrean, Drinking at the River of Light* (Tate Gallery).

> I looked;
> And, in the likeness of a river, saw
> Light flowing, from whose amber-seeming waves
> Flashed up effulgence, as they glided on
> 'Twixt banks on either side, painted with spring,
> Incredibly how fair . . .
>
> (29: 59–64)

Blake makes the stream vertical and has it flow down from the sun. Dante drinks from it at the left while Beatrice makes an explanatory gesture at the right. Near her are some tiny pencilled figures that may personify the 'flowers and sparkles' (95) that leave and re-enter the river. Above her is sketched a cowled female who has no relation to the text, and who may be meant to suggest a sibyl. On Dante's side of the stream a bearded man, perhaps a poet or prophet, with a scroll on his lap looks upward as if for inspiration. Below him some small pencilled figures appear to be engaged in engraving and painting, with two others peering out of the plant behind Dante. It is hard to find a unified meaning behind these details. Perhaps they are meant to imply that the true exercise of vision is in creating poetry and art.

The last of Dante's scenes that Blake illustrates, *The Queen of Heaven in Glory* (99, National Gallery of Victoria, Melbourne), depicts the celestial rose of cantos 31 and 32.

---

[135] For the view that Blake's angels are true to Dante's view of them, see Fuller, pp. 367–8.

In fashion, as a snow-white rose, lay then
Before my view the saintly multitude,
Which in his own blood Christ espoused.

(31: 1–3)

The Virgin Mary sits near the top, naked and holding a fleur-de-lis
sceptre in her right hand and a looking-glass in her left. (Leaving no
doubt, Blake inscribed 'Mary Scepter Looking Glass' here.) Blake's
familiar symbols of the *ancien régime* (cf. the fleur-de-lis sceptres pic-
tured in *Europe* 14) and the illusion of nature make us realize that
this is one of the designs in which Blake projects a vision opposite
to Dante's, and they give a special twist to Bernard of Clairvaux's
characterizing Mary as ' "the queen, that of this realm | Is sovran" '
(108–9). Beatrice, also naked, is seated below her. Blake has left
inscriptions (E 690) identifying some of the other details. Two
sphinxes sitting on closed books are labelled 'Dominions' (right) and
possibly 'Thrones' (left); the books are inscribed respectively 'Bible |
Chaind round' and 'corded round'. In contrast two open books near
them are 'Aristotle' and 'Homer', indicating that for Blake Dante's
inspiration was classical (derivative) rather than biblical (inspired).
Thus Blake ends his series (as we have seen, 100–2 belong earlier)
with a satire on the poet whom he accused of making 'This World the
Foundation of All' (E 689) but whose vision he often succeeded in
illuminating brilliantly.

The ending of the Dante series on an ironical note should not
divert us from the fact that most of Blake's illustrations do show
what is going on in the text. The remarkable features of the series as
a whole have less to do with the relatively few pictures in which Blake
deliberately subverted Dante's meaning and substituted his own than
with the subjects he chose and the manner in which he developed
them. Perhaps the most significant single decision Blake made was to
concentrate to such an extent upon Hell. Although he may have
intended to add more drawings to Purgatory and Paradise, he must
have realized he could never hope to counterbalance the seventy-two
Inferno subjects that he drew. As we have seen, Blake's Hell is often
a mirror of life on earth, and sequences like those of the Devils and of
the human/serpent transformations convey with awful conviction
one aspect of the polarized vision of Blake's later years. Another, dia-
metrically opposed aspect is seen in the truly paradisaical designs
93–6, showing man and woman in harmony and both in harmony

with the celestial world. Between these, Purgatory, although Blake produced some striking designs for it, does not involve him in the way in which Dante intended to engage the reader. Blake does not believe in the purgation of sin leading to heaven, does not at all believe in Purgatory itself (the word appears nowhere in his writings except for his notes on Dante), and so gives little attention to its whole reason for existence in the *Comedy*. Instead, he substitutes the themes of occluded vision signified by clouds, of the poet's struggle upwards to true vision, and of the true nature of the Earthly Paradise. With respect to the last subject, Blake shows himself as once again unwilling to accept the Church and its sacraments as mediating between humanity and the divine. On the whole, Blake took Dante's *Comedy* not as a subject for a systematic artistic interpretation but as providing a series of targets of opportunity for visual representation. He seized the opportunity of Linnell's Dante commission to produce during the last three years of his life some of the most memorable works of art of his career.

APPENDIX

The Dante illustrations were first catalogued by William Michael Rossetti, who saw them while they were still in the possession of the Linnell family and published his list in Gilchrist's *Life* in 1863 and again in 1880 (see 1880, ii. 227–34). Rossetti counted 98 designs, plus 'a slight inscribed diagram of the Hell-circles, and two other mere sketches, one of them of uncertain subject' (ii. 227). The first of these was later catalogued by Butlin as 812.101, *The Circles of Hell*, while the sketch of uncertain subject may have been 16, *The Goddess of Fortune*. *Unidentified Scene in Hell*, 100, would then be the other sketch. The one drawing that Rossetti appears to have missed altogether is catalogued by Butlin as 102, *The Punishment of the Thieves*. Although a remarkable piece of scholarship for its time, and still valuable for some of its short but perceptive comments, the Rossetti list would be difficult to employ as a source of reference because of its use of lower-case letters instead of numbers, beginning anew after the twenty-sixth and fifty-second entries for the *Inferno* and again for the *Purgatorio* and once again for the *Paradiso*.

Prior to the sale of the illustrations by the Linnell family, a facsimile was prepared by the National Art-Collections Fund.

Published as *Illustrations to the Divine Comedy of Dante by William Blake* in 1922, this edition used Rossetti's list as a basis, though differing from it in some details. It also established a numerical sequence for the whole series and included all 102 pictures, although it relegated three *Inferno* subjects to its end as nos. 100–2. It was this numeration that Albert S. Roe used in his monograph *Blake's Illustrations to* The Divine Comedy, published in 1953. Consequently, in his magisterial *Paintings and Drawings of William Blake* of 1981, Martin Butlin adhered to the numbering that had been employed by scholars for almost six decades, 'despite the fact that some drawings appear to be misplaced, while others cannot be firmly tied to a particular passage in Dante's text; see Nos. 812.45, 70, 73, 100, 101, and 102' (i. 535). Three subsequent editions or catalogues have employed their own numbering systems. Those of Milton Klonsky (1980) and of Corrado Gizzi (1983) independently arrive at identical arrangements of the series, while David Bindman's (2000) differs in some instances from all the others. The differences among the three systems are partly owing to the placing of Butlin 100–2 in the *Inferno* by Klonsky/Gizzi and by Bindman, and partly to the relocation of a few individual drawings by each. As every changed number affects all the numbers that follow it, the differences in the overall sequences may appear much greater than in fact they are. For the purposes of the present study, the use of a single reference source for all Blake's paintings and drawings has been thought to outweigh other considerations, and so Butlin's numbering has been employed. Those who consult the Klonsky/Gizzi and Bindman editions may find the following concordance useful.

A CONCORDANCE TO THE NUMBERING OF THE DESIGNS

	Butlin	Klonsky/Gizzi	Bindman
Dante Running from the Three Beasts	1	1	1
Dante and Virgil Penetrating the Forest	2	2	2
The Mission of Virgil	3	3	3
The Inscription over Hell-Gate	4	4	4
The Vestibule of Hell and the Souls Mustering to Cross the Acheron	5	5	5

	Butlin	Klonsky/ Gizzi	Bindman
Charon and the Condemned Souls	6	6	6
Homer Bearing the Sword, and His Companions	7	7	7
Homer and the Ancient Poets	8	8	8
Minos	9	9	9
The Circle of the Lustful: Francesca da Rimini ('The Whirlwind of Lovers')	10	10	10
The Circle of the Gluttons, with Cerberus	11	11	11
Cerberus (First Version)	12	12	12
Cerberus (Second Version)	13	13	13
Plutus	14	14	14
The Stygian Lake, with the Ireful Sinners Fighting	15	16	16
The Goddess of Fortune	16	15	15
Dante and Virgil about to Pass the Stygian Lake	17	17	17
Virgil Repelling Filippo Argenti from the Boat of Phlegyas	18	18	18
The Angel Crossing the Styx	19	19	19
The Angel at the Gate of Dis	20	20	20
Dante Conversing with Farinata degli Uberti	21	21	21
The Minotaur	22	23	23
The Centaurs and the River of Blood	23	24	24
The Wood of the Self-Murderers: The Harpies and the Suicides	24	25	25
The Hell-Hounds Hunting Destroyers of Their Own Goods	25	26	26
The Blasphemers, the Usurers, and the Sodomites	26	28	28
Capaneus the Blasphemer	27	29	29
The Symbolic Figure of the Course of Human History Described by Virgil	28	30	30
The Punishment of Jacopo Rusticucci and His Companions	29	31	31
The Usurers	30	32	32
Geryon Conveying Dante and Virgil Down Towards Malebolge	31	33	33

	Butlin	Klonsky/ Gizzi	Bindman
Demons Tormenting the Panders and Seducers in Malebolge	32	34	34
Dante and Virgil Gazing into the Ditch of the Flatterers	33	35	35
The Devils Under the Bridge	34	39	39
The Simoniac Pope	35	36	36
The Necromancers and Augurs	36	37	37
The Devils Carry the Lucchese Magistrate to the Boiling-Pitch Pool of Corrupt Officials	37	38	38
Virgil Abashing the Devils	38	40	40
The Devils Setting Out with Dante and Virgil	39	41	41
The Devils with Dante and Virgil by the Side of the Pool	40	42	42
Ciampolo the Barrator Tormented by the Devils	41	43	43
The Baffled Devils Fighting	42	44	44
Dante and Virgil Escaping from the Devils	43	45	45
The Hypocrites with Caiaphas	44	46	46
The Laborious Passage Along the Rocks	45	47	47
The Laborious Passage Along the Rocks	46	48	48
The Thieves and the Serpents	47	49	49
The Serpent Attacking Vanni Fucci	48	51	51
Vanni Fucci 'Making Figs' Against God	49	52	52
The Centaur Cacus	50	53	53
The Six-Footed Serpent Attacking Agnello Brunelleschi	51	54	54
Agnello Brunelleschi Half Transformed by the Serpent	52	55	55
The Serpent Attacking Buoso Donati	53	56	56
Buoso Donati Transformed into a Serpent; Francesco De' Cavalcanti Transformed from a Serpent into a Man	54	57	57
Ulysses and Diomed Swathed in the Same Flame	55	58	58

	Butlin	Klonsky/Gizzi	Bindman
The Schismatics and Sowers of Discord: Mohammed	56	59	59
The Schismatics and Sowers of Discord: Mosca De' Lamberti and Bertrand de Born	57	60	60
The Pit of Disease: The Falsifiers	58	61	61
The Pit of Disease: Gianni Schicchi and Myrrah	59	62	62
The Primaeval Giants Sunk in the Soil	60	63	63
The Complaint of the Giant Nimrod	61	64	64
Ephialtes and Two Other Titans	62	65	65
Antaeus Setting down Dante and Virgil in the Last Circle of Hell	63	66	66
The Circle of Traitors: The Alberti Brothers	64	67	67
Dante Striking Against Bocca Degli Albati	65	68	68
Dante Tugging at Bocca's Hair	66	69	69
Ugolino Relating His Death	67	70	70
Ugolino and His Sons in Prison	68	71	71
Lucifer	69	72	72
Virgil Girding Dante's Brow with a Rush	70	73	74
Dante, Virgil and Cato	71	74	73
The Angel in the Boat Departing After Wafting over the Souls for Purgation	72	75	75
The Rest on the Mountain Leading to Purgatory	73	77	77
The Ascent of the Mountain of Purgatory	74	76	76
The Souls of Those Who Only Repented At the Point of Death	75	78	78
The Lawn with the Kings and Angels	76	79	79
Lucia Carrying Dante in His Sleep	77	80	80
Dante and Virgil Approaching the Angel Who Guards the Entrance of Purgatory	78	81	81
The Angel Marking Dante with the Sevenfold 'P'	79	82	82

	Butlin	Klonsky/ Gizzi	Bindman
The Rock Sculptured with the Recovery of the Ark and the Annunciation	80	83	83
The Proud under Their Enormous Loads	81	84	84
The Angel Descending at the Close of the Circle of the Proud	82	85	85
The Terrace of Envious Souls	83	86	86
The Angel Inviting Dante to Enter the Fire	84	87	87
Dante at the Moment of Entering the Fire	85	88	88
Dante and Statius Sleeping, Virgil Watching	86	89	89
Beatrice on the Car, Matilda and Dante	87	90	90
Beatrice Addressing Dante from the Car	88	91	91
The Harlot and the Giant	89	92	92
Dante Adoring Christ	90	94	94
The Spiral Stairway	91	93	93
The Recording Angel	92	95	95
Dante and Beatrice in the Constellation of Gemini and the Sphere of Flame	93	96	96
St. Peter Appears to Beatrice and Dante	94	97	97
St. Peter and St. James with Dante and Beatrice	95	98	98
St. Peter, St. James, Dante and Beatrice with St. John Also	96	99	99
The Vision of the Deity, from Whom Proceed the Nine Spheres	97	100	100
Dante in the Empyrean, Drinking at the River of Light	98	101	101
The Queen of Heaven in Glory	99	102	102
Unidentified Scene in Hell	100	27	27
The Circles of Hell	101	22	22
The Punishment of the Thieves	102	50	50

4 'Thou readst black where I read white': The Bible

'THE OLD & NEW TESTAMENTS are the Great Code of Art', Blake wrote in ח׳ & his two Sons, and his lifelong engagement with the Bible culminated in several works, poetic and pictorial, during his late years. These comprise the manuscript poem *The Everlasting Gospel*; Blake's last illuminated book, *The Ghost of Abel*; the great engraved *Illustrations of The Book of Job*, seven pencil drawings for the apocryphal Book of Enoch (which Blake would nevertheless have regarded as a product of the Poetic Genius); an illustrated manuscript of the first four chapters of Genesis; and comments on a new translation of the Lord's Prayer, along with his own version. As we would expect, all these creations are interpretive, and none of them conform to received or generally accepted views of their subjects. Collectively, they may be considered Blake's last attempt at a 'Bible of Hell',[1] although they do not attempt to present a unified, consistent view among themselves. 'Blakean' terms and images do turn up, but each of these productions, finished and unfinished, is self-contained; and in viewpoint they range from a generally understandable though highly individual Christianity in the *Job* engravings to Blake at his most 'Manichaean' in *The Everlasting Gospel* and in his annotations to the Lord's Prayer.

The Everlasting Gospel

In 1818 or later,[2] Blake began to write a poem, which in the course of composition he entitled *The Everlasting Gospel*. Because Blake was

---

[1] 'I have also: The Bible of Hell: which the world shall have whether they will or no', Blake wrote in *The Marriage of Heaven and Hell* (24, E 44), possibly referring to the not-yet-written Lambeth Books; and on the back of a drawing 'The Bible of Hell in Nocturnal Visions collected' (Butlin 221ᵛ).

[2] The separate leaf (Rosenbach MS) that Erdman considers to have preceded the drafts Blake wrote in his Notebook and on one other piece of paper is watermarked 1818. See E 335 and Erdman, ' "Terrible Blake in His Pride" ', in *From Sensibility to*

a poor man, he hoarded paper for future use, and one section of the poem was written on part of a leaf of the 1802 Hayley *Ballads*,[3] another on a leaf watermarked 1818. To the best of our knowledge, Blake never made a fair copy of *The Everlasting Gospel*, and he may never have considered it as completed, but an editorial reconstruction of his probable last intention is to be found in Erdman's *Complete Poetry and Prose* (E 518–24), with passages considered to have been rejected supplied in the textual notes (E 874–80). While it is important to note that Erdman considers his entire arrangement as provisional, the detailed rationale he gives for it[4] is for the most part convincing, and it will therefore be the text followed here, with due attention to the parts printed as textual notes. The poem was composed at considerable speed, judging both from the hurried handwriting of some of the Notebook sections and from the relative indifference Blake shows in it toward the craft of its iambic tetrameter couplets. At the same time, it addresses subjects on which Blake had thought deeply and projects attitudes characteristic of some other late works, and it is therefore a work of considerable interest. A gnomic, subversive, sometimes savage reinterpretation of parts of the Gospels, shot through with references to other parts of the Bible, it gives Blake's own rendering of the character of Jesus.

The sections designated [m] and [n], though not written first, appear as a preface,[5] in which a figure of considerable importance to Blake appears.

> I will tell you what Joseph of Arimathea
> Said to my Fairy was not it very queer

Romanticism: Essays Presented to Frederick A. Pottle, ed. Frederick W. Hilles and Harold Bloom (New York: Oxford University Press, 1965), p. 335. *William Blake's Writings*, ed. Bentley, ii. 1720, agrees.

[3] See *The Notebook of William Blake*, ed. David V. Erdman with the assistance of Donald K. Moore (Oxford: Clarendon Press, 1973), pp. N117 n., N120. For another example of Blake's hoarding of paper for later use, see G. E. Bentley, Jr., 'The Date of Blake's Pickering Manuscript *or* The Way of a Poet with Paper', *Studies in Bibliography*, 19 (1966): 232–43.

[4] See Erdman, ' "Terrible Blake in His Pride" ', and E 874.

[5] These were published as the preface for the first time in 1982, E 518; see E 874 for Erdman's reason for so doing. In Keynes's 1966 *Complete Writings* they appear as, respectively, an independent Notebook fragment (p. 552) and as lines 23–4 (p. 751) of the section of *The Everlasting Gospel* that Keynes designates as *d* and Erdman as [k]. Blake wrote the lines on p. 52 of his Noteboook; see *The Notebook of William Blake*, p. N52.

> Pliny & Trajan what are You here
> Come listen to Joseph of Arimathea
> Listen patient & when Joseph has done
> Twill make a fool laugh & a Fairy Fun

Joseph of Arimathea appears in all four Gospels as the man who took away the body of Jesus for entombment.

> When the even was come, there came a rich man of Arimathaea, named Joseph, who also himself was Jesus' disciple:
> He went to Pilate, and begged the body of Jesus. Then Pilate commanded the body to be delivered.
> And when Joseph had taken the body, he wrapped it in a clean linen cloth, And laid it in his own new tomb, which he had hewn out in the rock: and he rolled a great stone to the door of the sepulchre, and departed. (Matt. 27: 57–60)

The other references are Mark 15: 43–6 (where Joseph is called 'an honourable counseller'), Luke 23: 50–3 (where he is called 'a counseller . . . a good man, and a just' who 'had not consented to the counsel and deed [i.e. the condemnation and execution of Jesus] of them'), and John 19: 38. For Blake the laying of Jesus' body in a tomb hewn out of the rock is a means of preserving it for the Resurrection, a role assigned to Los in *The Four Zoas*, where

> . . . Los & Enitharmon took the Body of the Lamb
> Down from the Cross & placd it in a Sepulcher which Los had hewn
> For himself in the Rock of Eternity . . .
>
> (110, first portion: 30–2, E 385)

According to legend, Joseph of Arimathea brought the Holy Grail with him to England and founded the Abbey of Glastonbury, where his staff was miraculously transformed into a blossoming thorn tree.[6] This may be the subject of the colour-printed relief etching that has been given the title *Joseph of Arimathea Preaching to the Inhabitants of Britain* (Butlin 262 and 286, Essick XII), showing an old bearded man with his right arm extended and his left holding a staff that appears rooted to the ground, addressing an audience of

---

[6] Robert N. Essick cites a pamphlet on the subject, published *c.*1770 and several times afterward, in which Blake could have found these details. See Essick, *The Separate Plates of William Blake: A Catalogue* (Princeton: Princeton University Press, 1983), pp. 44–6. This catalogue will be cited as 'Essick'.

young men and women.[7] A much later pencil drawing of the same subject (Butlin 780, repr. pl. 1028) has been dated *c*.1820–5 by Butlin on stylistic grounds. Whether or not Joseph of Arimathea was meant to be the protagonist in these designs, Blake certainly meant him to play that role when *c*.1810–20 he extensively reworked an early apprentice plate (Essick I) and entitled it *Joseph of Arimathea among the Rocks of Albion*.[8] The figure, made more powerful by Blake's extensive burnishing and strongly incised lines, is identified in Blake's new caption as 'One of the Gothic Artists who built the Cathedrals in what we call the Dark Ages . . .'. Thus Joseph of Arimathea combines for Blake the roles of disciple of Jesus, Los-like preserver of Jesus' body until his resurrection, and primeval artist.

The Fairy is a very odd figure for Joseph of Arimathea to address. Blake has no sentimental liking for the 'Fairies of Albion afterwards Gods of the Heathen'[9] who personify the amoral drives of human nature. A case in point is the Fairy who, caught by the poet, is forced to dictate *Europe*, and who, when the poet gathers flowers for him, 'laugh'd aloud to see them whimper because they were pluck'd . . .'.[10] Joseph and the Fairy inhabit different universes, and the fact that the former should address the latter begins the poem on a deliberately dissonant note. The invitation to Pliny and Trajan to listen as well is at least as odd, for both were associated with the persecution of the early Christians.[11] Blake may well have known of the letter in which Pliny, as Trajan's legate in Bithynia, asked the emperor whether his procedure was correct. 'The method I have observed towards those who have been denounced to me as Christians', wrote

---

[7] This print is related to a pencil drawing of *c*.1780 (Butlin 76 [repr. pl. 69], Rosenbach Museum and Library, Philadelphia). The subject has been questioned by Damon (*A Blake Dictionary*, p. 225), who points out that the audience appears to receive the speaker's message with consternation rather than joy, that the staff is not flowering, and that there is no suggestion of the Abbey of Glastonbury. The subject was first identified as Joseph of Arimathea by A. G. B. Russell, *The Engravings of William Blake* (London: G. Richards, 1912), p. 56, no. 5.

[8] See Essick, *Separate Plates*, no. I (second state). As Essick, p. 8, points out, Blake's original engraving was taken after a figure in Michelangelo's *The Crucifixion of Saint Peter* (Pauline Chapel, Vatican), through the intermediacy of a drawing that may itself have been copied from an engraving.

[9] *The Four Zoas*, Night the First, 4: 3, E 301.

[10] *Europe* iii. 21, E 60; this page exists in only two of the twelve copies of *Europe* (see Bentley, *Blake Books*, p. 142). Cf. the speaker of Blake's Notebook poem 'The Fairy', who exults in the idea that 'a tear or a smile | Will a man beguile' (3–4, E 475).

[11] As E 875 notes.

Pliny, 'is this: I interrogated them whether they were Christians: if they confessed it I repeated the question twice again, adding the threat of capital punishment; if they still persevered, I ordered them to be executed.' 'The method you have pursued, my dear Pliny,' Trajan replied, 'in cases of those denounced to you as Christians is extremely proper.'[12] That Blake does not expect this audience of three to benefit from Joseph's discourse is clear: 'Twill make a fool laugh & a Fairy Fun'. The Fool is a stock figure in Blake's writings, one whose opacity might well cause him to laugh at hearing about the true nature of Jesus, just as the incorrigible Fairy would. The idea that Joseph of Arimathea would bother talking to these three is one of the discordant aspects of this discordant poem.

On the same Notebook page (N58) that Blake wrote these lines he also wrote a section [k] bearing the title 'The Everlasting Gospel'. Attempts have been made to link this title with the frequent use of this term by radical dissenters in the seventeenth century,[13] but its importance in the book of Revelation (from which, of course, the dissenters derived it) makes it unnecessary to suppose such intermediacy:

And I saw another angel fly in the midst of heaven, having the everlasting gospel to preach unto them that dwell on the earth, and to every nation, and kindred, and tongue, and people,
    Saying with a loud voice, Fear God, and give glory to him; for the hour of his judgment is come: and worship him that made heaven, and earth, and the sea, and the fountains of waters.[14]

The following verses take up the point on humility made by Joseph of Arimathea at the end of [n]: 'I was standing by when Jesus died | What I calld Humility they calld Pride'. The polar opposition of these terms in their common sense and in what Blake would call their spiritual sense is taken up in the opening verses of [k], which are presumably still spoken by Joseph of Arimathea. (It would nevertheless have been more consistent in the light of what follows for him to

[12] The Letters of Pliny, trans. William Melmoth, rev. W. M. L. Hutchinson (2 vols., London: Heinemann, 1927), pp. 401, 407. This exchange of letters is discussed by Elaine Pagels, The Gnostic Gospels, pp. 92–3.
[13] Most notably by A. L. Morton in The Everlasting Gospel (London: Lawrence & Wishart, 1958).
[14] Rev. 14: 6–7. In Blake 'the Everlasting Gospel' also occcurs in the annotations to Bishop Watson (E 619), the Descriptive Catalogue (E 543), and Jerusalem 27 (E 171).

have said 'What they call Humility I calld Pride'.) The denial of humility is part of Blake's strategy of presenting an antinomian Christ who transgressed the Law and violated all common conceptions of virtue. As is generally recognized, there is a close relationship between the view of Jesus Blake expresses here and that of the Devil in *The Marriage of Heaven and Hell* (1790):

... now hear how he has given his sanction to the law of ten commandments: did he not mock at the sabbath, and so mock the sabbaths God? murder those who were murderd because of him? turn away the law from the woman taken in adultery? steal the labor of others to support him? bear false witness when he omitted making a defence before Pilate? covet when he pray'd for his disciples, and when he bid them shake off the dust of their feet against such as refused to lodge them? I tell you, no virtue can exist without breaking these ten commandments: Jesus was all virtue, and acted from impulse: not from rules. (Plates 23–4, E 43)

In *The Everlasting Gospel* Blake will present a Jesus who is neither humble, nor chaste, nor proud, nor gentle. Curiously, his immediate examples of the first of these is the story in Luke 2: 42–51 of the tarrying of the 12-year-old Jesus in Jerusalem unknown to Mary and Joseph, who 'sorrowing' retrace their steps only to find him 'sitting in the midst of the doctors, both hearing them, and asking them questions'. In answer to Mary's admonition, Jesus says, 'How is it that ye sought me? wist ye not that I must be about my Father's business?' Blake makes his retort much sharper: 'No Earthly Parents I confess | I am doing my Fathers business' (9–10). Blake's Jesus may be remembering words from a different context, where in Matt. 12: 46–9 Jesus is told, 'Behold, thy mother and thy brethren stand without, desiring to speak with thee.' Jesus' answer is 'Who is my mother? and who are my brethren?' and, indicating his disciples, 'Behold my mother and my brethren!' This extension of love to the community of believers, however, no more indicates a lack of humility than the statement that he must do his Father's business. In any event, although rejections of family ties are to be found in the New Testament, line 9 of *The Everlasting Gospel* is Blake's invention.

The instance immediately following also seems somewhat off-centre as a proof of Jesus' pride:

> When the rich learned Pharisee
> Came to consult him secretly

Upon his heart with Iron pen
He wrote Ye must be born again

(11–14, E 518–19)

Elsewhere, the 'iron pen' is associated with Urizen, who after his fall in Night VI of *The Four Zoas*, 'still his books he bore in his strong hands & his iron pen' (71, second portion: 35). Here Blake is probably drawing on Jer. 17: 1: 'The sin of Judah is written with a pen of iron, and with the point of a diamond: it is graven upon the table of their heart . . .'. Yet the message appears inappropriate to the situation, in which Nicodemus tells Jesus 'Rabbi, we know that thou art a teacher come from God: for no man can do these miracles that thou doest, except God be with him' (John 3: 2); and after the Crucifixion (19: 39) it is Nicodemus who brings the myrrh and aloes for the body of Jesus. Although the literal-minded Nicodemus has trouble understanding 'Except a man be born again, he cannot see the kingdom of God' (John 3: 3), he would not seem to rate the 'iron pen' of Jeremiah and Urizen, nor does the Gospel account use this expression. Indeed, Blake may have also had in mind the only other, and more celebrated, instance of it in the Bible:

Oh that my words were now written! oh that they were printed in a book!
    That they were graven with an iron pen and lead in the rock for ever!
    For I know that my redeemer liveth, and that he shall stand at the latter day upon the earth:
    And though after my skin worms destroy this body, yet in my flesh shall I see God: (Job 19: 23–6)

This text would appear (with slight modifications) as part of the passage in the bottom margin of *Job* engraving 11, 'With Dreams upon my bed thou scarest me & affrightest me with Visions'. If, as has been suggested, Blake takes Job's view of God here as erroneous,[15] it as all the more difficult to see why he should have Jesus write the mystery of the second birth 'with iron pen' upon the heart of Nicodemus. Was Blake writing in such haste that he did not think through the implications of this and the preceding example?

    Some of the following statements are equally off-kilter, for example 17–20:

---

[15] See Jenijoy La Belle, 'Words Graven with an Iron Pen: The Marginal Texts in Blake's *Job*', in *The Visionary Hand*, ed. Robert N. Essick (Los Angeles: Hennessey & Ingalls, 1973), pp. 537–8. See also discussion in pp. 243–6 below.

> He says with most consummate Art
> Follow me I am meek & lowly of heart
> As that is the only way to escape
> The Misers net & the Gluttons trap

As has been pointed out, this glosses Matt. 11: 29 ('I am meek and lowly in heart') by making Jesus appear to have been a hypocrite.[16] Going on to contrast 'the Scribes and Pharisees Virtuous rules' with Jesus' 'honest triumphant Pride' (25–6), Blake asserts that in this way Jesus avoided becoming 'bloody Caesars Elf' and 'at last . . . Caesar himself' (35–6). Blake need hardly be blamed for accepting the common Christian view of the Pharisees[17] (though he who questioned so much else might well have questioned this), but his idea that Jesus was somehow opposed to the Roman rule of the holy land, one that is reasserted in 'Cursing the Rulers before the People' (66), is clearly contradicted by Jesus' advice to 'Render therefore unto Caesar the things which are Caesar's' (Matt. 22: 21; cf. Mark 12: 17 and Luke 20: 25). Blake wants Jesus to be opposed to the government, and so this too becomes a feature of his Pride. This condemnation becomes linked with two members of Blake's unholy Trinity—'Bacon & Newton', who in his view denied spiritual Christianity. Surprisingly, the third member is not, as usual, Locke:

> Like dr Priestly & Bacon & Newton
> Poor Spiritual Knowledge is not worth a button.

(37–8)

In this sole mention of Joseph Priestley in Blake's writings, the Unitarian is condemned, despite his opposition to arbitrary government, presumably because he taught the identity of matter and spirit—a view that might have been congenial to the Blake of *The Marriage of Heaven and Hell*[18] but decidely not to the Blake of *The Everlasting Gospel*.

---

[16] See Randall Helms, 'The Genesis of *The Everlasting Gospel*', *Blake Studies*, 9 (1980): 149, 151.

[17] On the Pharisees as mystically inclined, without power in secular or Temple affairs, and viewed with suspicion by the Romans, see Leo Baeck, *The Pharisees, and Other Essays* (New York: Schocken Books, 1947).

[18] See Priestley, *Disquisitions Relating to Matter and Spirit* (London: Joseph Johnson, 1777); and Morton D. Paley, *Energy and the Imagination* (Oxford: Clarendon Press, 1970), pp. 81–3.

Although at times Blake may seem to be wrenching the Gospels'
accounts into consistency with his own views, we certainly can see
his general point about Jesus' 'honest triumphant Pride' (25) as man-
ifested in rejection of Satan's temptations (31–4):

> He had only to say that God was the devil
> And the devil was God like a Christian Civil
> Mild Christian regrets to the devil confess
> For affronting him thrice in the Wilderness

Jesus resisted three temptations (see Matt. 4: 1–11, Luke 4: 1–13),
which Blake conflates into one, which is also the subject of Milton's
Paradise Regained 1: 342–50, and of Blake's depiction of it
(*c*.1816–20) in what is arguably the best of his illustrations to that
poem: *The First Temptation* (Fitzwilliam Museum, Butlin 544.2).
His 'He was too proud to take a bribe' (15) may also refer to this.
Certainly we see Blake's point that 'had he been Antichrist Creeping
Jesus | Hed have done anything to please us (55–6)'.[19] Yet the poem
immediately proceeds into confusing ambiguities once more. Blake
declares that 'God wants not Man to Humble himself' (61) and also
that Jesus was 'Humble to God Haughty to Man' (64). We might
think, then, that we could silently add 'to Man' at the end of line 61.
But 'when he Humbled himself to God | Then descended the cruel
Rod' (67–8). Now it appears that Jesus ought not to have humbled
himself to God either, and this is the burden of what we take to be
God's words to Jesus in lines 69–74:

> If thou humblest thyself thou humblest me
> Thou also dwellst in Eternity
> Thou art a Man God is no more
> Thy own humanity learn to adore
> For that is my Spirit of Life
> Awake arise to Spiritual Strife

This message is close to the words of *The Marriage of Heaven and
Hell*: 'God only Acts & Is, in existing Beings or Men' (16, E 40); and
line 72 recalls Swedenborg's idea of the Divine Humanity.[20] These six

---

[19] Bentley, *Blake's Writings*, ii. 1067 n. says 'Creeping Jesus was evidently a prover-
bial Sussex expression meaning a favour-seeking hypocrite', citing J. J. Robinson, 'A
Creeping Jesus', *TLS*, 27 August 1925, p. 557.
[20] The possible Swedenborgian connection is suggested by W. H. Stevenson, *Blake:
The Complete Poems* (2nd edn., London: Longman, 1989), p. 867 n.

lines have the ring of a doctrine Blake wishes to endorse—but what follows is surprising:

> And thy Revenge abroad display
> In terror at the Last Judgment day
> Gods Mercy & Long Suffering
> Is but the Sinner to Judgment to bring
> Thou on the Cross for them shall pray
> And take Revenge at the Last Day
>
> (75–80)

It appears that God wants Jesus to appear to pray for sinners and then to destroy them at the Last Judgment—a programme made all the more questionable by the original reading of line 80: 'Whom thou shalt Torment at the Last Day' (E 879). Can this be the same God who said 'Thy own humanity learn to adore'? Jesus does not respond to the injunction to take revenge, but seems to refuse to pray for sinners in asserting 'I never will pray for the World' (82). Of course Jesus did pray for his executioners when he said on the Cross 'Father, forgive them; for they know not what they do' (Luke 23: 34), but we learn from lines 83–4 that Blake has a different situation in mind here:

> Once [I] did so when I prayd in the Garden
> I wishd to take with me a Bodily Pardon

The reference is of course to his prayer in the garden at Gethsemane 'O my Father, if it be possible, let this cup pass from me' (Matt. 26: 39), which Blake represents Jesus as now repudiating.[21] The remaining eighteen lines of this section demonstrate why the body, 'born in a night to perish in a night' (101), is not worth saving. Blake seems to have been in a hurry here, forgetting that he has not supplied a main verb for the statement that begins on line 85 ('Can that which was of Woman born'[22]), and starting a new sentence with 'Humility is only Doubt' at line 93. The introduction of 'Humility' here seems a forced attempt to link with the main theme of [k], as the thrust of this

---

[21] Helms, 'The Genesis of *The Everlasting Gospel*', suggests that Blake is misremembering the words spoken by Jesus at the Last Supper: 'I pray for them [my disciples]: I pray not for the world, but for them which thou hast given me' (John 17: 9).

[22] As David Fuller observes, 'born of a woman' occurs in Job 14: 1, 15: 14, and 25: 4, and 'the first of these passages is particularly well known because of its use in the burial service of the Book of Common Prayer'. See *William Blake: Selected Poetry and Prose* (New York: Pearson, 2000), p. 344 n.

concluding passage has nothing to do with Humility but is an affirmation of the pre-existence of the soul and its degradation by entering material existence. It is, furthermore, adapted from a couplet in *Auguries of Innocence* that itself has nothing to do with Humility:

> If the Sun & Moon should doubt
> Theyd immediately Go out
>
> (109–10, E 494)

The last four lines of [k] are likewise adapted from *Auguries of Innocence* (lines 125–8, E 492–3). There is of course nothing wrong with a poet's re-contextualizing his own words, but this conclusion, with its emphasis on the valuelessness of sensory experience and the all-importance of the Soul, is another example of the poem's dissonance, especially as the next section (in Erdman's reconstruction) will begin 'Was Jesus Chaste or did he | Give any Lessons of Chastity' (f: 1–2, E 521).

ii

The question 'Was Jesus Chaste . . . ?' suggests a completely unorthodox reconstruction of Jesus to come, but despite Blake's powerful rhetoric, this turns out not to be the case. The central situation of section [f] is the story of the woman taken in adultery in John 8: 2–11. The episode takes place 'early in the morning' (2), which Blake colours by linking sexuality and blushing: 'the morning blushd fiery red' (3), as he also does in 'The Angel' (E 24), where, however, the speaker of the poem resists her erotic impulse.

> Mary was found in Adulterous bed
> Earth groand beneath & Heaven above
> Trembled at discovery of Love
>
> (4–6)

Although the woman is not named in the Gospel, Blake accepts the post-biblical tradition that she is to be identified as Mary Magdalene, and so names her Mary. The cosmic reverberations of the incident are also not to be found in Blake's Gospel source, but Michael Tolley compares the immediate response of Earth and Nature to the Fall in *Paradise Lost*:

Earth trembl'd from her entrails, as again
In pangs, and Nature gave a second groan,
Sky low'r'd and muttering Thunder, some sad drops
Wept at completing of the mortal Sin . . .[23]

Earth, female like Mary, seems to undergo the pangs of childbirth, underscoring the sexual content of the scene. Jesus is described in the Gospel as sitting in the temple, but Blake places him 'in Moses Chair' to prepare the way for the contrast of the old and the new dispensations that will follow (cf. Matt. 23: 2, where Jesus says 'The scribes and the Pharisees sit in Moses' seat'). 'Moses Chair' did not literally exist but, as Matthew Henry glosses Matt. 23: 2 in his *Commentary on the Whole Bible* (1706–20): '*The pulpit of wood*, such as was made for Ezra, *that ready scribe in the law of God* (Neh. 8: 4), is here called *Moses's seat*, because Moses had those in every city (so the expression is, Acts 15: 21), who in those pulpits preached him; this was their office, and it was just and honourable; it was requisite that there should be some at whose mouth the people might *enquire the law*, Mal. 2: 7.'[24] Henry immediately continues in a vein that Blake would have understood completely: 'Note, 1. Many a good place is filled with bad men; it is no new thing for the vilest men to be exalted even to Moses's seat (Ps. 12: 8); and, when it is so, the men are not so much honoured by the seat as the seat is dishonoured by the men. Now they that sat in Moses's seat were so wretchedly degenerated, that it was time for the great Prophet to arise, like unto Moses, to erect another seat.' This is of course precisely what Blake means by placing Jesus 'in Moses Chair'.

According to the Law (Lev. 20: 10), 'the man that commiteth adultery with another man's wife, even he that commiteth adultery with his neighbour's wife, the adulterer and the adulteress shall surely be put to death'. Therefore, the woman's captors say 'Moses in the law commanded us, that such should be stoned' (John 8: 5), though, interestingly, they say nothing of the adulter*er*, who must have been

---

[23] 9: 1000–3. See Michael J. Tolley, 'William Blake's Use of the Bible in a Section of "The Everlasting Gospel" ', *Notes and Queries*, 207 (1962): 172. There may also be, as Tolley observes in another article, an echo in both passages of Rom. 8: 22: 'the whole creation groaneth and travaileth in pain together until now'. See Tolley, 'Blake's "Edens Flood" Again', *Notes and Queries*, 213 (1968): 14.

[24] Matthew Henry, *Commentary on the Whole Bible* (1706–20), *Blue Letter Bible*, www.blueletterbible.org/Comm/mhc/Mat/Mat023.html (27 September 2003).

taken with her 'in the very act' (4). Jesus' immediate response to their 'what sayest thou?' in the Gospel is to stoop down and write with his finger on the sand, 'as though he heard them not' (5–6). This part of the episode is the subject of Blake's watercolour *The Woman Taken in Adultery* (Butlin 486, Boston Museum of Fine Arts) and, as Blake well knew, of numerous other paintings and engravings.[25] In *The Everlasting Gospel*, however, Jesus does not write in the sand. His response is cosmic in nature:

> He laid his hand on Moses Law
> The Ancient Heavens in Silent Awe
> Writ with Curses from Pole to Pole
> All away began to roll
>
> (11–14)

With this action, Jesus undoes the old order. As in Rev. 6: 14 'the heaven departed as a scroll when it is rolled together . . .'. This apocalyptic event lays bare the sexualized Earth of line 15:

> The Earth trembling & Naked lay
> In secret bed of Mortal Clay
> On Sinai felt the hand Divine
> Putting back the bloody shrine
> And she heard the breath of God
> As she heard by Edens flood
>
> (15–20)

The shrine could be any place of sacrifice but perhaps principally that of Exod. 20: 24, where God instructs Moses on Sinai 'An altar of earth thou shalt make unto me, and shalt sacrifice thereon thy burnt offerings, and thy peace offerings, thy sheep, and thine oxen . . .'.[26] 'Putting back the bloody shrine' means not restoring it but putting it away, in accordance with the new dispensation. With this, the world moves back toward its prelapsarian state: 'And she heard the breath of God | As she heard by Edens flood' (19–20). The divine breath, now that of Jesus, proclaims 'Good & Evil are no more | Sinais trumpets cease to roar' (21–2), referring to Exod. 19: 16, where 'it came to pass on the third day in the morning, that there were thunders and

---

[25] See Christopher Heppner, 'The Woman Taken in Adultery: An Essay on Blake's "Style of Designing" ', *Blake*, 17 (Fall 1983): 44–60. Blake's picture is reproduced on p. 46.
[26] See Tolley, 'William Blake's Use of the Bible', 172.

lightnings, and a thick cloud upon the mount, and the voice of the trumpet exceeding loud . . .'. This abrogation of good and evil and by implication of the Ten Commandments is once more reminiscent of *The Marriage of Heaven and Hell*. When Jesus goes on to order 'Cease Finger of God to Write' (23), he is again alluding to this antinomian doctrine, for the tablets given to Moses on Sinai were 'written with the finger of God' (Exod. 31: 18); cf. 'Jehovahs Finger Wrote the Law' in *For the Sexes* (5, E 259), and Blake's watercolour of *c*.1805 *God Writing upon the Tables of the Covenant* (Butlin 448, National Gallery of Scotland). The God who writes the Law is dismissed by Jesus entirely:

> The Heavens are not clean in thy Sight
> Thou art Good & thou Alone
> Nor may the sinner cast one stone
> To be Good only is to be
> A Devil or else a Pharisee
>
> (24–8)

Line 24 echoes the words of Eliphaz in Job 15: 15: 'yea, the heavens are not clean in his sight' and 25: 5: 'yea, the stars are not pure in his sight'. Of course since God created heavens and stars, there is a conundrum here. It cannot be merely that Eliphaz is 'wrongheaded',[27] for the whole material creation is condemned in the following lines. 'Thou art Good & thou Alone | Nor may the sinner cast one stone' is clearly ironical, but it is hard to see how the irony is supposed to work. Apparently we are to take John 8: 7, where Jesus says 'He that is without sin among you, let him first cast a stone at her', at face value; but not Luke 18: 19, where he says 'Why callest thou me good? none is good, save one, that is, God.' The couplet that follows, which Blake added after the rest and led in,[28] did have some bite in its original reading: 'To be Good only is to be | A God or else a Pharisee' (E 880), but Blake revised line 28 to begin 'A Devil', blunting the point.

Jesus next addresses the 'Angel of the Presence Divine', a being (see Chapter 2) that Blake could at various times present as positive or negative, but who in *The Everlasting Gospel* is entirely demonic

---

[27] As Helms, 'The Genesis of *The Everlasting Gospel*', 135, puts it.
[28] See *Notebook*, p. N49. Blake turned the notebook and wrote these two lines perpendicular to the rest, then led them in to appear at the top of the page.

because he 'didst create this body of Mine' and he 'writ these Laws |
And Created Hells dark jaws' (30–2). A link is evident between this
sentiment and the 'Prisons are built of stones of Law. Brothels with
bricks of Religion' (8, E 36). But this late poem, unlike *The Marriage*,
does not create an antithetical, positive vision of the joys of the body.
Instead, the Angel is here equated with the blind creator of the
colour-printed drawing *Elohim Creating Adam* (Butlin 289, Tate
Gallery). In a section that began by asking whether Jesus was chaste,
we have come after thirty lines to the creation of the human body
as parallel to the creation of the Law and of Hell.[29] Jesus says 'My
Presence I will take from thee' (33), implying a contrast between the
Divine Presence and his own, and curses the Angel: 'A Cold Leper
thou shalt be' (34)—like the 'leprous' Jehovah of *The Four Zoas*
and *Milton*.[30] The Angel, who here appears to be equated with a
demiurgic God, is accused of inverting the course of Genesis 1 and
making 'all to Chaos roll | With the Circle for its soul'. Yet this
address manages to end on a positive note in two beautiful lines: 'Still
the breath Divine does move | And the breath Divine is Love' (41–2).
This nevertheless leaves us with a completely bifurcated universe in
which Law, Serpent, Hell, and bodily existence are all negative and
only the Spiritual breath Divine is positive.

At this point Blake recalls Mary, whom he had left waiting for
Jesus' words over twenty lines earlier. 'Mary Fear Not', he begins,
echoing words spoken, as Tolley points out,[31] by the angel of the
Annunciation to the Virgin in Luke 1: 30 and by the angel at the
sepulchre to 'Mary Magdalene and the other Mary' in Matt. 28: 5.
It's as if both Marys were aspects of the same being for Blake, 'The
Seven Devils that torment thee' are those whom Jesus expelled from
Mary Magdalene in Mark 16: 9 and Luke 8: 2, and the two Marys
are also conflated in section [d], which according to Erdman's recon-

[29] S. Foster Damon compares Rom. 7: 7–8: 'Nay, I had not known sin, but by the
law: for I had not known lust, except the law had said, Thou shalt not covet. But sin,
taking occasion by the commandment, wrought in me all manner of concupiscence.
For without the law sin was dead.' See *William Blake: His Philosophy and Symbols*,
p. 296.

[30] *Four Zoas*, Night VIII, 115: 49, E 381; *Milton* 13: 24, E 107. Tolley, 'William
Blake's Use of the Bible', 174 notes the leprosy of Miriam (Numbers 12: 10), of Gehazi
(2 Kings 5: 27), and of Moses' hand (Exod. 4: 6). In the poem Blake sent to Thomas
Butts on 22 November 1802, 'The Moon . . . | Became leprous & white as snow'
(73–4, E 722), which is certainly an allusion to Gehazi's becoming 'a leper as white as
snow'.

[31] 'Blake's "Edens Flood" Again', 17.

struction was not to be used in the final text, where Blake says of Jesus that

> If he intended to take on Sin
> The Mother should have an Harlot been
> Just such a one as Magdalen
> With Seven Devils in her Pen
>
> (2–5)

Blake then inserted between 5 and 6, without a line break, the couplet 'Or were Jew Virgins still more Curst And more sucking devils nurst'.[32] As Jeanne Moskal remarks, 'This section wanders directionless with couplets on various stories and a gratuitous anti-Semitic remark', and that may be why Blake abandoned it and wrote section [f] instead.[33] The 'Fallen Fiends of Heavnly birth' whom Jesus addresses in [f] 50–6 are presumably the seven devils, but they suggest the angels who fell with Satan as well, and also 'the sons of God' who 'took wives of the daughters of men' in Gen. 6: 2, 4.[34] Blake represents these Fiends, once devoted to Love but now to Hate, as having 'driven away my trembling Dove' (52), who with her trembling recalls the Heaven and Earth of line 6.[35] Jesus' prediction that 'You shall bow before her feet | You shall lick the dust for Meat' (53–4) assigns the Fiends the punishment of the serpent in Gen. 3: 14–15.[36] This makes it seem as if the love apparently represented by Mary will triumph, but her answer to the question as to whether it was 'love or Dark Deceit' complicates the issue. Since it was 'dark deceit to earn my Bread' (60), it was not love at all, and it gives the Fiends an opportunity to

---

[32] See *Notebook*, p. 120.

[33] See Jeanne Moskal, *Blake, Ethics, and Forgiveness* (Tuscaloosa, Ala.: University of Alabama Press, 1994), p. 44.

[34] The latter is suggested by Helms, 'The Genesis of *The Everlasting Gospel*', 139.

[35] Tolley ('Blake's "Edens Flood" Again', 12) compares Hosea 11: 11: 'They shall tremble as a bird out of Egypt, and as a dove out of the land of Assyria . . .' and also William Cowper's Olney Hymn 'Walking with God':

> Return, O holy Dove, return,
>   Sweet messenger of rest;
> I hate the sins that made thee mourn
>   And drove thee from my breast. (ll. 13–16)

[36] Stevenson, *Complete Poems*, p. 864 n., points out that the actual words 'lick the dust' appear in Micah 7: 17.

> call a Shame & Sin
> Loves Temple that God dwelleth in
> And hide in secret hidden Shrine
> The Naked Human form divine
>
> (63–6)

Although Mary can affirm both St Paul's metaphor of the body as 'the temple of the Holy Ghost which is in you' (1 Cor. 6: 19) and the divinity of the naked human form, she represents these as it were from outside, from the position of one who knows they are true by *not* having exemplified them. Furthermore, her initial Sin was not the sexual act but her letting in the Seven Devils, which Blake links with her 'dark pretence to Chastity' (71). 'Thence Rose Secret Adulteries' is perhaps an unconscious echo of the theme of 'The Sick Rose' of *Songs of Experience*, where the 'dark secret love' of 'The invisible worm' (E 23) destroys the life of the Rose. Mary says that what appeared to be her love was 'my blasphemy', and she asks Jesus whether he can forgive it. Of course he can, as in John 8: 11: 'Neither do I condemn thee: go, and sin no more', and in accordance with Blake's declaration, in what may have been the starting point of the whole poem, that 'Forgiveness of Sins' was the only thing that separated Christianity from classical ethics (section [a], E 875). However, what began as a questioning of Jesus' chastity and by implication a declaration of the holiness of physical love has become completely transformed. Unlike Oothoon of *Visions of the Daughters of Albion* (1793), who proclaims the joy of 'happy copulation' (7: 1, E 50), Mary presents herself as a sinner in need of forgiveness.

The forgiveness of Jesus impels his Spectre, 'the shadowy Man', categorized in typical Spectre terms as 'An Ever devo[u]ring appetite', to roll away from Jesus' limbs 'to make them his prey' (81–3). 'Glittering with festering Venoms bright' (85), this Spectre is the Serpent who will be named in line 95, and he speaks with the voice of the crowd in the Gospels: 'Crying Crucify this cause of distress' (85).[37] The Spectre contines in the first person plural, embodying all the enemies of Jesus in the poem and contrasting their activities and his:

---

[37] Cf. Mark 15: 13: 'And they cried out again, Crucify him'; also Matt. 27: 23, Luke 23: 21, and John 19: 6, 15. 'Crucify' was a second thought on Blake's part—the original line was 'Crying Ive found hi[m]' (E 880).

All Mental Powers by Diseases we bind
But he heals the Deaf & the Dumb & the Blind
Whom God has afflicted for Secret Ends
He comforts & Heals & calls them Friends

(87–90)

This chorus of villains contrasts Jesus' healing ministry with its own power to bind 'All Mental Powers by Diseases' (87). For this alone Jesus deserves death. The plural then turns back to the singular at the Crucifixion, fully revealing the Serpent nature of the Spectre:

But when Jesus was Crucified
Then was perfected his glittring pride[38]
In three Nights he devourd his prey
And still he devours the Body of Clay
For Dust & Clay is the Serpents meat
Which never was made for Man to Eat

(91–6)

Jesus' triumph here is achieved at the cost of Blake's completely separating matter and spirit. The Serpent devours his material body— 'the Body of Clay' may allude to the Hebrew meaning of Adam as 'red earth'—while Jesus in some other form descends to Limbo and harrows Hell in the traditional 'three Nights' between death and resurrection. In Blake's eyes this outcome is appropriate, 'For Dust & Clay is the Serpents meat | Which never was made for Man to Eat'.[39] Line 95 echoes the end of Isaiah's millennial prophecy, where 'dust shall be the serpent's meat' (65: 25). However, Isaiah's great vision is of a reborn world populated by joyful human beings, while Blake's, so dissociated from the mortal body that he leaves it to the Serpent, is very close to the Gnostics' view of a complete separation of matter and spirit.

iii

Section [i], the next in Erdman's editorial arrangement, begins with a rhetorical parallel to the openings of the first two sections, 'Was Jesus gentle, or did he | Give any marks of Gentility?' 'Gentle' is not a word

---

[38] Cf. the Spectre of *Jerusalem* 64: 26, E 215.
[39] These last two lines of [f] were written over a drawing to the right of line 94 and led in to follow it. It was presumably before that that Blake wrote '94 lines' below 94.

applied to Jesus in the New Testament, but it is familiar through the
first line of the Wesleys' Hymn 72, part 1: 'Gentle Jesus, meek and
mild . . .'.[40] Such gentleness would be appropriate to the world of
Innocence, but hardly to the speaker of *The Everlasting Gospel*, who
has paid the Price of Experience. The first example of Jesus' lack of
'Gentility' (a word that from the first bears upper-class overtones;
OED, s.v.) is the same as that given in [k]—he 'left his parents in dis-
may', to be found three days later among the doctors in the Temple.
This time Jesus' admonition includes a denunciation of obedience.
'Ye understand not what I say', he says, 'And angry force me to obey'
(10–11). It appears as if it is the parents who are angry (which they
are not in Luke 2), but the adjective slides over to Jesus himself, anti-
cipating the anger he will display later in this section. 'Obedience is
a duty then', he sarcastically continues, 'And favour gains with God
& Men' (12–13).[41] The example of John the Baptist, whom Satan
declares to have died because of disobedience, follows. It has been
suggested that Blake is confused about this episode (in Matt. 14:
1–11), but it is more likely that he regards John the Baptist's denun-
ciation of Herod's having married his sister-in-law as a form of dis-
obedience to the powers of this world and therefore to Satan.[42] 'But
you can turn the stones to bread', Satan tells Jesus (18),[43] alluding to
Matt. 4: 3: 'And when the tempter came to him, he said, If thou be
the Son of God, command that these stones be made bread' (cf.
Luke 4: 3). Blake was interested in this passage because it exemplified
for him the fallacy of demanding faith by miracle. 'Come hither
into the desart & turn these Stones to Bread', says the Spectre in
Jerusalem; 'Vain foolish Man! Wilt thou believe without Exper-
minent?' (54: 21–2, E 204). In *Paradise Regained*, Milton's Satan,
having assumed the disguise of 'an aged man in Rural Weeds'
(1: 314), says:

---

[40] See *The Poetical Works of John and Charles Wesley*, ed. G. Osborn (13 vols.,
London: Wesleyan-Methodist Conference, 1870), vi. 441, Part 1, line 1. This hymn
was first published in 1742.

[41] Keynes's quotation marks (*Complete Writings*, p. 748) give only lines 10–11 to
Jesus, but I agree with Stevenson (*Complete Poems*, p. 863) that 12–13 belong to this
speech as well.

[42] For the former view, see Helms, 'The Genesis of *The Everlasting Gospel*', 145.

[43] Helms is certainly correct in his assertions that 'this entire scene bears the stamp
of hasty writing', and that no connection is established 'between John's bleeding and
Jesus' ability to turn stones into bread'. This line, which like most others bears no end

But if thou be the Son of God, Command
That out of these hard stones be made thee bread;
So shalt thou save thyself and us relieve
With Food . . .

(1: 342–5)

In *The First Temptation* (Butlin 544.2, Fitzwilliam Museum), Blake
pictures Satan pointing downward to the stones and Jesus pointing
upward, in illustration of the reply of Milton's Jesus: 'man lives not
by Bread only, but each Word | Proceeding from the Mouth of God
. . .' (1: 348–9). The Second Temptation is elided in *The Everlast-
ing Gospel*, and Satan goes rapidly on to the third, offering Jesus
the 'Glories' that king and priest will confer on him if he will obey
Caiaphas, sacrifice to Herod, and 'be | Obedient fall down worship
me' (24–5). Having already denied obedience to his parents, Jesus is,
we know, not going to accept; but his response is far different in tone
than the comparatively restrained refusals he gives in the Gospels
and in Milton.

Following line 24 of [i] Blake presents the wrathful Jesus.

Thunders & lightnings broke around
And Jesus voice in thunders sound
Thus I sieze the Spiritual Prey
Ye smiters with disease make way
I come your King & God to sieze
Is God a Smiter with disease

(25–30)

Smiting with disease (in contrast to Jesus' healing) is frequently
employed by Blake as symbolizing oppression, as where the plagues
of Albions Angel attack America in *America* 14. There is ample
precedent in the Old Testament for God as a smiter with disease, the
most powerful being the plagues of Egypt. This aspect of the Old
Testament God—for that Blake recognized other aspects we will see
in *The Ghost of Abel*—is the being whom Blake calls 'the God of this
World', an expression he probably derived from 2 Cor. 4: 3–4:

punctuation in Blake's manuscript, is given a question mark by Stevenson (*Complete
Poems*, p. 863), making it more appropriate to the idea of temptation. However,
there is no apparent reason for the inversion of the order of 'you' and 'can', as the
rhythm would not be affected. Keynes (*Complete Writings*, p. 749) supplies a
period.

But if our gospel be hid, it is hid to them that are lost:
  In whom the god of this world hath blinded the minds of them which believe not, lest the light of the glorious gospel of Christ, who is the image of God, should shine unto them.

Despite the rage of the God of this world (31), Jesus

> . . . bound Old Satan in his Chain
> And bursting forth his furious ire
> Became a Chariot of fire
>
> (32–4)

Chaining Satan is a task performed by an angel in Rev. 20: 2 as a prelude to the Millennium, but here it is performed by Jesus himself. The metaphor that follows is an audacious one: Elijah is translated to heaven by 'a chariot of fire' in 2 Kings 2: 11, Milton described Jesus' 'fierce Chariot' with its 'burning Wheels' in *Paradise Lost* 6: 829–33, and Blake cried 'Bring me my Chariot of fire!' in *Milton* 1 (E 95); but here Jesus himself 'Became a Chariot of fire', and his defeated adversary, Satan, 'Dragd at his Chariot wheels' (43). This is a parallel to the kind of literal situation that Blake deplored in *The Iliad*, Achilles' chariot dragging Hector's body around the walls of Troy,[44] but it is 'Spiritual War' (42), not Corporeal. The same displacement from the external to the internal occurs in Blake's rendition of Christ's scourging the money-changers from the Temple in John 2: 13–16 (cf. Matt. 12): 'He scourgd the Merchant Canaanite | From out the Temple of his Mind' (48–9). The expulsion of the money-changers becomes part of a psychomachia in which Jesus purges himself of the greed they represent. The binding of Satan is likewise internalized as Jesus 'in his Body tight does bind | Satan & all his Hellish Crew' (50–1). In an ironical reversal of the Gospel narrative,

> . . . thus with wrath he did subdue
> The Serpent Bulk of Natures dross
> Till he had naild it to the Cross
>
> (52–4)

Milton's Michael, as David Fuller points out, in giving Adam a foreknowledge of the Crucifixion of Jesus, adds:

---

[44] As suggested by Hazard Adams, *William Blake: A Reading of the Shorter Poems* (Seattle: University of Washington Press, 1963), p. 196.

> But to the Cross he nails thy Enemies,
> The Law that is against thee, and the sins
> Of all mankind . . .[45]

The section ends, ironically:

> He took on Sin in the Virgins Womb
> And put it off on the Cross & Tomb
> To be Worshipd by the Church of Rome
>
> (55–7)

The last line is a deliberately anticlimactic comedown, reinforced by the triplet culminating in a half-rhyme, and in meaning comparable to Christians' worship of a 'Dead Corpse' in 'For the Sexes' (7, E 259).

iv

The last part of the text proper as Erdman reconstructs it, [e], comprises, with the exception of two marginal comments by Blake, seven couplets. Predicated on a series of antitheses, these provide a witty conclusion to the poem. Abandoning the 'Was Jesus —' structure that opened the three preceding units, Blake begins:

> The Vision of Christ that Thou doest see
> Is my Visions Greatest Enemy
>
> (1–2)

But who is 'Thou'? The next couplet makes it clear that the reference is not to the reader in general, but to a special kind of reader, the Jew:

> Thine has a great hook nose like thine
> Mine has a snub nose like to mine

By defining the Jew as his Contrary (or Negation?), Blake reverts to a stereotype he had employed before.[46] As early as 'A Song of Liberty' in *The Marriage of Heaven and Hell* (1790), Blake calls 'O Jew, leave counting gold! return to thy oil and wine', intimating that although modern Jews are misers and money-lenders, Jews were

---

[45] *Paradise Lost*, 12: 415–17; see Fuller in *William Blake: Selected Poetry and Prose*, p. 352 n. As Fuller remarks, in his illustrations of this passage, *Michael Foretells the Crucifixion* (e.g. Huntington Library and Art Gallery, Butlin 529.11), Blake shows both Jesus and the serpent nailed to the Cross.

[46] On this general subject, see Karen Shabetai, 'The Question of Blake's Hostility Toward the Jews', *ELH* 63/1 (1996): 139–52. Shabetai does not, however, discuss *The Everlasting Gospel*.

different when every man sat under his own vine and fig-tree. Elsewhere, however, Blake has much to say against the ancient Hebrews as well, and the statement in the address 'To the Jews' in *Jersualem* 27 that 'If Humility is Christianity; you O Jews are the true Christians' (E 174) is hardly complimentary in view of Blake's condemnation of humility. And in section [d] of *The Everlasting Gospel* (which is not considered by Erdman to be part of Blake's attempt at a final text), Caiaphas is made to say:

> He turnd the Devils into Swine
> That he might tempt the Jews to Dine
> Since when a Pig has got a look
> That for a Jew may be mistook[.]
>
> (28–31, E 877)

Blake seems to have realized, before abandoning the entire section, that it would be out of character for the Temple high priest to be an anti-Semite. Of course these lines, along with section [e], remained in Blake's Notebook, and there can be little doubt that Blake wished no harm to the Jews themselves, although he was capable of giving expression to deplorable anti-Semitic stereotypes. Lines 3–4 of [e] are often compared to a statement in Blake's Notebook: 'I always thought Jesus Christ was a Snubby or I should not have worshipd him if I had thought he had been one of those long spindle nosed rascals' (E 695). But a spindle is long and thin, though it may be rounded at the very end; it is therefore not the shape of the stereotypically Jewish 'great hook nose'. (Pinocchio's nose might be described as 'spindly'.) The self-reflective irony of the Notebook entry displays genuine wit lacking in the *Everlasting Gospel* lines.

Blake goes on in lines 5–6 to reject liberal Christianity such as that taught by the Unitarians—'Thine is the Friend of All Mankind'—for a proto-Kierkegaardian one—'Mine speaks in parables to the Blind'; and the radical oppositions go on with 'Thine loves the same world that mine hates | Thy heaven doors are my hell gates' (7–8). These irreconcilable differences continue with the examples of Socrates, a figure with whom Blake identified,[47] and his accuser Meletus. Blake

[47] When asked by Henry Crabb Robinson what resemblance he supposed there was between his Spirit and the Spirit of Socrates, Blake replied 'The same as between our countenances' (*BR*, p. 310, 10 December 1825), and continued 'I was Socrates', and then corrected this to 'A sort of brother'. Robinson himself thought Blake had 'a Socratic countenance' (*BR*, p. 309); as Damon points out, 'they were both "snubbies" ' (*Blake Dictionary*, p. 376).

made Meletus part of the triple Accuser pictured in *Jerusalem* 95,
with the inscription 'Anytus | Melitus | & Lycon | thought Socrates a
Very Pernicious Man | So Caiphas thought Jesus'. And Caiphas
comes next in *The Everlasting Gospel* as well, with 'And Caiphas
was in his own mind | A benefactor of Mankind' (11–12). The last
antithesis of this highly antithetical poem employs the colours of the
printed page to express the unbridgeable gap between the 'I' and the
'thou': 'Both read the Bible day & night | But thou readst black where
I read white.'

The Ghost of Abel

If *The Everlasting Gospel* represents the 'Manichaean' aspect of the
late Blake, *The Ghost of Abel* expresses his urge to reconcile seem-
ingly opposed aspects of the divine. Blake may have realized at the
time that this was to be his last work in illuminated printing. At the
very bottom of the second and last plate, he asserted the continuity
of his illuminated books by linking *Abel* with his very first, *All
Religions Are One*, with the line '1822 W Blake's Original Stereotype
was 1788'.[1] He cast this poem, for the first time since the dramatic
pieces in *Poetical Sketches* of 1783 (E 423–40), in the form of a play.
It may be that his decision to do this was stimulated by Blake's play-
going with John Linnell. On 27 March 1821, they went to the Drury
Lane Theatre to see *Pizarro* by R. B. Sheridan after Kotzebue, and
Thérèse, the Orphan of Geneva by J. H. Payne with music by Horn;
on 8 June to *Dirce, or the Fatal Urn*, an opera based on Metastasio's
Demofoonte, with music by Horn; followed by *The Midnight Hour*,
a farce translated from French; and in November 1821 they saw
John Dryden and Nat Lee's *Oedipus*.[2] One cannot imagine *The
Ghost of Abel* at Drury Lane, but it nevertheless has something of the
'feel' of a play. It opens with a four-line prologue, and continues with
a stage direction that is followed in the course of the poem by seven
more, one of which indicates a sound effect ('*Thunders*' at 2: 19).
The concluding lines are a 'Chorus',[3] after which '*The Curtain falls*'

---

[1] An etched plate is not, properly speaking, a stereotype, but Blake also refers to his
'types' in *Jerusalem* 3: 11, E 145.

[2] See Keynes, 'Blake and John Linnell', *Blake Studies*, pp. 216–17; and G. E.
Bentley, Jr., *Blake Records Supplement* (Oxford: Clarendon Press, 1988), pp. 77–9.

[3] It has been pointed out that the Dryden and Lee *Oedipus* that Blake attended with
Linnell ends with a chorus. See Essick and Viscomi, p. 262.

(E 272). There are three spatial levels, with Jehovah standing above, Adam and Eve on the ground, and Satan rising from Abel's grave as through a trapdoor. Although not intended for performance as a play, *The Ghost of Abel* is meant to be imagined as one.

The entire story of Cain and Abel is told in the first sixteen verses of Genesis 4. Eve's elder son Cain is a tiller of the ground, her younger, Abel, a keeper of sheep. They sacrifice, respectively, fruit of the ground and firstlings of the flock; Abel's offering is accepted, and Cain's is not.

And Cain talked with Abel his brother: and it came to pass, when they were in the field, that Cain rose up against Abel his brother, and slew him.

And the Lord said unto Cain, Where is Abel thy brother? And he said, I know not: Am I my brother's keeper?

And he said, What hast thou done? the voice of thy brother's blood crieth unto me from the ground.

And now art thou cursed from the earth, which hath opened her mouth to receive thy brother's blood from thy hand;

When thou tillest the ground, it shall not henceforth yield unto thee her strength; a fugitive and a vagabond shalt thou be in the earth.

And Cain said unto the Lord, My punishment is greater than I can bear.

Behold, thou hast driven me out this day from the face of the earth; and from thy face shall I be hid; and I shall be a fugitive and a vagabond in the earth; and it shall come to pass, that every one that findeth me shall slay me.

And the Lord said unto him, Therefore whosoever slayeth Cain, vengeance shall be taken on him sevenfold. And the Lord set a mark upon Cain, lest any finding him should kill him.

And Cain went out from the presence of the Lord, and dwelt in the land of Nod, on the east of Eden. (8–16)

This is the entire biblical story. All other details belong to artistic and literary creations, among which is the one to which Blake's *Ghost of Abel* responded—Lord Byron's *Cain, A Mystery* (1821). However, there was in Blake's time an earlier, famous literary treatment of the story, one which was almost certainly known to Blake. The Swiss artist and poet Salomon Gessner first published his *Der Tod Abels* in 1760, and it was first translated into English by Mary Collyer in 1761, with the author's first name Anglicized as Solomon. In her Translator's Preface Collyer observes that it is written 'in a kind of loose poetry, unshackled by the tagging of rhymes, or counting of syllables'.[4] This would have appealed to a poet who considered

---

[4] *The Death of Abel in Five Books* (3rd edn., London, 1762), p. xxiii.

even blank verse to be 'derived from the modern bondage of Rhyming' (*Jerusalem* 3 prose; E 145). According to the *Gentleman's Magazine*, Gessner's '*Death of Abel* has made his name famous throughout Europe'.[5] In 1814 the *Quarterly Review* declared 'No book of foreign growth has ever become so popular as *The Death of Abel.* . . . It has been repeatedly printed at country presses, with worn types and on coarse paper; and it is found at country fairs, and in the little shops of country towns almost as certainly as the *Pilgrim's Progress* and *Robinson Crusoe*.'[6] Moreover, Gessner was a friend of Henry Fuseli's, who admired his work. In an edition of *The Death of Abel* of 1802, the anonymous 'Translator's Preface' asserts 'Mr. Fuselin [*sic*], His countryman, in his "Historical Essay on the Painters, Engravers, Architects, and Sculptors, who have done honour to Switzerland," gives a distinguished place to Gessner, though then alive'.[7] This edition includes illustrations by Blake's friend Thomas Stothard, at least four of which were engraved by Robert Hartley Cromek, whom Blake was not to meet until 1805 but who was a friend of John Flaxman's. Stothard also illustrated *The Death of Abel in Five Books*, published by T. Heptinstall, London, in 1797. The plate (engraved by Blackberd) facing page 21 is captioned 'Speak Adam is this Death!' These are Eve's words upon finding a dead bird.[8] In *The Ghost of Abel*, Adam, beside the body of Abel, asks Jehovah 'Is this Death?' (1: 2, E 271). The digging of Abel's grave and his burial are prominently featured in both Gessner and Blake, but not even mentioned by Byron. Gessner even seems to imagine a sequel very like *The Ghost of Abel* when his Cain says 'If ever sleep shall seal my languid eyes, horror and fear will chase it from my brow, in fancy I shall behold my murdered brother, I shall see his mangled head, his blood-stained form' (i. 155). Most important, however, the theme of God's mercy—Jehovah's 'Covenant of the Forgiveness of Sins' in Blake's *Abel* (2: 24), completely without interest to Byron—is also an element of Gessner's work, in which an angel reports God's words 'I will not turn my face

---

[5] *Gentleman's Magazine*, 46 (1776): 80.

[6] Cited by Bertha Reed, *The Influence of Solomon Gessner upon English Literature* (Philadelphia: Americana Germanica Press, 1905), p. 116.

[7] *The Works of Solomon Gessner translated from the German with some account of His Life and Writings* (3 vols., Liverpool: Cadell & Davies, 1802), i, p. viii. Further references to this edition will generally be given parenthetically in the text. The *Death of Abel* occupies most of volume i (pp. 1–170); the rest (pp. 171–99) is devoted to Gessner's *Letter on Landscape Painting*, addressed to Fuseli.

[8] See *Works of Solomon Gessner*, i. 36.

from the sinner; the earth shall bear witness of my mercy' (i. 46). In these respects, though Gessner's sentimentalism is alien to Blake, *The Ghost of Abel* has more in common with *The Death of Abel* than it does with *Cain.*

Why did Blake address his *Ghost of Abel* to Byron at all? *Cain, A Mystery* had been published just the previous year, and it had occasioned a great deal of public comment, most of it condemnatory, but this alone cannot account for Blake's sole published reference to a living poet. How much of *Cain* he read, we do not know, but if we take a Blake's-eye view of Byron's 'Mystery', we may imagine what would most have drawn his interest. Byron's Cain is of course a powerfully drawn character, but there is little about him to have drawn Blake. His self-pitying longing for 'those | Gardens which are my just inheritance' (I. i. 86–7) would elicit no sympathy from Blake, and neither would his grudge against Adam for depriving him of them. 'Many persons such as Paine & Voltaire', Blake wrote in *A Vision of the Last Judgment*, 'say we will not Converse concerning Good & Evil we will live in Paradise & Liberty You may do so in Spirit but not in the ⟨Mortal⟩ Body as you pretend till after the Last Judgment' (E 564). As for Lucifer, Blake would no doubt have recognized as Urizenic the God he characterizes:

> But let him
> Sit on his vast and solitary throne,
> Creating worlds, to make eternity
> Less burthensome, to his immense existence
> And unparticipated solitude!⁹

However, Blake would have been unimpressed by Lucifer's grandiose claim to be one of those

> Souls who dare look the Omipotent tyrant in
> His everlasting face, and tell him, that
> His evil is not good!
>
> (I. i. 137–9)

'You might as well quote Satans blasphemies from Milton & give them as Miltons Opinions,' Blake had written earlier.¹⁰ Nor would

---

⁹ See Byron, *The Complete Poetical Works*, ed. Jerome J. McGann and Barry Weller (Oxford: Clarendon Press, 1991), vi. 237, Act I, scene i, ll. 147–51. Further references to *Cain* will be to this edition, by act, scene, and line numbers.

¹⁰ Annotations to Swedenborg's *Heaven and Hell*, E 601. Byron would make a similar argument in his own defence, though perhaps less ingenuously.

the cosmic theatrics of Act II have been likely to impress Blake. 'As to that false appearance which appears to the reasoner, | As of a Globe rolling thro Voidness, it is a delusion of Ulro' (*Milton* 29: 15–16, E 127). We can imagine Blake as more sympathetic to Cain's ironic account of his father's moralizing:

> I lately saw
> A lamb stung by a reptile: the poor suckling
> Lay foaming on the earth . . .
>
> .   .   .   .
>
> My father pluck'd some herbs, and laid them to
> The wound: and by degrees the wretch
> Resumed its careless life . . .
>
> (II. ii. 289–91, 292–4)

When Adam says 'Behold my son! . . . how from evil | Springs good!' (298–9), Cain thinks:

> . . . that 'twere
> A better portion for the animal
> Never to have been *stung at all*, than to
> Purchase renewal of its little life
> With agonies unutterable, though
> Dispell'd by antidotes.
>
> (300–5)

This is much in the spirit of Blake's remark in *A Vision of the Last Judgment* that 'First God Almighty comes with a Thump on the Head Then Jesus Christ comes with a balm to heal it' (E 565), though Blake's belief in the balm was real enough. Blake might also have relished Byron's portrayal of the meat-loving God who rejects Cain's offered fruits, along with his prayer

> . . . If a shrine without victim,
> And altar without gore may win thy favour,
> Look on it!
>
> (III. i. 266–8)

Blake would surely have been repelled by Eve's curse on Cain, with its vision of a never-ending cycle of murder 'till his children do by him | As he did by his brother!' (424–5), and would have regarded its cause as the failure of the living to forgive sin, though Cain thinks the dead Abel 'wilt forgive him, whom his God | Can ne'er forgive, nor his own soul' (532–3). At least part of Blake's motive in *The Ghost of Abel* is to supply what he sees as missing from Byron's universe.

In a passage of the Preface to *Cain* that was not published during Blake's lifetime, Byron wrote 'I am prepared to be accused of Manicheism—or some other hard name ending in "*ism*" which make[s] a formidable figure and awful sound . . .'.[11] A frequent critical response to Byron's *Cain*, though the word 'Manichaean' may not have been used, was the accusation of blasphemy.[12] *The Gentleman's Magazine* for December 1821 said it was full of 'Hideous Blasphemy', and in *Blackwood's Edinburgh Magazine* for January 1822 J. G. Lockhart wrote (anonymously) that *Cain* was 'a wicked and blasphemous performance'.[13] *The Eclectic Review* for May 1822 also called Byron 'a blasphemer';[14] *The Literary Gazette* for December 1821 asserted that 'A more direct, more dangerous, or more frightful production than this miscalled Mystery, it has never been our lot to encounter'.[15] In December 1821 the Reverend Henry Todd[16] published, under the name 'Oxoniensis', the longest of all the attacks on *Cain*, declaring that it was full of 'moral poisons' and 'blasphemous impieties'. Byron's 'Mystery' was widely regarded as subversive of both Church and State. Blake can hardly have been unaware of this reaction. What would have been his attitude toward Byron's sceptical view of religion? We can have some idea from Blake's conversation with Henry Crabb Robinson on the subject of Voltaire on 18 February 1826. As we have seen, Blake strongly disagreed with Voltaire's and Paine's views. Nevertheless, Blake told Robinson: 'I have had much intercourse with Voltaire and he said to me ["]I blasphemed the Son of Man and it shall be forgiven me[.] But *they* [the enemies of V.] blasphemed the Holy Ghost in me and shall not be forgiven them—["]'.[17] As for Paine, Blake wrote in response to Bishop Robert Watson's *Apology for the Bible*, 'let the Bishop

---

[11] *Complete Poetical Works*, vi. 229.

[12] On the contemporary reviews, see Truman Guy Steffan, *Lord Byron's Cain: Twelve Essays and a Text with Variants and Annotations* (Austin: University of Texas Press, 1968), pp. 336–426. Since, as Steffan points out, these reviews often reprinted long excerpts from the work at hand, 'varying from one-fifth to almost a third of the play' (p. 335), if he read one of the reviews, Blake could have also read a substantial part of the play itself. See also Essick and Viscomi, p. 223.

[13] Steffan, *Lord Byron's Cain*, pp. 339 and 356.

[14] Ibid., pp. 374, 337.   [15] Ibid., p. 337.

[16] Todd's *Remonstrance Addressed to Mr. Murray* bears the date 1822, but for its date of publication and other details, see Steffan, *Lord Byron's Cain*, pp. 383–4.

[17] *BR*, p. 322.

prove that he has not spoken against the Holy Ghost who in Paine strives with Christendom as in Christ he strove with the Jews' (E 614). Byron was famous as a defender of liberty and an opponent of empire. His maiden speech in the Lords was in opposition to capital punishment for frame-breaking. He had excoriated Castlereagh for his bloody policy in Ireland after the uprising of 1798, and he had condemned the tyranny of Napoleon. He denounced the political stasis of Europe after the Congress of Vienna. For all these reasons, and more, Blake would surely have regarded Byron, no matter how much he sapped a solemn creed with solemn sneer, as a prophetic spirit. However, Byron also believed in retribution, as expressed in the famous 'foregiveness curse' of *Childe Harold* IV. In dedicating and addressing *The Ghost of Abel* 'To LORD BYRON in the Wilderness' (E 270), Blake hopes to convert the author of *Cain* to the forgiveness of sins.

The subtitle of Blake's poem offers an alternative to Byron's as explained in the Preface to *Cain*: 'The following scenes are entitled "a Mystery," in conformity with the ancient title annexed to dramas on similar subjects, which were styled "Mysteries, or Moralities"'.[18] How much Byron—or Blake, for that matter—could have known about medieval drama is a matter for speculation. E. H. Coleridge, in the still invaluable notes to his edition of Byron, suggests that information could have been derived from Robert Dodsley's introduction to *A Select Collection of Old Plays*, from John Stevens's continuation of Sir William Dugdale's *Monasticon*, and from Thomas Warton's *History of English Poetry*.[19] A limited edition of two authentic Chester Plays from manuscripts owned by Frances Douce was published in 1818,[20] but it is doubtful whether Byron in Italy had the occasion (or Blake in London the means) to obtain it. What is certain is that, apart from its biblical subject, Byron's *Cain* has nothing in common with the Mysteries. Blake, in subtitling his poem 'A Revelation In the Visions of Jehovah | Seen by William Blake', is already correcting Byron. The latter claims affinity with a literary tradition; Blake claims direct experience—not Mystery but

---

[18] *Complete Poetical Works*, vi. 228.
[19] See *The Works of Lord Byron*, ed. Ernest Hartley Coleridge, *Poetry* (rev. edn., London: John Murray, 1901), v. 200. See also Philip W. Martin, *Byron, a Poet before His Public* (Cambridge: Cambridge University Press, 1982), pp. 164–8.
[20] *Chester Mysteries. De Deluvio Noe. De Occisione Innocentium*, ed. J. H. Markham (London: Roxburghe Club, 1818). Only fifty-six copies were printed.

Revelation, inevitably associated with the Apocalypse of St John. The assertion 'Seen by William Blake' may perhaps be modelled on the phrase 'as heard and seen' that Emanuel Swedenborg frequently used in his subtitles.[21] Like John of Patmos and like Swedenborg, Blake wants to declare the first-hand nature of his visionary experience. It may be said that this is in itself a literary genre, but even so it is one distinctly different from the genre of 'Mystery'.

Why 'in the Wilderness'?[22] Cain, of course, says 'now for the wilderness' (III. i. 544) before he exits, but the phrase is rich in adumbrations both in the Bible and in Blake's writings, and could have either a positive or negative charge. The 'wilderness' bears a special meaning in the Bible's spiritual topography, as Blake knew. It is the desert in which the Israelites wandered for forty years, in the course of which they built the Tabernacle; for example, in Num. 1: 1 'the LORD spake unto Moses in the wilderness of Sinai, in the tabernacle of the congregation, on the first day of the second month, in the second year after they were come out of the land of Egypt'. In the New Testament, the word first refers to John the Baptist. 'In those days came John the Baptist, preaching in the wilderness of Judaea . . . The voice of one crying in the wilderness, Prepare ye the way of the Lord, make his paths straight' (Matt. 3: 1, 3; cf. Mark 1: 3, Luke 3: 4, John 1: 23). Plate 1 of Blake's first illuminated book, *All Religions are One*, bears the image of John the Baptist and the legend 'The Voice of one crying in the Wilderness'.[23] The voice here is clearly Blake's, affirming the value of Poetic Genius and declaring that 'The Religions of all Nations' (pl. 8) derive from it. (Ironically, when R. H. Cromek wrote to Blake 'Believe me, yours is "*the voice of one crying in the wilderness!*" ',[24] he was saying something that Blake already believed.) It was in the wilderness that Satan tempted Jesus three

---

[21] For example, *A Treatise concerning Heaven and Hell, and of the Wonderful Therein, as Heard and Seen, by Emanuel Swedenborg*, is the full title of the 1784 edition that Blake owned and annotated.

[22] For some views on this question, see S. Foster Damon, *A Blake Dictionary*, p. 153; Leslie Tannenbaum, 'Lord Byron in the Wilderness: Biblical Tradition in Byron's *Cain* and Blake's *The Ghost of Abel*', *Modern Philology*, 72 (1975): 351; Irene Tayler, 'Blake Meets Byron on April Fool's', *English Language Notes*, 16 (1978): 91–2; Essick and Viscomi, p. 295.

[23] See Blake, *The Early Illuminated Books*, ed. Morris Eaves, Robert N. Essick, and Joseph Viscomi (London: William Blake Trust/Tate Gallery, 1993), p. 44.

[24] See *The Letters of William Blake*, ed. Geoffrey Keynes (rev. edn., Cambridge, Mass.: Harvard University Press, 1968), p. 126.

times in Matt. 4. And in יה *& his two Sons* 'The Spoilers say Where are his Works That he did in the Wilderness' (E 274). The 'wilderness' is thus a waste place, but one that provides the background for sacred drama.

Byron is then addressed by Blake as if he were an Old Testament Prophet: 'What doest thou here Elijah?' The source of the question is 1 Kings 19, and it too should be taken in context.

But he himself went a day's journey into the wilderness, and came and sat down under a juniper tree: and he requested for himself that he might die; and said, It is enough; now, O Lord, take away my life; for I am not better than my fathers.

And as he lay and slept under a juniper tree, behold, then an angel touched him, and said unto him, Arise and eat.

And he looked, and, behold, there was a cake baken on the coals, and a cruse of water at his head. And he did eat and drink, and laid him down again.

And the angel of the Lord came again the second time, and touched him, and said, Arise and eat; because the journey is too great for thee.

And he arose, and did eat and drink, and went in the strength of that meat forty days and forty nights unto Horeb the mount of God.

And he came thither unto a cave, and lodged there; and, behold, the word of the Lord came to him, and he said unto him, What doest thou here, Elijah? (1 Kings 19: 4–9)

Elijah has a special importance to Blake. Seen 'on his fiery Chariot' in *A Vision of the Last Judgment*, 'he comprehends all the Prophetic Characters' (E 560). In *Jerusalem* the Friends of Albion 'gave their power to Los | Naming him the Spirit of Prophecy, calling him Elijah' (39. 30–1, E 187). In the passage in Kings, Elijah, like John after him, is in 'the wilderness'; but unlike John, he is for the moment abandoning his prophetic function. He is not a voice crying in the wilderness, but a man hiding in a cave. In the Old Testament account, the voice of the Lord comes to Elijah as 'a still small voice' and asks again: 'What doest thou here, Elijah?' (13). Impelled by the voice, Elijah goes out to begin the overthrow of the idolatrous King Ahab and Jezebel his queen.

Blake's initial question to Byron/Elijah is elucidated in the following one: 'Can a Poet doubt the Visions of Jehovah?' Clearly, he cannot. There follow five statements affirming the superiority of Imagination over nature, very much in the absolutist spirit of יה *&*

his two Sons, culminating with 'Imagination is Eternity' (E 270). Then comes the first, very interesting stage direction:

> Scene. A rocky Country. Eve fainted over the dead body
> of Abel which lays near a Grave. Adam kneels by her Jehovah
> stands above[25]

There is no grave or burial of Abel in Genesis. Nor are these to be found in Byron's *Cain,* where the body of Abel is last seen on the ground watched over by the newly widowed Zillah. But in Gessner's *Death of Abel* an angel conveys God's order: 'Adam! The Almighty commands thee to restore this mouldering body to the dust from which it sprang: commit it to the bosom of the earth' (i. 133). Soon we are told 'Adam was employed in preparing the grave' (i. 148), and then that 'Adam had now finished digging the grave' (i. 150). Blake's scene resembles Gessner's in this respect.[26] Blake had previously followed Gessner when he pictured the subject in his watercolour *The body of Abel found by Adam and Eve* (Butlin 664, Fogg Art Museum), which was one of the pictures Blake showed in his exhibition of 1809, its full title continuing: *Cain, who was about to bury it, fleeing from the face of his Parents.—A Drawing* (E 548). Both this picture and the striking version in tempera that Blake executed *c.*1826 (Butlin 806, Tate Gallery)[27] show the open grave with a spade lying next to it, with Eve lamenting over the body of Abel and Adam looking on in horror, as Cain runs away, enveloped in the flames of divine wrath. There is nothing like this either in Genesis or in *Cain, A Mystery,* but Gessner's Cain characterizes himself as 'pursued by hell . . .' (i. 157), and later exclaims 'Pursued by the wrath of my Creator, frantic with despair, I fly to hide me in the wilderness' (i. 164). The same scene is shown in a small replica of the watercolour (Butlin 666, Fitzwilliam Museum) that is thought by Butlin to be a copy by John Linnell, who noted that Blake brought a drawing of Cain and Abel to him on 11 September 1821, and that he began to copy it on 12 September and finished on 14 September. As we can see,

[25] Erdman prints these and other stage directions in italics, but as Blake used the same script for them as for the rest, I render them in roman.

[26] Bertha Reed observes that Blake's opening bears more resemblance to Gessner than to the Bible. See *The Influence of Solomon Gessner upon English Literature,* p. 110.

[27] William Vaughan suggests that both pictures were 'inspired by Gessner's poem'; see Vaughan, *German Romanticism and English Art* (New Haven and London: Yale University Press, 1979), p. 109.

Blake had been interested in the aftermath of the fratricide as an artistic subject long before *The Ghost of Abel*, and he and Linnell were involved with it not long before the illuminated book was created. In the latter, however, it is not possible to tell whether Cain dug the grave before fleeing, as the title of the watercolour tells us, or whether the gravedigger was Adam, as in Gessner's narrative.

The situation is thematically amplified by small designs in the upper third of the first plate, on either side of 'Seen by William Blake'. To the right, a vengeful God, arms outspread, pursues a fleeing Cain. To the left, a lion pursues a stag. The latter could be intended as parallel to the former, but Cain is hardly an innocent victim, and it more likely is an emblem of life in the postlapsarian world as figured in the murder of Abel. (Among the results of the Fall that Blake noted on the verso of his watercolour *The Fall of Man* (Butlin 641, Victoria and Albert Museum) are 'The Lion seizes the bull, the Tiger the Horse'.) After the first word spoken, by Jehovah— 'Adam!'—we see Cain with a knife running from the body of Abel, behind which large flames—no doubt from the sacrificial altar[28]— are visible. Adam, refusing to listen to Jehovah, asks 'Is this Death?' Immediately to the right of his question we see a looping serpent approaching a fruited bough—tempter and forbidden fruit. And just below the word 'Adam' is a vignette, one of three on this page, in which prelapsarian Adam and Eve stand naked beneath a tree drooping with fruit. This reminder of the lost paradise stands to the left of Adam's question: 'Is this thy Promise that the Womans Seed | Should bruise the Serpents head: Is this the Serpent? Ah!' (1: 3–4). Faced with the brute fact of Abel's murder, Eve too rejects the promised redemption: 'Is this the Promise of Jehovah! O it is all a vain delusion | This Death & this life & this Jehovah!' The promise to which both allude is of course part of God's curse on the serpent in Gen. 3: 15: 'And I will put enmity between thee and the woman, and between thy seed and her seed; it shall bruise thy head, and thou shalt bruise his heel.' If the prophecy lacks truth, then life is meaningless. Since Adam and Eve do not understand this, they must find their way to its

[28] Leslie Tannenbuam compares the design in *Milton* 12, where the figures are similar and the altar is shown between them, and he points out that 'Significantly to the left of the flames and above Jehovah's name is the inspirational falling star that we have seen in *Milton*, intended here as a contrast to the sacrifical fire'. See Tannenbaum, 'Blake and the Iconography of Cain', in *Blake in His Time*, ed. Robert N. Essick and Donald Pearce (Bloomington and London: University of Indiana Press, 1978), p. 28.

meaning through the appearance of what claims to be the ghost of Abel.

Its first words are of a nameless 'Voice [that] is heard coming on': 'O Earth cover not thou my Blood! cover not thou my my Blood' (1: 8). These words derive of course from the Lord's words to Cain: 'And now art thou cursed from the earth, which hath opened her mouth to receive thy brother's blood from thy hand.' The apparition's insistence upon revenge, so unlike the nature of the real Abel, gives it away:

> Among the Elohim a Human Victim I wander I am their House
> Prince of the Air & our dimensions compass Zenith & Nadir
> Vain is thy Covenant O Jehovah I am the Accuser & Avenger
> Of Blood O Earth Cover not thou the Blood of Abel
>
> (1: 10–13)

As we have seen in the Introduction, Henry Crabb Robinson noted that when he pointed out to Blake that God created the heaven and the earth, 'I was triumphantly told that this God was not Jehovah but the Elohim, and the doctrine of the Gnostics repeated with sufficient consistency to silence one so unlearned as myself' (*BR*, p. 545). This 'Gnostic' use of 'Elohim' is for the most part typical of Blake, but it will be revised later in *The Ghost of Abel*. The 'Prince of the Air' is Satan, as in Eph. 2: 2: 'in time past ye walked according to the course of this world, according to the prince of the power of the air, the spirit that now worketh in the children of disobedience'. The supposed Ghost maintains that the Satanic powers he encompasses embrace the entire material world, from zenith to nadir, as the fallen Zoas in *Milton*:

> Four Universes round the Universe of Los remain Chaotic
> Four intersecting Globes, & the Egg form'd World of Los
> In midst; stretching from Zenith to Nadir, in midst of Chaos.
>
> (34 [38]: 32–4, E 134)

To the left of the Ghost's lines is a tiny image of the recumbent Eve with the Ghost floating in the air above her.[29] Eve has not been

---

[29] This is also the view of Erdman, *Illuminated Blake*, p. 382; and of Essick and Viscomi, p. 30. Essick and Viscomi remark that this is one of the emblems derived from a sheet of pencil sketches (British Museum) on a sheet from *Designs to a Series of* [Hayley's] *Ballads* (1802), which they reproduce as Supplementary Illustration 2, p. 249.

deceived, saying 'Thou Visionary Phantasm thou art not the real Abel' (1: 9). The Ghost insists on vengeance: 'Life for Life! Life for Life!' This is the doctrine Jehovah himself pronounced in Exod. 21: 23–5:

> And if any mischief follow, then thou shalt give life for life,
> Eye for eye, tooth for tooth, hand for hand, foot for foot,
> Burning for burning, wound for wound, stripe for stripe.

However, it is Blake's motive to have God abrogate this law for a new Covenant that will be introduced at the end of the poem.

The Ghost created by Blake has a curious resemblance to one in a work that Blake could not have read. Samuel Taylor Coleridge wrote part of *The Wanderings of Cain* in 1797, and he began work on a continuation in 1807; but as nothing of it was published until 1828,[30] Blake could not have read it. As Coleridge's works had a way of circulating orally and in manuscript, it is just possible that Blake may have known something of it, but any parallels may also be owing to the general influence of Gessner on both. When Coleridge's Cain encounters 'the Shape that was like Abel' (2: 113–14), the Shape shrieks, rends its garments, and throws itself on the ground.

> But Cain said—'Didst thou not find favour in the eyes of the Lord thy God?'
> —The Shape answered, 'The Lord is God of the living only, the Dead have another God. . . . Wretched shall they be all the days of their mortal life,' exclaimed the Shape, 'who sacrifice worthy and acceptable sacrifices to the God of the dead; but after death their toil ceaseth.' (2: 116–22)

Both ghosts are portrayed as suffering horribly and their Otherness is emphasized by their strange language. In what Coleridge intended as Part III, moreover, 'Abel' turns out to be an evil impostor, just as he does in Blake's poem. Coleridge has him take Cain and his son into 'an immense meadow' and there 'persuades Cain to offer sacrifice for himself & his son Enoch by [letting *del.*] cutting his Child's arm & letting the blood fall from it'.

Cain is about to do it when Abel himself [with *del.*] in his Angelic

---

[30] My source of Coleridge texts and dates is the *Poetical Works*, ed. J. C. C. Mays (3 vols., Princeton: Princeton University Press, 2001). The 'reading texts' are to be found in vol. i, with that for *The Wanderings of Cain* in part 1, pp. 361–5. The variorum texts are contained in vol. ii, with that for *The Wanderings of Cain* in part 1, pp. 492–504.

appearance. attended by Michael is seen [in *del.*] the heavens whence they sail slowly down. Abel addresses Cain with terror warning him not to offer up his innocent child. The Evil spirit throws off the countenance of Abel. & assumes his own shape, flies off pursuing a flying battle with Michael, & Abel carries off the Child.[31]

The idea of a demonic Abel and a heavenly Abel is also a remarkable coincidence. The great difference between the two is of course that Cain does not appear at all in Blake's *Ghost of Abel*.

After Blake's false Abel demands blood, Jehovah says, in line with Gen. 4: 15, that 'He who shall take Cains life must also Die O Abel' (1: 15). Both Gessner (i. 119) and Byron (III. i. 496–7) have an angel make the pronouncement, but Blake follows Genesis in having Jehovah act without intermediacy here. At this point Blake's Adam attempts to dismiss all they have seen and heard as 'all a Vain delusion of the all creative Imagination' (1: 17), much as near the beginning of *Jerusalem* Albion calls the Saviour 'Phantom of the over heated brain!' (4: 24, E 146). Then a brilliant effect occurs in the middle of Adam's speech.

> Eve come away & let us not believe these vain delusions
> Abel is dead & Cain slew him! We shall also Die a Death
> And then! what then? be as poor Abel a Thought: or as
> This! O what shall I call thee Form Divine! Father of Mercies
> That appearest to my Spiritual Vision: Eve seest thou also.
>
> (1: 18–22)[32]

After 'or as' Adam is suddenly overcome by spiritual vision. (On the literal plane, we should note that Adam has twice refused to *hear* Jehovah, and calls him 'thou Spiritual Voice'; the audience is to imagine that Adam does not *see* Jehovah until this moment, when he finds him within.) Eve responds: 'I see him plainly with my Minds Eye. I see also Abel living: | Tho terribly afflicted as We also are' (1: 23–4). This is not to be found in the Bible, nor of course in Byron, but in *The Death of Abel* Abel's widow, Thirza, says: 'I have seen him, arrayed in celestial splendour he appeared before me: the majesty of Heaven sat on his radiant brow, and yet his eyes beamed with their wonted tenderness for me' (i. 150). To the left of Adam's speech,

---

[31] *Poetical Works*, ii. 496.

[32] Is it mere coincidence that in canto I of *Don Juan*, published in 1819, Byron writes: '. . . we die, you know, *and then*— | *What then?*—I do not know, no more do you—' (lines 1064–5, emphasis mine)? See *Complete Poetical Works*, ed. McGann, v. 51.

between the 'Adam' of line 17 and the 'Eve' of line 23, we see another vignette of Adam and Eve. They are still naked beneath the tree, but it is now bare of fruit, and, though their hands are linked, they appear to be moving in opposite directions. Presumably the eating of the forbidden fruit has taken place some time since the scene depicted earlier, and we now see the first result of the Fall. In the text, Eve's speech continues onto the second plate in magnificent words that show the way out of their fallen state: 'were it not better to believe Vision | With all our might & strength tho' we are fallen & lost' (2: 1–2).

Adam and Eve kneel before Jehovah's feet, but the Ghost cannot abide 'the Sacrifices of Eternity', which, alluding to Psalm 34: 18,[33] he calls 'a Broken Spirit | And a Contrite Heart' (2: 4–5). More and more revealing his true nature, the obdurate Ghost cries 'My desire is unto Cain | And He doth rule over Me' (2: 7–8). Although Cain is not literally present here, he inhabits the simulacrum of his victim's ghost. In a vignette to the left of this speech, a figure is seen in the running posture of Cain in Blake's pictures but reversed—i.e. toward the right and with his back to us—and pushing away a seated figure who may be female. This may be the Ghost repulsing Eve as he exits, although there are almost as many interpretations of this image as there are interpreters.[34] To the Ghost's demand for Sacrifice and Blood, Jehovah replies 'Lo I have given you a Lamb for an Atonement instead | Of the Transgres[s]or, or no Flesh or Spirit could ever Live' (2: 10–11). He is the obverse of the Urizen who saw 'That no flesh nor spirit could keep | His iron laws one moment'.[35] After a last cry, the Ghost 'sinks down into the Grave. from which arises Satan | Armed in glittering scales with a Crown & a Spear'. It is a stage effect analogous to the appearance of the armed head conjured up by the witches in *Macbeth*. No longer speaking through the victim's mask, Satan bellows like a stage villain: 'I will have Human Blood & not the blood of Bulls or Goats | And no Atonement . . .' (2: 13–14). Although denying Atonement, Satan goes on to predict what he does not understand: 'Thou shalt Thyself be sacrificed to Me thy God on Calvary' (18). In a vignette to the left of these lines, and

---

[33] As pointed out by Damon, *William Blake*, p. 476.

[34] Erdman also sees the figures as Cain and Eve (*Illuminated Blake*, p. 383); Tannenbaum sees Cain slaying Abel ('Iconography of Cain', p. 30); Essick and Viscomi suggest that the runner is 'Abel's soul', depicted as female, 'rejecting Jehovah' (p. 235).

[35] *The [First] Book of Urizen*, 23: 26, E 81.

between the word 'Satan' and the word 'Jehovah', are two naked fig-
ures, one in the air above the other, gesturing as if in conversation.
These are probably Satan and Jehovah, respectively.[36] In contrast to
Satan's speech, Jehovah's is calm and full of authority—reinforced
by the stage direction 'Thunders'—'Such is My Will'. Manifestly,
Jehovah agrees to be sacrificed, but his words have a twofold mean-
ing, referring as well to what follows them:

> that Thou Thyself go to Eternal Death
> In Self Annihilation even till Satan Self-subdud Put off Satan
> Into the Bottomless Abyss whose torment arises for ever & ever.

> (2: 19–21, E 272)

The last marginal vignette, to the left of these words, brings back the
elements of the first and third—Adam, Eve, and the tree—and adds
the serpent entwined around the tree trunk. This is a flashback to
what makes the future sacrifice necessary. The Chorus then enters to
point the moral.

Here Blake changes a conception he had occasionally employed
before. Usually (but not always) the word 'Elohim' has a negative
valence for him, as in *Elohim creating Adam*, and the same is true of
Jehovah, as in *Milton* 13: 24 'And Jehovah was leprous; loud he
call'd, stretching his hand to Eternity' (E 107). The combination of
the two names is also negative in *A Vision of the Last Judgment*,
where the 'Angel of the Divine Presence . . . is frequently called by
the name of Jehovah Elohim The I am of the Oaks of Albion' (E 559).
Yet in *Jerusalem* 61: 1–2, the two words together (no matter which
comes first) indicate a benevolent view of the Old Testament God:
'Behold: in the Visions of Elohim Jehovah, behold Joseph & Mary |
And be comforted O Jerusalem in the Visions of Jehovah Elohim' (E
211). This notion of a combined Jehovah Elohim is carried forward
into *The Ghost of Abel*. 'The Elohim of the Heathen swore
Vengeance for Sin!' exclaims the Chorus, 'Then Thou stoodst | Forth
O Elohim Jehovah' (2: 22–3). This combined figure is clothed in his
'Covenant of the Forgiveness of Sins' (24). The heathen Elohim are
not destroyed, however, but roll apart to their proper stations to
become the Cherubs over the Mercy Seat (itself an image that can

---

[36] As Erdman (*Illuminated Blake*, p. 233) and Essick and Viscomi (p. 236) agree.
Tannenbaum, however, sees 'Cain attempting to defend himself before God'
('Iconography of Cain', p. 30).

elsewhere have highly negative value for Blake), 'each in his station fixt in the Firmament by Peace Brotherhood and Love' (E 272) 'The Curtain falls' is the last line of text proper, but not the last words on the second page. Those are inscribed on the only comparatively large design in the booklet, in which 'The Voice of Abels | Blood' is pictured as swirling across the page from the anguished figure at our right, down to the ground (Fig. 29). There, prone over Abel's corpse, lies a despairing mourner wearing only what appears to be a skirt of fur. This figure has been variously identified as Adam, Cain, or Eve.[37] As its back is to us, we cannot see its features—but since the initial stage direction specifies 'Eve fainted over the dead body of Abel', Eve appears the likeliest candidate. The blood that emanates from Abel's 'Voice' is both the blood that Cain shed and the blood demanded by the Ghost. (Gessner's *Death of Abel*, it may be noted, has an intense emphasis on imagery of blood—for example, Cain exclaims 'I fly, but his blood pursues me: the purple torrent bathes my very footsteps. . . . Away, trembling feet! haste from the fast-pursuing blood. . . .—Drag me, ye faultering knees, sprinkled with a brother's blood', and 'I hear his dying groans! I see his streaming blood!'[38]) Tannenbaum calls attention to Heb. 12: 24: '[Ye are come] to Jesus the mediator of the new covenant, and to the blood of sprinkling, that speaketh better things than that of Abel.'[39] The 'better things' are of course redemption through the sacrifice of Jesus, promised by Blake's Jehovah in response to Satan. Nothing could be further from the view that Blake had expressed in *The Everlasting Gospel*.

What can explain the disparity of these doctrines? It cannot have been a sudden change of belief, for the 'Manichaean' view of *The Everlasting Gospel* is consistent with some of the statements in יה *& his two Sons* and, as we will see, with some of those in Blake's marginalia to Dr Thornton's translation of the Lord's Prayer. It is true that one poem was written in Blake's personal Notebook, while the other was etched and printed, but *The Ghost of Abel*, which exists in five known copies,[40] is not known to have been offered for sale and

---

[37] Damon (*William Blake*, p. 477) identifies it as Adam; Erdman (*Illuminated Blake*, p. 383) and W. H. Stevenson (*Complete Poems*, p. 872 n.) as Cain; Tannenbaum ('Iconography of Cain', p. 29) as either Adam or Cain; Essick and Viscomi (p. 236) as Eve.

[38] i. 118 and i. 121.

[39] Tannenbaum, 'Biblical Tradition', 361.

[40] See Bentley, *Blake Books*, p. 335; *Blake Books Supplement*, p. 80; and Essick and Viscomi, p. 239. Copy E consists of plate 1 only.

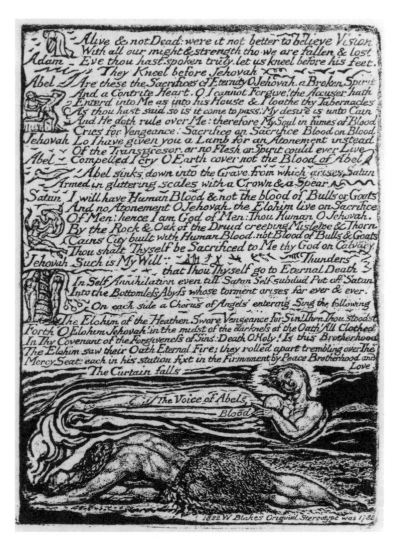

FIG. 29. William Blake, *The Ghost of Abel*, pl. 2. Relief
etching, 1822.

was probably given by Blake to friends (Linnell and Thomas Butts owned copies). This limited issue can hardly have caused Blake to revise his doctrines even were he tempted to do so. It is more likely that Blake, like many of us, was capable of holding contradictory attitudes at different times or even at the same time. For example Blake reportedly told his friend and patron the Swedenborgian C. A. Tulk 'that he had two different states, one in which he liked Swedenborg's writings and one in which he disliked them'. He then continued, no doubt in deference to his friend's convictions on the subject, that 'the second was a state of pride in himself', while 'The first was a state of humility, in which he received and accepted Swedenborg' (*BR*, p. 38). We may assume that Blake's 'two different states' applied to other subjects as well. No longer creating large symbolic structures, Blake was now freed, as it were, from his own 'System', free to be inconsistent. In *The Ghost of Abel*, a major theme is the unity of Jehovah and Jesus, as it would also be in plate 17 of the *Job* engravings.

Illustrations of the Book of Job

In Robert Frost's dramatic poem *A Masque of Reason*, Job's Wife says: 'It's God. | I'd know him by Blake's picture anywhere.'[1] Job's Wife speaks for many, for Blake's *Illustrations of the Book of Job* is a work known to large numbers of people who may be otherwise unfamiliar with Blake's art. Among Blake's very late works, it is as a whole the most powerful and the most completely realized. Confronting themes with which Blake was much occupied in other works of the period, it embodies them in a way more generally accessible to those outside his immediate circle, and the engravings show him at the height of his ability. If Blake succeeded no more than other interpreters in demonstrating a credible moral universe in the Book of Job—and this, of course, may have been far from his intention— he did achieve in this series a magnificently coherent work of art.

The *Illustrations of the Book of Job* constitute what is probably Blake's best-documented project.[2] Blake had previously executed

---

[1] *The Poetry of Robert Frost*, ed. Edward Connery Latham (New York: Henry Holt, 1979), ll. 17–18, p. 474.

[2] Unless otherwise indicated, the details in this summary are from the 'Documentary Record' by David Bindman and Barbara Bryant in David Bindman, Barbara Bryant, Robert N. Essick, Geoffrey Keynes, and Bo Ossian Lindberg, *William*

nineteen watercolours on the subject (Butlin 550.1–16, 18–20, Pierpont Morgan Library). In September 1821 Blake borrowed them back so that he could make a set for John Linnell. The two artists spent 8 and 10 September tracing the outlines, and Blake then took the Butts drawings home to return to their owner. The tracings became the basis for a second set of drawings produced by Blake for Linnell, twenty-one in number because Blake added watercolours on the subjects of Job's vision of the true God and Job and his three daughters.[3] At some point, generally thought to be after the completion of the Linnell drawings,[4] pictures on the same subjects were added to the Butts collection. In general, as Butlin remarks, the Linnell series shows more emphasis on subtleties of modelling rather than line, and is freer in handling, and the colours 'richer and often more dramatic'. On 23 March 1823 Blake and Linnell signed a Memorandum of Agreement according to which Blake would engrave for Linnell twenty plates 'from his own Designs of Job's Captivity' at the price of one hundred pounds, with Linnell to pay for the copperplates, and Blake to receive an additional hundred pounds out of the profits of the sale of the engravings 'as the receipts will admit of it'.[5] (Presumably either 17 or 20 was already in existence, and Blake added the other after the Memorandum had been drawn up and signed.) Blake began by making pencil drawings, one of which was not used, in reduced size in a notebook (now in the Fitzwilliam Museum). He started engraving the plates on 2 May 1823. On 4 and 5 March 1825 Blake and Linnell proved the plates, and Blake did some further work after the first proofs. A contract between Blake and Linnell was signed and dated 25 March 1825, which is also the date that Blake inscribed on every plate. However, we do not hear of the plates being printed until February 1826, and the labels for the set (Linnell optimistically had 500 printed) bear the date 'March 1826'. The printing history of the *Job* is summarized in

---

Blake's Illustrations of the Book of Job: The Engravings and Related Material with Essays, Catalogue of States and Printings, Commentary on the Plates and Documentary Record (London: William Blake Trust, 1987). This edition is hereafter cited as BTJ. Most of the factual data on the *Job* project can also be found in BR. As the 'Documentary Record' in BTJ is arranged according to date, I have not thought it necessary to provide page numbers in references from it.

[3] Butlin 551.1–21, Fogg Art Museum except for numbers 2 (private collection) and 20 (Lessing J. Rosenwald Collection, National Gallery of Art).

[4] See Butlin's entries for 550.17 and 550.20.   [5] BR, p. 277.

a letter sent by Linnell's son, John Linnell, Jr. to Bernard Quaritch on 6 May 1892:

The first printing for sale of the Job plates Mr Linnell had executed after the plates were finished and delivered to him by Blake in the latter part of 1825—at this date, after a very limited number of copies of the 'proofs'—the India and the French—had been taken, the word 'proof' was removed from the plates,—and 100 Copies of 'prints' were struck off—these completed the original printing, which was finished in time for the publication of the work in March 1826. Mr. Linnell then put the plates away, & they were never again used after this time until the year 1874. At this time my father wishing to have some prints of the Job to offer for sale (the original 100 [plain] copies having long since been exhausted), he had 100 copies printed from the plates upon India paper. These are the copies, 6 of which we forward[ed] to you yesterday.[6]

A total of 315 sets of Job were printed (*BR*, p. 590 n.); the price was three guineas for an ordinary copy, five for a proof copy, six for an India paper proof copy. On 14 July 1826 Linnell paid Blake 150 pounds for the plates and copyright.

Sales of the *Job* began more than two years before its publication.[7] Among the pre-publication subscribers were John Flaxman, John Robert Thornton, Thomas Butts, and Henry Crabb Robinson; buyers soon after publication included Edward Calvert, Charles Aders, Thomas Griffiths Wainewright, and Sir Thomas Lawrence. The engravings were nevertheless slow in gaining appreciation for the great works of art they are. Even some who admired some of Blake's other works demurred at their deliberate antiquity of style. On 15 March 1827 Blake wrote to John Linnell that Blake's long-time friend George Cumberland had informed him that Cumberland's 'Bristol Friends' considered the *Job* 'too much Finished, or over Labour'd . . .'; Cumberland himself wrote to his son on 26 December 1827: 'I could never consider it as equal to his other performances.' Allan Cunningham wrote in his *Lives of the Most Eminent Painters, Sculptors, and Architects* (1830): 'They are in the early fashion of workmanship, and bear no resemblance whatever

---

[6] Bo Ossian Lindberg, *William Blake's Illustrations to the Book of Job* (Åbo: Åbo Akademi, 1973), pp. 50–1.

[7] Unless otherwise indicated, this information may be found in the 'Documentary Record' in BTJ, and those wishing to find the context of quoted references may consult the chronological arrangement there. Much of this material also appears in BR either at the appropriate date or in 'Linnell's Job Accounts', pp. 598–608.

to the polished and graceful style which now prevails.' The Quaker poet Bernard Barton wrote to John Linnell on 12 April 1830:

There is a dryness and hardness in Blake's manner of engraving which is very apt to be repulsive to print-collectors in general—to any, indeed, who have not taste enough to appreciate the force and originality of his conceptions, in spite of the manner in which he has embodied them. I candidly own I am not surprised at this; his style is little calculated to take with admirers of modern engraving. It puts me in mind of some old prints I have seen, and seems to combine somewhat of old Albert Durer with Bolswert. I cannot but wish he could have clothed his imaginative creations in a garb more attractive to ordinary mortals, or else given simple outlines of them. The extreme beauty, elegance, and grace of several of his marginal accompaniments induce me to think that they would have pleased more generally in that state.

'Dryness and hardness' goes back to the vocabulary of the age of Sir Joshua Reynolds, in which the very artists Blake wished to emulate were condemned. In his first Prospectus for his engraving of *The Canterbury Pilgrims*, Blake proposed to engrave that work 'in a correct and finished Line manner of Engraving, similar to those original Copper Plates of Albert Durer, Lucas, Hisben, Aldegrave and the old original Engravers, who were great Masters in Painting and Designing' (E 567). The style of 'the old original Engravers' was still far from being appreciated by the mainstream of connoisseurs.

However, some artists and collectors of more advanced taste were appreciative of Blake's style of engraving. First among these were the 'Ancients', the group of young artists, including Samuel Palmer, George Richmond, and Edward Calvert, who gathered around Blake in his last years, and whose chosen cognomen expresses their enthusiasm for the 'primitive'. Samuel Palmer recalled to Gilchrist: 'At my never-to-be-forgotten first interview, the copper of the first plate—"Thus did Job continually"—was lying on the table where he had been working at it. How lovely it looked in the lamplight, strained through the tissue paper!'[8] In the next two decades some young Victorians were deeply impressed by the *Job*. The poet Edward Fitzgerald called it 'terrible, awful, wonderful' in 1836, and in 1845 F. T. Palgrave, then a student at Balliol, wrote to his mother:

---

[8] See Gilchrist, *Life*, p. 299.

Yesterday evening Mr Jowett asked me to have tea with him, after he had looked at some Greek of mine. . . . He showed me a book which I dare say papa knows—W. Blake's 'Illustrations of the Book of Job'. They are a number of little etchings, drawn and etched by Blake; and certainly they show immense power and originality. Though often out of drawing and grotesque, they are most interesting—far more than Flaxman, for instance. Schiavonetti's etchings in the 'Grave' though far more correct, give but a faint idea of the force and vigour of these. If you can possibly borrow them, I am sure you will be exceedingly interested by them—I have seen nothing so extraordinary for a long time. Some, as of Job in misery and of the Morning Stars singing for joy, are beautiful, some, as of a man tormented by dreams and The Vision of the night, are most awful; and what adds much to the pleasure of seeing them, is that every stroke seems to do its utmost in expression, and to show that one mind both planned and executed them . . .

A copy of the *Job* was acquired by the British Museum Print Room in 1847. John Ruskin's view of Blake was mixed, but his judgement of the *Job* engravings was not. In volume 3 of *Modern Painters* (1856) he wrote: 'Blake, always powerful in the etched grotesque of the book of Job, fails always more or less as he adds colour'; and in *Elements of Drawing* (1857): '*The Book of Job* engraved by himself, is of the highest rank in certain characters of imagination and expression; in the mode of obtaining certain effects of light it will also be a very useful example to you. In expressing conditions of glowing and flickering light, Blake is greater than Rembrandt.' But the watershed of further appreciation was Alexander Gilchrist's *Life of William Blake*, published in 1863.

'The engravings [of *Job*] are the best he ever did,' Gilchrist flatly asserted, 'vigorous, decisive, and, above all, in a style of expression in keeping with the designs, which the work of no other hand could have been in the case of conceptions so austere and primeval as these.'[9] Gilchrist valued in the *Job* engravings precisely what Blake had attempted and what some earlier critics condemned, the 'primitive' nature of their style. 'They are', Gilchrist wrote, 'incisive and richly toned . . . and have equally a style of execution all their own.' He continued:

In spirit and character they are no less independent, having more real affinity, perhaps, with Orcagna than with any other of the greatest men. In their unison of natural study with imagination, they remind one decidedly of him; and also of Giotto, himself the author of a now almost destroyed series of

[9] Ibid., p. 289.

frescoes from Job, in the Campo Santo at Pisa, which it will be interesting to compare, as far as possible, with these inventions of Blake.[10]

The effect of the Gilchrist *Life* was, moreover, not limited to the biographer's praise. Volume 2 included the first comprehensive attempt at a complete catalogue of Blake's art—William Michael Rossetti's *Descriptive Catalogue*, first published in 1863 and augmented in 1880.[11] These editions also contained the first published facsimile of the *Job* plates, executed in photo-intaglio process by W. J. Linton.[12] Between the two editions of Gilchrist, John Linnell published a second edition of 100 copies printed from the original plates in 1874, and Charles Eliot Norton published a facsimile with his own commentary in the United States in 1875.[13] The *Job* engravings were well on the way to becoming the best known and most admired of all Blake's works.

The *Job* engravings show Blake at the height of his artistic power. As Robert N. Essick has demonstrated, part of the credit for this belongs to John Linnell.[14] It is true that Blake had always been proud of having been trained in the shop of John Basire, a practictioner of a style emphasizing line, one that was considered old-fashioned by the time Blake began earning his living. Typical of many of Blake's statements on the subject is: 'The more distinct, sharp, and wirey the bounding line, the more perfect the work of art' (*A Descriptive Catalogue*, E 550). Of his own *Canterbury Pilgrims* he declared:

---

[10] See Gilchrist, *Life*, p. 294. It should of course be remembered that attributions to 'Orcagna' and to 'Giotto' in the mid-19th c. are not necessarily reliable—but the substance of Gilchrist's comparison is nevertheless understandable.

[11] See Gilchrist, *Life* (1880), ii. 205–23. The lists of *Job* watercolours (25) are confined to those which Rossetti considered 'the most noticeable': 117 (*a–m*) and 118 (*a–l*) for the Butts and Linnell sets, respectively. Rossetti gave the watercolours titles, which are not, however, those by which they are generally known today. The first use of the latter that I have been able to find is in *Illustrations of The Book of Job by William Blake*, ed. Laurence Binyon and Geoffrey Keynes (New York: Pierpont Morgan Library, 1935). However, as Blake did give titles to the engravings in form of the main caption for each, I have used those titles either complete, or, if necessary, in foreshortened form for both engravings and watercolours.

[12] On Linton and the Gilchrist *Life*, see Joseph Viscomi's comprehensive online article 'Blake after Blake: A Nation Discovers Genius', http://sites.unc.edu/viscomi/blakeafterblake.html. 8 March 2003.

[13] Norton, *William Blake's Illustrations of the Book of Job* (Boston: James R. Osgood, 1875). Norton's commentary is heavily indebted to Gilchrist but also includes some important new insights.

[14] See Essick, 'John Linnell, William Blake, and the Printmaker's Craft', in *Essays on the Blake Followers*, ed. G. E. Bentley, Jr. (San Marino, Calif.: Huntington Library, 1983), pp. 18–32.

'This Print is the Finest that has been done or is likely to be done in England where drawing ⟨its foundation⟩ is Contemnd and absurd Nonsense about dots & Lozenges & Clean Strokes made to occupy the attention to the Neglect of all real Art' ('Public Address', E 582). Nevertheless many of Blake's graphic productions over his long career had been far less uncompromising than such statements would imply. Most of Blake's commercial productions are 'mixed method' works—that is, combining etching and engraving and employing dots, lozenges, and crosshatching as well as line. This is also true of some works that Blake produced independently, such as the very early separate plate that he later reworked and entitled *Joseph of Arimathea Among the Rocks of Albion*.[15] The late version might be regarded as something of a testament to the influence of John Linnell. By working for Linnell on one portrait engraving and collaborating with him on another,[16] Blake absorbed such techniques as hatching with very fine lines, leaving areas unengraved for whites, burnishing other areas so as to make whites stand out sharply against darks, and flick work (short engraved strokes),[17] as well as gaining renewed faith in 'the hard and wirey line of rectitude' (*Descriptive Catalogue*, E 550). Gilchrist was not mistaken when he asserted with specific reference to the *Job* engravings that 'Blake's manner of handling the graver had been advantageously modified since his acquaintance with Mr. Linnell'.[18]

Blake began with rough pencil drawings, in the notebook now in the Fitzwilliam Museum, scaled to the size of the plates. These became the basis of drawings that were used for counterproofing—transferred to the copperplates, preserving the right and the left of the original drawings (unlike copy engraving, in which a mirror image is produced). The work on the plates was done entirely with engraving tools, without any etching. It was at this stage that Blake had an inspired afterthought. Without, for the most part, prelimi-nary drawings—we have John Linnell's authority[19] for this—he drew

[15] Essick, *The Separate Plates of William Blake*, no. I.

[16] The plates are, respectively, *James Upton* (1818–19) and *Wilson Lowry* (1824–5); Essick, *The Separate Plates of William Blake*, nos. XL and XLII.

[17] See Essick, 'John Linnell, William Blake, and the Printmaker's Craft'.

[18] Gilchrist, *Life*, p. 289. Gilchrist was, however, incorrect in ascribing to Linnell Blake's introduction to the works of Dürer, Marcantonio Raimondi, and Julio Bonasone, engravers whom Blake had long admired.

[19] See Geoffrey Keynes, 'The Development of the Job Designs', BTJ, p. 21, quoting a letter from Linnell to C. W. Dilke dated 27 September 1844.

in the margins of each plate, probably with a drypoint needle,[20] images that exist in a pictorial space distinct from but related to that of the main design, and he also inscribed in the upper and lower margins biblical texts that had a literal or thematic relation to the subject. That Blake became interested in the idea of border designs in the 1820s is attested by those in copy Y of the *Songs of Innocence and of Experience* (Metropolitan Museum of Art), bearing 1825 watermarks.[21] Copy W of the *Songs* (King's College, Cambridge), with 1818 and 1825 watermarks, also has border designs,[22] and so do the first two plates of copy E of *Jerusalem*. All these, however, are simple and ornamental in contrast to the rich, thematically significant border designs of *Job*. The result is that an alternative reality is created outside the ruled lines of the central design, one which both comments on and amplifies the significance of the main image. There are no works of art quite like this, but it too has its tradition.

One of the artists Blake most admired was Albrecht Dürer. In his *Descriptive Catalogue* he ranked Dürer with Raphael and Michelangelo in their use of the 'distinct, sharp, and wirey' bounding line (E 550), and he declared his *Canterbury Pilgrims* plate to be in 'the style of Alb Durers Histries & the old Engravers' (E 572). Blake can hardly have been unaware that Dürer's illustrations for the work now known as *The Book of Hours of the Emperor Maximilian the First* consisted of images in the margins around a rectangular area of text with ruled borders. Blake must also have known that in 1817 Rudolph Ackermann had published a facsimile edition entitled *Albert Durer's Designs of the Prayer Book*. This lithographic facsimile,[23]

---

[20] Robert N. Essick, 'Blake's Engravings to the Book of Job', BTJ, p. 43. However, Butlin (557.7, 9, and 11; and 559.1–6) reports that three of the preparatory sketches do have marginal sketches, as also do six of the trial proofs in the Rosenwald Collection.

[21] See Bentley, *Blake Books*, pp. 368 and 424.

[22] Bentley (*Blake Books*, pp. 423 and 429) accepts George Richmond's view that the borders of copy W (King's College, Cambridge), bearing 1818 and 1825 watermarks, were drawn by Mrs Blake; but this is disputed by Andrew Lincoln, who writes 'there is no reason to think that the borders, with their delicate brushwork and their Blakean motifs, were not devised and executed by Blake himself'. Lincoln, Introduction to *Songs of Innocence and of Experience* (London: William Blake Trust/Tate Gallery, 1991), p. 23.

[23] Walter L. Straus, editor of *The Book of Hours of the Emperor Maximilian the First* (New York: Abaris Books, 1974), writes that in 1808 the decorations were published 'in the first book of note printed by means of the newly invented process of lithography', by the Aretin-Senefelder Press, Nuremberg. Ackermann says in his 'Advertisement': 'I regret much that, in the edition published at Munich by Messrs. Strixner and Pilotz, from which this is copied, the text was omitted.'

taken from a German facsimile drawn by Johann Nepomuk Strixner, lacked the texts of the prayers, but these would not in any event have been to Blake's purpose. Ackermann was also the publisher of the second edition (1813) of Blair's *Grave*, with Blake's designs engraved by Lewis Schiavonetti. In 1821, when the Blakes moved to Fountain Court, Strand, they were within a few steps of Ackermann's print shop and showroom at 101 The Strand; the two premises were in fact so close that the large display room in which Ackermann also had weekly receptions during March and April had a private door leading to Fountain Court.[24] There can be little doubt that Blake had an opportunity to see *Albert Dürer's Designs of the Prayer Book*, and that, considering his interest in Dürer, he would have taken advantage of it. He appears to have learned from them how marginal designs on a relatively small scale could be used both decoratively and significantly.

For example, in no. 6 John of Patmos is seen writing in a book with a pen, and an eagle stands to his right. In the sky above appears a woman holding a baby (who holds a crown) in her left arm; her right hand holds a sceptre, and the crescent moon is at her feet. This subject from Revelation was of course a favourite one of Blake's as well. In his preface to the Ackermann edition J. B. Bernhart quotes an author of 1805 as saying that St John here 'is all prophetic greatness and sublimity'.[25] But perhaps more representative of these designs is no. 38 (Fig. 30), where we see at the upper right an angel with a book kneeling on a cloud at the right, a vine going counter-clockwise across the top and down the left margin with a bird and a grotesque head, and in the bottom margin bunches of grapes growing, a bacchic figure sitting on a cask and drinking from a pitcher, a faun sitting on a tree stump and playing a syrinx, and, at the lower right, an eagle perching. Of course Blake did not copy the details of this or any other of Dürer's marginal illustrations, but adapted the mode to his own purposes in what proved to be an inspired afterthought.

Dürer was not the only possible influence on Blake's marginal designs. One tantalizing parallel is with one of the graphic masterpieces of the early nineteenth century, the *Tageszeiten* (1805, 1807) of Philipp Otto Runge. Like Blake, Runge exploits the margins of his

---

[24] See 'W. P.', 'Rudolph Ackermann of the Strand, Publisher', *Notes and Queries*, 4th ser., 4 (7 August 1869): 109–12; and Robert N. Essick and Morton D. Paley, *Robert Blair's The Grave Illustrated by William Blake* (London: Scolar Press, 1982), p. 39.

[25] *The Book of Hours*, p. 3. Bernhart was Keeper of the Royal Library, now the Staatsbibliothek, Munich, owner of the Dürer orginals.

FIG. 30. Johann Nepomuk Strixner after Albrecht Dürer,
Albert Durer's Designs of the Prayer Book (London: R. Ackermann,
1817), p. 38. Lithographic facsimile.

FIG. 31. *Illustrations of the Book of Job*, 5: *Then went Satan forth from the presence of the Lord.* Engraving, 1825.

engravings to create another plane of visual existence, and the visionary qualities in the works of both artists also suggest that they could have been sympathetic to each other's work.[26] However, there is no evidence of any first-hand knowledge of Blake on Runge's part or vice versa, although such a notion is all the more tantalizing because the first essay on William Blake to appear in Germany was published in January 1810 in the *Vaterländisches Museum*, edited in Hamburg by Dr Friedrich Christoff Perthes, and Runge was a member of the artistic and literary circle that gathered around Perthes and his publication. However, the *Tageszeiten* had been published several years before, and, as Runge died in December 1810 he would have had little opportunity to pursue any affinity he might have felt for Blake. As for Blake, there is nothing to prove that he knew any of Runge's work. Karl Aders may have acquired a copy of the *Tageszeiten* around 1810–11,[27] but we have no way of knowing whether Blake would have seen it in 1825, when his first contact with the Aderses is recorded (*BR*, p. 309). It is possible that the interesting resemblance between Blake's and Runge's use of marginal space is partly a matter of artistic affinity and partly owing to common sources. It has been suggested that the latter, in addition to Dürer, could include the engravings Tommaso Piroli made for *Le Antichità di Ercolano*, published at Rome in 1789, in which border designs are also featured.[28] In addition to comparisons there are also, of course, some important distinctions to be made. The Herculaneum designs Piroli engraved have side borders that are mirror images of each other. This is sometimes true of Blake's side margins but sometimes not. It is never true of Dürer's, whose figures are, in addition, often larger than Blake's. Runge's side margins are mirror images but, like Blake's and unlike Piroli's they are significative as well as decorative. What all four have

---

[26] David Bindman discusses their common interest in Jakob Böhme in 'Blake and Runge', in *Runge, Fragen und Antworten*, ed. Hanna Hohl (Munich: Prestel, 1979), pp. 86–95.

[27] See Georg Symaken, 'Die "Tageszeiten" von Philipp Otto Runge und "The Book of Job" von William Blake', *Jahrbuch der Hamburger Kunstsammlungen*, 20 (1975): 63. I thank D. W. Dörrbecker for drawing this important paper to my attention, and also for other information about Runge.

[28] See Symaken, 'Die "Tageszeiten" von Philipp Otto Runge und "The Book of Job" von William Blake', 6 and figs. 6 and 7. Symaken sees a decisive difference between Runge and Blake in that 'the cosmic themes of the German stand opposed to Old Testament experience', while Blake's 'dynamic world-picture' is apocalyptic and prophetic.

in common is using marginal spaces to create an additional realm of existence. Something unique to Blake is the inscribing of biblical texts above and below the double ruled border that frames the main image of each of the *Job* engravings. These were obviously chosen with some care. Each plate bears a main caption below the lower border, and this may be taken as the title of that particular engraving, although it is necessary to shorten some of them for ease of reference. All the caption quotations are, as one would expect, from the Book of Job. Others are from different books of the Old and New Testaments, which is in itself an important feature, as it is Blake's purpose here (in direct opposition to, for example, *The Everlasting Gospel*) to reconcile our ideas of the Father and of the Son. The specific texts will be discussed in the context of each plate, but it should be said that in general the quotations often interact with and resonate against each other, and we have in them yet another dimension of meaning that enriches the work as a whole.

At the top of the title page are the Hebrew words for 'Book of Job', separated by a horizontal bar from the elegantly lettered 'ILLUS-TRATIONS of | The | BOOK | of | JOB' at the centre of the page. The title page design, for which no watercolour or pencil drawing exists, may well have been drawn directly onto the copperplate in drypoint like the marginal designs. Showing seven angels moving clockwise in a graceful U-shaped arc, this image has prompted some critics to try to identify sections of Blake's *Job* with the concept of the Seven Eyes of God used in *The Four Zoas*, *Milton*, and *Jerusalem*.[29] Such a schematization of Blake's series is difficult to sustain, especially as five of the Eyes have Hebrew names, the fourth being Shaddai, and Blake would have known that in the Book of Job Shaddai is the principal name of God,[30] leaving little room for the others. It is probable that Blake pictured seven angels partly for design reasons, and partly

---

[29] S. Foster Damon offers such an interpretation in *Blake's Job* (Providence, RI: Brown University Press, 1966), p. 5 and *passim*, but he had previously outlined it in his great pioneering work *William Blake: His Philosophy and Symbols* (1924), pp. 223–34. Joseph H. Wicksteed, in the second (1924) edition of another seminal work, *Blake's Vision of the Book of Job* (London: J. M. Dent), partially accepted this idea of 'a sevenfold structure' (pp. 33–4). Both these books remain of great value in the interpretation of individual features of the *Job* designs.

[30] See, for example, Matthew Henry on Job: 'He lived while God was known by the name of *God Almighty* more than by the name of *Jehovah*; for he is called *Shaddai—the Almighty*, above thirty times in this book.'—*Blue Letter Bible*, www.blueletterbible.org/Comm/mhc/Job/Job000.html

because of the generally mystic resonance of the number seven. The title page is a doorway into the world of Job, with the last angel already turned with his back to us, leading the way.

In the background of the first plate, captioned *Thus did Job continually*, a Gothic cathedral in the background, no doubt built by one of those 'Gothic Artists who Built the Cathedrals . . . of whom the World was not worthy',[31] indicates the persistent availability of vision. Job's prosperity is suggested by five storehouses (substituted for two small pyramids in Linnell's drawing that in turn replaced two tents in Butts's), and a flock of some of his seven thousand sheep. A tent-like form in the upper margin may be a visual equivalent of the 'tents of prosperity' in *The Four Zoas* (36: 12, E 325), and written above it is the beginning of the Lord's Prayer (Matt. 6: 9; Luke 11: 2), which was inscribed in the sun of Butts's watercolour but absent from Linnell's. Everything seems propitious. Blake follows the Bible in giving Job seven sons (each with a shepherd's crook), and three daughters. All are on their knees in prayer except Job and his wife, who sit under a massive tree reminiscent of the great central tree of 'The Ecchoing Green' of *Songs of Innocence*. The sun is setting, the cresent moon is waning, and the evening star shines in the sky. All of this might be taken as creating a Gray's *Elegy*-like atmosphere were we not led to look for signs of foreboding by our knowledge of the night to come. Having that knowledge, we notice the unused musical instruments hanging on the tree and the opened books on the laps of Job and his wife at prayer. Regarding the latter, Charles Eliot Norton observed as early as 1875 that the inscriptions on the flaming altar in the lower margin had special significance.[32] These are: 'The Letter Killeth | The Spirit giveth Life', and 'It is Spiritually Discerned', slightly modified quotations of 2 Cor. 3: 6 and 1 Cor. 2: 14.[33] Job's

---

[31] This is part of Blake's inscription on the second state of *Joseph of Arimathea Among the Rocks of Albion* (Essick, *Separate Plates*, no. I, p. 3).

[32] Charles Eliot Norton, *William Blake's Illustrations of the Book of Job*, n.p.

[33] In the first quotation the AV has 'but' after 'Killeth', and in the second 'they are' rather than 'it is'. S. Foster Damon remarks that 'Some of Blake's variations seem to be slips of an imperfect memory, but others are intentional', and we must be alive to the latter possibility as we consider the biblical texts in Blake's margins. See Damon, *Blake's Job*, p. 55. Damon gives a complete recension of Blake's biblical inscriptions together with the the wording of each passage in *Blake's Job*, pp. 55–66. It should be added that plate 1 originally included the statement 'Prayer to God is the Study of Imaginative Art', but Blake expunged this as he did 'Praise to God is the Exercise of Imaginative Art' in the last plate. Perhaps his reason was that these lines would have been the only marginal inscriptions not from the Bible. They appear in condensed form in יהוה *& his two Sons*: 'Prayer is the Study of Art' and 'Praise is the Practise of Art'.

prayers and sacrifices in the days of his prosperity were, in Norton's words, 'but the proprietary and selfish sacrifices of the law'. This is reinforced by the context of the second quotation: 'But the natural man receiveth not the things of the Spirit of God: for they are foolishness unto him: neither can he know *them*, because they are spiritually discerned.'[34] In the beginning Job is shown as the natural man in his religious devotions. The bullock and the ram in the lower corners of the engraving and the rams' heads at the ends of the altar are emblematic of his blood sacrifices. The words *Thus did Job continually* are also subversive of the seeming pastoral tranquillity of the scene, for 'continually' takes on the connotation of 'automatically', and the whole passage (Job 1: 5) both indicates Job's religious anxiety and prompts us toward the next design: 'And it was so, when the days of their feasting were gone about, that Job sent and sanctified them, and rose up early in the morning, and offered burnt offerings according to the number of them all: for Job said, It may be that my sons have sinned, and cursed God in their hearts. Thus did Job continually.'

This religious anxiety of Job's is the subject of the lower part of 2, *When the Almighty was yet with me. When my Children were about me* (Job 29: 5), a scene not in the Bible. The locale has changed—the Gothic cathedral is not visible, and there are now three trees, each with a disturbingly serpent-like vine climbing up its trunk. The scene is still one of apparent pastoral domesticity, including a son with a wife and child (absent from the text of Job), two more grandchildren (likewise absent) to the right, sheep safely grazing, and a dog sleeping in what Gilchrist characterizes as 'a recessed settle . . . much in the spirit of Orcagna',[35] that in the engraving alone also contains books. The significant action going on is a comparison of texts. Two angels with opened scrolls at the left make eye contact with Job, who, with worried glance indicates with his right thumb a passage in the book he grips with his left hand. (Butlin remarks that in tracing the Linnell from the Butts watercolour Job's expression was 'misunderstood'; to leave no doubt in the engraving Blake turned Job's face from profile to three-quarter view and made his concern evident.) Job's wife still has her book on her lap but looks over to her husband's. One son has entered from the right with an opened book and

---

[34] As pointed out by Ben F. Nelms, 'Text and Design in *Illustrations of the Book of Job*', in *Blake's Visionary Forms Dramatic*, ed. David V. Erdman and John E. Grant (Princeton: Princeton University Press, 1970), p. 337 n.

[35] Gilchrist, *Life*, p. 292.

the one behind Job has opened a scroll. The question before the house appears to be whether the sons 'have sinned and cursed God in their hearts'. (Even the children at the far right have a book, but they may be using theirs as a hymnal.) These textual comparisons have their result in heaven above, where one angel flies up with a book, another with a scroll, and two more lay scrolls at the base of the heavenly throne. There sits the Chief Bookkeeper of all, whom Job has created in his image (except for the upper figure's frizzled hair), with a volume opened on his lap, pointing downward with his right index finger. Satan leaps balletically into the centre of the picture space, arms upraised toward the heavenly throne. 'There was a day', as Blake's lower marginal inscription says, 'when the Sons of God came to present themselves before the Lord & Satan also came among them to present himself before the Lord' (Job 2: 1). Satan has of course requested power over Job, and the gesture is his answer. The faces of Job and his wife appear in the flames under Satan's arms, indicating that all that they have on earth will be in Satan's power. Heavy black clouds, corresponding to the dark clouds in the Linnell watercolour, ascend up the sides of the design space from the middle of the image to its upper margin. These dramatically contrast with the radiance of the Lord's nimbus, which lights up the faces of the angels below him. Such powerful contrasts of dark and light are a hallmark of the *Job* engravings.

Both the marginal designs and inscriptions mirror these radical dualities and ambiguities. Woody stems form Gothic traceries that go up each side margin in a beautiful 'Tree of Jesse' composition of the kind we see in the 'Introduction' to *Songs of Innocence*. However, in the first compartment of one we see a peacock and of the other a parrot, birds aptly characterized by Damon as 'the peacock of pride and the parrot of vain repetitions'.[36] In larger spaces higher up are the pillar of fire and the column of smoke that showed the Israelites under Moses the way to the Promised Land, but the pairs of angels above each appear to incline their heads in grief, perhaps because that path will first lead to Sinai, where the Law was delivered. In the lower margin's corners stand a bearded shepherd and a shepherdess, both with crooks, inside the fence of a sheepfold. Its gate is open, sheep sleep within, and a dog (perhaps the one of the main design) sleeps in the gateway. This is a trace of the Innocence

---

[36] Damon, *Blake's Job*, p. 14.

also indicated by the main design. In contrast, the upper margin inscriptions introduce elements of conflict. Above the two Hebrew words meaning 'King Jehovah' in the centre, Blake inscribed 'The Angel of the Divine Presence'. We have seen that this expression could be at best ambiguous in יְהוָֹה *& his two Sons*, and entirely negative in *The Everlasting Gospel*. Arching over these six words is the question 'Hast thou considered my Servant Job' that the Lord puts to Satan twice (Job 1: 8 and 2: 3), in effect tempting Satan to do his worst. And above this is a fragment of Dan. 7: 9: 'I beheld . . . the Ancient of Days', part of a vision which, it has been pointed out, leads to the coming of 'One like the Son of Man', and to his being given universal dominion.[37] Other fragmentary quotations prefigure Job's redemption. 'We shall awake up in thy Likeness', which the reader-viewer must put together from the far left and the far right, is from Psalm 17, but with its meaning somewhat changed from the original, which reads 'I shall be satisfied, when I awake, with thy likeness' (15). What in the source is meant to signify daily personal experience is expanded by Blake to mean communal resurrection. This is reinforced by the text in the white cloud to the right of 'We shall wake up', which is from Job 19: 26: 'I shall see God.' As the context of the latter passage shows, this meets Blake's purpose in combining the idea of the Son of Man coming to judge the world and the resurrection of the flesh: 'For I know that my redeemer liveth, and that he shall stand at the latter day upon the earth: And though after my skin worms destroy this body, yet in my flesh shall I see God' (Job 19: 25–6). The sole remaining quotation in the upper margin, 'Thou art our Father', on the cloud to our right is from a statement in Isaiah 63: 16 reiterated in 64: 8, the former of which reads in part 'thou, O LORD, art our father, our redeemer; thy name is from everlasting'. Thus the marginal inscriptions present both positive and negative views of the divine, the former stressing redemption, resurrection, and millennial Judgement.

'And the lord said unto Satan Behold All that he hath is in thy power', reads the inscription from Job 1: 12 that arches over 3. Satan, quick to take advantage of the Lord's permission, is seen here as a grotesque black, bat-winged figure, perched on top of the eldest son's house, gleefully enjoying the act of bringing it down with flames and

---

[37] See Jenijoy La Belle, 'Words Graven with an Iron Pen: The Marginal Texts in Blake's *Job*', in *The Visionary Hand*, ed. Robert N. Essick, p. 530.

thunderbolts. (His is the agency here, rather than the 'great wind from the wilderness' from the line, Job 1: 19, that provides the caption for this engraving.) Although Job's sons and daughters are specified in the biblical text, it is a family group that dominates the centre of the picture, with a naked, athletic-looking man pulling a woman up towards him while he carries a baby on his left shoulder. (Perhaps this is the same family group seen to Job's left in 2; though the sons have neither wives nor children in the Bible story.) This group of three is very similar to the one depicted among flames and collapsing architecture in *Europe* 18, the resemblance of which to that in John Flaxman's ambitious sculpture *The Fury of Athamas* (National Trust, Ickworth) has been noted.[38] However, there are problems of dating here, since Flaxman executed *Athamas* at Rome between 1790 and 1794, while Blake (who had never been to Rome) published *Europe* in 1794. There may be a common classical source behind both.[39] All the women in this scene appear to be the brothers' wives (not mentioned in the Bible), as there are seven of them and Job had only three daughters. The feet of the dead woman in the foreground rest on a tambourine and there are objects for drinking and eating at the lower right (there were more of them in Butts's watercolour but they were 'simplified', to use Butlin's term, in Linnell's, and the engraving follows the Linnell picture in this respect, though the details are clearer in the engraving). Above them, the corpse of one son sprawls vertically upside down, loins above heart and head; and the figure behind him appears to be hermaphroditic.[40] The margins are dominated by flames and by clouds, behind which we glimpse the scaly surface of some huge monster. In the lower right-hand corners, scorpions raise their tails, ready to deliver their poisonous stings.

How are we to interpret Blake's treatment of the story so far? It is certainly possible to consider the Job of 1 a man in a state of error, religious by rote, avoiding the spontaneous joys of life. His anxiety about the observance of the Law, we may easily believe, is what creates the Satan within him, a counter-self who challenges the God Job

[38] See Stephen C. Behrendt, '*Europe* 6: Plundering the Treasury', *Blake*, 21 (1987–8): 87, 90, and 94 n. 9.

[39] See Lindberg, *William Blake's Illustrations to the Book of Job*, p. 208; Dörrbecker in *William Blake: The Continental Prophecies*, pp. 205–6.

[40] As Joseph H. Wicksteed observes; see *Blake's Vision of The Book of Job*, p. 107. Wicksteed also thinks the seven women are wives (p. 99).

has made in his own image. However, what happens in 3 must give us pause. We might apply the words in Night 1 of *The Four Zoas* where Blake says of Urthona (the unfallen Los): 'In Eden; in the Auricular Nerves of Human life | Which is the Earth of Eden, he his Emanations Propagated' (4: 1–2, E 301). Then the destruction of the sons and daughters (or sons and wives) could be interpreted as symbolic, part of, to use Damon's words, 'a spiritual act' in which 'the sons are as dead to the father'.[41] The Book of Job, at least through Blake's eyes, could then be read as a psychomachia in which all events take place within a single self—Job's wife would then be his Emanation, his accusers his superego, and his losses confined to his own psyche. Would this, as Lindberg argues, deprive the tale of its terror?[42] On the other hand, would Blake have endorsed the idea of Satan's murdering Job's sons in order for God to test his belief? Would Blake have regarded feasting, drinking, and sexual pleasure as deserving death by fiery immolation? Or may we interpret Blake's meaning as unfolding on two different levels, literal and symbolic, either alternatively or simultaneously? We must return to such questions later.

A messenger (his flesh colour striking and wearing a brown garment in the Linnell drawing) arrives in engraving 4, captioned 'And I only am escaped alone to tell thee', from Job 1: 15. The beginning of this passage arcs across the top margin: 'And there came a Messenger unto Job & said The Oxen were plowing & the Sabeans came down [AV 'fell upon them'] & they have slain the young Men [AV 'servants'] with the edge of the sword' (Job 1: 14–15). On receiving this terrible news, Job and his wife react—she wringing her hands above her head in despair, he looking heavenward with hands prayerfully together. They sit on a massive piece of outdoor furniture, with a Gothic cathedral once more in the left background. They do not yet see a second messenger approaching, but his words are inscribed in the lower margin: 'While he was yet speaking came also another & said | The fire of God is fallen from heaven & hath burned up the flocks [AV 'sheep'] & the | Young Men [AV 'servants'], & consumed them; and I only am escaped alone to tell thee' (Job 1: 16). Far away on a mountain slope is the figure of a third bearer of evil

---

[41] *Blake's Job*, p. 16.
[42] *William Blake's Illustrations to the Book of Job*, p. 311. I cannot, however, agree with Lindberg's view that Blake thought the young men and women deserved punishment.

tidings. A female angel lies supine at each of the inner right-hand corners of the picture, while bat-winged Satan, the instigator of all this, stands on top of the curved earth in the margin above. He is 'Going to & fro in the Earth | & walking up and down in it', as he says in answer to God's question 'From whence comest thou?' (Job 2: 2). Having heard of the loss of his sons, servants, and flocks, Job is about to endure more, as in their second interview God grants Satan the right to attack Job's flesh, sparing only his life. Once more, Blake follows the general story fairly closely, while freely changing some details. He does not introduce any elements that would induce anything but a literal reading of what happens to Job and his children and servants, although on a literal level the latter no more deserve to die for Job's mistakes than the crew of an entire ship for a sailor's shooting of an albatross. Blake allows himself greater freedom in depicting the Lord. In 5 (Fig. 31), 'Then went Satan forth from the presence of the Lord' (Job 1: 12), the expression and bodily attitude of the enthroned father-figure have changed radically as compared with 2. His head now inclines to his right, and his face has an expression of mixed apathy and despair. His right leg is swung over further, knee up, making his posture even more 'Urizenic'. In his right hand he loosely holds a book, in his left a scroll. Having handed power over to Satan, he now repents having made humankind: 'And it grieved him at his heart', part of a sentence from Gen. 6: 6 that Blake used in ךך‭ & his two Sons, is inscribed below the caption. Below that we read 'Who maketh his Angels Spirits & his Ministers a Flaming Fire' (Ps. 104: 4), implying that Satan is doing God's work by pouring flame upon Job from a vial, flame that backfires into the heavens, causing the nearest angels around God's throne to shrink away. Job's wife leans her head against his shoulder and clasps his arm as he gives one of his two loaves to an old man with a crutch (similar to figures in 'London' and in *Jerusalem* 84, except that those are guided by a little boy while this one has a dog on a leash). Wicksteed thinks that the fact that Job gives the loaf with his left hand indicates that his charity is based on 'a false conception of material values',[43] and in Damon's view the replacement of the Gothic church by 'Druid architecture' in the left mid-ground indicates that 'Job is now in

---

[43] Some of Wicksteed's identifications of right with spiritual and left with material are convincing, as is this one, while others are less so. See Wicksteed, *Blake's Vision of the Book of Job*, p. 117.

error'.[44] Yet Job must be doing something right, as the presence of two prayerful angels on either side of the lower scene suggests. It is, rather, his view that such charity will save him from disaster that is in error: 'Did I not weep for him who was in trouble? Was not my Soul afflicted for the Poor[?]' he asks in the upper margin (Job 30: 25). The border designs make their own visual comment: huge briars interlace woody vines along the sides in a parody of the Tree of Jesse motif, at the bottom two enormous serpents swim in fire, their tails twining upwards, and two angels look down in horror from the right and left corners of the inset frame.

Satan goes on to do what the Lord gave him permission to do— 'And smote Job with sore boils from the sole of his foot to the crown of his head' (Job 2: 7). Plate 6 shows a naked Satan, scaly and without genitals, smiling cheerfully in the manner of one of Blake's demons in the *Inferno* as he stands on Job's body. Flames pour from a vial in his left hand and arrows of disease fly down from his right. Ironically, he has a halo (first acquired in the Linnell water-colour), and he stands in a position very similar to those of the central figures in *The spiritual form of Nelson guiding Leviathan* (Butlin 649, Tate Gallery) and in *Albion rose* (Butlin 262.1 and 274). I have discussed the relation among these images elsewhere,[45] and need only say here that the figures of Satan and Nelson are parodies of Albion, the last giving himself as a sacrifice for humankind, the first two sacrificing it. Supine Job has covered his loins with a twilled fabric that Blake may intend as sackcloth, and he lies on straw. His wife, like one of Flaxman's funerary angels, is hunched over in grief at his feet. This is in contradiction to the Bible, which has her play an adversarial role:

And he took him a potsherd to scrape himself withal; and he sat down among the ashes.

Then said his wife unto him, Dost thou still retain thine integrity? curse God, and die.

But he said unto her, Thou speakest as one of the foolish women speaketh. What? shall we receive good at the hand of God, and shall we not receive evil? In all this did not Job sin with his lips. (Job 2: 8–10)

---

[44] See Damon, *Blake's Job*, p. 20. The introduction of the cromlech is certainly deliberate, for the structure in the left mid-ground has $3\frac{1}{2}$ pillars in the Butts water-colour and $2\frac{1}{2}$ in the Linnell.

[45] See *Energy and the Imagination*, pp. 195–6.

As Elizabeth Rigby, Lady Eastlake, pointed out in 1864, Blake deliberately gives Job's wife a sympathetic role: 'It would seem,' she wrote

as if the English painter knew and resented the calumnious treatment of Job's wife by older Art, and had devoted these most remarkable illustrations in some degree to her vindication. Throughout the series she appears tenderly compassionating the afflicted partner of her life—sunk at his feet in grief, or kneeling in prayer by his side. The painter also adds a trait omitted by Scripture, for the same gentle sympathising woman figures in the last plate as the mother of the second fair family that was given to Job.[46]

It would be hard to believe that in this Blake was not thinking of the sharer of his own life, Catherine, especially as Job's wife disappears from the biblical narrative after chapter 2 but remains with her husband throughout Blake's series of engravings. As for Job, his boils recall those of Albion in *Jerusalem* 43: 64 (E 192), 'Coverd with boils from head to foot' because of his own repressed feelings, 'the terrible smitings of Luvah'. The landscape reflects Job's desolate state—the background buildings are now ruins, and the sun is setting. The lower margin is filled with images of decay, including a broken shepherd's crook, the 'grasshopper that shall be a burden' and the 'pitcher . . . broken at the fountain' of Ecclesiastes 12: 5–6,[47] a frog, and nettles. Two spiders are about to join these, lowered on filaments from the upper corners of the inner 'frame' by bat-winged parodies of angels.

Job has managed to pull himself up to a sitting position in 7, leaning against his horrified wife in a position that, Lindberg observes, suggests a pietà.[48] His eyes look up to a piece of massive architecture

---

[46] See Anna Jameson and Elizabeth Rigby, Lady Eastlake, *The History of Our Lord As Exemplified in Works of Art* (4th edn., 2 vols., London: Longmans, Green, 1881), i. 231. Mrs Jameson began this book but died fairly early in its composition, and the remainder was written by Lady Eastlake. As the parts Mrs Jameson wrote are identified as hers and this one is not, it must be by Lady Eastlake. The author explains what she means by 'calumnious treatment' earlier. 'In the cycles of the 14th and 15th century, she is made second only to Satan in acts of torment. Job appears invariably seated on the ground, in the deepest dejection, with Satan scourging him on one side, and his wife scolding him on the other, and looking as if he relished the one as little as the other' (i. 227).

[47] See Damon, *Blake's Job*, p. 22; and Jenijoy La Belle, 'Words Graven with an Iron Pen', p. 535.

[48] *William Blake's Illustrations to the Book of Job*, p. 231; Lindberg further suggests that it is modelled specifically upon Michelangelo's *Pietà*, which he says Blake could have known through an engraving of 1547 by Antonio Salamanca.

at the right, the upper part of which is cross-shaped.[49] He will need what solace this can bring even more, as his 'friends' Eliphaz the Temanite, Bildad the Shuhite, and Zophar the Naamathite, enter, gesticulating with upraised hands, from the right. They will do their best to convince Job that his sufferings are somehow his own fault. As Northrop Frye remarks, they are 'representatives of the continuous social anxiety . . . that makes human misery constant by trying to rationalize and explain it away in every crisis'.[50] At the bottom of the lower margin, Blake has inscribed part of James 5: 11: 'Ye have heard of the Patience of Job and have seen the end of the Lord'. Indeed, the whole of this passage is relevant: 'Behold, we count them happy which endure. Ye have heard of the patience of Job, and have seen the end of the Lord; that the Lord is very pitiful, and of tender mercy.' Blake's Job will endure, though his patience will be tried by his would-be comforters. The marginal designs offer a non-verbal comment on them: an aged shepherd and a shepherdess (presumably Job and his wife) sleep standing up in the lower corners, propped by a barren tree, and in the top corners of the inset frame sit two more sleeping figures.

'Let the Day perish wherein I was Born', from Job 3: 3, is the caption of 8, and there is something remarkable about the desolation of this plate. Job's wife kneels, head down in despair to Job's right, and the three friends assume similar positions to his left. A massive arch is partially visible further to his left and rugged hills surmounted by huge dark clouds form the background. The sun has set, leaving just a little light tingeing the edges of the clouds and a tiny bit of the sky; otherwise the picture is almost black, except for light from an unknown source striking the human figures and the immediate foreground. Job, covered with boils, gestures dramatically upward, with both hands high and palms up. There are no buildings in the background, and no trees; the only plants are some thorns and spiked blades of grass at the lower left edge of the picture space. Although there is life in the lower margin, it is debased and forbidding—branches with poisonous-looking berries, an enormous briar, (probably) poisonous mushrooms of two kinds, and a thistle. A

---

[49] As Charles Eliot Norton was the first to note, in *William Blake's Illustrations of the Book of Job*, n.p.

[50] 'Blake's Reading of the Book of Job', in *William Blake: Essays for S. Foster Damon*, ed. Alvin Rosenfeld (Providence, RI: Brown University Press, 1969), p. 222.

cloud extends from the top margin down the sides, and raindrops fall from it to water these baneful plants. All three marginal inscriptions are from the Book of Job itself, increasing the sense of enclosedness in this scene.[51]

This dark night of the soul at first appears to be pierced by light in 9, 'Then a Spirit passed before my face | the hair of my flesh stood up' (Job 4: 15). The Spirit stands erect, robed, with a long white beard, and with radiance streaming from a disc of light around his head and shoulders. In the Butts watercolour the spirit is almost an outline and the nimbus an undefined area of light; in the Linnell version the figure is filled in and the nimbus circular; and these aspects of the latter are carried through further in the engraving. The Spirit stands erect, wearing a long garment with his arms concealed beneath it, and gazing seriously ahead. This is the vision of Eliphaz the Temanite, who in the world below gestures upward so that Job, his wife, Bildad, and Zophar also see the Spirit. In the vision Eliphaz in bed recoils with his hair standing on end. It is the Spirit who speaks the words Blake inscribed in the upper parts of the margins: 'Shall mortal Man be more Just than God? Shall a Man be more pure than his Maker? Behold he putteth no trust in his Saints [AV 'servants'] & his Angels he chargeth with Folly' (4: 17–18). In context, this is part of a speech in which Bildad declares that Job must be at fault to merit the punishments he has received from God, and that he ought to receive chastisement gladly. The facts that we cannot see the Spirit's hands and that he stands on the horizontal part of a U-shaped black cloud should make us wary of his pronouncements. He is as much Bildad's erroneous projection as was the Lord of 2 and 5 Job's, and his teaching is as barren as the leafless trees that alone occupy both the right and the left margins.

How erroneous the counsels of all three friends are is revealed in both the design and texts of 10, 'The Just Upright Man is laughed to scorn' (Job 12: 4). On the left side of Job the comforters assume the dramatic pose of the three accusers of Socrates in the upper design of *Jerusalem* 93, both derived, as Blunt points out, from Henry Fuseli's drawing *The Three Witches* (Courtauld Institute of

---

[51] As La Belle points out, this plate is the only one with inscriptions 'not containing the words "God", "Lord", or "Father"'. See 'Words Graven with an Iron Pen', p. 530.

Art, London).[52] Job's wife sits weeping to his right, earnestly looking into his face. The gesture of her hands appears to suggest not so much agreement with the friends,[53] as the question 'How can this be?' Blake's Job appears to be speaking the lines engraved in the upper margin, culminating with 'Though he slay me yet will I trust in him' (Job 13: 15). Between and behind Job and his accusers a single flower springs, but far from striking a note of hope, this alludes to part of the inscription below the caption: 'Man that is born of a Woman is of few days, & full of trouble | he cometh up [AV 'forth'] like a flower & is cut down: he fleeth also as a shadow | & continueth not' (Job 14: 1–2). In the engraving alone a bright area of light begins below the cornice at the far left and continues along the top of the whole mountain range in the background. This may be a premonition of hope, but the marginal designs are much in the vein of those immediately preceding. At the lower right an owl grasps a mouse or rat with its talons; at the lower left another bird, difficult to identify,[54] grasps a snake. At the top inset frame corners two chained male figures hold on to keep from falling down the margins. Bat wings emerge from behind the two lower corners. Worse is still to come with Job's terrible dream.

The caption of 11—'With Dreams upon my bed thou scarest me & affrightest me with Visions'—is a rephrasing of Job 7: 14, 'Then thou scarest me with dreams, and terrifiest me through visions'. This design's composition owes much to Blake's own colour-printed drawing *Elohim Creating Adam* (Butlin 289): in both a monstrous father-god floats vertically over a horrified supine figure helpless beneath him. In Blake's *Job* the head of the demonic figure also resembles that in *Night Thoughts*, watercolour 133 (engraved for the Edwards edition, facing page 80), illustrating the Job-like

[52] Blunt, *The Art of William Blake*, p. 40 and figs. 51a and 51b. This resemblance is probably what Lady Eastlake had in mind when she described the three friends as 'pointing at him with ominous arms, like the witches in Macbeth'. See Jameson and Rigby, *The History of Our Lord*, i. 230.

[53] As suggested by Wicksteed, *Blake's Vision of the Book of Job*, p. 139; Damon, *Blake's Job*, p. 30; Lindberg, *William Blake's Illustrations to the Book of Job*, p. 242; and Andrew Wright, *Blake's Job: A Commentary* (Oxford: Clarendon Press, 1972), p. 29.

[54] Damon (*Blake's Job*, p. 30) suggests it is 'the cuckoo of slander', but cuckoos feed on insects not snakes; Lindberg (*William Blake's Illustrations to the Book of Job*, p. 241) identifies it as a raven, but this bird is not black; and Blake elsewhere emphasizes the raven's blackness.

question 'shall I question loud | The thunder, if in that the ALMIGHTY dwells?' Although Young means this positively, Blake did not believe that the glory of God was manifested in loud noises, and this is one of the numerous *Night Thoughts* illustrations that undermines Young's text. In the strange head of the demon Anthony Blunt observes a 'fusion of the Gothic with the classical type', combining the characteristics of ancient heads of Jupiter with 'the character of those grotesque heads familiar in Gothic sculpture in which the hair round a mask is transformed into foliage'.[55] As if to leave no doubt as to its true identity, the figure is entwined by a serpent, as in *Satan Watching the Endearments of Adam and Eve* in the *Paradise Lost* drawings,[56] and his cloven hoof is exposed, like that of 'The Angry God of This World' in Dante illustration 3, *Dante and the Mission of Virgil* (see Chapter 3). With his right hand he points to the twin tablets of the Decalogue on which a few Hebraic characters faintly appear, while with his left he reaches for a chain being offered to him by a scaly demon in the black flames below. Another demon grasps Job's loins and one more his ankles (are these three nightmare transformations of Job's comforters?). This is the only one of the engravings in which Job's wife does not appear, and his isolation reinforces his—and our—sense of terror. As most critics agree, this is the nadir of Job's afflictions.

As if to compensate for the unsually dense imagery of its main design, 11 bears only a simple image of flame in its margins, but it is nonetheless rich in texts. Three of the upper ones come from the Book of Job itself, the two in the corners (30: 17 and 30: 30) giving details of his sufferings, the third announcing 'The triumphing of the wicked | is short, the joy of the hypocrite is | but for a moment' (20: 5). More difficult to understand is the quotation from 2 Corinthians just above the top horizontal inner frame: 'Satan himself is transformed into an Angel of Light, & his Ministers [AV 'his ministers also be transformed'] into Ministers of Righteousness' (11: 14–15). Although it may seem like a statement of literally incredible opti-

---

[55] Blunt, 'Blake's Pictorial Imagination', *Journal of the Warburg and Courtauld Institutes*, 6 (1943): 199. Blunt suggests that Blake knew this type from sculptures in St Stephen's Chapel, Westminster, engraved by Basire for the Society of Antiquaries in 1795. He cites plate 13 of *Plans, Elevations and Sections . . . of St. Stephen's Chapel, Westminster*, engraved by Basire 1795.

[56] There are several versions of this watercolour, the most striking of which is the rich, full-bodied one Blake executed for John Linnell in 1822 (Butlin 537.1, National Gallery of Victoria).

mism—Wicksteed is probably not alone in taking it to mean 'No depth of error is irredeemable'[57]—in its context, this passage is a companion to the one about 'the joy of the hypocrite' above it, as it continues 'whose end shall be according to their works'. As Matthew Henry expounds the passage:

And no marvel (says the apostle); hypocrisy is a thing not to be much wondered at in this world, especially when we consider the great influence Satan has upon the minds of many, who *rules in the hearts of the children of disobedience*. As he can turn himself into any shape, and put on almost any form, and look sometimes *like an angel of light*, in order to promote his kingdom of darkness, so he will teach his ministers and instruments to do the same. But it follows, *Their end is according to their works* (v. 15); the end will discover them to be deceitful workers, and their work will end in ruin and destruction.[58]

More immediately obvious in meaning is the lowermost marginal quotation: 'Who opposeth & exalteth himself above all that is called God, or is Worshipped' (2 Thess. 2: 4). Here Blake clearly has in mind the exposure of Satan, in line with what immediately precedes the quotation—'and that man of sin be revealed, the son of perdition . . .'. The longest marginal statement, however, is irrefutably positive. It differs in many details from the AV original and is evidently Blake's own translation of Job 19: 22–7:

Blake: Why do you persecute me as God & are not satisfied with my flesh. Oh that my words | were printed in a Book that they were graven with an iron pen & lead in the rock for ever | For I know that my Redeemer liveth & that he shall stand in the latter days upon | the Earth & after my skin destroy thou This body yet in my flesh shall I see God | whom I shall see for Myself and mine eyes shall behold & not Another tho consumed be my wrought Image

AV: Why do ye persecute me as God, and are not satisfied with my flesh? Oh that my words were now written! oh that they were printed in a book! That they were graven with an iron pen and lead in the rock for ever! For I know that my redeemer liveth, and that he shall stand at the latter day upon the earth: And though after my skin worms destroy this body, yet in my flesh shall I see God: Whom I shall see for myself, and mine eyes shall behold, and not another; though my reins be consumed within me.

---

[57] *Blake's Vision of the Book of Job*, p. 148.
[58] *Blue Letter Bible*, www.blueletterbible.org/Comm/mhc/2Cr/2Cro11.html (27 September 2003).

Job's words, part of which, as Lindberg points out, form the end of the Church of England Burial Service,[59] are especially moving in a plate that depicts the horrors of Job's dream of Satan masquerading as God, the reason for the two quotations previously discussed and the reference of 'and not another' here. The words 'Oh that my words | were printed in a Book that they were graven with an iron pen' must have had special meaning for Blake, as that was exactly what he was doing in the *Illustrations of the Book of Job*.

'I am Young & ye are very Old wherefore I was afraid' (Job 32: 6), the caption to 12, is from the beginning of the long speech of Elihu, which continues to the end of chapter 37. The tenor of Elihu's words is not radically different from that of the three others, but Blake chooses to accentuate his youth, his emotional nature, and the energy of his discourse as positive elements. Elihu wears a transparent body stocking of the kind worn by the son to the right in 2, and he points to the heavens with his left hand while stretching his right toward his audience. Of these, the men, including Job, listen attentively, while Job's wife is hunched over with her hands clasped between her knees, in a pose Blake uses to indicate despair, as for example in the central figure of *Jerusalem* 51. There are twelve stars in the sky, but Elihu seems not to point at these—indeed, there are no stars in his speech—but out of the picture space into the upper margin. There, and in the bottom margin as well, Blake has excerpted fragments of Elihu's speech that suit his own purpose.[60] Among these are a version of Job 33: 23–4: 'If there be with him an Interpreter One in a Thousand | Then he is gracious unto him | & saith Deliver him from going down to the Pit | I have found a Ransom'. Blake has made one significant change from the AV text in verse 23: he has substituted 'Interpreter' for 'messenger'. This is probably because it was he himself whom Blake thought of as the Interpreter, a name given him by the young artist friends who called themselves the Ancients.[61] In the lower margin the sleeping Job, his left hand on a scroll, bears more of Elihu's words on his garment: 'Look upon the heavens & behold the clouds | which are higher | than thou' (Job 35: 5). In the

---

[59] Lindberg, *William Blake's Illustrations to the Book of Job*, p. 268.

[60] Lindberg, 'William Blake's Illustrations of the Book of Job', BTJ, n.p. observes that there are 166 words from Elihu's pronouncements, 'surpassed only by Jesus, who, in plate 17, has 170 words'.

[61] See Nelms, 'Text and Design in *Illustrations of the Book of Job*', p. 344 n.

lower left corner two angels are encouraging a horde of tiny humans to do just that: they rise from sleep and stream up both vertical margins to form a design near the top much like the tent-like shape at the top of 1. There stars appear above and below them, the ones above forming Orion's belt and the Pleiades; above these are clouds with some of Elihu's words on them. Elihu's speech, mediated by the angels, has freed Job's thoughts to rise. Although his body will not stand erect until 18, his ordeal is about to end.

In 13, perhaps the most dramatic engraving of the series, 'Then the Lord answered Job out of the Whirlwind' (Job 38: 1), an enormous swirl goes clockwise around the picture space, causing the comforters to bend over but leaving Job (although his hair is blown back) and his wife sitting upright with their hands prayerfully together. This is a day scene in the Butts watercolour, but it is far more effective as a night scene in Linnell's, which Blake follows in the engraving. Blake also follows the Linnell watercolour in making the structure in the background a balustrade rather than a cromlech. God appears in the whirlwind with his arms cruciform, suggesting the union of Father and Son, and looking compassionately at Job. His feet are reassuringly human. In the lower margin trees have been blown down by the mighty wind, and in the upper one five or perhaps six Job-like figures arc from left to right parallel to the movement of the wind in the main design. In keeping with the powerful simplicity of the design, the marginal texts are also simple, consisting of short quotations from Job 38: 2, Psalm 14: 3, and Job 38: 28. The God presented here is obviously the opposite of the false god of 11; the fact that the heads of both resemble Roman sculptures of Jupiter (Blunt compares this one to a relief of Jupiter Pluvius with outstretched arms on the column of Marcus Aurelius[62]) sets them apart all the more from each other. The way is now prepared for Job to share the divine vision in 14, 'When the morning Stars sang together, & all the Sons of God shouted for joy' (Job 38: 7). Here the Butts watercolour has the advantage of a cerulean sky, perhaps faded in the Linnell version. This is the design that Samuel Palmer recalled singling out when he wrote to Gilchrist: 'In Westminster Abbey were his earliest and most sacred recollections. I asked him how he would like to paint on glass, for the great west window, his *Sons of God shouting for Joy*, from his designs in the *Job*. He said, after a pause, "I

[62] Blunt, *The Art of William Blake*, pp. 36, 41.

could do it!" kindling at the thought'.[63] However, the engraving (Fig. 32) has at least one advantage over either watercolour: in the latter there were four angels, but in the engraving Blake added the arms and hands of two more on either side of the design area, to suggest an infinite succession of angels. Blake had previously depicted just such a frieze of angels in *Night Thoughts*, watercolour 437, referring to Young's 'Chorus of the Skies'.[64] Below a thin line of cloud the Lord appears, again cruciform, with Helios conducting the horse of the sun under his right arm and Selene bearing the moon drawn by two serpents under his left. (Despite his condemnation of classical mythology, Blake could employ it in a subordinate role when it suited his artistic purposes.) Another cloud layer forms a cavern from which Job and his wife, with the three comforters, look up in awe. This sublime view of the created world is continued in the margins. In the side margins are six little vignettes of the days of Creation, three on each side, each with an appropriate quotation from Genesis 1. An angel stands at each of the upper inner frame corners, with a thread passing from one to the other and back again. Above the left-hand one are seven stars, above the right three—so perhaps the thread is metaphorically related to the text above it: 'Canst thou bind the sweet influences of Pleiades or loose the bands of Orion' (Job 38: 31). In the bottom margin we see Leviathan in the sea, flaming at either end; and below him the worm of mortality winding around a cylindrical object. In the main design and its margins we have a composite picture of the natural world from the perspective of the eternal world, one that could be compared in this respect with the long vision that ends Book the First of *Milton a Poem*, concluding 'Thus Nature is a Vision of the Science of the Elohim' (29 [31]: 65, E 128).

Accepting the physical universe necessarily means accepting the enormous forces within it. 'Behold now Behemoth which I made with thee' (Job 40: 15), says the Lord in 15, with an angel at either side, pointing with his downstretched left arm. Job and his companions now sit in a space in the upper part of the picture, but still separated from God by a layer of cloud. Directly below his left index finger is the terraqueous globe, in which are a hippotamus-like

---

[63] Gilchrist, *Life*, p. 303.

[64] See Keynes, *Blake Studies*, p. 26 and plate 12. Keynes points out that such a frieze of figures with arms upraised appears in one of the unsigned engravings for Jacob Bryant's *New System* (1774–6).

FIG. 32. *Illustrations of the Book of Job*, 14: *When the morning Stars sang together, & all the Sons of God shouted for joy.* Engraving, 1825.

(though tusked) creature on dry land among reeds and bulrushes, suggestive of Egypt, and a huge crocodile-headed serpent, coiling in the sea. The upper one, Behemoth, is 'the chief of the ways of God', in the words from Job 40: 19 that Blake engraved in the right margin; while Leviathan is 'King over all the Children of Pride' (Job 41: 34). These two monsters previously figured in Blake's 'spiritual portraits' of Pitt and Nelson (Butlin 651 and 652, Tate Gallery), embodying war by land and war by sea. Here they are represented, as so many of Blake's monsters, as grotesque. If we were within that transparent sphere we would see them as terrifying embodiments of natural energy, but from a divine perspective outside the bound circle of the natural world, they look absurd, 'sharers', as Milton O. Percival puts it, 'in the colossal joke of their success as realities'.[65] At the top corners of the inset border two bearded angels write in books, while at the lower right corners are two eagles, each perhaps 'a portion of genius' as in *The Marriage of Heaven and Hell* (E 37), and the sea has washed two empty conch shells up into the bottom corners. The artistry of this engraving is astutely described in Charles Eliot Norton's early commentary. Noting that Behemoth and Leviathan 'are represented as if from some medieval bas-relief', Norton goes on to say 'The design exhibits the marked tendency, in much of Blake's work, to an architectural mode, and strongly ornamented character of composition', and he links this to 'his skill as an engraver in the production and the bold distribition of strongly contrasted light and shade'.[66]

After the instruction of Job by the Lord in plates 13, 14, and 15 comes the downfall of Satan in 16, 'Thou hast fulfilled the Judgment of the Wicked' (Job 36: 17). The little apocalypse in which Satan is cast out is not in the Book of Job, but Blake has decided to have God give Job, his wife, and the three comforters a preview of the Last Judgement. Three of the marginal texts give his authority from the New Testament for doing so:

The Accuser of our Brethren is Cast down | which accused them before God day & night (Rev. 12: 10)

The Prince of this World shall be cast out (John 12: 31)

[65] See Percival, *William Blake's Circle of Destiny* (New York: Columbia University Press, 1938), p. 270.
[66] Norton, *William Blake's Illustrations of the Book of Job*, n.p.

Even the Devils are Subject to Us through thy Name. Jesus [AV 'And he'] said unto them, I saw Satan as lightning fall from Heaven (Luke 10: 17–18)

In the centre of the picture space, which he dominated leaping horizontally in 2 and soaring diagonally in 5, Satan now plummets down, with two other figures who may be Job and his wife in their former state of error,[67] in a flaming thunderbolt. More fires await him below, and in the bottom and side margins as well. The two angels of 15 have moved down a little so as to observe him with satisfaction from above, while Job and his wife look on (she crossing her arms in wonder) from the lower left and the friends shrink away at the lower right. In the top centre the enthroned Lord is seen in a new form. No longer the passive and even drooping *dieu fainéant*, as Northrop Frye calls him,[68] of 2 and 5, God now sits with attentive regard and blesses the event with his open right palm. In his egg-shaped white nimbus, which is not all visible because part of it meets the upper edge of the picture space, are two weeping cherubs and four more child angels (of which at least three have their own haloes) crowding around God's body. There are traces of these, pencilled in the Linnell drawing, none in Butts's, and none in the Fitzwilliam Notebook; Blake must have drawn them directly onto the copper with an etching needle, as he did the marginal designs. Butlin compares Blake's pictorial key to *A Vision of the Last Judgment*, in which, Blake says, 'Jesus is surrounded by Beams of Glory in which are seen all around him Infants emanating from him these represent the Eternal Births of Intellect from the divine Humanity' (E 562). In the upper inset corners appear the two angels of the former engraving, but without their writing materials.

One of the two pictures that Blake added to the original *Job* series is 17, which has been given the editorial title *The Vision of Christ*.[69] However, Blake did not use that title. The caption he gave to the engraving (Fig. 33) was *I have heard thee with the hearing of the Ear but now my Eye seeth thee*'. (It has been pointed out that since the AV text has an 'of' between 'heard' and 'thee', Blake here chooses the

[67] See Wicksteed, *Blake's Vision of the Book of Job*, p. 117; Damon, *Blake's Job*, p. 42; Lindberg, *William Blake's Illustrations to the Book of Job*, p. 317.

[68] Frye, 'Blake's Reading of the Book of Job', p. 227.

[69] So far as I can determine, this title was first given it in *Illustrations of The Book of Job by William Blake*, ed. Laurence Binyon and Geoffrey Keynes (New York: Pierpont Morgan Library, 1935).

FIG. 33. *Illustrations of the Book of Job, 17: I have heard thee with the hearing of the Ear but now my Eye seeth thee.* Engraving, 1825.

Vulgate text because Job has indeed heard God's voice.)[70] The possible circumstances of production of the Linnell and Butts watercolours of this subject have already been discussed above. One thing that is certain is that the engraving follows the Linnell watercolour in placing the three friends with their backs to Job and his wife instead of facing the Lord in a row behind them, as in the Butts version. Also, both in the Linnell picture and in the engraving God's hands, outstretched with palms down in benediction, are much closer to the heads of Job and his wife than in the Butts picture. The placement of the friends is far more effective here than in the Butts watercolour, as they are all the more set off by having their backs turned to God, in contrast to Job and his wife, and in the engraving alone a somewhat comic touch is added by the middle one's attempting to sneak a look over his right shoulder. These false comforters are shrinking away from the radiance of God's magnificent mandorla, which streams radiantly from concentric discs of light, and even passes out of the inner frame into the upper margin. In the lower right margin (the upper margin is taken up only with inscriptions, one of them on a cloud) is a beautiful, winged female angel holding in her right hand a quill pen with which she is inditing texts from the Gospel of John. The statement in one of her texts, 'I and my Father are one', comes from John 10: 30, asserting the unity of Father and Son. All the other quotations in this lower margin are from John 14, and have as their theme the unity of the divine and the further unity of the divine and the human. The one that begins furthest to the left reads 'He that hath seen me hath seen my Father also' (9). In a book opened in the lower left corner we read an amplification of this message, from 7; and in another book, in the right-hand corner still another, from 21 and 23. The right-hand page of the latter book brings in another element: 'And [AV: I will pray] the Father [AV: and he] shall give you Another Comforter, that he may abide with you for ever' (16). This is glossed in verse 26, which Blake does not include: 'But the Comforter, which is the Holy Ghost, whom the Father will send in my name, he shall teach you all things . . .'. This divine unity is completed by the words in the scroll at the bottom centre—'At that day ye shall know that I am in my Father, and ye in me, and I in you' (20). The proposed title

[70] See Lindberg, *William Blake's Illustrations to the Book of Job*, p. 322; and La Belle, 'Words Graven with an Iron Pen', p. 543.

'The Vision of Christ' is not so much wrong as incomplete—the subject of this engraving is the unity of Father, Son, Holy Ghost, and Humanity.

Job's altar in 18, *And my Servant Job shall pray for you* (Job 42: 8), is made of unhewn stones, an important detail because in Exod. 20: 25 God commanded: 'And if thou wilt make me an altar of stone, thou shalt not build it of hewn stone: for if thou lift up thy tool upon it, thou hast polluted it.' This makes for a significant difference between the engraving and both watercolours, in which the surfaces of the altar are smooth. Job stands erect for the first time in the entire series so far, in the cruciform palms-up bodily attitude that indicates the giving up of self in imitation of Christ, as in the full-page *Jerusalem 76* design. This view of Job began with the Linnell watercolour, the Butts drawing having shown him from the front, with his left leg on a step of the altar. In both the Butts and the Linnell watercolours there is a three-pillared structure in the mid-ground (turned at an angle in the Linnell drawing), but in the engraving this has been eliminated and replaced by trees. In appearance and dress (a loose, long-flowing robe) Job is virtually identical with the God who blessed him in the preceding plate. Job's wife to his left, her long hair flowing down her back, is bowed with her hands held together in prayer; and the three friends to his right are also bowed. The upright form of Job is continued by the pointed triangle of flame that rises from his altar, while the curve formed by his arms is echoed first by a swag of cloud and then by the lower part of the disc of an enormous, radiant sun—so enormous that part of its disc continues into the upper margin. Because of its size, and because the natural sun will not rise until 21, this must be the spiritual sun, a Swedenborgian notion that Blake retained, according to which the spiritual sun is the Lord, its light divine truth, and its heat divine good.[71] Here we see Job and his wife adoring its beams, and even the three friends are worshipping it. As the line from Job 42: 10 below the caption reminds us, Job has 'prayed for his Friends'. An opened book in the left-hand corner begins with the words of Jesus from Matt. 5: 44, beginning 'I say unto you Love your Enemies . . .'. In line with this spirit of harmony, the foremost of three angels in the upper right

---

[71] Emanuel Swedenborg, *Heaven and its Wonders and Hell* (New York: Swedenborg Society, 1956), p. 86 (no. 117). 'I have conversed with the—Spiritual Sun—I saw him on Primrose hill', Blake told Henry Crabb Robinson in 1825 (*BR*, pp. 311–12; cf. Lindberg, *William Blake's Illustrations to the Book of Job*, p. 328).

margin plays a harp and his counterpart on the upper left plays a double horn or double recorder. Wheat ready for harvest bends gently below. Two personal touches are added in the lower margin by a painter's palette and brushes, above which Blake placed his signature, and in the centre and just above, an engraver's implement identified by Robert Essick as 'a knife tool' of just the sort Blake employed 'to cut the lines of intense illumination on pl. 18 and elsewhere in the second half of the series'.[72]

Though now rich in spirit, Job and his wife are poor in material possessions, and so they go from having been donors of charity in 5 to becoming the recipients of it in 19. In the words of the caption, 'Every one also gave him a piece of Money' (Job 42: 11). Although the AV text says 'every man', Blake changed this to 'Every one', which is indeed true to the spirit of the passage:

> Then came there unto him all his brethren, and all his sisters, and all they that had been of his acquaintance before, and did eat bread with him in his house: and they bemoaned him, and comforted him over all the evil that the LORD had brought upon him: every man also gave him a piece of money, and every one an earring of gold.

In the Butts watercolour there were only two female givers of charity, but Blake introduced one more in Linnell's—indeed, this is one of the two plates (the other being 20) in which there are more women than men. These women, as well as those in the following two plates, are, in Gilchrist's words, 'of exquisite beauty', and he adds, touchingly, 'These women are given to us no less noble in body than in soul; large-eyed, and large-armed also; such as a man may love with all his life'.[73] The foremost one extends an earring to Job and his wife, who are seated under a tree on a piece of primitive furniture, and one of those behind holds a net purse from which she will extract a gift. The figure nearest to us is a dark-bearded man of great dignity, bearing a large, heart-shaped purse (on which an angel is depicted in both watercolours but not in the engraving). The entire scene is rich with fertility—figs hang from the tree, and ripe wheat stands in the field. This is carried over to the marginal designs: palm trees bear thick bunches of grapes at both right and left, two females float in the lower margin, bearing fruit and flowers, in the upper margin two more scatter petals, the one to the right also bearing a sprig on

---

[72] Essick, *William Blake, Printmaker*, p. 237.   [73] Gilchrist, *Life*, p. 292.

which there may be berries. Two more young women appear in the palm fronds above each of the upper inset corners, and three go down the two side margins, and at the very bottom corners are huge roses (left) and lilies (right). The inscription from Job 38: 41 at the upper centre, 'who provideth for the Raven his food [AV 'food?']' when his young ones cry unto God' reinforces this theme of abundance. All the marginal figures, it is worth noting, are female. A line of light over the hills in the central background suggests that the dawn is nigh.

The extraordinary design for 20, *There were not found Women fair as the Daughters of Job* (Job 42: 15), is one of the two that was not present in the original Butts set, the Butts watercolour being like 17 on laid paper instead of the woven paper of the rest. Indeed, Butlin and most other scholars consider it to have been executed after the Linnell version.[74] The episode is not in the Bible and so in all versions was completely invented by Blake. The Butts watercolour is of an outdoor pastoral scene with sheep, dog, and greensward. Job and two of his daughters sit on a couch in the meadow with one daughter kneeling in the middle as Job indicates three scenes in the sky above them. The left-hand daughter has drawing or writing paper, the middle one is reading a book, and the one at the right has a scroll in her left hand. It has been considered since W. M. Rossetti's catalogue[75] that this rather poor drawing is largely by a hand other than Blake's, and that it even may have been completed after Blake's death. The Linnell version is closer to the engraving, though it cannot have been the source for it. It is a mixture of outdoors and indoors. The daughters here hold no objects, all three incline towards Job. The scenes Job relates appear on a wall, but there are a meadow and sheep in the foreground. Even the Fitzwilliam Notebook drawing still includes some sheep. Blake's prior rendition of this subject closest to the engraving is, as Butlin points out, a drawing of a tempera done for Butts *c.*1799–1800 (Butlin 394, Rosenwald Collection, National Gallery of Art). There the scene is an interior, and Job's arms extend sideways as he tells his daughters his story. Similarly, the engraving (Fig. 34) takes place indoors, and is in fact the only indoor scene in the series. The floor and lower levels

---

[74] An exception is Lindberg, *William Blake's Illustrations to the Book of Job*, p. 345.

[75] See Rossetti, 'Descriptive Catalogue', in Gilchrist, *Life* (1880), ii. 224, 117 (*l*).

FIG. 34. *Illustrations of the Book of Job*, 20: *There were not found Women fair as the Daughters of Job.* Engraving, 1825.

of the walls, indistinct in the tempera, have been developed in the engraving. Three scenes are readily identifable behind Job: from left to right, the destruction of Job's servants by the Chaldeans (1: 17) with Satan overhead, God appearing out of the whirlwind as in 13, and the destruction of a ploughman by Satan himself (and not by the Sabeans as in Job 1: 15). Lindberg notes the apsidal nature of the space and suggests they are in a house or church adorned with frescos; if the latter, 'they are sitting on the altar in front of the apse under the altar-piece'.[76] There is a lower level of paintings to the left and right. Each contains four elements: a human slumped over in despair, a round arch above him or her, jagged lines of lightning, and a bearded head above with arms outstetched (or possibly bat wings on the left), controlling the thunderbolts. Both slumping figures resemble Job's wife in 8 and 12, and the bearded heads may belong to the demonic false god of 11. Serpents decorate the walls between the two levels of pictures. Whether church or palace, the room as a whole suggests the passage in *Jerusalem* 16 where the archetypes of all things that happen on earth are represented:

> All things acted on Earth are seen in the bright Sculptures of
> Los's Halls & every Age renews its powers from these Works
> With every pathetic story possible to happen from Hate or
> Wayward Love & every sorrow & distress is carved here[77]

The two levels of pictures are separated by a band, in each of which is a serpent. The floor is made up of an interesting design, a large circle containing many intersecting small circles—perhaps emblematizing human interdependence and the containment of all humanity in the divine. The margins continue the sense of harmony and plenitude conveyed by the main design—grape vines, bearing bunches of grapes at the middle and the bottom of the frames, climb all over the marginal space; angelic couples converse at the upper corners of the inset margins; and a harp and a mandolin occupy the two bottom corners. Cued by these musical instruments, Lindberg argues that the entire scene originates in the apocryphal *Testament of Job*, pointing out that although the text of this book was not available in Blake's time, Blake could have been aware of its content through visual

---

[76] *William Blake's Illustrations to the Book of Job*, pp. 339, 342.
[77] 16.61–4, E 161, as suggested by Wicksteed, *Blake's Vision of the Book of Job*, p. 203 n.

sources.[78] One element that is indeed from the Bible is the granting of a separate inheritance (unusual for women in the Old Testament) to the daughters—Jemima, Kezia, and Kerenhappuch. 'And in all the land were no women found so fair as the daughters of Job,' reads the caption in full, 'and their father gave them inheritance among their brethren' (42: 15).

In a brilliant stroke that goes back to the first watercolour series, Blake makes the last plate correlative with and yet contrary to the first, with Job and his family underneath a tree with sheep in the foreground. Where the moon was waning at our right in 1, it is waxing at our left in 21, and the sun that was setting at our left in 1 is now rising at our right. Most important, the musical instruments that were hanging on a tree at the beginning are now being used. At the front centre Job plays a harp, his wife a mandolin, and between them a beautiful daughter ('no women . . . so fair as the daughters of Job') sings from a text on a scroll, as one of her sisters sings from a booklet. The remaining daughter and the seven sons vigorously play various musical instruments, some singing at the same time. Even the two foremost sheep have awakened and gaze at the viewer. The tentlike form that we saw in the upper margin of 1 appears in the same place here, and in the lower margin the bull and the ram have changed corners. Before the sheep is a shepherd's crook (unbroken, in contrast to the one in 6), while the altar in the centre is now inscribed 'In burnt offerings for Sin | thou hast had no pleasure' (Hebrews 10: 6). In both watercolours the sun's disc bears an inscription beginning 'Great & Marvellous', but this has been transferred to the two sides of the top margin with the rest of Rev. 15: 3: 'Great & Marvellous are thy Works | Lord God Almighty || Just & true are thy ways || O thou King of Saints'. This is part of 'the song of Moses the servant of God, and the song of the Lamb' (Rev. 15: 3), which is presumably what is being sung to musical accompaniment in the design.[79] 'So', in the words of the caption, 'the Lord blessed the latter end of Job more than the beginning' (Job 42: 12).

[78] Acording to Lindberg, 'the direct source of Job's design' is a 'very dilapidated *al secco* of about 1350' showing Job telling his daughters the story, from the cycle of Job illustrations from St Stephen's Chapel, Westminster, which was included in the *Vestuta Monumenta* (1785–1811) of Richard Gough with engravings by Robert Smirke. See *William Blake's Illustrations to the Book of Job*, pp. 139 n., 343–4. Lindberg also argues that 'The catholic tradition of Job as the patron saint of musicians and singers derives from this apocryphal source' (p. 343).

[79] As Damon says, 'The Justice of the Old Testament and the Mercy of the New are united . . .' (*Blake's Job*, p. 52).

In the *Illustrations of the Book of Job* Blake created a masterpiece that exemplifies his own desideratum: 'when a Work has Unity it is as much a part as in the Whole' (*On Homers Poetry*, E 269). He could not of course resolve the fundemental dilemma that theologians have so often addressed in vain: of how the children and servants could in the biblical story be regarded as so many chattels to be destroyed and then replaced so that God could in effect win a bet with Satan. He chose rather to address the subject on different levels at different times, sometimes as literal illustration, sometimes as symbolic of intrapsychic events. In so doing, he emphasized the unity of Father, Son, and Holy Spirit, and the unity of God and man—and woman. In no other late work of Blake's do women have so important and so positive a role. He also introduced the subject of music and the other arts prominently where the text does not call for them at all. Although a knowledge of Blake's other works and of his characteristic ideas is important for a thorough understanding of the series, it is accessible on at least one level to viewers with no knowledge of these. Of all Blake's works it is the one that has to the greatest degree passed into the general consciousness of our culture.

Genesis and Enoch

The work known as the 'Genesis Manuscript' (Butlin 828.1–11, Huntington Library and Art Gallery) was commissioned by John Linnell, according to Gilchrist,[1] who probably had this information from Linnell himself. According to William Michael Rossetti, it was executed 'in the year of Blake's death',[2] and this seems probable because two of the leaves are watermarked 1826.[3] Blake had once created his own version of Genesis, in *The [First] Book of Urizen* (1794). Now he was creating an illuminated manuscript of the biblical text, but his intention, as we would expect, went far beyond decoration. His designs are largely symbolic rather than illustrative, and he created his own headings, sometimes far from the usually accepted significance of the texts beneath them, for each chapter to convey the meaning he desired. He also made some deliberate

---

[1] *Life*, p. 259. It was owned by Linnell, and then by his estate.
[2] Gilchrist, *Life* (1863), ii. 246 (1880, ii. 264).
[3] See Robert N. Essick, 'Illustrated Manuscript of Genesis', in *The Works of William Blake in the Huntington Collections* (San Marino, Calif.: Huntington Library, 1985), p. 89. Pages 88–115 are devoted to a description of the manuscript.

changes in the texts themselves. The result is to turn the biblical book of Genesis, from its beginning to verse 15 of Chapter 4 into a Blakean myth.

One of the numerous puzzles presented by the Genesis Manuscript is that it has two title pages, neither of them completed. The two have a great deal in common: the letters GE | NE | SIS, the central figure of Adam with a halo and his right arm upraised, three figures occupying the left, right, and top, and four more at the bottom. In both, the three figures are the persons of the Trinity. God the Father, bearded, occupies an elliptical space at the right. In the first version his robe is tinted blue, and his right arm raised like Adam's, but Blake's rendition of him lacks conviction, as if the artist's heart were not in giving the Father's figure equal status with the other two. The Son in the initial version extends his left arm through the disc he inhabits at the right. Athletically leaping through the air at the top, arms and legs extended, is the Holy Ghost, tinted red. Near the bottom of the leaf are four indistinct figures with flames above their heads, three of them extending their arms like Adam above them. In the second title page (Fig. 35), the title is teeming with vegetation. Some of these plants have been identified as exotic flowers that Blake could have known from the plates in Dr Thornton's *Temple of Flora* (London: 1799–1807), and that, along with the ears of wheat in the letter G, suggest fertility; while red roses and a possible Lily of Calvary suggest martyrdom.[4] Serpentine forms, whether meant to be snakes or tendrils, prefigure the Temptation and Fall. The figure at the top of the page now has huge wings, making him more easily identifiable. On the mid-level the Son, wearing a filmy garment, stands with arms cruciform, as in the *Paradiso* design *Dante Adoring Christ* (Butlin 812.90),[5] and he is clearly passing a scroll down to Adam (which he may indeed be doing less distinctly in the previous version). The Father is much as he was before, though lacking any tint, and he still lacks any semblance of power. In the lower part the heads of the four figures are more clearly defined, the flames are gone, and behind them are two trees, one bearing fruit. Presumably the latter are the Tree of the Knowledge of Good and Evil and the Tree of Life. As for the four forms, W. M. Rossetti may have been correct in identifying

---

[4] See Piloo Nannuvutty, 'A Title Page in Blake's Illustrated Genesis Manuscript', in *The Visionary Hand*, ed. Robert N. Essick, pp. 127–46. This article was first published in 1947.

[5] A comparison made by Essick, 'Illustrated Manuscript of Genesis', p. 94.

FIG. 35. William Blake, Genesis Manuscript: Second Title
Page, *c.*1826–7. Pencil, pen, watercolour, and liquid gold.

the four as 'the four living creatures used as the Evangelical Symbols',[6] but there is something decidedly comical about them. From right to left they appear to be a sad ox or bull, a caricature of a lion, a crowned eagle, and a scaly, at least partly human being with left arm upraised. They are sitting or sprawling on the ground, and they seem to partake less of the reality of the 'Four Mighty Ones . . . in every Man'[7] than that of Dorothy, the Cowardly Lion, the Scarecrow, and the Tin Woodman in *The Wizard of Oz*. They appear to inhabit the fourth and lowest tier of a reality that descends from the Holy Spirit at the top, to divine beings in human form in the middle, then to the human form, and last to these grotesques.

Blake's first chapter heading, 'The Creation of the Natural Man', gives a certain cast to the text of Gen. 1: 1–18 below. Of course Genesis 1 says no such thing, but rather, as Blake faithfully indited two leaves later, 'So God created man in his own image, in the image of God created he him; male and female created he them' (Gen. 1: 27). There is also something disquieting in the way in which God reaches down with his left arm in Blake's headpiece drawing, a gesture that reminds us of that of the demiurge in the famous frontispiece of *Europe* (1794), though mitigated, as Essick observes, by his right hand held in blessing,[8] as well as by the two graceful angels flanking him. Blake's text of 1: 1–18 is accurate save for one significant exception: after God's creation of the 'two great lights', verse 18 of Genesis in the AV reads 'And to rule over the day and over the night, and to divide the light from the darkness: and God saw that it was good'. Blake's line ends with 'the darkness', leaving out 'and God saw that it was good'. So with both word and image Blake alters the meaning of the beginning of Genesis.

In leaves 4 and 5, acts of creation are illustrated as performed by three figures, which may be the Persons of the Trinity, or God and two angels, or three angels. This culminates with the newly created Adam walking in wonder toward the three figures, who appear to both welcome him and show him the way. The only unsettling note is Blake's rendering of Gen. 1: 25, in the AV 'And God made the beast of the earth after his kind, and cattle after their kind, and every thing that creepeth upon the earth after his kind: and God saw that it was good'. The words after the second 'earth' have been rubbed out, and

---

[6] Gilchrist, *Life* (1880), ii. 264.   [7] *The Four Zoas*, Night I, 1: 4, E 300.
[8] See Essick, 'Illustrated Manuscript of Genesis', pp. 98–9.

so, as in 1: 18, God no longer 'saw that it was good'. Once more Blake has altered the meaning of the text by leaving out a positive statement. He next creates a heading for chapter 2 expressing his own interpretation of God's creation of Adam from the dust of the ground and of Eve from Adam's rib: 'The Natural Man divided into Male & Female & of the Tree of Life & of the Tree | of Good & Evil.' This notion of the creation of the sexes as a division is of course very far from 'And the LORD God said, It is not good that the man should be alone; I will make him an help meet for him' (Gen. 2: 18). Blake also introduces two important changes in wording. In Gen. 2: 7 'the LORD God formed man of the dust of the ground', and Blake first copied this, but then wrote 'adamah' over 'ground'; and where Gen. 2: 9 reads in the AV 'And out of the ground made the LORD God to grow every tree that is pleasant to the sight . . .', Blake began 'And out of the ground (Adamah) . . .'. *Adamah*, the Hebrew feminine noun, is used to mean 'earth',[9] but without the pejorative sense that Blake attaches to it. (Cf. ‏יהוה‎ *& his two Sons*: 'He repented that he had made Adam (of the Female, Adamah) & it grieved him at his heart'.) Blake will go on inserting 'adamah' in negative contexts. On leaf 7, it is written over the word 'ground' in the recension of 'And out of the ground the LORD God formed every beast of the field' (Gen. 2: 19); on leaf 9 Blake adds the word 'Adamah' in parentheses after 'In the sweat of thy face shalt thou eat bread, till thou return unto the ground' (Gen. 3: 19); it is added after 'to till the ground' in Gen. 3: 23, and three times after 'ground' in God's curse on Cain in Gen. 4: 11–13. By substituting or adding the word 'adamah' Blake repeatedly denigrates the female principle.

The design at the head of page 6 shows God the Father having just created Adam and Eve, with Eve as in Gen. 1: 27: 'So God created man in his own image, in the image of God created he him; male and female created he them.' A figure in a tree or shrub at the left may possibly be Satan, as Butlin (828.6) suggests. If so, the Fall is being prepared even as Eve is being created. At the bottom of leaf 7 there is another drawing of the creation of Eve, with horizontal figures on three levels. In the upper part flies the triad of beings last seen at the bottom of page 5; at the bottom Adam lies supine on the ground with what appears to be a wound in (or a belt around?) his chest; between the two, Eve floats in the air, her feet almost touching the wound. The

---

[9] See Damon, *A Blake Dictionary*, p. 6.

implication is that, as in Gen. 2: 21, 'the LORD God caused a deep sleep to fall upon Adam, and he slept: and he took one of his ribs, and closed up the flesh instead thereof . . .'. This, unlike the previous design,[10] would correspond to Blake's myth of sexuality as expressed in his chapter title 'The Natural Man divided into Male & Female . . .' and his myth of the division of a primordial androgynous humanity into male and female. According to Blake's view in the Genesis Manuscript, this division is the cause of the Fall, as expressed in the heading for chapter 3 (leaf 8): 'Of the Sexual Nature & its Fall into Generation & Death'. Above this inscription is a drawing of Adam and Eve kneeling before the fruited Tree of Knowledge, and a serpent with an enormous head crawling toward them from the tree trunk. Eve's hands are in the position of a *Venus pudica*, much as Cambel's in *Jerusalem* 81. Sexual shame has come into existence as a result of eating the fruit (a piece of which is on the ground near Adam's forward knee). The drawing after the end of this chapter represents the expulsion of Adam and Eve from Paradise, though it is so sketchy that we might not guess this if it were not for this event's being the conclusion of chapter 3. As it is, we can make out three heads at the right, presumably indicating the triad we have seen several times previously, and two figures on the right, bent at an angle toward the left. From this we move to the story of Cain and Abel in chapter 4.

As we have seen, *The Ghost of Abel* introduces the theme of the forgiveness of sins where it does not exist in the Genesis account. The heading to chapter 4 gives this element even more emphasis: 'How Generation & Death took Possession of the natural Man | & of the Forgiveness of Sins written upon the Murderers Forhead'. In the headpiece illustration, Cain (a surprisingly small figure in relation to the others) flees while either Adam or Eve mourns over Abel's body, with the other parent possibly indicated by a head bowed behind the first figure. A large figure in the sky is pursuing Cain, perhaps Jehovah or possibly Abel's ghost. This is unlike Blake's other renditions of the subject, in which the murderer is pursued by flame. Nevertheless, in the tailpiece design God is shown embracing the kneeling Cain and appears to be marking his forehead with a kiss. The depiction of the two figures is widely recognized as recalling, no

---

[10] It may well be, as Essick suggests ('Illustrated Manuscript of Genesis', p. 104 and p. 138 n.), that Blake was aware of the existence of the 'Elohim' and 'Jahweh' accounts of creation.

doubt intentionally, engravings of the return of the Prodigal Son.[11] Thus, although it has some negative elements, the Genesis Manuscript ends on a highly positive note.

In the Genesis Manuscript Blake reinterprets his biblical subject in both word and image. As in *The Everlasting Gospel*, physical existence is viewed as entirely negative; and forgiveness of sins is the dominant theme of the Cain and Abel story, as in *The Ghost of Abel*. This freedom in handling the text is even more pronounced in Blake's illustrations for the *Book of Enoch*. *Enoch* is of course not a canonical book but an apocryphal one, but Blake would have made little distinction between the two, and the fact that *Enoch* had only become available in English in 1821 would have made his interest in it all the keener.

ii

The existence of the pseudepigraphical work known as the *Book of Enoch* was long known. The first part of it was accepted by the early Christian Church, but it was excluded from the canon at the Council of Nicaea in 325 CE.[12] The Greek text was extant until the eighth century, and the book remained canonical for the Church of Ethiopia. Its survival has been attributed 'to the fascination of marginal and heretical Christian groups, such as the Manichaeans'.[13] It is quoted in Jude 14–15: 'And Enoch also, the seventh from Adam, prophesied of these, saying, Behold, the Lord cometh with ten thousands of his saints, To execute judgment upon all, and to convince all that are ungodly among them of all their ungodly deeds which they have ungodly committed, and of all their hard speeches which ungodly sinners have spoken against him.' (Jude, too, was excluded by the Council of Nicaea but was restored at the Council of Trent in the

[11] Leslie Tannenbaum argues convincingly for *The Prodigal Son* of Marten de Vos as a model. See Tannenbaum, 'Blake and the Iconography of Cain', in Essick and Pearce, eds., *Blake in His Time*, p. 31 and plate 53.

[12] General information about the *Book of Enoch* is from 'Enoch, First Book of', *Encyclopædia Britannica*. http://search.eb.com/eb/article?eu=33262 (1 November 2002); and from *The Old Testament Pseudepigrapha*, ed. James H. Charlesworth (Garden City, NY: Doubleday, 1983), i. 5–12 (by E. Isaac). Known to scholars as *1 Enoch*, this book is now considered, as E. Isaac puts it, 'composite, representing numerous period and writers' (i. 6). This is not, however, pertinent to a discussion of the book as it was understood by Blake and his contemporaries.

[13] *Encyclopædia Britannica*, s.v.

mid-sixteenth century.) As one who read the Bible day and night, Blake would have known of the existence of the *Book of Enoch* through Jude, which provided the material for his watercolour of *c.*1805 *The Devil Rebuked; The Burial of Moses* (Butlin 449, Fogg Art Museum).[14] He would also, of course, have known the lines of Genesis in which an extraordinary distinction is given to Enoch:

And Enoch lived sixty and five years, and begat Methuselah:
    And Enoch walked with God after he begat Methuselah three hundred years, and begat sons and daughters:
    And all the days of Enoch were three hundred sixty and five years:
    And Enoch walked with God: and he was not; for God took him. (Gen. 5: 21–4)

Verse 24 is usually taken to mean that Enoch did not die in the mortal fashion, but was taken up directly into heaven. This is what no doubt led the authors of the pseudepigraphic book to speak in his name. Blake, however, could not have had an opportunity to read the text until, after having been brought to England in manuscript by the African explorer James Bruce in the later eighteenth century, it was published in English translation by Richard Laurence in 1821.[15]

The earlier part of the *Book of Enoch* is built around lines in Genesis that recount the intercourse of heavenly males with earthly females:

And it came to pass, when men began to multiply on the face of the earth, and daughters were born unto them,
    That the sons of God saw the daughters of men that they were fair; and they took them wives of all which they chose. (Gen. 6: 1–2).

The fruit of their union was a race of giants:

There were giants in the earth in those days; and also after that, when the sons of God came in unto the daughters of men, and they bare children to them, the same became mighty men which were of old, men of renown.
    And GOD saw that the wickedness of man was great in the earth, and that every imagination of the thoughts of his heart was only evil continually. (6: 4–5)

[14] See Allan R. Brown, 'Blake's Drawings for the *Book of Enoch*' [1940], in *The Visionary Hand*, ed. Robert N. Essick, p. 107.
[15] *The Book of Enoch the Prophet*, trans. [from the Ethiopic] by Richard Laurence [Regius Professor of Hebrew] (Oxford, 1821). This edition is hereafter referred to as the *Book of Enoch* or *Enoch*.

God's decision to cause the Deluge follows. To these elements *Enoch* added others equally daring in their imaginative scope; in the words of Laurence, the reader will be 'disposed to admire the vivid imagination of a writer, who transports him far beyond the flaming boundaries of the world . . . displaying to him every secret of creation; the splendours of heaven, and the terror of hell; the mansions of departed souls; and the myriads of the celestial hosts, the Seraphim, Cherubim, and Ophanim, which surround the blazing throne, and magnify the holy name, of the great Lord of spirits, the Almighty Father of men and of angels.'[16]

It is not surprising that such a combination of the supernatural-erotic and the apocalyptic stimulated the imaginations of poets such as Lord Byron and Thomas Moore[17] and artists such as John Flaxman and William Blake. In October 1821 Byron wrote *Heaven and Earth, A Mystery*, about the doomed loves of two seraphs and two women, culminating with the Deluge. It is doubtful that Byron had read *Enoch*: he did not claim to have done so, and his subtitle quotes Gen. 6: 1–2, not Laurence's translation. Nevertheless, the interest stirred by the latter may have led Byron to undertake the subject at this particular time.[18] Thomas Moore did read Laurence's *Enoch*, as references in his *Loves of the Angels* indicate,[19] but the three poems that his work comprises are erotic romances with no trace of *Enoch*'s apocalyptic energy, and the four illustrations that Richard Westall produced for the book are in keeping with Moore's sentimental treatment of his subject matter.[20] John Flaxman, who appears to have produced about a dozen *Enoch* illustrations[21] for his

---

[16] *The Book of Enoch*, 'Preliminary Dissertation', pp. xlvii–xlviii.

[17] See Philip W. Martin, 'The Angels of Byron and Moore—Close Encounters of Another Kind', in *Romanticism and Millenarianism*, ed. Tim Fulford (New York and Basingstoke: Palgrave, 2002), pp. 153–66.

[18] Lord Byron, *The Complete Poetical Works*, vol. vi, ed. Jerome J. McGann and Barry Weller, Commentary, p. 682.

[19] See Thomas Moore, *The Loves of the Angels* (2nd edn., London, 1823), title page, pp. 125 n. and 134 n.

[20] Three of these pictures, including the one on the title page, were engraved by Charles Heath, one by E. Portbury. These engravings are discussed, as are John Flaxman's drawings for *Enoch*, by G. E. Bentley, Jr. in 'A Jewel in an Ethiop's Ear', in *Blake in His Time*, ed. Robert N. Essick and Donald Pearce (pp. 213–40 and figs. 122–38).

[21] In 'A Jewel in an Ethiop's Ear', figs. 126–38 Bentley reproduces thirteen Flaxman drawings, of which seven are clearly illustrations of the *Book of Enoch* and six are hypothetically associated with it. The connection of several of the latter group with *Enoch* is highly doubtful.

own pleasure rather than for any book project, does capture some of
the dynamism of the descent of the angels to the daughters of men.
Yet, although the Flaxman drawings that are certainly *Enoch*
subjects all relate to the erotic encounters narrated in chapter 7, the
artist's representations of these are almost decorous. In contrast,
William Blake's drawings for the *Book of Enoch* present scenes of
sexual ferocity and visionary power.

Blake had been interested in Enoch long before Laurence's
translation was published. He may, as John Beer suggests, have read
extracts from the *Book of Enoch* published in the *Monthly Review*
for 1 February 1801.[22] Enoch was the subject of Blake's only litho-
graph, produced in 1806–7 and itself connected with some much
earlier drawings.[23] Although Blake's *Enoch* did not appear in the
second edition of *Specimens of Polyautography*, published by Georg
Jacob Vollweiler in 1806–7 or in its predecessor, Philipp André's
Specimens of Polyautography of 1803, his execution of it as a litho-
graph (partially etched) was certainly prompted by the invention of
the new medium by Alois Senefelder in the mid-1790s and its con-
tinuation by André and then by Vollweiler.[24] Blake presents Enoch as
the father of the arts, seated in the centre with a book in his lap, as
Job in *Job* 1 and drawings associated with it. Indeed, Blake's *Enoch*
was for a time thought to be a representation of Job,[25] but its Hebrew
inscriptions are determinative. In Blake's design Enoch is presented
as presiding over the arts. Long-bearded and looking serious or
even sorrowful, he sits on a two-stepped dais decorated with Gothic
arches. Written vertically on one page of his book is the name
'Enoch' in Hebrew. He is flanked by a seated young man writing with

[22] See John Beer, 'Blake's Changing View of History: The Impact of the Book of
Enoch', in *Historicizing Blake*, ed. Steve Clark and David Worrall (Basingstoke:
Macmillan, 1994), pp. 159–78.
[23] See Robert N. Essick, 'Blake's "Enoch" Lithograph', *Blake*, 14 (1980–1): 180–4;
and Essick, *Separate Plates*, no. XV, pp. 55–9. The related early drawings are: *Moses
and Aaron (?) Flanked by Angels* (Butlin 112, Princeton University Library, 1780–5);
Enoch Walked with God (?) (Butlin 146, Cincinnati Art Museum, c.1780–5); see also
Essick, *Separate Plates*, figs. 31 and 32 with their captions. '*In Maiden Meditation,
Fancy Free*' (Butlin 582, c.1807, University of California, Los Angeles) and its verso
drawing are probably sketches for *Enoch*; see also Essick, *Separate Plates*, figs. 33 and
34.
[24] Essick, *Separate Plates*, p. 58, suggests that Vollweiler probably furnished the
stone for Blake and did the printing (or had it done).
[25] As by A. G. B. Russell, *The Engravings of William Blake* (London: G. Richards,
1912), p. 91.

a quill pen and a seated young woman playing the harp. Standing to his right is a young man with brush and palette. Further to his right is a diagonally floating youth holding an opened scroll and behind him two male onlookers; further to his left a diagonally floating man holding a page or a tablet, with another young man pointing to an inscription in Hebrew on it, which is the Hebrew text of Gen. 5: 24, beginning in the AV 'And Enoch walked with God . . .'. At least three of the male figures are naked. A grape vine goes up the left and the right sides of the picture, with a large cluster of grapes at the lower end of each, suggesting, as so often in Blake's works, human productivity. And so we have in a single image the 'Four Arts: Poetry, Painting, Music, | And Architecture' that Blake designated as 'The Four Faces of Man'—Architecture being, of course, represented by the 'Living Form' of the Gothic arches—along with the 'Naked Beauty displayed' without which 'Art can never exist'.[26]

Blake recognizes Enoch's importance in another way by making him, as the seventh in Adam's line, the seventh Church of human history in *Milton* and *Jerusalem*.[27] And c.1820 he included Enoch in his *Epitome of James Hervey's 'Meditations Among the Tombs'* (Butler 770, Tate Gallery), showing Enoch holding an opened scroll which may be meant to signify the Book of Enoch itself. But an entirely different perspective opened after Blake had an opportunity to read Laurence's translation of the whole *Book of Enoch*. A brief survey of its contents will show what elements of *Enoch* must have appealed to Blake's imagination. It opens with the crime of a group of angels called 'the Watchers' (1: 15), who descend to the earth and have sexual relations with the 'elegant and beautiful' daughters of men (7, sect. 2: 1–15), resulting in the birth of a race of giants.[28] These devour everything produced by men, and then turn against them and devour them as well as birds, beasts, reptiles, and fishes, until the angels Michael, Gabriel, Raphael, Suryal, and Uriel look down from

---

[26] *Milton* 27 [29]: 55–6, E 125; *On Virgil*, E 270; הד *& his two Sons*, E 275.

[27] See the identical passages in *Milton* 37: 35–6, E 138 and *Jerusalem* 7: 25, E 149:

And these the names of the Twenty-seven Heavens and their Churches
Adam, Seth, Enos, Cainan, Mahalaleel, Jared, Enoch . . .

[28] This part of the account is of course based on Gen. 6: 1–2. Although Blake uses the term 'a Watcher & a Holy-One' among the verses prefixed to chapter 4 of *Jerusalem* (E 232), his source is the Book of Daniel, which is also a major source for *Enoch* 4: 13 and 4: 23.

heaven, see the amount of blood shed on the earth, and hear how 'The earth deprived *of her children* has cried even to the gate of heaven' (9: 1–2). Then 'the Most High, the Great and Holy One' tells Gabriel to destroy the children of the Watchers, saying 'Let every oppressor perish from the face of the earth . . .' (10: 13–19), and this is followed by a millennial vision in which 'all the earth shall be cultivated in righteousness; it shall be wholly planted with trees, and filled with benediction . . .' (10: 21). Enoch has a vision in which 'I beheld the Ancient of days, whose head was like white wool, and with him another, whose countenance resembled that of man' (46: 1). The latter is revealed to be the Son of man. The Ancient of days sends the Deluge but then repents and places a sign in the heavens (54: 1–3). Another millennial vision follows, which includes the prophecy that 'In that day shall be distributed *for food* two monsters; a female monster, whose name is Leviathan, dwelling in the depths of the sea, above the springs of waters; And a male *monster*, whose name is Behemoth, which possesses, *moving* on his breast, the invisible wilderness . . .' (58: 7–8). Noah, Lamech's son, is born, and Mathusla [*sic*] describes him to Enoch in almost supernatural terms: 'His colour is whiter than snow; he is redder than the rose; the hair of his head is whiter than white wool; his eyes are like the rays of the sun; and when he opened them he illuminated the whole house' (105: 10). Enoch prophesies that the child 'shall survive upon the earth, and his three sons with him' but that his posterity shall 'beget upon the earth giants, not spiritual, but carnal'. The Deluge begins, and Noah's vision of it is recounted, beginning at chapter 64. We can see how such a combination of the visionary, the sexual, the apocalyptic, and the millennial would have appealed to Blake's imagination, stimulating him to create a series of remarkable though unfinished illustrations, of which six are known, some time between 1824 and 1827.[29]

In the first of these (Fig. 36), *The Descent of the Angels to one of the Daughters of Men*[30] (Butlin 827.1), the central figure is a woman in an exaggeratedly seductive posture similar to those of the figures

---

[29] In Butlin's *Catalogue* these are numbered 827.1–5 (Lessing J. Rosenwald Collection, National Gallery of Art), with an additional drawing (Fogg Art Museum) on the verso of a sketch for one of the Dante illustrations, numbered 812ᵛ.

[30] It should be noted that no Blake titles exist for these drawings. William Michael Rossetti catalogued them simply as 'Five Designs to the Book of Enoch' in Gilchrist, *Life* (1880), ii. 270, no. 157.

FIG. 36. William Blake, *The Descent of the Angels to one of the Daughters of Men*, c.1824–7. Pencil.

of the two central female figures of Dante illustration 812.99, *The Queen of Heaven in Glory*.[31]

It happened after the sons of men had multiplied in those days, that daughters were born to them elegant and beautiful.

And when the angels, the sons of heaven, beheld them, they became enamoured of them, saying to each other; Come, let us select for ourselves wives from the progeny of men, and let us beget children. . . .

Then they took wives, each choosing for himself; whom they began to approach, and with whom they cohabited; teaching them sorcery, incantations, and the dividing of roots and trees. (7, sect. 2: 1–2, 10)

It is Blake who has decided to present the daughter as a seductress, perhaps in accordance with 19: 2, where the angels are said to have been led astray by their wives, and he accentuates this by making the fingers of her right hand appear to be turning into fibres, as are perhaps her right toes as well. She is drawing the angels on each side of her down into the world of vegetation, and her doleful expression indicates her own entrapment in what Blake sees as the torments of sexuality. The two angels that are descending to her are part human, part star; a star beams from the crotch of each and each has an enormous penis. The woman, whose vulva is clearly indicated, appears to be stroking the one at the right. Although nothing is said about the angels' phallic attributes in the early part of *Enoch*, Blake may be drawing on a much later passage, 87: 5, where the Watchers are seen as 'great stars, whose parts of shame resembled horses'.[32]

The second design is known by the title *An Angel Teaching A Daughter of Men the Secrets of Sin*.[33] Actually, there is no way of telling what if anything the angel is saying to the naked woman at the centre, as he swoops down to touch her vulva with his left hand. She is ironically placed in the posture of a *Venus pudica*, but with her left arm touching the angel's instead of covering her breasts and her right hand below her genitals rather than covering them. On the left and right sides are two of the giant children mentioned by Enoch. They

[31] See Brown, 'Blake's Drawings for the *Book of Enoch*', p. 114.

[32] This may be what Brown means when he refers to 'a later vision of Enoch where, with disconcerting bluntness, they are so represented' ('Blake's Drawings for the *Book of Enoch*', p. 110). The passage is identified by G. E. Bentley, Jr. in 'A Jewel in an Ethiop's Ear', p. 232.

[33] See Geoffrey Keynes, ed., *Blake's Pencil Drawings*, 2nd ser. (London: Nonesuch Press, 1956), no. 45, and Butlin 827.2.

are not much bigger than the other figures, but their large heads and unmuscled limbs suggest that these are babies who will grow to full gigantic size.

Then they took wives, each choosing for himself; whom they began to approach, and with whom they cohabited; teaching them sorcery, incantations, and the dividing of roots and trees.

And the women conceiving brought forth giants;

Whose stature was each three hundred cubits. These devoured all *which* the labour of men *produced*; until it became impossible to feed them; (7, sect. 2: 10–12)

The vegetation at the centre illustrates the 'dividing of roots and trees', which for Blake would be associated with the 'Stems of Vegetation'[34] on which humanity is bound. Lines that may indicate flames, suggesting the punishment about to befall the giants,[35] emanate from the one at our left. Punishment is also pictured in the third drawing, where a male figure, presumably a dead Watcher, lies at the foot of a tree, to the right of which a naked woman raises her arms in horror. At the left of the tree another woman, much of her body covered with scales, soars upward as if in triumph. It has been suggested that this second woman is the woman of the previous picture, 'now become a siren',[36] and indeed this drawing is known as *The Daughter of Men Becomes a Siren*. However, the word 'siren' does not occur in Laurence's translation,[37] and neither does the scaly woman appear in the text. Blake is supplying his own imagery here, specifically with respect to the scaly woman, who is also the subject of a Notebook poem:

> A Woman Scaly & a Man all Hairy
> Is such a Match as he who dares
> Will find the Womans Scales Scrape off the Mans Hairs
>
> (E 517)

---

[34] Cf. for example 'Unless my beloved is bound upon the Stems of Vegetation' in Night VIII of *The Four Zoas*, 109 [105]: 53, E 379.

[35] See Bentley, 'A Jewel in an Ethiop's Ear', p. 234. Bentley also points out that 'there may be a tiny human on the arm, or against the chest, of one or both giants' (p. 240 n. 49). There are no flames at this point in the text of *Enoch*, nor are there tiny humans, but these details are indeed suggested by the drawing.

[36] See Keynes, *Blake's Pencil Drawings*, 2nd ser., no. 45; see also Brown, 'Blake's Drawings for the *Book of Enoch*', pp. 100–12.

[37] See Peter Alan Taylor, 'Blake's Text for the *Enoch* Drawings', *Blake*, 7 (1973–4): 85.

Hairiness is an attribute of Orc, the revolutionary 'Hairy youth' of *America* (1: 11, E 51), while scales can be an attribute of the seductive nature-goddess Vala—Luvah says in Night II of *Vala*: 'she [Vala] grew | A scaled serpent, yet I fed her tho' she hated me' (26: 8–9, E 317).[38] This is not to say that the picture should be read as emanating from one of Blake's other works, so that the naked woman is Jerusalem and the supine male Albion.[39] Rather, the threatening aspect of femality that Blake personifies in Vala is also embodied in the woman to the left. All three of these *Enoch* drawings represent sexuality as entrapping and monstrous.

With the fourth design (Fig. 37), *Enoch Before the Great Glory* (Butlin 827.4), Blake's subject shifts to chapter 14: 14–25, where Enoch is given a vision of God enthroned: a spacious habitation '*in the midst of* a vibrating flame' and containing 'an exalted throne'. Rivers of flame emanate from under the throne, and 'One in great glory sat upon it'.

Then the Lord with his own mouth called me, saying: Approach hither, Enoch, at my holy word.

And he raised me up, making me draw near even to the entrance. My eye was directed to the ground.

Wavy lines suggest the fire on the floor, and two robed figures stand before a seated one who may have a book opened in his lap (as does the Almighty in *Job* 2). The two angels beside the throne that stand with their giant wings forming a canopy over it are not to be found in the text, as Butlin (827.4) points out, though they do occur elsewhere in Blake's *œuvre*, as in *Christ Girding Himself with Strength* (Butlin 464, City of Bristol Museum and Art Galleries). The figure standing at the left is slightly taller than the other and appears to be making a gesture with his right hand; it may be that he is a guiding angel[40] introducing the 'One in great glory'. Alternatively, the drawing may be related to a similar description later in *Enoch* 46: 1:[41]

There I beheld the Ancient of days, whose head was like white wool, and with him another, whose countenance resembled that of man. His

---

[38] The *Vala* example is cited by Brown, 'Blake's Drawings for the *Book of Enoch*', p. 114.

[39] As suggested by Brown, ibid.

[40] See Keynes, *Blake's Pencil Drawings*, 2nd ser., no. 45.

[41] As suggested by Bentley, 'A Jewel in an Ethiop's Ear', p. 233.

FIG. 37. William Blake, *Enoch Before the Great Glory*,
c.1824–7. Pencil.

countenance was full of grace, like *that of* one of the holy angels. Then I inquired of one of the angels, who went with me, and who shewed me every secret thing, concerning the Son of man; who he was; whence he was; and why he accompanied the Ancient of days.

The Son of man would then be the slightly taller figure on the left, Enoch the one on the right. In either case, the expression of the seated figure, to the extent that we can determine it from a few sketched lines, looks stern, appropriately for a God who will shortly decide to send the Deluge.

There is also more than one possibility for the reference of the design that has been given the number 5 and the title *The Vision of the Lord of the Spirits*, but here the difference in meaning, depending on which possibility one chooses, is considerable. The drawing shows a nude male, with prominent genitalia, surrounded by four figures who form an ellipse around him. The central figure is usually taken as the Lord of the Spirits ringed by four archangels,[42] as in *Enoch* 40: 1–9, where Enoch sees an 'infinite number of people, standing before the Lord of the Spirits' and hears 'the voices of those upon the four sides magnifying the Lord of glory'. He asks 'Who are those *whom* I have seen on the four sides, and whose words I have heard and written down?' The 'angel of peace' identifies them as Michael, Raphael, Gabriel, and Phanuel. 'These are the four angels of the most high God, and their four voices, which at that time I heard', he concludes. The composition has been compared by Anthony Blunt to medieval roof bosses such as one at York Cathedral, and to Blake's own *God Blessing the Seventh Day* (Butlin 434, private collection) and *Job* 5.[43] However, as at least two of the figures have what could be indications of breasts, and as Blake nowhere pictures the Messiah with genitalia, it may be that Blake is freely treating the earlier part of *Enoch* here, and showing a fallen angel surrounded by four of the Daughters of Men.[44]

---

[42] See Brown, 'Blake's Drawings for the *Book of Enoch*', p. 112; and Keynes, *Blake's Pencil Drawings*, 2nd ser., no. 45.

[43] See Blunt, 'Blake's Pictorial Imagination', 198. Blunt points out that the York boss was reproduced by Flaxman for one of his lectures; although these were published after Blake's death, Blake nevertheless would have had ample opportunity to see Flaxman's drawing even if he had not seen the original. Blunt observes that the pattern of a figure or figures enclosed in a circle of flying angels is a regular formula in the medieval boss. See also Blunt, *The Art of William Blake*, pl. 42b.

[44] See Bentley, 'A Jewel in an Ethiop's Ear', p. 231. As Bentley recognizes, there is nothing in the text of *Enoch* to indicate polygamy.

The only other known presumed *Enoch* illustration is one drawn on the verso of the Dante watercolour *The Circle of the Gluttons, with Cerberus* (Butlin 812.11, Fogg Art Museum). It bears both the name 'ENOCH' in block capitals and 'Enoch' is handwritten, but not by Blake, at the lower left (drawings 1–5 are similarly inscribed in a hand other than Blake's). The drawing shows a figure with arms upraised and feet manacled together leaping upward from a rock. Four large stars are at the level of his waist and below them is a huge star. No passage of *Enoch* combines these elements, though in 18: 14–16 one of the Watchers is confined with 'seven great stars',[45] and, as we have seen, the starry genitals of the Watchers in the first drawing may relate to 87: 5, where the Watchers are described as 'great stars, whose parts of shame resembled horses'. Visions of stars also occur in several other passages: in 81: 9 'the ordinance of the stars' is introduced, and in 81: 11 we are told 'Four conductors of them first enter . . .'; in the vision of 85: 2 'a single star fell from heaven'. However, there is nothing to relate these to the leaping man who spreads his arms aspiringly in the drawing but who is held back by a chain. This motif occurs in one of the best known of Blake's illustrations to *Night Thoughts*, Butlin 330.35 (British Museum), where it is the poet, holding a lyre, who is restrained by a chain from flying further upward; and this subject was engraved for the Edwards edition of 1797 ironically illustrating the line 'Oft bursts my song beyond the bounds of life'.[46] It is possible that Blake intends in the *Enoch* drawing to represent Enoch himself,[47] and this drawing may therefore suggest the limitations of his vision.

While only the first part of the *Book of Enoch* concerns the Watchers and the daughters of men, it is the subject of three or possibly four of Blake's illustrations. Clearly, when Blake made these drawings the elements about them that most appealed to him were the sexual and the primordial. These are not presented as noble and joyful, but as savagely debased (as indeed they are in the text). The apocalyptic aspects of *Enoch* also interested him, but he represents these as ambiguous at best. If in *The Illustrations of the Book*

---

[45] As suggested by Bentley, 'A Jewel in an Ethiop's Ear', p. 234. The design is reproduced there as fig. 144 and in Butlin's *Catalogue* as plate 1052, captioned *A Soaring Figure amid Stars, probably for 'Enoch'*.

[46] Edward Young, *The Complaint, and the Consolation; or, Night Thoughts* (London: R. Edwards, 1797), p. 16. See also Bentley, 'A Jewel in an Ethiop's Ear', p. 234.

[47] As suggested by Beer, 'Blake's Changing View of History', p. 166.

of Job, Blake tried to unify the divine and the human, in the *Enoch* sketches his 'Manichaean' side comes to the fore.

The Lord's Prayer

The publication of Thornton's *Virgil* did not end Blake's contact with Dr Robert John Thornton. Indeed, as far as we can tell, the relations between them were cordial. Blake executed one more commission for Thornton: a small ($2\frac{3}{4} \times 4$ in.) engraving after his own water-colour *Moses Placed in the Ark of the Bulrushes* (Butlin 774, Huntington Library). This was published as *The Hiding of Moses* in Thornton's new annual *Remember Me! A New Years Gift or Christmas Present*, dated 1825 (but published in late 1824). Thornton was now conscious enough of Blake's importance to say in his Prospectus: 'The Plates are by Linnell, Blake, and other eminent Artists . . .'.[1] In 1826, possibly in May, Dr Thornton visited Blake in his illness.[2] Nevertheless, Blake regarded Thornton as a typical example of the pseudo-Christian who betrays his ostensible faith by compromising with the powers of this world. This is shown by Blake's annotations to Thornton's *The Lord's Prayer, Newly Translated from the Original Greek, with Critical and Explanatory Notes* (London, 1827). Blake's marginalia to this booklet have the considerable interest of almost certainly being the last words he wrote on the subject of the Bible.

It may first be asked how and why Blake acquired Thornton's publication. A reasonable supposition is that it was obtained by Thornton's friend Linnell and loaned or given to Blake for the specific purpose of annotation. Such a practice would not have been unusual at the time. Coleridge's friends would lend him books with the hope that they would be returned with marginalia. That something like this may have happened is further suggested by the fact that at least one mutual friend asked Linnell to lend him the book. About a year after Blake's death, on 19 August 1828, Samuel Palmer wrote to Linnell: 'My Father presents best respects—I think he would be very much amused by a sight of Mr. Blake's annotations on Dr. T.s Lord's Prayer.'[3] It may be that the words 'amused by' reflect more of the attitude of the younger Palmer than that of his Baptist

---

[1] *BR*, pp. 295–6.   [2] See Bentley, *The Stranger from Paradise*, p. 435 n.
[3] *BR*, p. 369.

father. Nor is there any evidence that Linnell, himself a Baptist, did not take Blake's marginalia seriously. The salient fact is that others in Linnell's circle knew of the existence of Blake's Thornton marginalia and were interested in seeing them. This suggests that Blake wrote them with the expectation of an audience, fit though few, rather than for his own private reference.

What was the nature of the book that Blake annotated? While even the best editions of Blake can only be expected to print passages from the original in the proximity of the marginalia, it is important to describe the book as a whole, both its form and its content, as Blake was not reacting merely to isolated passages but to the entire work. *The Lord's Prayer, Newly Translated from the Original Greek* is a folio-sized volume with blue paper wrappers, which have been preserved in the copy that Blake annotated.[4] It is composed of a title page, two columns of prose on the verso of the title page, a frontispiece, a page beginning with Thornton's new translation, pages numbered 2–8 headed 'Critical and Explanatory Notes', and a last page headed 'Reasons for a New Translation of the Whole Bible', with a blank verso. Although it is slim, the booklet is quantitatively more substantial than one might imagine from reading the marginalia in an edition of Blake: its pages are for the most part densely packed, and it comprises perhaps fourteen thousand words. If we begin by taking a Blake's-eye view of the pages of Thornton's volume, we will gain a sense of the marginalia in their original context.

Blake probably read the entire booklet (or as much of it as he was ever going to read) before he wrote his title page comment, just as his general comments on Bishop Watson's *Apology for the Bible* (E 611) and on Bacon's *Essays* (E 620) indicate that he had already read those books. Blake wrote his general remark in a large hand. At first he may have written only the lines 'I look upon this as Most Malignant & Artful | Attack upon the Kingdom of Jesus'. After this he could have added a few words before reaching the right-hand

---

[4] In the Henry E. Huntington Library (San Marino, Calif.). My discussion of this volume and its annotations is based on an examination of the original copy. I am grateful to the Huntington Library for the courtesies extended to me, and to Professor Robert N. Essick for giving me a photocopy for reference and for helpful information. I have compared my readings of Blake's MS notes against the texts of the two principal modern editions: Erdman's *Complete Poetry and Prose of William Blake*; and Bentley's *William Blake's Writings*.

margin, but he realized that he would not have room to say what he wanted to say in horizontal lines before running into the printed text, so he curved the continuation down the margin: 'by the Classical Learned thro the Instrumentality of Dr Thornton'. Then he continued laterally below this: 'The Greek & Roman Classics is the Antichrist | I say Is & not Are as most expressive & correct too'. Blake regards Dr Thornton, producer of *The Pastorals of Virgil* and therefore epitomizing the Classical Learned, as engaged in an act of imperialism whereby the New Testament, which in Blake's view is antithetical to classical values, is absorbed by them. This represents a theme present throughout the annotations, as the point about what is 'correct' represents another. Of course Blake knows that 'Classics' is plural and that the verb would ordinarily be plural too. However, for him the 'Greek & Roman Classics' compose a single composite entity, a sort of two-headed beast, which demands a singular verb. Blake is calling the reader's attention—and it is clear from the size of the handwriting alone that he expects his comments to be read—to how the choice of words—or in this instance a word—affects meaning, which will be a major concern in the annotations that follow.

Thornton's next page, the verso of the title page, collects statements from various sources on the Lord's Prayer, the necessity of learning to an understanding of the Bible, the ethics of Christ, and the quality of Dr Thornton's new translation. Two of the three notes that Blake wrote on this page have to do with a passage from Dr Johnson, beginning 'The Bible is the *most difficult* book in the world to *comprehend*, nor can it be understood at all by the *unlearned*, except through the aid of Critical and Explanatory notes'. Blake counters: 'Christ & his Apostles were Illiterate Men Caiphas Pilate & Herod were Learned.' By juxtaposing the names of those to whom the Synoptic Gospels assign responsibility for the Crucifixion against Jesus and the Apostles, Blake gives dramatic emphasis to his point. Blake returns to this subject at the bottom of the page, writing in a large hand: 'The Beauty of the Bible is that the most Ignorant & Simple Minds Understand it Best—Was Johnson hired to Pretend to Religious Terrors while he was an Infidel or how was it[?]' Blake may have been thinking here of Johnson's posthumously published *Prayers and Meditations*, in which Johnson's friend and editor George Strahan wrote of Johnson's 'morbid melancholy' that 'To the prevalence of this infirmity, we may certainly ascribe that anxious fear, which seized him on the approach of his dissolution . . .'.[5] Johnson himself wrote 'My terrours and perplexities have so much encreased, that I am under great depression and discouragement', and on another occasion 'Calm my inquietude, and relieve my terrours . . .'.[6] Blake did not condemn what he regarded as genuinely spiritual terror. Samuel Palmer recalled visiting Blake as Blake was working on his Dante designs: 'He said he began them with fear and trembling. I said "O! I have enough of fear and trembling." "Then", said he, "you'll do."'[7] Just as Blake asserted in his annotations to Reynolds that Sir Joshua 'was Hired to Depress Art' (E 635), he here insinuates that the Tory Anglican Johnson manufactured his 'Religious Terrors' in the interests of Church and State. This is hardly fair to Dr Johnson, but it must be conceded that fairness is not a hallmark of Blake's late writings. Blake's other note on this page is placed under a subsection headed 'Lord Byron *on the Ethics of* Christ'. Thornton quotes Byron's *Letter . . . on the Rev. W. L. Bowles' Strictures on the Life and Writings of Pope*, to the effect that the highest poetry is ethical and moral. Byron then asks: 'What made Socrates *the greatest of men?* His *moral truths—his ethics.* What proved Jesus Christ to be the son of God, hardly less than his miracles did? *His moral precepts.*' Blake counters by quoting himself: 'If Morality was Christianity | Socrates was The Savior.' (This same aphorism had been inscribed in יה *& his two Sons*, where it may have been a late thought, as the lettering is very small, squeezed in between the title inscription and the engraved plinth above it.) Blake distances himself from the liberal dissenting Christianity of his day as much as he distances himself from the established Church. At this point in his life, Blake is far beyond any affinity with either liberal or conservative Christian movements. His general attitude is similar to Gnosticism in that he places an intuitive knowledge of the divine above any texts, including even the text of the Bible.

Thornton's frontispiece is an engraving signed 'Harlow, of the Academy of St. Luke, and of the Academy at Florence del.' and 'H. Cook, Sculp.' It illustrates verses 20–2 of Matt. 9 (inscribed in the engraver's hand below the design), in which a woman with an issue of blood touches Christ's garment and is healed. Blake had also exe-

[5] Samuel Johnson, *Prayers and Meditations*, ed. George Strahan (London: T. Cadell, 1785), pp. xiv–xv.
[6] Ibid., pp. 38, 76.   [7] *BR*, p. 391.

cuted a design on this subject, a watercolour for Thomas Butts, c. 1803–5.[8] Harlow's picture shows Jesus with his back to us, flanked by two men, turning his head to see the woman as she crouches in the left foreground and touches his cloak. At the top in engraved script we read: 'This pencil sketch was done in 15 minutes by the great Harlow in the presence of Doctor Thornton, his early Patron and Fosterer of his extraordinary genius; in which every stroke, however trifling, tells, and is published as a curious Specimen of departed Genius!' 'The great Harlow' was George Henry Harlow (1787–1819), a one-time pupil of Sir Thomas Lawrence's, well known for portraiture, history painting, and religious subjects.[9] The first picture that Harlow exhibited at the Royal Academy was a portrait of Dr Thornton, and his portraits of James Northcote and of Felicia Dorothy Hemans are in the National Portrait Gallery. In 1818 he travelled to Italy, where his work was admired by Canova, who presented him to the pope. He painted a copy of Raphael's *Transfiguration* that was much celebrated in Rome, and that was exhibited after his return to England. Blake saw it in the company of Linnell in August 1819,[10] but his response to it is unknown. The featuring of Harlow's drawing, which has of course nothing to do with biblical translation, is yet another example of Thornton's rambling eccentricity, and it could well have reminded Blake of the less positive aspect of his own past artist–publisher relationship with Thornton, and could perhaps have made him wonder whether he himself might not have been a more fitting recipient of Thornton's boasted patronage than the creator of this rather insipid design.

Thornton's translation of the Lord's Prayer opens page 1. Blake's comments on this page are of three kinds. One continues the attack on learning. Thornton's note at the bottom of the page begins 'Men from their *childhood* have been so accustomed *to mouth* the LORD's PRAYER that they continue this *through* life . . .'. Blake's tartly rejoins: 'It is the Learned that Mouth & not the Vulgar'. Another kind of annotation appears in a large hand in the bottom margin and vertically going up the right-hand margin. These notes are the first in

---

[8] *Christ Healing the Woman with an Issue of Blood* (Victoria and Albert Museum); see Butlin 482 and plate 560.

[9] E. Bénézit, *Dictionnaire critique et documentaire des peintres, sculpteurs, dessinateurs et graveurs* (new edn., rev. Jacques Busse, 14 vols., Paris: Gründ, 1999), vi. 758–9.

[10] *BR*, p. 259.

which Blake moves toward his own version and pseudo-version of the Lord's Prayer, which are best considered together later. The third type has to do with Thornton's actual translation, about which Blake has surprisingly little to say. In the top margin above the title 'The Lord's Prayer', Blake writes:

Such things as these depend on the Fashion of the Age
  In a book where all may Read & ⎫
  In a book which all may Read & ⎬ are Equally Right
  In a book that all may read   ⎭ That Man who &c is equally So
                                    the man that & the Man which

Blake's first example is of course self-referential, taken from the 'Introduction' to *Songs of Innocence*:

> Piper sit thee down and write
> In a book that all may read—
>
> (E 7)

Blake's note asserts that what linguists call 'relative markers'[11] in his examples are interchangeable. This may indeed appear puzzling as there are no relative markers either in the AV text of the Lord's Prayer or in Dr Thornton's version. Is Blake saying that all differences in biblical translation are as inconsequential as his examples, and that all merely reflect 'the Fashion of the Age'? The only other comment, if it can be called that, on Thornton's translation at this point is two lines from the Greek New Testament written above the lines corresponding to Matt. 6: 9–10. Here Blake gives the last ten words of the first verse and the first eight words of the next. It may be that Blake thought that the Greek alone was sufficient to show up the inadequacy of Thornton's version. A quantitative indication of this is that Thornton's text is one hundred words long, compared to seventy-four words in the AV. The translation itself is to be sure a very odd one. Parts of it appear very far from the original, and it introduces words and phrases that have no counterparts in the Greek. The AV and the modern *New English Bible* translations are far closer to each other than either is to Dr Thornton's. The reason for this is quite simply that Dr Thornton's text is only in part a new translation; in part it is an explication or paraphrase. Blake's objections, however, are not directed to its lack of accuracy or to its verbosity, but to the world-view he sees as represented by Thornton's entire booklet.

---

[11] For information about relative markers I am grateful to Professor Gunnel Tottie.

The right-hand column of page 1 is taken up by 'Lines on Eternity' in iambic tetrameter. This turgid poem, by an unidentified author (could it be Thornton himself?), is unlikely to have caught Blake's attention, but that is not true of a very short quotation in the footnote on this page: ' "The Heavens declare the Glory of God," and as Young says, "an undevout astronomer is mad." ' Blake, of course, had executed the largest number of drawings he ever did on a single subject in illustrating *Night Thoughts*. In the 1745 edition that Blake used for his project the line Thornton quotes as line 801 of Night IX, and the line preceding it—'Devotion! daughter of Astronomy!'— was marked with a + sign on the page used for watercolour 458. However, the lines actually illustrated were 792–4, and 792 was marked with a *. This closely related passage reads:

—But tho' Man, drown'd in Sleep,
With-holds his Homage, not *alone* I wake;
Bright Legions swarm unseen, and sing, unheard,
By mortal ear . . .

This sentiment Blake could easily endorse, and his design shows a man sleeping in a tent, with sheep asleep in the foreground, and to our left three angels looking on. The third, playing a lute, has risen into the night sky, which is spangled with stars. However, the passage continues:

the glorious Architect,
In This His universal Temple, hung
With Lustres, with innumerable Lights,
That shed Religion on the Soul: At once,
The *Temple*, and the *Preacher*! O how loud
It calls Devotion! Genuine Growth of *Night*!
Devotion! Daughter of Astronomy!
An *undevout* Astronomer is *mad*.

With his thorough knowledge of Young, Blake could easily have placed the passage quoted by Thornton in the context of what Blake called Natural Religion. In *Jerusalem* he had represented the architectural aspect of this, linked, as by Young, with astronomy, but with a much different valorization, on plate 66:

They build a stupendous Building on the Plain of Salisbury; with chains
Of rocks round London Stone: of Reasonings: of unhewn Demonstrations
In labyrinthine arches. (Mighty Urizen the Architect.) thro which

The Heavens might revolve & Eternity be bound in their chain.
Labour unparalleled! a wondrous rocky World of cruel destiny
Rocks piled on rocks reaching the stars: stretching from pole to pole.
The Building is Natural Religion & its Altars Natural Morality
A building of eternal death: whose proportions are eternal despair[.]¹²

Thornton's quotation of Young may also be responsible for Blake's derisive expression 'seen thro a Lawful Telescope' in the note on the bottom margin to be discussed later.

On page 2 Blake, still occupied with his own incipient Lord's Prayer, wrote another line of it in the bottom margin, and nothing else elsewhere. Actually, there is at least one passage, in the first paragraph on this page, that might have been expected to draw Blake's attention. Thornton wrote: '. . . In the Greek, we address *God*, as the *Common Parent of all mankind*, hence we are ALL brothers, as is beautifully expressed in a Medallion having on the one side a praying African, and on the other, "Am I not also a *Brother*".' Thornton is referring to a medallion originally made by Josiah Wedgwood and reproduced as an engraving in Erasmus Darwin's *The Botanic Garden* (facing i. 87). It is a circular emblem showing a black slave kneeling in chains and extending his manacled hands forward, with the inscription 'AM I NOT A MAN AND A BROTHER' arching above him. This image, the details of which Thornton is evidently misremembering slightly, became a popular icon of the abolitionist movement, and Blake (who also executed five engravings for this volume of Darwin¹³) would no doubt have been familiar with it and, always an opponent of slavery, would have sympathized with its message. The text of page 2 continues with quotations from Matthew, Milton, and Isaiah, and two unidentified blank verse poems, 'Lines on the Love of God' and 'Creation a Proof of the Love of God', the latter running over into page 3. That page includes a number of further quotations, one of which is likely to have caught Blake's attention. Discussing the notion that the name of God 'is not to be mentioned without *religious awe*', Thornton writes: 'The great Sir Isaac Newton was so impressed with *this Idea*, that whenever he heard the *name of* God, he constantly bowed his head, and when *in*

¹² 66: 2–9, E 218; cf. the building of the Temple of Urizen in Night the Seventh of *The Four Zoas*, 96: 1–18, E 361.
¹³ These include *The Fertilization of Egypt* after Henry Fuseli, which Blake signed, and four engravings of the Portland Vase, assigned to Blake on documentary evidence. See Bentley, *Blake Books*, p. 547.

the open air, took off *his hat.*' Blake has nothing to say on the subject
of his *bête noire* Newton here, but Thornton's remark, along with
a longer quotation about Newton on page 5, may have coloured
Blake's note on 'Newtonian & Baconian Philosophers' on the recto
facing page 8, although neither Newton nor Bacon is mentioned by
Thornton there.

Page 4, which is devoid of marginal notes, contains among its
many quoted passages—Dr Thornton was nothing if not generous in
providing the reader with texts by others—at least one that could
have struck a responsive chord in Blake. It is the first two lines of a
verse paraphrase of a passage in Matthew, identified by Thornton as
8: 12 but actually part of 7: 12: 'whatsoever ye would that men
should do to you, do ye even so to them'. The two lines of verse as
Thornton renders them are:

> Precept Divine! to Earth in mercy given,
> O sacred rule of action, worthy *Heaven*!

Although the poet is unidentified here, the lines are the opening of
'Paraphrase' by Helen Maria Williams. Nevertheless, the fact that
Thornton could cite lines by a poet often defamed as an unregener-
ate supporter of the French Revolution is surely significant, as is his
previous statement opposing slavery (still legal, although the slave
trade was not, in British colonies in 1827). So are Thornton's further
remarks on slavery, war, and women on this page. 'Wherever
Christianity prevails,' Thornton wrote, 'it has discouraged, and in
some degree, abolished *slavery*. It has introduced *more equality*
between the two sexes, and rendered the *conjugial union* more *ratio-
nal* and *happy*.' On these statements Blake, who expresses agreement
with Thornton nowhere in the marginalia, is silent.

Page 5 opens with a poem in six quatrains beginning:

> There is *a land of pure delight*,
> Where SAINTS *immortal* reign;

The author, though again not identified by Thornton, is Isaac Watts,
and the poem is his Hymn 66: 'A Prospect of Heaven Makes Death
Easy'. Blake's affinities with Dr Watts as a writer of lyrics are
well known,[14] and this poem in particular bears some interesting

[14] See Vivian de Sola Pinto, 'William Blake, Isaac Watts, and Mrs Barbauld', in *The
Divine Vision*, ed. V. de Sola Pinto (London: Gollancz, 1957), pp. 67–80.

resemblances to Blake's Pickering Manuscript poem 'The Land of Dreams', in which mortals are also represented as separated from the blessed by a body of water. What drew a comment from Blake, however, is a passage from Addison's *Spectator* beginning 'How doth a genius like Sir Isaac Newton, from amidst the darkness that involves the human understanding, break forth, and appear like one of another species!—the vast machine, we inhabit, lies open to him; he seems not unacquainted with the general laws that govern it; and while with the transport of a philosopher he beholds and admires the glorious work, he is capable of paying at once *a more devout* and *more rational homage* to his Maker.' We can easily imagine Blake's reaction to positing Urizen's 'dark machines'[15] as an object of worship, and as I have suggested, the reference to Newton probably contributed to his comment at the end of Thornton's text. However, on page 5 his note has to do with a passage a little further on in the Addison quotation: 'Dim at best are the conceptions we have of the Supreme Being, who, as it were, keeps the human race in suspense, neither discovering nor hiding Himself . . .'. Blake tartly remarks: 'a Female God'. He is of course alluding to the notion of woman as tease he presents elsewhere under the figure of Vala and is suggesting that Addison's and Thornton's God coyly plays with the human race.

On page 6, after the conclusion of the long quotation from Addison, Thornton begins a diatribe on the word 'Will', relating to his translation. In the course of this, he introduces two lines from Alexander Pope's poem 'The Universal Prayer': 'Who binding Nature fast in *fate* | Let free the *human will*.' Thornton had previously quoted one line of 'The Universal Prayer' in his booklet, and he would go on to reproduce twelve more in succeeding pages. He appears to have regarded Pope's poem as a British equivalent of the Lord's Prayer, as indeed Pope himself implies. At the bottom of the verso of the title page Thornton asserts: 'The Lord's Prayer is then an *Universal Prayer*', and then quotes Pope's line: 'Father of All, in *every age* adored!' Pope and Dryden, according to Blake, were poets who 'did not understand Verse' ('Public Address', E 575), and he satirized Pope in an epigram in his Notebook (E 506). Although Blake's sole comment on page 6 is not directed toward Pope, Blake would have regarded 'The Universal Prayer' as an example of what he called

[15] *The Four Zoas*, Night VIII, 101: 7, E 373.

Deism—the worship of Nature and Reason under the name of God—with its concluding stanza (not quoted by Thornton) opening 'To Thee, whose Temple is all Space, | Whose Altar, Earth, Sea, Skies . . .'. Thornton's own text through page 6 continues to the end with a series of statements on the subject of 'Will', and it is probably the last of these that stimulated Blake's response. 'It is the WILL of Him,' Thornton wrote, 'who is *uncontrolably powerful*; whose WILL therefore must prevail one way or other: either with our *will* or against it, either so as to bow and satisfy us, or so as to break and plague us . . .'. Going up the right-hand margin, Blake wrote: 'So you See that God is just such a tyrant as Augustus Caesar & is not this Good & Learned & Wise & Classical'. Blake opposes the idea that God must be worshipped because of the arbitrary power of his will, a view he identifies not with Christianity, characterized by a God who sacrifices himself and forgives sins, but with the pagan gods. In so rejecting the idea of God as a tyrant, Blake is also alluding to Augustus in Thornton's *Pastorals of Virgil*, a subject to which he will return at the very end of these annotations. Once more, this is hardly fair to Dr Thornton, whose stated views were, as we have seen, highly critical of Augustus Caesar.

Blake had nothing to say to Thornton's remaining 'Critical and Explanatory Notes', which continue through page 8. He was moved to write again at the end of the unnumbered page that is the recto of leaf 6, headed 'Reasons for a New Translation of the Whole Bible'. In the bottom margin he inscribed in a large hand: 'The only thing for Newtonian & Baconian Philosophers to Consider is this Whether Jesus did not suffer himself to be Mockd by Caesars Soldiers Willingly &'; at some point he added in pencil 'I hope they will' but then deleted this, inserted the word 'to' and made the note conclude 'Consider this to all Eternity will be Comment enough'. It may be that the last nine words were written as part of the original statement, and that Blake realized he was creating a syntactical problem and so revised; but in any event, the note is remarkably distant from Thornton's subject on this page. Blake appears to be picking up Thornton's earlier references to Newton previously noted, and his word 'Comment' probably refers to a parenthetical remark at the conclusion of Thornton's proposal, advocating a new translation 'by an assemblage of the first scholars of the age, (with marginal, or other notes, if thought necessary) . . .'. Blake replies that such a team of scholars would represent the scientific attitude he associates with

Newton and Bacon, and that all marginal or other notes ('Comment') are useless, in contrast with faith in the miraculous as represented by Jesus' sacrifice.

At first Blake's indifference to the subject of biblical translation may seem surprising, especially as there is reason to believe that this had not always been the case. Most of the English Bibles published in his lifetime used the Authorized Version as their texts—this was true of the two Bibles for which Blake provided five engravings each early in his career[16]—but there are two projects of biblical translation in which he may have been interested at one time or another. One was that of Dr Alexander Geddes, who was known in the late eighteenth century as an authority on the German scholarship later to be called the Higher Criticism of the Bible. As Jerome McGann argues, Geddes's ideas about biblical texts may well have affected the structure of *The [First] Book of Urizen*.[17] The other was Bishop Robert Lowth's new translation of Isaiah, which, as I have suggested elsewhere, may have influenced the prosody of *Jerusalem*.[18] However, during his last years, Blake appears to have lost interest in the translation of the Bible to the point of what can only be called nihilism. As we have seen, Blake dismissed differences in translation as mere quibbles. He appears at this very late point of his life to have regarded the real meaning of the Bible as something to be intuited rather than translated, and this is nowhere so evident as in his own versions of the Lord's Prayer in these marginalia.

In the bottom margin of page 1, which begins with Thornton's own translation, Blake wrote three lines of a parodic comment that then continues up the right margin. These read in their final form:

Lawful Bread Bought with Lawful Money & a Lawful Heaven seen | thro a Lawful Telescope by means of Lawful Window Light | The Holy Ghost & whatever cannot be Taxed is Unlawful & Witchcraft. Spirits are Lawful but

---

[16] *The Protestant's Family Bible 'By a Society of Protestant Divines'* (London: Harrison, 1780–1) and *The Royal Universal Family Bible* (London: J. Fielding, 1780/1). For details see Bentley, *Blake Books*, pp. 514–17. Blake appears not to have known the Unitarian Gilbert Wakefield's *A Translation of the New Testament* (3 vols., London: Philanthropic Press, 1791).

[17] See Jerome J. McGann, 'The Idea of an Indeterminate Text: Blake's Bible of Hell and Dr. Alexander Geddes', *Studies in Romanticism*, 25 (1986): 303–24.

[18] Paley, *The Continuing City: William Blake's Jerusalem* (Oxford: Clarendon Press, 1983), pp. 45–7.

not Ghosts especially Royal Gin is Lawful Spirit | No Smuggling real British Spirit & Truth[19]

The reiteration of the word 'Lawful' emphasizes what Blake regards as the fatal accommodation made by those who, like Thornton, see Christianity as part of the social order instead of radically opposed to it. In הי & *his two Sons*, Blake had declared 'For every Pleasure Money is Useless', but in the view Blake imputes to Thornton everything is determined by the cash nexus—'Lawful Bread Bought with Lawful Money'. Blake's anger is no doubt directed to Thornton's translation of the line that appears in the AV as 'Give us this day our daily bread' as 'Grant unto *me, and the whole world, day by day*, an abundant supply of *spiritual* and *corporeal* Food'. It is a generous sentiment, but the word 'corporeal' may have triggered Blake's response, as Blake characteristically opposes 'corporeal' and 'spiritual' rather than linking them. To this Blake would contrast the view of apostolic Christianity as rendered in Mark 6: 8, where Jesus, unconcerned with 'Lawful Bread Bought with Lawful Money', commands his disciples 'that they should take nothing for their journey, save a staff only; no scrip, no bread, no money in their purse'. The 'Lawful Heaven seen | thro a Lawful Telescope' that follows may, as suggested above, be a reference to Young's 'undevout astronomer' near the bottom of this page, bringing with it associations of Urizen's Newtonian heavens in which the stars move in their assigned order. The reference to 'Lawful Window Light' immediately following is to the window tax, introducing one aspect of a major theme of the Thornton annotations, that of taxation.

The denunciation of taxes is a theme taken up only late in Blake's career (*Concordance*, s.v.). It first appears in two contexts in *Jerusalem*:

Human Miseries turnd fierce with the Lives of Men along the Valley
As Reuben fled before the Daughters of Albion Taxing the Nations

(64: 33–4, E 215)

. . . when the Triple Headed Gog-Magog Giant
Of Albion Taxed the Nations into Desolation & then gave the Spectrous Oath

(98: 52–3, E 258)

---

[19] The words '& whatever' are a substitution for a deleted word E 668 reads as 'who'; the word 'real' was first written after 'Spirit' and then deleted and inserted in pencil after 'Smuggling'.

In both these passages, 'taxing' has the force of exacting tribute, as it does in 2 Kings 23: 35: 'And Jehoiakim gave the silver and the gold to Pharaoh; but he taxed the land to give the money according to the commandment of Pharaoh: he exacted the silver and the gold of the people of the land, of every one according to his taxation, to give it unto Pharaoh-nechoh.' Of Blake's eight remaining uses of words related to 'tax', all but one occur in the Thornton annotations. The other is from יה *& his two Sons* and has a link with the New Testament:

There are States in which all Visionary Men are accounted Mad Men such are Greece & Rome Such is Empire or Tax See Luke Ch 2 v I (E 274)

In the passage to which Blake refers, 'it came to pass in those days, that there went out a decree from Caesar Augustus, that all the world should be taxed'. Again, the people, among them Joseph and Mary, are taxed for the sake of a domineering empire. In the Thornton annotations, Blake leaps from taxation in biblical times to his own time and place, where the Gog-Magog Giant is not a foreign power but the British government taxing its own subjects in multifarious ways.

Blake would probably not have had to pay the income tax, since it started at £60 a year, and those who earned their income by their own work were partially exempt.[20] However, Blake would have been only too aware that he contributed to manifold taxes. Some of these are enumerated by William Cobbett, writing in the *Political Register* in April 1825:

Here comes my jolly landlord with his foaming pot of beer in one hand, and with his other grimy paw held out for the '*Sixpence*, if you please.' Sixpence, you vile extortioner! Why, I can take barley (in spite of the Corn Bill), turn it into malt, and make a better pot of beer for *three halfpence*. 'Aye, master,' says my landlord, 'but this pot of mine has paid malt tax, beer tax, license tax, my house tax, window tax, candle tax, coal tax, and taxes besides without number.' I am silenced, of course.[21]

Another imaginary conversation, this time with a farmer on the price of a bushel of wheat, follows:

---

[20] See J. Stephen Watson, *The Reign of George III 1760–1815* (Oxford: Clarendon Press, 1960), pp. 375–8; Elie Halévy, *England in 1815*, trans. E. I. Watkin and D. A. Barker (New York: Barnes & Noble, 1968), pp. 370–81.

[21] William Cobbett, *Selections from Cobbett's Political Works*, ed. John M. Cobbett and James P. Cobbett (6 vols., London: Ann Cobbett, 1835), vi. 461–2.

'Nine *shilling*s, you rogue, when I can buy wheat in France for less than *four*?' 'Yes,' says the farmer; 'but consider the *Waterloo taxes* that *I have paid* upon this bushel of wheat.' 'What taxes?' 'Why, land tax, poor tax, window tax, beer and malt tax, leather tax, iron tax, and all those taxes for my labourers and wrights as well as for myself, for their taxes are included in what I pay them for *work*.' Am I not, then, as completely silenced, as I was in the case of the jolly landlord?

These lists were not exhaustive. In addition to the taxes already mentioned, in March 1822 Cobbett lists in the *Political Register* taxes on salt, hops, leather for shoes, sugar, soap, candles, tea, brandy, rum, gin, and wearing apparel, among others. In addition to the nationally levied taxes there were the locally levied rates, and these were paid by tenants as well as by owner occupiers; if a landlord rented out a house, the rates were paid by his tenant. Nor can Blake have been happy with the use to which much of his taxes were put, whether to pay off the war debt as Cobbett's 'Waterloo taxes'[22] implies, or to raise buildings—£1,000,000 in 1818 and £500,000 more in 1824—for a Church which he believed 'Crucifies Christ with the Head Downwards' ('A Vision of the Last Judgment', E 564). Blake's attack upon taxes in the Thornton annotations thus combines, in a manner typical of Blake, the biblical and the contemporary.

As the insubstantial Holy Ghost 'cannot be taxed', it is degraded in the eyes of Church and State to a form of witchcraft. Indeed ghosts are because untaxable illegal, unlike that taxable commodity, the ironical synonym to 'Ghosts'—'Spirits', in this case 'Royal Gin'. Blake's allusion conjures up associations with Hogarth's famous engraving *Gin Lane*, which shows the terrible depredations of gin upon the population. This is 'Lawful Spirit' because it contributes to the Excise, but when smuggled it ceases (like 'Witchcraft' and 'Ghosts') to exhibit 'real British Spirit' because it is then not productive of tax revenue. These bitterly satirical lines are much in the same tone as the full parody of Thornton's Lord's Prayer that Blake wrote at the end of the booklet. First, however, he began a straightforward version of his own.

What might be called Blake's Lord's Prayer, as distinguished from his parody of Thornton's, begins as a single sentence in two lines in

---

[22] Ibid., vi. 245; David V. Erdman, *Blake: Prophet Against Empire* (Princeton: Princeton University Press, 1977), p. 492.

the bottom margin of page 2: 'Give us the Bread that is our due & Right by taking away Money or a Price or | Tax upon what is Common to all in thy Kingdom'. The one element in this sentence not so far discussed is the reference to the lives of the early Christians as described in Acts 4: 32: 'And the multitude of them that believed were of one heart and of one soul: neither said any of them that ought of the things which he possessed was his own; but they had all things common.' (Once more there is an overlap here with an aphorism in יה *& his two Sons*: 'The whole Business of Man Is The Arts & All Things Common'.) Nothing could be further from the lives of humans in what Blake calls 'Satans Kingdom' in the full version of his own Lord's Prayer that he wrote out in the bottom and right-hand margins of page 3. These lines are in places very difficult to read because of deletions, revisions, and erasures (as E 669 notes). A version of this text in the form in which Blake left it, ignoring deletions for the moment and incorporating additions and revisions, would read as follows:

Jesus our Father who art in thy Heavens calld by thy Name the Holy Ghost Thy Kingdom on Earth is Not nor thy Will done but Satans Will who is the God of this World The Accuser Let his Judgment be Forgiveness that he may be consumd in his own Shame

Give us This Eternal Day our own right Bread & take away Money or Debt or Tax & Value or Price as we have all things common among us Every Thing has as much right to Eternal Life as God who is the Servant of Man His Judgment shall be Forgiveness that he may be consumd in his own Shame

Leave us not in Parsimony Satans Kingdom liberate us from the Natural Man & want or Jobs Kingdom

For thine is the Kingdom & the Power & the Glory & not Caesars or Satans Amen.[23]

Blake begins his own Lord's Prayer by addressing Jesus as 'the Holy Ghost', that untaxable and therefore unlawful entity. He continues by making a complete bifurcation between our world, which is relegated to Satan, and the Kingdom of God. The Accuser, Satan, will in the end be destroyed by being forgiven—Blake's transformation of Satan's being thrown into the lake of fire and brimstone in Rev. 20: 10. In the next sentence, Blake repeats the ideas and some of

[23] Bentley's text and notes (ii. 516) should be consulted for variants between his and Erdman's readings of the text, but as far as the state of the text after deletions is concerned, there are few important differences.

the words of the note on page 2, but adds that God is the servant of Man, entitled to eternal life only in so far as everything else is. This is very much in the spirit of Jesus' declaration in *The Everlasting Gospel*:

> Thou art a Man God is no more
> Thy own humanity learn to adore
>
> (E 520)

There follows an appeal not to be left in 'Parsimony', after which is inserted 'Satans Kingdom'. Blake certainly had no illusions about the spiritualizing effects of poverty, having so often lived close to it. (In הי *& his two Sons* he calls money 'the lifes blood of Poor Families'.) In the final line of his own version, Blake equates Caesar's kingdom, the State, with Satan's. His attitude is unabashedly Gnostic and Manichaean, which is not to say that he had been reading books on those subjects but rather that the values usually associated with those attitudes came to life again in him.

The version of the Lord's Prayer on page 3 represents what Blake truly thought. On the blank verso of leaf 6 of Thornton's booklet, he wrote another, satirical version, rendering what he regarded as the subtext of the Thornton translation. He preceded it with a note on Thornton's whole enterprise: 'This is Saying the Lords Prayer Backwards which they say Raises the Devil'. Thornton says the Lord's Prayer backwards in one sense because his modern version gives a meaning opposite to what Blake believes the spiritual message of Jesus to be. More literally, saying it backwards would be an act of black magic invoking Satan. Since Satan is in Blake's view the god of this world, the second meaning reinforces the first. A third meaning may hark back to Blake's earlier use of the word 'Devil' in *The Marriage of Heaven and Hell*; if so, this additional meaning would be that Thornton's text brings out the truth-revealing Devil in William Blake. The ensuing title ironically designates what will follow as 'Doctor Thorntons ⟨Tory⟩ Translation Translated out of its disguise in the ⟨Classical⟩ & Scotch language into [plain] ⟨the vulgar⟩ English'. Dr Thornton was not, of course, Scottish; but the 'Scotch language' here may imply the Scottish philosophy of Thomas Reid and his disciples, known for its emphasis on 'common sense'. (Another possibility might be the scepticism of David Hume.) 'Classical', an afterthought, links Thornton as a classicist with Blake's condemnation of 'The Greek and Roman Classics' as 'the Antichrist'; 'Tory', another afterthought, imparts what Blake regards as a political dimension to Thornton's translation. (Far from being a reactionary, Thornton was to all appearances broad-minded and eclectic in his views, but, as in the instance of Dr Johnson, these annotations do not aspire to even-handedness.) The words 'the vulgar' are substituted for 'plain' perhaps because 'the vulgar' appears to have more to do with matters of language. This mock-title is followed by Blake's parody of Thornton's translation.

A rendition of Blake's parodic version, incorporating later additions and leaving out deletions, would read as follows (line breaks not significant):

> Our Father Augustus Caesar who art in these thy Substantial
> Astronomical Telescopic Heavens Holiness to thy Name or Title &
> reverence to thy Shadow Thy Kingship come upon Earth first &
> then in Heaven Give us day by day our Real Taxed Substantial
> Money bought Bread deliver from the Holy Ghost so we call Nature
> whatever cannot be Taxed for all is debts & Taxes between
> Caesar & us & one another lead us not to read the Bible but let
> our Bible be Virgil & Shakspeare & deliver us from Poverty in
> Jesus that Evil one For thine is the Kingship or Allegoric
> Godship & the Power or War & the Glory or Law Ages after Ages in
> thy Descendents for God is only an Allegory of Kings & nothing Else
> Amen

Blake's satirical text has something in common with George Orwell's transformation of 1 Corinthians 13 in his epigraph to *Keep the Aspidistra Flying*, which begins: 'Though I speak with the tongues of men and of angels, and have not money, I am become as a sounding brass, or a tinkling cymbal.' Orwell seeks to unmask the hypocrisy of a supposedly Christian society by a simple strategy—the substitution of the word 'money' for 'love' or 'charity', brilliantly culminating with 'And now abideth faith, hope, money, these three, but the greatest of these is money'. Blake's procedure is more complex, for the object of his attack is the interconnectedness of Church and State that he elsewhere, as in *Jerusalem* 89: 52–3 (E 249), represents as the conjunction of Rahab and Tirzah. Some of the themes of Blake's parody have already been discussed with respect to his preceding annotations. These include the worship of Caesar as God, the materiality of the 'Telescopic Heavens', the omnipresence of Tax and the cash nexus, the 'Substantial' nature of the bread that is prayed for (though Thornton specifies '*spiritual* and *corporeal* Food'), the substitution of the Classics (now, surprisingly, including Shakespeare) for the

Bible, and the poverty of those who follow Jesus. The imagined speaker of this prayer regards whatever is immaterial as non-existent. His 'God' is a dissimulation, 'only an Allegory of Kings & nothing Else'—an imaginary projection of earthly power. For him the Holy Ghost is not spirit but 'Nature', and the 'Power' and 'Glory' in the Lord's Prayer are really 'War' and 'Law'. The 'Kingship' that the speaker twice invokes is the subject of a note immediately following the parody.

Still speaking in his imagined persona, Blake writes: 'I swear that Basilea βασιλεια is not Kingdom but Kingship'. This appears to be the one point Blake makes that actually concerns the correctness of Thornton's translation. βασιλεια appears twice in the Lord's Prayer, both times rendered in the AV as 'kingdom', as indeed it is in the New English Bible and in the Revised Standard Version. Thornton translates it first as 'reign' and then as 'sovereignty'. Blake retranslates the first of these as 'Kingship'. He disregards the second but what he evidently means by his subsequent note is that Thornton's words are more appropriate to a present-day earthly realm than to a spiritual one (or possibly to a millennial one). Indeed, Thornton had elaborated on his rendering of βασιλεια in the explanatory notes on page 3, but evidently not in such a way as to satisfy Blake. The speaker who translates Basilea as Kingship proceeds to identify himself: as 'I Nature Hermaphroditic Priest & King'. 'Hermaphroditic' is of course Blake's term for a being or state of unresolved contradictions, as exemplified by the union of the State and its Church. (Cf. the 'terrible indefinite Hermaphroditic Form' of the Covering Cherub in *Jerusalem* 89: 3, E 248.) This being asserts that he exists in the material world—'in Real Substantial Natural Born Man'—and that this is the only world, the rest being 'the Ghost of Matter or Nature', just as God is merely 'the Ghost of the Priest & King'. God, Blake's speaker candidly asserts, 'exists not', being a mere Ghost of 'the Priest & King who Exist'. This ironical use of 'Ghost' to mean a being in the realm of fantasy is peculiar on Blake's part to the Thornton annotations. (It is interesting that apart from its very different meanings in 'the Holy Ghost' and the very specific 'Ghost of Abel', the word 'ghost(s)' appears only four times in Blake's writings after *Poetical Sketches*, and that three of these occur here, along with a deleted 'ghostly'.[24])

---

[24] *Concordance*, s.v. I do not count Blake's titles for and descriptions of his own pictures, where the word has an entirely different function. The other occurrence is in *Jerusalem* 63: 13, 'The Giants & the Witches & the Ghosts of Albion' (E 214).

Blake's next note—'Here is Signed Two Names which are too Holy
to be written'—apparently alludes to the Jewish belief that the name
of God is too holy to be spoken aloud. One of the 'Two Names'
would presumably be that of 'I Nature', the speaker of the lines
above—or perhaps they are the true names of the dual parts of his
'Priest & King' identity. Next Blake associates the conceptions that
he has been satirizing with quantitative measurement: 'Thus we see
that the Real God is the Goddess Nature & that God Creates noth-
ing but what can be Touch'd & Weighed & Taxed & Measured'.
Weighing and measuring are attributes of Blake's Urizen, as in Night
the Second of *The Four Zoas* where under Urizen's direction the stars
move 'In right lined paths outmeasurd by proportions of number
weight | And measure. mathematic motion wondrous. along the
deep' (33: 23-4, E 322). Thus Blake links what he considers to be
Thornton's God to his own mythology. His annotations then con-
clude with a dig at Thornton himself: 'all else is Heresy & Rebellion
against Caesar Virgils Only God See Eclogue i & for all this we thank
Dr Thornton'. As we have seen, Blake had alluded to Thornton's
Virgil earlier in these annotations. What he has in mind now are
the lines from Virgil's First Eclogue discussed in Chapter 1: 'O
Meliboeus, it is a god who wrought for us this peace—for a god he
shall ever be to me . . .'. Blake reminds anyone who may read these
annotations that Thornton's paraphrase of lines 37-40 of Eclogue I
begins: 'He [Tityrus] calls Augustus "a God" . . .'.[25] Blake's annota-
tions to Thornton's *Lord's Prayer* end, as they begin, with a personal
attack upon its author.

Blake's annotations to Thornton have several points in common
with his more or less contemporary יה *& his two Sons* aphorisms.
Both were written for tiny audiences of readers in the Blake–Linnell
circle. Both are uncompromising, sometimes fiercely so, presenta-
tions of Blake's very late ideas, and both display attitudes that can be
called Gnostic. In Thornton's *Lord's Prayer*, Blake found a bloated
translation set in an equally bloated farrago of opinions and quota-
tions, and he annotated it with a view not of being fair to Dr
Thornton and the authorities and poets he quotes but of exposing the
basic compromise that he saw as underlying Thornton's entire book-
let. Blake, who could read New Testament Greek and at least some

---

[25] See Annabel Patterson, *Pastoral and Ideology* (Berkeley and Los Angeles:
University of California Press, 1987), pp. 258-9.

Hebrew, regarded the meaning of the Bible not as the province of scholars but rather as something to be intuited. In Thornton's proposal for an entire new translation, he saw only a new opportunity for priest and king to subject the Bible, and especially the most uncompromising doctrines of the New Testament, to the language of accommodation. For Blake at the end of his life the spiritual and earthly kingdoms were distinct, though linked, and projects like Thornton's were an attempt to blur the distinction. This attitude is expressed in Blake's response to the death of his friend John Flaxman, in a letter sent to George Cumberland on 12 April 1827, in terms that conclude with the language of the Lord's Prayer: '. . . So must we All soon follow every one to his Own Eternal House Leaving the Delusive Goddess Nature & her Laws to get into Freedom from all Law of the Members into The Mind in which every one is King & Priest in his own House God Send it so on Earth as it is in Heaven' (E 784).

Supplementary Note:
The Visionary Heads

DURING 1819 AND FOR a few years following, Blake made a large number of pencil drawings known as Visionary Heads,[1] largely in three sketchbooks.[2] The first of these, known as the Blake–Varley Sketchbook (Butlin 692, dispersed), contained drawings by both Varley and Blake.[3] The second, the Larger Blake–Varley Sketchbook, was made public in 1989,[4] and the Folio Blake–Varley Sketchbook does not now exist, though individual drawings from it have been identified.[5] In addition, a number of Visionary Heads exist on loose sheets and may have been drawn on them rather than extracted from a sketchbook. The total of known subjects, traced or untraced, is approximately 187. Although no plan or sequence appears to be followed, most of these subjects are from British history, with some from biblical times and classical antiquity, and a few others from disparate sources. Blake's friends John Linnell and John Varley copied and counterproofed some of them, as may have Blake himself.

Blake's Visionary Heads owe their existence most of all to John Varley, a successful landscape artist who was very interested in astrology and physiognomy. John Linnell had been a pupil of Varley's and no doubt introduced him to Blake. According to Gilchrist the meetings during which the drawings were made took place 'during the favourable and fitting hours of night; from nine or ten in the evening to one or two, perhaps three and four o'clock in the morning'.[6] Like Varley, Blake was interested in physiognomy and

---

[1] G. E. Bentley, Jr. notes that a few were made after 1821 and at least one as late as 1825. See *The Stranger from Paradise*, p. 372 n.

[2] See G. E. Bentley, Jr., 'Blake's Visionary Heads: Lost Drawings and a Lost Book', in *Romanticism and Millenarianism*, ed. Tim Fulford (New York and Basingstoke: Palgrave, 2002), pp. 186–205.

[3] See *The Blake–Varley Sketchbook of 1819, in the Collection of M. D. E. Clayton-Stamm*, ed. Martin Butlin (London: Heinemann, 1969).

[4] See L.M.C.K., Introduction to *The Larger Blake–Varley Sketchbook*, Christie's Catalogue (Tuesday, 21 March 1989), pp. 9–12.

[5] See Bentley, 'Blake's Visionary Heads', p. 193.   [6] *Life*, p. 263.

astrology, and in the related 'science' of phrenology as well.[7] He had engraved four plates for Henry Hunter's English edition of Lavater's *Essay on Physiognomy*, and also a separate plate portraying Lavater, after an unknown artist.[8] On 14 October 1807 Blake wrote to Richard Phillips, editor of the *Monthly Magazine*, to protest against the imprisonment of an astrologer (E 769); and in *Jerusalem* 91: 36–7 'Los reads the Stars of Albion! the Spectre reads the Voids | Between the Stars' (E 251). The most extensive account of how Blake drew the Visionary Heads by someone who had known him is Allan Cunningham's,[9] but Cunningham, though sympathetic, is not always reliable, while John Varley was present, was a friend of Blake's, and a believer in the enterprise. His account of the drawing of *The Ghost of a Flea* is therefore worth quoting at length:

This spirit visited his imagination in such a figure as he never anticipated in an insect. As I was anxious to make the most correct investigation in my power, of the truth of these visions, on hearing of this spiritual apparition of a Flea, I asked him if he could draw for me the resemblance of what he saw: he instantly said: 'I see him now before me.' I therefore gave him paper and pencil, with which he drew the portrait, of which a fac-simile is given in this number. I felt convinced by his mode of proceeding that he had a real image before him, for he left off, and began on another part of the paper, to make a separate drawing of the mouth of the Flea, which the spirit having opened, he was prevented from proceeding with the first sketch, till he had closed it. During the time occupied in completing the drawing, the Flea told him that all Fleas were inhabited by the souls of such men, as were by nature blood-thirsty to excess, and were therefore providentially confined to the size and form of insects; otherwise, were he himself for instance the size of a horse, he would depopulate a great portion of the country. He added, that if in attempting to leap from one island to another, he should fall into the sea, he could swim, and should not be lost. This spirit afterwards appeared to Blake, and afforded him a view of his whole figure, an engraving of which I shall give in this work.[10]

The engraving (Fig. 38) occupies the upper part of a plate facing page 54. It shows not the whole figure[11] but the Flea's head and shoulders,

---

[7] See Anne K. Mellor, 'Physiognomy, Phrenology, and Blake's Visionary Heads', in *Blake in His Time*, ed. Essick and Pearce, pp. 53–74.

[8] See Essick, *Separate Plates*, p. 156.

[9] See Cunningham, 'Life of Blake', in *BR*, pp. 496–9.

[10] John Varley, *A Treatise on Zodiacal Physiognomy* (London, 1828), pp. 54–5.

[11] The drawing for this may be *The Ghost of a Flea, Full-length* (Butlin 694, Private Collection).

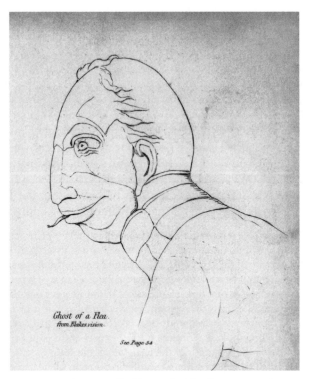

FIG. 38. John Linnell, *Ghost of a Flea*. Engraving after a
drawing by John Varley after William Blake, from *Zodiacal
Physiognomy* by John Varley, 1828.

and the plate is signed: 'J. Linnell sc. | J. Varley inv.'[12] The fact that
all three were involved—Varley presumably copied Blake's original
drawing (Butlin 692.98, Tate Gallery), and Linnell engraved it—
shows how much of a group enterprise the production of the
Visionary Heads was. *The Ghost of a Flea* is also the subject of a
tempera of *c.*1819–20 (Butlin 750, Tate Gallery), in which the Flea
is shown full-length on what appears to be a stage with curtains
and holding a bowl (presumably for blood).

What is clear from Varley's account is that the images Blake drew
as Visionary Heads were perceived rather than invented. This phe-
nomenon has rightly been characterized as an example of eidetic

[12] See Essick, *Separate Plates*, no. LVII, p. 246.

imagery.[13] What defines an eidetic image is that it is actually seen rather than remembered or made up. As E. R. Jaensch, who pioneered the study of this subject, wrote, 'When the influence of the imagination is at its maximum, they are ideas that, like after-images, are projected outward and literally *seen*.'[14] So when Blake would tell Varley, for example, 'I can't go on—it is gone! I must wait till it returns',[15] he was not imposing on his credulous friend, as Gilchrist believed, but reporting what he actually saw. This does not mean, of course, that the materials for these images came from nowhere. Geoffrey Keynes has shown, for example, that parts of Blake's Flea derive from an engraving of a flea seen under a microscope first published in Dr Robert Hooke's *Micrographia* in 1665;[16] and the facial features and costumes of his human subjects must also have derived from Blake's own prior visual experience.

Another Visionary Head of considerable interest is *The Man who Taught Blake Painting in His Dreams* (Butlin 753, Fitzwilliam Museum), which also exists as a counterproof (Butlin 754, Tate Gallery). Seen full-face, this strange countenance with its unusually large eyes set in an ovoid head with wavy, though not overabundant, long hair, might well provide the model for a benevolent extraterrestrial being. A phrenological analysis made according to the system of Spurzheim, according to Anne K. Mellor, reveals him to be, among other things, artistic, imaginative, and enthusiastic—in other words, very like Blake himself.[17] On his forehead this oneiric instructor bears an enigmatic mark or growth, which Keynes likens to a Jewish Menorah (seven-branched candlestick), which in turn 'gains in significance from being placed in the central point of the forehead . . . in Indian yoga an important meditational centre (*cakra*) or "third

---

[13] See Joseph Burke, 'The Eidetic and the Borrowed Image: An Interpretation of Blake's Theory and Practice of Art', in *The Visionary Hand*, ed. Essick, pp. 261–6. Burke's essay was first published in 1964.

[14] See E. R. Jaensch, *Eidetic Imagery* (New York: Harcourt, Brace, 1930), pp. 1–2.

[15] See Gilchrist, *Life*, p. 264.

[16] See Geoffrey Keynes, 'Blake's Visionary Heads and the Ghost of a Flea', in *Blake Studies*, ed. Keynes, p. 134 and p. 33.

[17] See Mellor, 'Physiognomy, Phrenology, and Blake's Visionary Heads', p. 66. Spurzheim himself was not always on the mark. After examining the head of Samuel Taylor Coleridge, whose identity was unknown to him, at a dinner party, Spurzeim pronounced the subject to be devoid of '*Ideality*' but as having 'an unusual share of *Locality*'. See my *Portraits of Coleridge* (Oxford: Clarendon Press, 1999), p. 82.

eye" '.[18] This would of course suggest that Blake received the benefit of his teacher's spiritual insight as well as his knowledge of painting.

There are, of course, some other Visionary Heads of interest, but a great many of them illustrate what Gilchrist had in mind when he wrote that 'critical friends would trace in all these heads the Blake mind and hand—his *receipt* for a face: every artist has his own, his favourite idea, from which he may depart in the proportions, but seldom substantially'.[19] However, they do illustrate an aspect of Blake that appears to have been given freer play in his late years—his imaginative sportiveness.

[18] See Geoffrey Keynes, *The Complete Portraiture of William and Catherine Blake* (London: William Blake Trust/Trianon Press, 1977), p. 132 and plate 22a. Butlin sees eight branches and suggests it 'may rather be a more general allusion to the flames of inspiration'. It is hard to decide precisely how many branches there are because of marks indicating blood vessels that may or may not be intended as part of a candle-stick, and this effect is more pronounced in Blake's counterproof (Butlin 754, Tate Gallery) and in the copy probably made by Linnell (Butlin 755).

[19] *Life*, p. 264.

Bibliography

ADAMS, HAZARD, *William Blake: A Reading of the Shorter Poems* (Seattle: University of Washington Press, 1963).

ALPERS, PAUL, *The Singer of the Eclogues* (Berkeley and Los Angeles: University of California Press, 1979).

BAECK, LEO, *The Pharisees, and Other Essays* (New York: Schocken Books, 1947).

BAKER, C. H. COLLINS, *Catalogue of William Blake's Drawings and Paintings in the Huntington Library*, enlarged and revised by R. R. Wark (San Marino, Calif.: Huntington Library, 1957).

BARKAN, LEONARD, *Unearthing the Past: Archaeology and Aesthetics in the Making of Renaissance Culture* (New Haven and London: Yale University Press, 1999).

BAYLE, PIERRE, *A General Dictionary, Historical and Critical*, ed. and trans. John Peter Bernard, Rev. Thomas Birch, John Lockman, et al. (rev. edn., 10 vols., London, 1734–41).

BEER, JOHN, *Blake's Humanism* (Manchester: Manchester University Press, 1968).

—— *Blake's Visionary Universe* (Manchester: Manchester University Press, 1969).

—— 'Influence and Independence in Blake', in *Interpreting Blake*, ed. Michael Phillips (Cambridge: Cambridge University Press, 1978), pp. 196–261.

—— 'Blake's Changing View of History: The Impact of the Book of Enoch', in *Historicizing Blake*, ed. Steve Clark and David Worrall (Basingstoke: Macmillan, 1994), pp. 159–78.

BEHRENDT, STEPHEN C., '*Europe 6*: Plundering the Treasury', *Blake: An Illustrated Quarterly*, 21 (1987–8): 85–94.

BÉNÉZIT, E., *Dictionnaire critique et documentaire des peintres, sculpteurs, dessinateurs et graveurs* (new edn., rev. Jacques Busse, 14 vols., Paris: Gründ, 1999).

BENTLEY, G. E., Jr., *Blake Books* (Oxford: Clarendon Press, 1977).

—— *Blake Records* (Oxford: Clarendon Press, 1969).

—— *Blake Records Supplement* (Oxford: Clarendon Press, 1988).

—— 'Blake's Visionary Heads: Lost Drawings and a Lost Book', in *Romanticism and Millenarianism*, ed. Fulford, pp. 183–206.

—— 'The Date of Blake's Pickering Manuscript *or* The Way of a Poet with Paper', *Studies in Bibliography*, 19 (1966): 232–43.

BENTLEY, G. E., Jr., 'A Jewel in an Ethiop's Ear', in *Blake in His Time*, ed. Essick and Pearce, pp. 213–40.

—— *The Stranger from Paradise: A Biography of William Blake* (New Haven and London: Yale University Press, 2001).

BIEBER, MARGARET, *Laocoon: The Influence of the Group Since Its Rediscovery* (rev. edn., Detroit: Wayne State University Press, 1967).

BINDMAN, DAVID, *Blake as an Artist* (Oxford: Phaidon, 1977).

—— 'Blake and in Runge', in *Runge, Fragen und Antworten*, ed. Hanna Hohl (Munich: Prestel, 1979), pp. 86–95.

—— 'Text as Design in Gillray's Caricature', in *Icons—Texts—Iconotexts: Essays on Ekphrasis and Intermediality*, ed. Peter Wagner (Berlin and New York: Walter de Gruyter, 1996), pp. 309–23.

—— *William Blake: His Art and Times* (London: Thames & Hudson, 1982).

—— 'William Blake and Popular Religious Imagery', *The Burlington Magazine*, 128 (1986): 712–18.

—— BARBARA BRYANT, ROBERT N. ESSICK, GEOFFREY KEYNES, and BO OSSIAN LINDBERG, *William Blake's Illustrations of the Book of Job: The Engravings and Related Material with Essays, Catalogue of States and Printings, Commentary on the Plates and Documentary Record* (London: William Blake Trust, 1987).

—— ed., *John Flaxman, R.A.* (London: Royal Academy, 1979).

—— and FRANCES CAREY, eds., *Apocalypse and the Shape of Things to Come* (London: British Museum, 1999).

BINYON, LAURENCE, 'The Engravings of William Blake and Edward Calvert', *Print Collector's Quarterly*, 7 (1917): 305–32.

—— Introduction to *Little Engravings Classical & Contemporary Number II. William Blake, Being All His Woodcuts* (London: Sign of the Unicorn, 1902).

BLAIR, ROBERT, *The Grave* (London, 1808).

BLAKE, WILLIAM, *Blake's Poetry and Designs*, ed. Mary Lynn Johnson and John E. Grant (New York: W. W. Norton, 1979).

—— *The Complete Poems*, ed. W. H. Stevenson (2nd edn., London and New York: Longman, 1989).

—— *The Complete Poetry and Prose of William Blake*, ed. David V. Erdman (rev. edn., Berkeley and Los Angeles: University of California Press, 1982).

—— *Complete Writings of William Blake*, ed. Geoffrey Keynes (Oxford: Oxford University Press, rev. edn., 1972).

—— *William Blake: The Continental Prophecies*, ed. Detlef W. Dörrbecker (London: Tate Gallery/William Blake Trust, 1995).

—— *The Divine Comedy*, ed. David Bindman (Paris: Bibliothèque de l'Image, 2000).

—— *The Early Illuminated Books*, ed. Morris Eaves, Robert N. Essick, and Joseph Viscomi (London: Tate Gallery for the William Blake Trust, 1993).

—— *The Four Zoas* by William Blake, ed. Cettina Tramontano Magno and David V. Erdman (Lewisburg, Pa.: Bucknell University Press, 1987).

—— *Illustrations of The Book of Job by William Blake*, ed. Laurence Binyon and Geoffrey Keynes (New York: Pierpont Morgan Library, 1935).

—— *Illustrations to the Divine Comedy of Dante by William Blake* (London: National Art-Collections Fund, 1922).

—— *Jerusalem/The Emanation of the Giant Albion*, ed. Morton D. Paley (London: William Blake Trust/Tate Gallery, 1991).

—— *The Letters of William Blake*, ed. Geoffrey Keynes (rev. edn., Cambridge, Mass.: Harvard University Press, 1968).

—— *Milton a Poem*, ed. Robert N. Essick and Joseph Viscomi (London: Tate Gallery/William Blake Trust, 1993).

—— *The Notebook of William Blake*, ed. David V. Erdman with the assistance of Donald K. Moore (Oxford: Clarendon Press, 1973).

—— *The Prophetic Writings of William Blake*, ed. D. J. Sloss and J. P. R. Wallis (2 vols., Oxford: Clarendon Press, 1926).

—— *Songs of Innocence and of Experience*, ed. Andrew Lincoln (London: William Blake Trust/Tate Gallery, 1991).

—— *William Blake: The Gates of Paradise*, ed. Geoffrey Keynes (3 vols., London: Trianon Press for the William Blake Trust, 1968).

—— *William Blake: Selected Poetry and Prose*, ed. David Fuller (New York: Pearson, 2000).

—— *William Blake's Writings*, ed. G. E. Bentley, Jr. (2 vols., Oxford: Clarendon Press, 1978).

BLUMER, M.-L., 'La Commission pour la recherche des objets de sciences et arts en italie (1796–1797)', *La Révolution Française*, 86 (1933): 62–88, 124–50, 222–5.

BLUNT, ANTHONY, *The Art of William Blake* (New York: Columbia University Press, 1959).

—— 'Blake's Pictorial Imagination', *Journal of the Warburg and Courtauld Institutes*, 6 (1943): 190–212.

BOGAN, JAMES, 'From Hackwork to Prophetic Vision: William Blake's Delineation of the Laocoon Group', *Publications of the Arkansas Philological Association*, 6 (1980): 33–51.

BOTTICELLI, SANDRO, *The Drawings for Dante's Divine Comedy*, ed. Hein.-Th. Schulze Altcappenberg (London: Royal Academy, 2000).

BOUTANG, PIERRE, *William Blake manichéen et visionnaire* (Paris: La Différence, 1990).

BOYD, HENRY, *A Translation of the Inferno of Dante Alighieri in English Verse, with Historical Notes, and the Life of Dante* (2 vols., Dublin, 1785).

BRILLIANT, RICHARD, *My Laocoön: Alternative Claims in the Interpretation of Artworks* (Berkeley: University of California Press, 2000).

BROWN, ALLAN R., 'Blake's Drawings for the *Book of Enoch*' [1940], repr. in *The Visionary Hand*, ed. Essick, pp. 105–16.

BRUMMER, HANS HENRIK, *The Statue Court in the Vatican Belvedere*, Acta Universitatis Stockholmiensis/Stockholm Studies in History of Art, No. 20 (Stockholm: Almqvist & Wiksell, 1970), pp. 75–119.

BRYANT, JACOB, A *New System, or an Analysis of Ancient Mythology* (3 vols., London, 1774–6).

BURKE, JOSEPH, 'The Eidetic and the Borrowed Image: An Interpretation of Blake's Theory and Practice of Art' [1964], in *The Visionary Hand*, ed. Essick, pp. 253–302.

BURWICK, FREDERICK, 'Blake's *Laocoön* and *Job*: or, On the Boundaries of Painting and Poetry', in *The Romantic Imagination*, ed. Frederick Burwick and Jürgen Klein (Amsterdam and Atlanta: Rodopi, 1996), pp. 125–55.

BUTLIN, MARTIN, ed. *The Blake–Varley Sketchbook of 1819, in the Collection of M. D. E. Clayton-Stamm* (London, Heinemann: 1969).

——— *The Paintings and Drawings of William Blake* (2 vols., New Haven and London: Yale University Press, 1981).

——— *William Blake* (London: Tate Gallery, 1978).

——— and TED GOTT, *William Blake in the Collection of the National Gallery of Victoria* (Melbourne: National Gallery of Victoria, 1989).

——— MOLLIE LUTHER, and IAN WARRELL, *Turner at Petworth* (London: Tate Gallery, 1989).

BYRON, LORD, *The Complete Poetical Works*, vol. v, ed. Jerome J. McGann (Oxford: Clarendon Press, 1986); vol. vi, ed. Jerome J. McGann and Barry Weller (Oxford: Clarendon Press, 1991).

——— *The Works of Lord Byron*, ed. Ernest Hartley Coleridge, vol. v, *Poetry* (rev. edn., London: John Murray, 1901).

CAREY, FRANCES, ed., *Apocalypse and the Shape of Things to Come* (London: British Museum, 1999).

CHARLESWORTH, JAMES H., ed., *The Old Testament Pseudepigrapha* (2 vols., Garden City, NY: Doubleday, 1983).

Christie's, Catalogue, Tuesday, 21 March 1989, Lot 184, *The Larger Blake–Varley Sketchbook*, Introduction by L.M.C.K.

CHURCHILL, CHARLES, *The Poetical Works of Charles Churchill* (2 vols., London: Bell & Daldy, 1866).

CLARK, KENNETH, *The Romantic Rebellion: Romantic versus Classic Art* (New York: Harper & Row, 1973).

COBBETT, WILLIAM, *Selections from Cobbett's Political Works*, ed. John M. Cobbett and James P. Cobbett (6 vols., London: Ann Cobbett, 1835).

[COLE, HENRY], 'The Vicar of Wakefield. With thirty-two Illustrations. By W. Mulready, R. A. Van Voorst', *The Athenaeum* (1843), pp. 65–8.

COLERIDGE, SAMUEL TAYLOR, *Lectures 1808–1819 On Literature*, ed. R. A. Foakes (2 vols., Princeton: Princeton University Press, 1987).

——*Poetical Works*, ed. J. C. C. Mays (3 vols., Princeton: Princeton University Press, 2001).

CREHAN, STUART, *Blake in Context* (Dublin: Gill and Macmillan, 1984).

CUMBERLAND, GEORGE, *An Essay on the Utility of Collecting the Best Works of the Italian School; Accompanied by a Critical Catalogue* (London, 1827).

CURRAN, STUART, 'Blake's Gnostic Hyle: A Double Negative', *Blake Studies*, 4 (1972): 117–34.

CUZIN, JEAN-PIERRE, JEAN-RENÉ GABORIT, and ALAIN PASQUIER, eds., *D'après l'antique* (Paris: Réunion des Musées, 2000).

DAMON, S. FOSTER, *A Blake Dictionary: The Ideas and Symbols of William Blake* (Hanover, NH: University Press of New England, rev. edn., 1988).

——*Blake's Job* (Providence, RI: Brown University Press, 1966).

——*William Blake: His Philosophy and Symbols* (Gloucester, Mass.: Peter Lang, 1958 [1924]).

DAMROSCH, LEOPOLD, *Symbol and Truth in Blake's Myth* (Princeton: Princeton University Press, 1980).

DANTE ALIGHIERI, *Comento di Christophoro Landino Fiorentinto sopra la Comedia di Danthe Alighieri* (Florence, 1481).

——*Dante con l'espositione di Christoforo Landino, et di Alessandro Vellutello* (Venice, 1564).

——*A Translation of the Inferno of Dante Alighieri in English Verse, with Historical Notes, and the Life of Dante*, by Henry Boyd (2 vols., Dublin, 1785).

——*The Vision; or Hell, Purgatory, and Paradise, of Dante Alighieri*, trans. Henry Francis Cary (2nd edn., London: Taylor & Hessey, 1819).

——*The Inferno of Dante Alighieri*, ed. Henry Oelsner, trans. Herman Oelsner and John Aitken Carlyle (London: J. M. Dent (Temple Classics), 1958 [1900]).

——*The Purgatorio of Dante Alighieri*, ed. Herman Oelsner, trans. Thomas Okey (London: J. M. Dent (Temple Classics), 1956 [1901]).

——*The Paradiso of Dante Alighieri*, ed. Henry Oelsner, trans. Philip Henry Wicksteed (London: J. M. Dent (Temple Classics), 1958 [1899]).

DIDEROT, DENIS, *Encyclopédie, ou Dictionnaire raisonné des sciences, des arts, et des métiers* (17 vols., Neuchâtel, 1765).

——*Recueil de planches sur les sciences et les arts* (11 vols., Paris, 1763).

DÖRRBECKER, DETLEF W., 'A Survey of Engravings After Flaxman's Outline Compositions', in *John Flaxman, R.A.*, ed. Bindman, pp. 184–5.

DRYDEN, JOHN, *The Works of John Dryden*, ed. Edward Niles Hooker and H. T. Swedenberg, Jr., vol. v, *The Works of Virgil in English* (Berkeley: University of California Press, 1987).

DÜRER, ALBRECHT, *Albert Durer's designs of the Prayer Book* (London: R. Ackermann, 1817).

—— *The Book of Hours of Emperor Maximilian the First*, ed. Walter L. Straus (New York: Abaris Books, 1974).

EASTLAKE, ELIZABETH RIGBY, Lady. See Jameson, Anna.

EAVES, MORRIS, *The Counter-Arts Conspiracy: Art and Industry in the Age of Blake* (Ithaca, NY, and London: Cornell University Press, 1992).

ECO, UMBERTO, *The Name of the Rose*, trans. William Weaver (New York: Harcourt Brace, 1983).

ERDMAN, DAVID V., *The Illuminated Blake* (Garden City, NY: Anchor Books, 1974).

—— *Blake: Prophet Against Empire: A Poet's Interpretation of the History of his Own Times* (Princeton: Princeton University Press, 1977).

—— ' "Terrible Blake in His Pride" ', in *From Sensibility to Romanticism: Essays Presented to Frederick A. Pottle*, ed. Frederick W. Hilles and Harold Bloom (New York: Oxford University Press, 1965), pp. 331–65.

—— ed., *A Concordance to the Writings of William Blake* (2 vols., Ithaca, NY: Cornell University Press, 1967).

—— and JOHN E. GRANT, eds., *Blake's Visionary Forms Dramatic* (Princeton: Princeton University Press, 1970).

ESSICK, ROBERT N., 'Blake's "Enoch" Lithograph', *Blake: An Illustrated Quarterly*, 14 (1980–1): 180–4.

—— 'John Linnell, William Blake, and the Printmaker's Craft', in *Essays on the Blake Followers*, ed. G. E. Bentley, Jr. (San Marino, Calif.: Huntington Library, 1983), pp. 18–32.

—— 'A Relief Etching of Blake's Virgil Illustrations', *Blake: An Illustrated Quarterly*, 25 (Winter 1991/2): 117–26.

—— *The Separate Plates of William Blake: A Catalogue* (Princeton: Princeton University Press, 1983).

—— *A Troubled Paradise: William Blake's Virgil Wood Engravings* (San Francisco: John Windle, 1999).

—— *William Blake, Printmaker* (Princeton: Princeton University Press, 1980).

—— *William Blake's Commercial Book Illustrations* (Oxford: Clarendon Press, 1991).

—— *The Works of William Blake in the Huntington Collections* (San Marino, Calif.: Huntington Library, 1985).

—— ed., *The Visionary Hand: Essays for the Study of William Blake's Art and Aesthetics* (Los Angeles: Hennessey & Ingalls, 1973).

—— and MORTON D. PALEY, ' "Dear Generous Cumberland": A Newly Discovered Letter and Poem by William Blake', *Blake: An Illustrated Quarterly*, 32 (1998): 4–13.

—— —— *Robert Blair's* The Grave *Illustrated by William Blake* (London: Scolar Press, 1982).

——and DONALD PEARCE, eds., *Blake in His Time* (Bloomington and London: Indiana University Press, 1978).

ETTLINGER, LEOPOLD, 'Exemplum Doloris: Reflections on the Laocoön Group', in *De Artibus Opuscula XL: Essays in Honor of Erwin Panofsky*, ed. Millard Meiss (2 vols., New York: New York University Press, 1961), i. 121–6; ii. 37.

[FERGUSON, ROBERT], 'Horae Germanicae (No. XVIII): Lessing's *Laocoon*', *Blackwood's Magazine*, 16 (September 1824): 312–16.

FLAXMAN, JOHN, *Compositions by John Flaxman, Sculptor, R.A., from the Divine Poem of Dante Alighieri, Containing Hell, Purgatory, and Paradise* (London: Longman, Hurst, Rees & Orme, 1807).

——'Cursory Strictures on Modern Art', in *The Artist*, ed. Prince Hoare (London, 1810), pp. (1–16).

FROST, ROBERT, *The Poetry of Robert Frost*, ed. Edward Connery Latham (New York: Henry Holt, 1979).

FRYE, NORTHROP, *Fearful Symmetry: A Study of William Blake* (Princeton: Princeton University Press, 1947).

FULFORD, TIM, ed., *Romanticism and Millenarianism* (New York and Basingstoke: Palgrave, 2002).

FULLER, DAVID, 'Blake and Dante', *Art History*, 11 (1988): 349–73.

FUSELI, HENRY, *Lectures on Art Delivered at the Royal Academy March 1801* (London: J. Johnson, 1801).

GESSNER, SALOMON, *The Death of Abel in Five books*, trans. Mary Collyer (3rd edn., London, 1762).

——*The Works of Solomon Gessner* (3 vols., Liverpool: Cadell & Davies, 1802).

GILCHRIST, ALEXANDER, *Life of William Blake* (2 vols., London: Macmillan, 1863).

——*Life of William Blake* (2nd edn., 2 vols., London: Macmillan, 1880).

——*Life of William Blake*, ed. Ruthven Todd (rev. edn., London: J. M. Dent, 1945).

GITTINGS, ROBERT, *The Mask of Keats* (Cambridge, Mass.: Harvard University Press, 1956).

GIZZI, CORRADO, ed., *Blake e Dante* (Milan: G. Mazzotta, 1983).

GOETHE, WOLFGANG VON, 'Observations on the Laocoon', *Monthly Magazine*, 1 June (1799): 349–52, 399–401.

GOSLEE, NANCY MOORE, *Uriel's Eye: Miltonic Stationing and Statuary in Blake, Keats, and Shelley* (Tuscaloosa, Ala.: University of Alabama Press, 1985).

GOTT, TED, 'Thornton's *Virgil*', in Butlin and Gott, *William Blake in the Collection of the National Gallery of Victoria*, pp. 135–6.

GRÉGOIRE, HENRI BAPTISTE, *Rapport sur les destructions opérées par le Vandalisme, et sur les moyens de le réprimer* (Paris, 1794).

HAGSTRUM, JEAN H., *William Blake: Poet and Painter* (Chicago: University of Chicago Press, 1964).

—— 'The Wrath of the Lamb: A Study of William Blake's Conversions', in *From Sensibility to Romanticism: Essays Presented to Frederick A. Pottle*, ed. Frederick W. Hilles and Harold Bloom (New York: Oxford University Press, 1965), pp. 311–30.

HALÉVY, ELIE, *England in 1815*, trans. E. I. Watkin and D. A. Barker (New York: Barnes & Noble, 1968).

HARPER, GEORGE MILLS, *The Neoplatonism of William Blake* (Chapel Hill, NC: University of North Carolina Press, 1961).

HASKELL, FRANCIS, and NICHOLAS PENNY, *Taste and the Antique: The Lure of Classical Sculpture, 1500–1900* (New Haven: Yale University Press, 1981).

HAVELY, NICK, ed., *Dante's Modern Afterlife: Reception and Response from Blake to Heaney* (New York: St Martin's Press, 1998).

HAYLEY, WILLIAM, *Essay on Epic Poetry* (London: J. Dodsley, 1782).

—— *An Essay on Sculpture* (London: T. Cadell & W. Davies, 1800).

HELMS, RANDALL, 'The Genesis of *The Everlasting Gospel*', *Blake Studies*, 9 (1980): 122–60.

HENRY, MATTHEW, *Commentary on the Whole Bible* (1706–20), *Blue Letter Bible*, www.blueletterbible.org/Comm/mhc

HEPPNER, CHRISTOPHER, 'The Woman Taken in Adultery: An Essay on Blake's "Style of Designing"', *Blake: An Illustrated Quarterly*, 17 (Fall 1983): 44–60.

HERRSTROM, DAVID STEN, 'Blake's Redemption of God in the *Laocoön*', *Bucknell Review*, 30 (1986): 37–71.

HILTON, NELSON, *Literal Imagination: Blake's Vision of Words* (Berkeley and Los Angeles: University of California Press, 1983).

—— ' "Under the Hill" ', *Blake: An Illustrated Quarterly*, 22 (1988): 16.

HOFF, URSULA, *William Blake's Illustrations to Dante's Divine Comedy* (Melbourne: National Gallery of Victoria, 1961).

HOLLSTEIN, F. W. H., *Dutch and Flemish Etchings, Engravings, and Woodcuts ca. 1450–1700* (58 vols., Amsterdam: Menno Hertzberger, 1949–).

IVINS, WILLIAM F., 'Ignorance, the End', *Bulletin of the Metropolitan Museum of Art*, NS 2 (1943): 3, 4 (3–10).

JAENSCH, E. R., *Eidetic Imagery* (New York: Harcourt, Brace, 1930).

JAMES, DAVID, 'Blake's *Laocoön*: A Degree Zero of Literary Production', *PMLA* 98 (1983): 226–36.

JAMES, G. INGLI, 'Blake's Woodcuts Illuminated', *Apollo*, 94 (1974): 194–5.

JAMESON, ANNA, *Sacred and Legendary Art* (3rd edn., 2 vols., Boston and New York: Houghton Mifflin, 1886).

——and ELIZABETH RIGBY, LADY EASTLAKE, *The History of Our Lord As Exemplified in Works of Art* (4th edn., 2 vols., London: Longmans, Green, 1881).

JANSON, H. W., 'Titian's Laocoön Caricature and the Vesalian–Galenist Controversy', *Art Bulletin*, 28 (1946): 49–53.

JOHNSON, SAMUEL, *Prayers and Meditations*, ed. George Strahan (London: T. Cadell, 1785).

KELLER, PETER, 'The Engravings in the 1481 Edition of the *Divine Comedy*', in Botticelli, *The Drawings for Dante's Divine Comedy*, ed. Schulze Altcappenberg, pp. 326–33.

KEYNES, GEOFFREY, *A Bibliography of William Blake* (New York: Grolier Club, 1921).

——'Blake's Copy of Dante's *Inferno*', in *Blake Studies* (2nd edn., Oxford: Clarendon Press, 1971), pp. 147–54.

——ed., *Blake's Pencil Drawings*, 2nd ser. (London: Nonesuch Press, 1956).

——ed., *Blake Studies: Essays on His Life and Work* (2nd edn., Oxford: Clarendon Press, 1971).

——*The Complete Portraiture of William and Catherine Blake* (London: William Blake Trust/Trianon Press, 1977).

——ed., *The Illustrations of William Blake for Thornton's Virgil* (London: Nonesuch Press, 1937), Keynes's Introduction, pp. 7–20 (repr. Keynes, *Blake Studies*, pp. 136–42).

——ed., *William Blake's Laocoön: A Last Testament: With Related Works: On Homers' Poetry and On Virgil, The Ghost of Abel* (London: The Trianon Press for the William Blake Trust, 1976).

KLONSKY, MILTON, *Blake's Dante: The Complete Illustrations to The Divine Comedy* (New York: Harmony Books, 1980).

KNOWLES, JOHN, *The Life and Writings of Henry Fuseli* (2 vols., London, 1831).

LA BELLE, JENIJOY, 'Words Graven with an Iron Pen: The Marginal Texts in Blake's *Job*', in *The Visionary Hand*, ed. Essick, pp. 527–50.

LAURENCE, RICHARD, trans., *The Book of Enoch the Prophet* (Oxford, 1821).

LESSING, GOTTHOLD EPHRAIM, *Laokoon and How the Ancients Represented Death*, trans. E. C. Beasley (London: G. Bell & Sons, 1914).

LINDBERG, BO OSSIAN, *William Blake's Illustrations to the Book of Job*, Acta Academiae Aboensis, Ser. A, vol. 46 (Åbo: Åbo Akademi, 1973).

LINNELL, DAVID, *Blake, Palmer, Linnell and Co.: The Life of John Linnell* (Sussex: The Book Guild, 1994).

McDANNELL, COLLEEN, and BERNHARD LANG, *Heaven: A History* (New Haven and London: Yale University Press, 1988).

MCGANN, JEROME J., 'The Idea of an Indeterminate Text: Blake's Bible of Hell and Dr. Alexander Geddes', *Studies in Romanticism*, 25 (1986): 303–24.

MARTIN, PHILIP W., 'The Angels of Byron and Moore—Close Encounters of Another Kind', in *Romanticism and Millenarianism*, ed. Fulford, pp. 153–66.

——*Byron, a Poet before His Public* (Cambridge: Cambridge University Press, 1982).

MEE, JON, *Dangerous Enthusiasm: William Blake and the Culture of Radicalism in the 1790s* (Oxford: Clarendon Press, 1992).

MELLOR, ANNE K., 'Physiognomy, Phrenology, and Blake's Visionary Heads', in *Blake in His Time*, ed. Essick and Pearce, pp. 53–74.

MILTON, JOHN, *Complete Poems and Major Prose*, ed. Merritt Y. Hughes (New York: Odyssey Press, 1957).

MITCHELL, W. J. T., *Iconology: Image, Text, Ideology* (Chicago and London: University of Chicago Press, 1986).

MONTFAUCON, BERNARD DE, *The Supplement to Antiquity Explained, and Represented in Sculptures, By the learned Father Montfaucon, Translated into English by David Humphreys* (5 vols., London: J. Tonson & J. Watts, 1725).

MOORE, THOMAS, *The Loves of the Angels* (2nd edn., London: Longman, Hurst, Rees, Orme, & Brown, 1823).

MORTON, A. L., *The Everlasting Gospel* (London: Lawrence & Wishart, 1958).

MOSHEIM, JOHN LAURENCE, DD, *Commentaries on the Affairs of the Christians Before the Time of Constantine the Great*, trans. Robert Studley Vidal (2 vols., London, 1813).

MOSKAL, JEANNE, *Blake, Ethics, and Forgiveness* (Tuscaloosa, Ala.: University of Alabama Press, 1994).

MÜNTZ, EUGÈNE, 'Les Annexations de collections d'art ou de bibliothèques', *Revue d'histoire diplomatique*, 10 (1896): 484 (481–508).

NANNUVUTTY, PILOO, 'A Title Page in Blake's Illustrated Genesis Manuscript', in *The Visionary Hand*, ed. Essick, pp. 127–46.

NELMS, BEN F., 'Text and Design in *Illustrations of the Book of Job*', in Erdman and Grant, eds., *Blake's Visionary Forms Dramatic*, pp. 336–58.

NORTON, CHARLES ELIOT, *William Blake's Illustrations of the Book of Job* (Boston: James R. Osgood, 1875).

NORVIG, GERDA S., *Dark Figures in the Desired Country: Blake's Illustrations to The Pilgrim's Progress* (Berkeley: University of California Press, 1993).

OKADA, KAZUYA, 'Orc Under a Veil Revealed', *Blake: An Illustrated Quarterly*, 34 (2000): 38–45.

ORWELL, GEORGE [Eric Blair], *Keep the Aspidistra Flying* (London: Secker & Warburg, 1969 [1936]).

OTTLEY, WILLIAM YOUNG, *An Inquiry into the Origin and Early History of Engraving* (2 vols., London, 1816).

OUSELEY, SIR WILLIAM, *Travels in Various Countries of the East* (3 vols., London: Bowdell & Martin, 1819–23).

PAGELS, ELAINE, *The Gnostic Gospels* (New York: Random House, Vintage Books, 1981).

PALEY, MORTON D., *Apocalypse and Millennium in English Romantic Poetry* (Oxford: Clarendon Press, 1999).

——*The Apocalyptic Sublime* (New Haven and London: Yale University Press, 1986).

——'The Art of "The Ancients"', in *William Blake and His Circle*, Papers Delivered at a Huntington Symposium (San Marino, Calif.: Henry E. Huntington Library and Art Gallery, 1989), pp. 97–124.

——*The Continuing City: William Blake's Jerusalem* (Oxford: Clarendon Press, 1983).

——*Energy and the Imagination: A Study of the Development of Blake's Thought* (Oxford: Clarendon Press, 1970).

——'The Fourth Face of Man: Blake and Architecture', in *Articulate Images: The Sister Arts from Hogarth to Tennyson*, ed. Richard Wendorf (Minneapolis: University of Minnesota Press, 1983), pp. 184–215.

——' "A New Heaven Is Begun": Blake and Swedenborgianism', *Blake: An Illustrated Quarterly*, 13 (1979): 64–90.

——'The Truchsessian Gallery Revisited', *Studies in Romanticism*, 16 (1977): 165–77.

——' "Wonderful Originals"—Blake and Ancient Sculpture', in *Blake in His Time*, ed. Essick and Pearce, pp. 170–93.

——*Portraits of Coleridge* (Oxford: Clarendon Press, 1999).

——*William Blake* (Oxford: Phaidon, 1978).

PALMER, A. H., *The Life and Letters of Samuel Palmer* (London: Seeley & Co., 1892).

——ed., *Catalogue of an Exhibition of Drawings, Etchings, and Woodcuts by Samuel Palmer and other Disciples of William Blake* (London: Victoria and Albert Museum, 1926).

PASSAVANT, JOHANN DAVID, *Tour of a German Artist in England* (2 vols., London: Sanders & Otley, 1836).

PATAI, RAPHAEL, *The Hebrew Goddess* (3rd edn., Detroit: Wayne State University Press, 1990).

PATTERSON, ANNABEL, *Pastoral and Ideology* (Berkeley and Los Angeles: University of California Press, 1987).

PENNY, NICHOLAS, *Reynolds* (London: Royal Academy, 1986).

PERCIVAL, MILTON O., *William Blake's Circle of Destiny* (New York: Columbia University Press, 1938).

PETERFREUND, STUART, *William Blake in a Newtonian World* (Norman, Okla.: University of Oklahoma Press, 1998).

PHILIPS, AMBROSE, *The Poems of Ambrose Philips*, ed. M. G. Segar (Oxford: Blackwell, 1937).

PINTO, VIVIAN DE SOLA, 'William Blake, Isaac Watts, and Mrs Barbauld', in *The Divine Vision*, ed. V. de Sola Pinto (London: Gollancz, 1957), pp. 65–80.

PIQUET, FRANÇOIS, *Blake et le sacré*, Études Anglaises, 98 (Paris: Didier, 1996).

PIROLI, TOMMASO, *Les Monumens antiques du Musée Napoléon dessinés et gravés par Thomas Piroli* (4 vols., Paris, 1804).

PLATO, *Works of Plato*, trans. Thomas Taylor (5 vols., Frome, Somerset: Prometheus Trust, 1995–6 [London, 1804]).

PLINY THE YOUNGER, *The Letters of Pliny*, trans. William Melmoth, rev. W. M. L. Hutchinson (2 vols., London: Heinemann, 1927).

——*Natural History*, trans. D. E. Eicholz (Cambridge, Mass.: Harvard University Press, 1962).

PRIESTLEY, JOSEPH, *Disquisitions Relating to Matter and Spirit* (London: Joseph Johnson, 1777).

REED, BERTHA, *The Influence of Solomon Gessner upon English Literature* (Philadelphia: Americana Germanica Press, 1905).

REES, ABRAHAM, *The Cyclopaedia; or, Universal Dictionary of Arts, Sciences, and Literature* (39 text volumes and 6 plates volumes, London: Longman, Hurst, Rees, Orme, & Brown, 1802–20).

RICHARDSON, JONATHAN, Sr., and JONATHAN RICHARDSON, Jr., *An Account of Some of the Statues, Bas-reliefs, Drawings and Pictures in Italy* (London: J. Knapton, 1722).

ROE, ALBERT S., *Blake's Illustrations to* The Divine Comedy (Princeton: Princeton University Press, 1953).

ROSENBLUM, ROBERT, *The International Style of 1800: A Study in Linear Abstraction* (New York: Garland, 1976).

——*Transformations in Late Eighteenth Century Art* (Princeton: Princeton University Press, 1967).

ROSENFELD, ALVIN, ed., *William Blake: Essays for S. Foster Damon* (Providence, RI: Brown University Press, 1969).

RUSSELL, A. G. B., *The Engravings of William Blake* (London: G. Richards, 1912), p. 91.

SCHIFF, GERT, *Johann Heinrich Füssli 1741–1825: Text und Oeuvrekatalog* (2 vols., Zurich: Verlag Berichthaus, Munich: Prestel-Verlag, 1973).

SCHLEGEL, AUGUST WILHELM, *A Course of Lectures on Dramatic Art and Literature*, trans. John Black (2 vols., London: Baldwin, Craddock & Joy, 1815).

SHABETAI, KAREN, 'The Question of Blake's Hostility Toward the Jews', *ELH* 63 (1996): 139–52.

SHAKESPEARE, WILLIAM, *King Lear*, ed. Kenneth Muir (Cambridge, Mass.: Harvard University Press, 1959).

SHELLEY, PERCY BYSSHE, *Shelley's Prose*, ed. David Lee Clark (Albuquerque: University of New Mexico Press, 1954).

SPECTOR, SHEILA A., 'Blake's Graphic Use of Hebrew', forthcoming in *Blake: An Illustrated Quarterly*.

—— '*Wonders Divine*': *The Development of Blake's Kabbalistic Myth* (Lewisburg, Pa.: Bucknell University Press, 2001).

STEFFAN, TRUMAN GUY, *Lord Byron's Cain: Twelve Essays and a Text with Variants and Annotations* (Austin: University of Texas Press, 1968).

STEPHEN, SIR LESLIE, and SIR SIDNEY LEE, *Dictionary of National Biography* (26 vols., London: Oxford University Press, 1959–60).

STORY, ALFRED T., *The Life of John Linnell* (2 vols., London: Richard Bentley & Son, 1892).

STUART, JAMES, and NICHOLAS REVETT, *The Antiquities of Athens* (5 vols., London: J. Haberkorn, 1762–1830).

SWEDENBORG, EMANUEL, *Arcana Cœlestia, Now first translated from the original Latin . . . by a Society of Gentlemen* (13 vols., London: J. & E. Hodson, 1802–16).

—— *Heaven and Its Wonders and Hell* (New York: Swedenborg Society, 1956), p. 86 (no. 117).

SYMAKEN, GEORG, 'Die "Tageszeiten" von Philipp Otto Runge und "The Book of Job" von William Blake', *Jahrbuch der Hamburger Kunstsammlungen*, 20 (1975): 61–70.

TAMBLING, JEREMY, 'Dante and Blake: Allegorizing the Event', in *Dante's Modern Afterlife*, ed. Havely, pp. 33–48.

TANNENBAUM, LESLIE, 'Blake and the Iconography of Cain', in *Blake in His Time*, ed. Essick and Pearce, pp. 23–34.

—— 'Lord Byron in the Wilderness: Biblical Tradition in Byron's *Cain* and Blake's *The Ghost of Abel*', *Modern Philology*, 72 (1975): 350–64.

TAYLER, IRENE, 'Blake Meets Byron on April Fool's', *English Language Notes*, 16 (1978): 85–93.

—— 'Blake's *Laocoön*', *Blake: An Illustrated Quarterly*, 10 (1976–7): 72–81.

TAYLOR, PETER ALAN, 'Blake's Text for the *Enoch* Drawings', *Blake: An Illustrated Quarterly*, 7 (1973–4): 82–6.

THORNTON, ROBERT JOHN, *The Pastorals of Virgil, with a Course of English Reading, Adapted for Schools* (London, 1821).

—— *The Lord's Prayer, Newly Translated from the Original Greek, with Critical and Explanatory Notes* (London, 1827).

TINKLER-VILLANI, V., *Visions of Dante in English Poetry: Translations of the Commedia from Jonathan Richardson to William Blake* (Amsterdam: Rodopi, 1989).

TODD, RUTHVEN, 'Blake's Dante Plates', *Book Collecting & Library Monthly*, 6 (1968): 164–71.

TOLLEY, MICHAEL J., 'Blake's "Eden's Flood" Again', *Notes and Queries*, 213 (1968): 11–18.

—— 'Thornton's Blake Edition', *University of Adelaide Library News*, 10 (1988): 4–11.

—— 'William Blake's Use of the Bible in a Section of "The Everlasting Gospel" ', *Notes and Queries*, 207 (1962): 171–6.

TOYNBEE, PAGET, *Dante in English Art* (Boston: Ginn & Co. for the Dante Society, 1921).

—— *Dante in English Literature from Chaucer to Cary* (2 vols., New York: Macmillan, 1909).

TURNER, JANE, ed., *The Dictionary of Art* (34 vols., London: Macmillan, 1966).

VAN GELDER, JAN G., and INGRID JOST, *Jan de Bisschop and His Icones & Paradigmata: Classical Antiquities and Italian Drawings for Artistic Instruction in Seventeenth Century Holland* (2 vols., Doornspijk, Netherlands: Davaco, 1985).

VARLEY, JOHN, *A Treatise on Zodiacal Physiognomy* (London, 1828).

VAUGHAN, WILLIAM, *German Romanticism and English Art* (New Haven and London: Yale University Press, 1979).

VIRGIL, *The Works of John Dryden*, ed. Edward Niles Hooker and H. T. Swedenberg, Jr., vol. v, *The Works of Virgil in English* (Berkeley: University of California Press, 1987).

Virgil, trans. H. Rushton Fairclough (rev. edn., 2 vols., Cambridge, Mass.: Harvard University Press, 1960).

VISCOMI, JOSEPH, 'Blake after Blake: A Nation Discovers Genius', http://sites.unc.edu/viscomi/blakeafterblake.html

—— *William Blake and the Art of the Book* (Princeton: Princeton University Press, 1993).

WAAGEN, G. F., *Treasures of Art in Great Britain* (3 vols., London, 1854).

WAGENKNECHT, DAVID, *Blake's Night: William Blake and the Idea of Pastoral* (Cambridge, Mass.: Belknap Press, 1973).

WATSON, J. STEPHEN, *The Reign of George III 1760–1815* (Oxford: Clarendon Press, 1960).

WELLS, WILLIAM, *William Blake's 'Heads of the Poets'* (Manchester: Manchester City Art Gallery, 1969).

WESLEY, JOHN and CHARLES, *The Poetical Works of John and Charles Wesley*, ed. G. Osborn (13 vols., London: Wesleyan-Methodist Conference, 1870).

WICKSTEED, JOSEPH, *Blake's Vision of the Book of Job* (2nd edn., London: J. M. Dent, 1924).

The William Blake Archive, ed. Morris Eaves, Robert N. Essick, and Joseph Viscomi, www.blakearchive.org.

WILLIAMS, HELEN MARIA, *Poems on Various Subjects: with Introductory*

Remarks on the Present State of Science and Literature in France (London: G. & W. B. Whittaker, 1823).

WILTON, ANDREW, *The Wood Engravings of William Blake for Thornton's Virgil* (London: British Museum, 1977).

WINCKELMANN, ABBÉ J. J., *Reflections on the Painting and Sculpture of the Greeks, Translated from the German Original by Henry Fusseli* [*sic*], *A.M.* (London: A. Millar, 1765).

'W.P.', 'Rudolph Ackerman of the Strand, Publisher', *Notes and Queries*, 4th ser., 4 (7 August 1869): 109–12.

WRIGHT, ANDREW, *Blake's Job: A Commentary* (Oxford: Clarendon Press, 1972).

WRIGHT, JULIA M., 'The Medium, the Message, and the Line in William Blake's *Laocoön*', *Mosaic*, 33 (2000): 101–24.

YATES, FRANCES A., 'Transformations of Dante's Ugolino', *Journal of the Warburg and Courtauld Institutes*, 14 (1951): 92–117.

YEATS, WILLIAM BUTLER, *Mythologies* (New York: Macmillan, 1959).

——'William Blake's Illustrations to Dante', in *Essays and Introductions* (New York: Macmillan, 1961), pp. 116–45.

YOUNG, EDWARD, *The Complaint, and the Consolation; or, Night Thoughts* (London: R. Edwards, 1797).

General Index

Index of Works by William Blake

(An asterisk * indicates a reproduction)